CHANGE AND CONTINUITY IN MINANGKABAU:

LOCAL, REGIONAL, AND HISTORICAL PERSPECTIVES ON

WEST SUMATRA

CHANGE AND CONTINUITY IN MINANGKABAU:

LOCAL, REGIONAL, AND HISTORICAL PERSPECTIVES ON

WEST SUMATRA

edited by

Lynn L. Thomas
and
Franz von Benda-Beckmann

Ohio University Center for International Studies
Center for Southeast Asian Studies

Monographs in International Studies
Southeast Asia Series Number 71

Athens, Ohio 1985

Library of Congress Cataloging in Publication Data
Main entry under title:

Change and continuity in Minangkabau.

   (Monographs in international studies. Southeast Asia
series ; no. 71)
   Papers presented at a symposium held in April 1981
in Amsterdam, under the auspices of the Inter-congress
of the International Union of Anthropological and
Ethnological Sciences.
   Bibliography: p.
   1. Minangkabau (Indonesian people)--Congresses.
2. Sumatera Barat (Indonesia)--Congresses. I. Thomas,
Lynn L. II. Benda-Beckmann, Franz von.
III. International Union of Anthropological and
Ethnological Sciences. Inter-congress. IV. Series.
DS632.M4C47 1985   306'.0899922   85-5026
ISBN 0-89680-127-6

Reprinted 1988.

ISBN: 0-89680-127-6

CONTENTS

Part III. Politics and Economics in Historical Perspective

THEMES AND ISSUES

Lynn L. Thomas
Pomona College
and
Franz von Benda-Beckmann
LBH Wageningen

A symposium on Minangkabau society, culture, and history
was held in September 1980 in Bukit Tinggi, West Sumatra, in
the Minangkabau heartland. It was organized by the University
and the Teachers´ Training College of West Sumatra in cooperation with the provincial government. In April of the next
year, a second symposium was held, in Amsterdam, under the
auspices of the Inter-Congress of the International Union of
Anthropological and Ethnological Sciences. The two symposia
indicate the growing interest in Minangkabau, both within
Indonesia and in the international scholarly community.
Actually it is more accurate to speak of a revived interest.
For since the early years of Dutch colonial rule in the 1820s,
the Minangkabau have continually intrigued and vexed people,
from the early Dutch and later Indonesian civil servants sent
to administer the area once it had been incorporated into the
colony of the Dutch East Indies and later into the Republic of
Indonesia, to foreign academic scholars, and many Minangkabau
themselves. Given the "credentials" of Minangkabau society,
this is hardly surprising.

The Minangkabau are the world´s largest matrilineal
people, their social and political organization seemingly
coming close to the state of "pure matriliny" in some anthro-
pologists´ interpretations. But they are equally well-known
for a strong adherence to Islam and for a markedly modern and
outward looking orientation. Minangkabau have a long tradition of voluntary, putatively temporary migration (merantau).
It is estimated that approximately two and a half million
Minangkabau live in West Sumatra, most of them (86%) in
villages and living off agriculture and closely related
activities. Nearly the same number of people live in the
rantau areas outside the West-Sumatran heartland of the
Minangkabau as traders, proprietors of restaurants, and administrative officials. In proportion to the Indonesian
population, an impressive number of Minangkabau have become
prominent scholars and politicians. These characterizations,

-1-

and, when set side by side, the apparent contradictions between them, have been sources of fascination and puzzlement.
How can a matrilineal society be strongly Islamic? How can
matriliny survive the onslaught of the state and the capitalist world economy? The additional fact that the Minangkabau have a highly developed verbal culture, manifest in
historical legends, myths, epics, and stories and in the complex elaborations of their adat (law, morals, customs, practices), makes it easy to see why foreign scholars in particular should have taken such a great interest in this
society. From the early years of Dutch colonial rule until
the invasion of Indonesia by the Japanese in World War II, the
body of literature covering most aspects of Minangkabau
social, economic, political, and cultural life has been significantly growing.[1] In addition there also has developed,
since the 1920s, a significant body of Minangkabau literature,
including both fiction and scholarly and exigetical interpretations of the Minangkabau society. However, as most of
these literatures are written in Dutch or Indonesian, it has
largely escaped the notice of the non-Dutch reading anthropological public.[2]

Little was published on Minangkabau during the 1940s and
1950s, but the two major publications, by P. E. de Josselin de
Jong (1951) and Schrieke (1955), had a great impact on the
orientation of subsequent researchers. De Josselin de Jong's
thesis on the Socio-Political Organization in Minangkabau and
Negeri Sembilan (1951) comprised a thorough and critical assessment of the available Dutch sources and interpreted Minangkabau social organization in terms of anthropological
theory. It presented Minangkabau society to a wider anthropological audience, and provided the most important source on
Minangkabau for non-Dutch reading scholars, in particular also
for the (somewhat unhappy) treatment of Minangkabau in Schneider and Gough's volume on Matrilineal Kinship (1961). Simultaneously, it interpreted Minangkabau social organization in a
critical discussion of the just published works of Murdock
(1949) and Lévi-Strauss (1969, originally published in 1949)
and was a major contribution and development of what is now

---

[1] The most important Dutch writings are probably these:
Francis 1839; Wilken 1885; Hasselt 1882; Resume 1872; v. Eerde
1901; Verkerk Pistorius 1871; Westenek 1918; Guyt 1936;
Schrieke et al. 1928; Joustra 1923; de Rooij 1890; Leyds 1926;
Willinck 1909; Kielstra 1887-1892; Korn 1941.
[2] For exceptions, in the older literature, see: in German,
Kohler 1910; Lublinsky 1927; in English Loeb 1934, 1935;
Cooper-Cole 1936, 1945; in French, Collet 1925.

generally known as the Leiden school of structuralist theory (J. P. B. de Josselin de Jong, Van Wouden being among the major figures in the establishment of this school). Closing the lid on previous, largely evolutionist approaches and controversies, it analyzed Minangkabau in terms of an "Indonesian field of ethnological study" (a concept originally elaborated by J. P. B. de Josselin de Jong), hypothesizing that Minangkabau social-political organization was a transformation of the structural core elements characterizing the Indonesian societies, with an emphasis on asymmetric connubium and double descent in particular (see also de Josselin de Jong's essay in this volume).

While his model has not been generally accepted by later researchers, with respect to both theoretical construction and historical and contemporary ethnographic evidence, de Josselin de Jong's hypotheses have set the background and standard for later enquiries and analyses.

Schrieke's The Causes and Effects of Communism on the West Coast of Sumatra (1955) has had a similar importance for subsequent analyses of Minangkabau social, economic, and political development. Originally published in 1929 in Dutch, it was the English translation of the sociological section of a Governmental Commission report on the conditions preceding and leading to the communist uprisings in 1926-27. Schrieke had concluded that increased monetarization of the West Sumatran economy, especially since the introduction of the tax system in 1908, formed the fundamental background for the uprisings. The subsistence economy gave way to rural capitalism; increasing land transfers and the development of inheritance rights within the conjugal family eroded the matrilineal adat system of communal land tenure and signaled its imminent breakdown.

After World War II had reached Sumatra, no research was reported for twenty years. Then, in the 1960s, a Minangkabau rush began. Beginning with Nancy Tanner's pioneering field research in the mid 1960s, nearly thirty scholars have carried out intensive field or archival research, or both, with a significant part played by Minangkabau social scientists, during the last twenty years. During the ten years preceding the two symposia, twelve doctoral dissertations or other books had been written in the English language alone. Some fifty-two working papers were given at the symposium in Bukit Tinggi in 1980 and thirteen in Amsterdam in 1981. Most of the papers were expressions of work in progress, preceding or elaborating upon more voluminous research reports.

This volume reports on the Amsterdam symposium by anthropologists, historians, sociologists, and area specialists.[3] The central substantive problem for virtually all of these studies is that of understanding changes in the light of continuities and continuities in the light of changes. They involve the rethinking of issues long important in the study of Minangkabau, the nature of Minangkabau matriliny, the relation of _adat_ and Islam, and the persistence of Minangkabau social and cultural forms despite their incorporation into the national and the world economies.

The major purpose of this volume is to focus critical attention on these themes in Minangkabau life and history as these are seen in current studies of the society, not to give a general introduction to Minangkabau.[4]

We have arranged the papers in three parts. Those in Part I focus on local organization and emphasize kinship patterning, but put these in wider contexts (whether theoretical, regional, or historical). The papers in Part II focus on social and especially cultural patterning and examine such patterning in wider regional and historical settings. The papers in Part III focus on political or economic patterning, or some combination of these in relation to social and cultural kinds of facts. It is the interplay in the papers between these substantive foci, the attention given to continuities or changes in these substantive areas, and the attention to Minangkabau-specific and more general concerns that provides for numerous threads among the parts, and among several combinations of the papers. We will discuss these briefly here, mostly in terms of the arrangement of the papers into the three parts.

The Papers in Part I

The papers in Part I are largely inspired by de Josselin de Jong's work and by the treatment Minangkabau has received in Schneider and Gough's book on _Matrilineal Kinship_ (1961). Prindiville, and Tanner and Thomas treat the organization and the workings of the organization of matrilineal descent in Minangkabau in the light of anthropological attempts to delin-

---

[3] The Peletz paper is an addition to the volume after the symposium; although Peletz was among those invited to the symposium who were unable to attend, it is most fortunate that at least one paper representing Negeri Sembilan can be included here. The paper Thomas delivered in Amsterdam was based upon a paper he co-authored with Richard Lando (Lando and Thomas 1983). The paper by Tanner and Thomas in this volume is a revision of the paper Nancy Tanner delivered in Amsterdam.
[4] For one such introduction, see Tanner 1976.

eate general understandings about matriliny. Both find the most influential understandings seriously wanting; both begin, in the present essays as well as in other works, the process of reconceptualizing the issues, particularly as regards women's and men's respective places in different realms in the society. They question and criticize the models on the basis of their own experience with the complex reality of the society, confronting the built-in assumptions of the model with interpretative and critical ethnography. Both observe that anthropologists have given primacy to presumed features of patrilineal societies in model building, taking matriliny as the odd case to be interpreted in view of how one understands patriliny to be constituted and how matriliny deviates from that norm. Both observe that male centering has been read into matriliny. Both observe the tendency to give primacy to male authority. Both papers insist upon more careful demarcation of social positions in gender associations and more careful delineation of central involvements of persons in groups.

While Prindiville, and Tanner and Thomas focus on gender relations and the mother-child linkage, Peletz stresses the importance of siblingship in the social structure of Negeri Sembilan. In his analysis of kinship and socio-political relations he argues that "principles of siblingship cannot be subsumed under the rubric of descent and may in fact enjoin behaviors and social linkages that are at sharp variance with a descent based logic." By focusing their analyses on key principles of social organization, these authors decompose the larger categories "matrilineal," "descent," "alliance," and clear the ground for the construction of new models. Naim's paper also is concerned with Minangkabau society as a functioning system. He focuses on the relations between voluntary, putatively temporary, migration and village life, one of the important aspects in the study of Minangkabau identified in de Josselin de Jong's introduction in this volume. Naim's discussion, like that of Kato (1977), whom he cites, emphasizes the view that merantau has been institutionalized in Minangkabau in historically and situationally variable ways. Moreover, merantau is seen as having significantly supported the matrilineal system. At the same time, it is proposed to have been both a response to that system and an integral part of it in terms of both its effects and its workings. In spite of the considerable diversity of its forms and involvements with other institutions, merantau is seen as having had and continuing to have a long-term, overall role in the society; it is viewed as a safety valve, siphoning off excess population and thereby sustaining the viability of the social system which engenders it. Contemporary developments in the Minangkabau homeland are analyzed in historical perspective, especially with respect to the incorporation of the region into the nation, and increased individualization and other changes in family life. Such changes are viewed as engendering new forms of _merantau,_ but preserved to a great extent are the core notions of what _merantau_ constitutes. Preserved also is the important hypothesized siphoning function. Thereby, in Naim´s view, _merantau_ has significantly helped preserve the modified matrilineal system of the homeland.

In the discussion of historically variable forms of _merantau,_ Naim´s paper is a natural entryway to the papers of Part II, which are united in their concern with the Minangkabau-wide (or in Watson´s case, comparative) processes of change in their relations to the outside. Here again a shift can be observed in the historical and theoretical focus of recent researches. The quest for the origins of Minangkabau matriliny which was well entrenched in the colonial literature (see citations to Wilken, Willinck, Van Ossenbruggen, in de Josselin de Jong 1951) has been given up (at least for the moment). As in the studies of kinship mentioned above, historical studies of other facets of Minangkabau life have also by and large given up the search for a model of social-structural principles of earliest Minangkabau society and for the putative spatial and historical transformations of these principles. Rather the emphasis is put on a historiographic account of changes in attested socio-political systems within specific periods of time in the Minangkabau and _rantau_ areas.

The Part II Papers

J. Kathirithamby-Wells sketches out the manner in which Minangkabau forms of state-craft were used in, and aspects in which they were adapted to, western _rantau_ areas. She views the basic concepts of rule as having been retained, in terms of the emphases on adherence to and endowment of laws, notions of supernaturally constituted talents, and notions of moral superiority of rulers. Modes of government administration reaching to supra-village levels were also Minangkabau derived and retained; the heartland traditions of _Koto-Piliang_ (the more royal, hierarchical form) and _Bodi-Caniago_ (the more egalitarian, or consensually oriented) were also retained and developed. A third ideologically constituted tradition was incorporated into the heartland traditions, that of the local raja, stemming directly from the Pagarruyung Tuanku. Kathirithamby-Wells does not argue that Minangkabau traditions simply "ruled" in Inderapura and Anak Sungai regions--rather, it is more that these traditions provided an appropriate mode of discourse adapted to local conditions for use in conflict management.

Kathirithamby-Wells' emphasis on royal forms of governance in the _rantau_ areas would seem to be fully consistent with the inference de Josselin de Jong (e.g. 1975a, 1975b) has made to the effect that in the _darat_ (heartland), the traditions of _adat katumanggungan_ are "associated with the coast," while the traditions of _adat parapatih_ are "associated with the interior." The evidently clear and unequivocal association of the former traditions with Koto-Piliang and of the latter with Bodi-Caniago, and of these in turn respectively with "royalty" and "egalitarian" norms, seems to be an important Minangkabau ideological contrast of some considerable antiquity. Whether it is a problem in understanding the contrasts to find Kathirithamby-Wells' noticing both traditions in the _rantau_, and not just the _adat katumanggungan_ there, remains to be worked out.

The linkages of these concepts with the _adat_/Islam contrast also need further explication (for excellent beginnings, see de Josselin de Jong 1951; Taufik Abdullah 1966, 1971, 1972). Taufik Abdullah's paper in this volume suggests the kind of caution needed in future investigations. He criticizes legalistic conceptions of the place of Islam in Minangkabau. The legalistic conceptions associate Islam too specifically and tightly with political forms such as _adat katumanggungan_ or with specific social structural forms, such as in inheritance law; or they place Islam too much in the realm of an ideological reflex of political or political economic forces. In the process of the criticism he is able to richly transcend the parochialisms that so often accompany discussions of "the place of religion in society." His purpose is not to divorce realms of abstract ideas from social realities; it is instead to suggest a much greater degree of autonomy from specific social structures and a much more intriguing delicateness of connections of Islam with other social facts than is often achieved. He criticizes both a "strictly cultural approach to understanding..." and "one-sided economic interpretations," and he is able to astutely avoid both an ahistorical structuralism and that variety of historicism devoid of attention to systematic connections.

To a large extent, the suggestions of Taufik Abdullah may be said to have been taken up in C. W. Watson's paper on the processes of adoption of Islam in Kerinci (to the south of Minangkabau). In this interpretation, these processes can be seen in three stages. There was, first, the establishment of Islam via the Sultan's influence and via attempts on the part of local leaders associated with the Sultan to establish higher authority than they had previously enjoyed in the village.

There were, second, the attempts especially on the part of
merchants to use Islamic modes of discourse to challenge the
higher structures of authority established in the first stage,
resulting in the conflict stimulated by resistance against the
attempts to establish newer modes of religious orthodoxy. In
the second stage, Islam is sufficiently well institutionalized
that "internal strife within villages soon gives to religious
issues a momentum of their own, and the question of religious
orthodoxy becomes a dimension added to the character of traditional intervillage disputes." In the third stage, in the
late nineteenth century, Kerinci is not completely Islamicized
but Islam has acquired fairly uncontroversial placements in
villages, placements in which it is partly integrated into
village governance and partly given its own place, in what is
an interesting balance of church and state. Watson's paper is
in part presented as amendment and further appreciation of
Christine Dobbin's excellent papers on eighteenth century
Minangkabau history (1975, 1977). Watson's paper can also be
seen in conjunction with Taufik Abdullah's work (this volume,
and 1971) as further indication of the need to examine Islam
more meaningfully in the context of the social and political
lives of its adherents. Perhaps, though, a disjunction in
Watson's as compared with Abdullah's interpretations needs
also to be seen. Whereas Abdullah stresses the ideology of
Islam in relation to Minangkabau thought, Watson stresses the
ideological uses of Islam in political conflict and finds the
ritual forms more than the doctrines to be of specific appeal;
perhaps the difference is one of Kerinci vs. Minangkabau.
Whether as coda, parallel, or counterpoint, further work on
interpretation of Islam in Minangkabau can certainly benefit
from Watson's work on Kerinci.

The relative autonomy of ideology from specific social
structures suggested in Taufik Abdullah's paper also is at the
heart of Umar Junus' paper. Ideology, or rather confrontations of ideologies (adat—Islam; traditional—modern; female-
male) expressed in Minangkabau literary works are examined for
their "evidence" concerning political and social changes.
Umar Junus attempts to place specific structural delineations
in specific historical perspectives. He sketches thematic
structures in two genres of literature, kaba (Minangkabau
narrative stories) and novels, both of which are treated differently according to their variants in history and in
thematic structure. Differences in conceptualization and
evaluation of aspects of "modernity" and "tradition" are
discussed in terms of the ideologies expressed in the literary
forms. One might be tempted to infer trends from Junus' delineations: from the focus on traditional (ostensibly closed)
life in the classical kaba to the problematic assertion of

tradition in the face of change in newer _kaba_ and in early
novels, to the denial of tradition in later novels, and finally to an ideology of mutual accommodation in the newer
novels.

The Part III Papers

The papers in Part III are also primarily concerned with
change. In contrast with the Part II papers, they focus more
on discontinuities in change which are seen as consequences of
historically located "impacts" of external political and
economic forms on Minangkabau village life. With the exception of Kahin's paper which deals with the revolutionary
struggle in West Sumatra just after World War II, the papers
focus upon the nature of change in the early 20th century in
relation to 19th century conditions. All three papers critically examine Schrieke's analysis and engage in a critical
discussion with each other's interpretations.

Akira Oki argues for more use in Minangkabau studies of
a socio-economic approach. While critically examining
Schrieke's pioneering and well-known West Coast report, Oki
considers how the approach might be improved upon by giving
greater joint attention to the economic and regional sides of
things. Oki is careful at the same time not to ignore social
aspects of economic facts. He agrees with Schrieke that increased monetarization of the West Sumatran economy in the
first quarter of this century was the "fundamental background"
of the 1926-27 uprising. But greater differentiation of what
"increased monetarization" might mean is called for. Oki
argues that examination of regional variations in production
of export commodities preceding the uprising helps make
regional variations in protest explicable. He also argues
that regional and social variations in income were insufficiently recognized by Schrieke. Oki agrees with Schrieke that
descent group ownership of land weakened, but he argues that
this weakening was not so profound as Schrieke thought and was
manifested in increased pawnings rather than in outright
selling, which Schrieke incorrectly thought to be the case.
Oki also agrees with Schrieke that the authority of _penghulus_
(heads of matrilineal descent groups) did indeed decline as a
result of Dutch policies and social-economic conditions. But
he disagrees with Schrieke on the important matter of the
burden of taxation; while Schrieke had held that the tax
burden was relatively unimportant, Oki holds that it and the
increased demand for imported goods that was concomitant with
it placed a rather heavy burden on the poor. Oki finds that
the tax burden itself was heavy, in real terms, and also that

its sanctions were onerous and morally offensive. In his closing remarks, Oki mentions a point also made by Joel Kahn elsewhere, that the survival of village institutions (such as matrilineal descent groups) in West Sumatra may owe as much to a politically enforced emphasis on subsistence in an under-developed economy as to some inherent strength of those in-stitutions.

Franz and Keebet von Benda-Beckmann approach the problem of change from a legal anthropological perspective in their treatment of Minangkabau property law in relation to the social conditions of the last two centuries. Throughout the paper, they take up the significant challenges which Joel Kahn (and in a different way also Taufik Abdullah) have presented to students of Minangkabau. The challenge is to investigate more closely the ways in which persistence and change are conceived and seen in relation to the society's political and economic history. The von Benda-Beckmanns argue that previous understandings of changes have been misinformed by legalistic interpretations of the Minangkabau adat of property and in-heritance and by equally legalistic associations of actual social, economic, and political conditions with these trans-formed notions of adat. Like Oki, they do not view the changes occurring in the early decades of this century as having been so profound a watershed as suggested by Schrieke and by Kahn in his previous publications (especially 1976). Kahn had suggested that "the" Minangkabau society--seen as being autonomous and static, and based on feudalized lineage and village organization--had been "created" by Dutch policies. The von Benda-Beckmanns see the "watershed," and the concomitant comparison between pre- and post-watershed conditions, as a dramatized result of several false com-parisons: (1) The transformation of Minangkabau adat through Dutch legalistic interpretations which too heavily emphasized the communal aspect of land holdings and the matrilineal ele-ments of social organization, which themselves had been fully developed in Dutch adat literature and jurisprudence only in the early 20th century. (2) The retrojection of this "system" into the 19th century. (3) the association of corresponding social and economic conditions to these transformed adat-notions. (4) The legalistically informed overinterpretation of the conditions observed in the 1910s and 1920s and the inferences for future developments based upon them, which unduly emphasized the individualistic aspects in Minangkabau land tenure. (5) The contraposition of the picture con-structed for the present and future with that of the past, producing the impression of radical change.

The irony, if the von Benda-Beckmanns' arguments are sustained in later analysis, is that Kahn is himself seen to

-10-

have fallen prey to Dutch misconceptions that descent groups were internally homogeneous groups. What the Dutch "saw" as intrinsic tradition, and what Kahn saw from the Dutch writings to be consequences of Dutch policies enforcing local autonomy, the von Benda-Beckmanns see as misconstrual of the nature and working of the descent groups. They were not, in the von Benda-Beckmanns' view, feudalized static organizations, except in the summary portrayals of the Dutch. And the Dutch policies, in their view, rather contributed to an increasing differentiation in land holding and the gradual disintegration of property holding descent groups long before the taxation system was introduced.

Whether these interpretations are borne out or not will require additional research. Perhaps most important at the present, though, especially for a reader new to Minangkabau studies, is the increasing refinement of interpretation, and the increased sharpening of sensibilities about the significance of issues of study; simultaneously the problematic character of such interpretations becomes evident. At the end of the paper dealing with changes in the 20th century, the exercise of critical reconstruction can be seen to close back upon itself. For it is mostly in view of the von Benda-Beckmanns' interpretations of contemporary Minangkabau social forms that their interpolations into the past are made. It then becomes a crucial matter of interpretation that the kinds of contingent systematicity they find in Minangkabau village life, expressed nowadays in the context of incorporation of Minangkabau into the national Indonesian state, be appropriate to the present as well as past contexts.

Joel Kahn's paper in this volume is a continuation of his efforts to understand the low level of development of the productive forces of small-scale economic enterprise in Southeast Asia in relation to larger political economic forms.

Kahn's paper is an intermediate taking of stock and a setting out of the directions in which his research has been leading. The petty commodity mode of the production, the workings of which are discussed in more detail elsewhere (e.g., Kahn 1980), and similar modes of production are discussed in terms of the variable commoditization of both productive inputs (land, labor, means of production) and outputs.

The reader will notice in Kahn's paper that more than the other contributions to the volume it addresses theoretical questions in their own right, and derivatively addresses Minangkabau-specific questions. He re-examines Schrieke's and his own previous interpretation of the "watershed" leading to a transformation of the Minangkabau economy. In his previous work, Kahn had accepted Schrieke's watershed thesis, disagreeing, however, about the nature of the transformation. Whereas

Schrieke saw rural capitalism emerge in Minangkabau, Kahn's
research saw petty commodity production becoming the dominant
mode of production in rural areas. In his paper he partially
revises and refines his analysis. He argues that despite superficial continuities in the Minangkabau economy, a transformation has occurred in the way small-scale rural enterprises are reproduced. Besides partly resulting from the introduction of taxation, Kahn views the transformation as a
result of large-scale land alienations following the introduction of the agrarian laws in the 1870s.

It would seem that this revised interpretation would not
lead to substantial changes in the criticism of the von Benda-
Beckmanns (in this volume). Also, Oki's critique of Schrieke
concerning the neglect of regional variations and the generalizations based upon events in fringe areas may well be extended to Kahn's new interpretation of the effects of land
alienations by the colonial government. Perhaps Kahn more
than any others of the contributors to the volume has left
himself open to doubts that theory too much guides substantive
interpretations away from local, Minangkabau realities. But
readers should note well that it is a clear enough implication
of many of Taufik Abdullah's and the von Benda-Beckmann's
comments that substantive interpretations are not so innocent
in ways that matter in any case. Kahn's potential for "over-
theorizing," then must be seen to be at least partly counterbalanced by (a) the great import of the facts he attends to in
everyday Southeast Asian lives, by (b) the potential already
realized in his work of avoiding commonplaces that turn out to
be wrong, and (c) in the clarifying of limits of theoretical
understanding.

Kahn points to several problems involving understandings
of economics in the modes of production under consideration;
first the linkages of political and economic structure to
actual action have been attended to too seldom and too super-
ficially—the best example of this is the apparent counterin-
tuitiveness of small-scale producers' responses to changes in
input prices. A common cliché has been that small-scale
producers are caught in something "we may designate as trad-
itionalism." Even those who are willing to grant "precapitalist" laborers some kind of rationality (even in the "traditional" mode) have been by and large unwilling to investigate
the considerable differentiation in kinds of reasoning invoked
under differing conditions. Part of the irony in this is that
the same scholars focusing on traditions focus also on differentiations among traditions—thereby one would have thought
necessitating even more the kind of investigation Kahn's work
is directed toward. Kahn's researches in West Sumatra and
Negeri Sembilan have had to much more finely differentiate

modes of commoditization with differing factor inputs and outputs. He is able to begin to enrich our substantive understandings of peasant economics as well as significantly improve the theoretical frameworks brought to bear on the problems involved. In the last part of his paper, he returns to
the larger problems of external connections and offers suggestions about the meanings of market penetration in the Southeast Asian systems he examines.

Audrey Kahin discusses important aspects of village
politics and government during the revolutionary struggle in
West Sumatra just after World War II. She mentions the early
attempts of Republican leaders to make use, partly for
efficiency's sake, of the Indonesian officials from Dutch
colonial and Japanese occupation administrations. Widespread
dissatisfaction with those attempts and with the policy of
letting British and Indian troops begin the process of re-
colonialization resulted in policy shifts. Elections,
strategic appointments, and the creation of village-based organizations for specific tasks such as tax collection and
security were achieved. Village-level and Residency Administration proved sufficient to carry out the struggle
against the determined Dutch effort to reassert control.
Although after their major (second) assault was begun in
December 1948 and the Dutch were able to take military control
of most towns, they nevertheless found themselves effectively
blocked. Contrary to their expectations, their old local
leadership, on which they counted for support, was not rally-
ing to their cause and the new forms of Residence and local
government and a mostly united population had them effectively
checkmated.

Connections between Kahin's paper and other papers in
the volume are most intriguing. Kahin herself, for example,
is tempted to see the considerable village autonomy and decentralized government of 1945-50 in the light not just of
immediate circumstances, and not just in the light of Dutch
colonial policies affecting village governance, but also in
the light of precolonial forms or ideas of government. Obviously the comparison cannot be direct. It remains unclear
whether there has been continuity through colonial times of
actual practices or abstract norms favoring decentralized
governance. One alternative would be a marked disjuncture in
governance stemming from newer, or more situationally specific
practices or norms of justice. These remain difficult questions.

Similar questions need to be asked about the role of
Islamic leaders in 1945-50. Taufik Abdullah's and C. W.
Watson's work suggest appropriate avenues of interpretation,
but, again, we have to contend with problems of potential con-

-13-

tinuities seen in situations in which the disjunctions of immediate situations or the more immediate past may be more important than, or just as important as, continuities.

It is worthwhile mentioning also the counterpoint in Kahin's paper when set in relation to Akira Oki's paper. Specifically, one wonders about the kind of balance between social-cultural constructions of justice and inchoate reflex notions of fairness in both the 1926-27 rebellion and the 1945-50 revolution. Oki does not deny the former and Kahin does not deny the latter, but the differences in emphasis are striking; and whether they are genuinely differences in local situations or ones of interpretative inclination, are not yet matters on which much can be said with any definiteness.

The discussions which accompanied the presentation of the papers in Amsterdam were lively, open, and critical. It was unfortunate that several scholars who have done, or are currently doing research in Minangkabau, such as Kato, Dobbin, Evers, Young, Ok-Kyung Pak, Ng, Scholz, and Persoon, were not able to attend the symposium, although the latter four had been present and given papers at the Bukit Tinggi symposium. The frequent references to their work, both in the papers and during the discussions, made clear that their absence was corporal only. On the basis of a large stock of shared knowledge, and united by the common focus on the same society—and to a large extent more specifically on the same historical processes and problems—the participants did not find it difficult to cross disciplinary boundaries and to look at "their own" problems from the point of view of others. The combined effort of various disciplines has indeed achieved a considerable improvement (and one might hope a deepening) of our understanding of change and continuity in Minangkabau. At the same time, it has opened new insights and perspectives for future research. The problem of "the survival of matrilineal institutions," for example, which is discussed most specifically by Tanner and Thomas, Prindiville, Naim, and the von Benda-Beckmanns, has to be seen as much more complex a problem of change and continuity than one would have gathered even just a few years ago.

Continuity and change are not treated in these papers as mutually exclusive categorical alternatives. Characteristic of the perspective taken in most of the papers is Prindiville's comment to the effect that the change of residence pattern from a room to a separate house need not be seen as a marked departure, given that "the room in a house" and "a house" are similarly viewed in Minangkabau, and given that the houses still remain on lineage land and near other lineage

houses, and are owned by the lineage of the woman most closely
associated with the house. There is both continuity here and
discontinuity; Prindiville suggests that the discontinuity is
strongly colored by the continuity and that the most obvious,
and rather narrow perception that "lineages are breaking down
into nuclear families" is insufficiently qualified by way of
understanding the conditions and contingencies involved. The
interplaying of different possibilities is considerable, as
for example in the incorporation of Islam into Minangkabau, or
in the placing of Minangkabau statecraft forms into the rantau
(Kathirithamby-Wells), or in the continuity in changes in the
presumed siphoning effect of merantau (Naim), or yet again, in
the Communist uprising of 1926-27 (Oki), or yet again, in the
events of the immediate post-war period (Kahin), where the
roles of specific actors add to the sense of problematicity in
the putting of continuities together. Ideological changes
seemingly can occur independently, as in the case discussed by
the von Benda-Beckmanns. Economic constraints can, in one
view, in one circumstance, lead to political conflict without
much in the way of cultural mediation (Oki's paper), while in
another view, in another circumstance, the dismantling of
prior political constraints frees people to work for culturally constituted notions of distributive justice (cf.
Kahin's paper).

With the partial exception of Kahn, the authors do not
strive to explain the various configurations of changes and
continuities in terms of general explanatory theory. This
restraint is largely due to the sharpened awareness of the
state of ethnographic knowledge as well as of the analytical
and theoretical complexities involved. Despite the large
research efforts during the past twenty years and the rich
body of colonial literature, and even anticipating the publications which can be expected to result from the research by
Prindiville, Young, Ng, Ok-Kyung Pak, Persoon (and others), it
cannot yet be claimed that Minangkabau is adequately understood, either in terms of general models or historical and
contemporary events and conditions. Pre-colonial history
largely remains obscure in the darkness of ignorance. The
early forms of Minangkabau socio-political organization--which
would provide in one view the proper basis for constructing a
model that would allow a systematic study of historical variations and transformations--remain subject to speculation.
As for the more accessible past and the contemporary situation, our knowledge still is inadequate, too. In his essay in
this volume, which was the opening address to the symposium,
de Josselin de Jong identified some major spheres which
deserve particular attention in future studies. Besides the
gaps in knowledge diagnosed by de Josselin de Jong, it was

-15-

felt that the intersections of political and economic organization remain perhaps the largest and most important lacunae which must be filled before comprehensive understandings—even if still in sketch—can be achieved. A particular problem is the still insufficient knowledge of inter-regional and village variations in Minangkabau and its various rantau. The field of ethnological study approach, originally introduced by J. P. B. de Josselin de Jong in 1935 and in the recent past mainly developed by P. E. de Josselin de Jong in several publications, may indeed serve as a valuable tool for the study of variations within Minangkabau. But more intensive research on the historical development and contemporary conditions of individual villages would be a necessary part of any analysis of intervillage variations as transformations of common underlying structural principles.

Generalizations about Minangkabau thus remain difficult. Kahn's challenge to the notion of "tradition" as disembodied "continuity" (1976, 1980) raised most sharply the specific substantive respects in which traditions cannot be seen to have "a life of their own." Continuity has to be seen to be "reproduced" and not just as "being there." This insight must be extended to the variations in the spatial dimension, and the conceptualization of research problems, however specific, must more systematically take into account the processes of reproduction. In this volume, Kahn's, Oki's, the von Benda-Beckmanns', and Kahin's papers already express the growing tendency to analyze these reproductions within the increasing complexity of legal, social, economic, political, and cultural relations and institutions in Minangkabau. The survival or persistence of Minangkabau matriliny consequently ceases to be the problem of change and continuity; it becomes one important issue within a larger and much more complex set of questions. It is also the awareness of these complexities which makes most authors wary of "explaining" Minangkabau in terms of "general" theory. Their concern is with problems of the understanding and conceptualization of these complexities. Their contribution to general social scientific understanding and to their respective disciplines is on the analytical level. If there is any central theoretical problem, it is that of understanding relations among social and structural sorts of facts, cultural and ideological sorts of facts, and concretely situated events, conditions, and actions (those undertaken and those foregone). Most of the volume's papers are analytical exercises which critically examine, dissect, and reinterpret historical descriptions, Minangkabau myths and ideologies, and simultaneously examine the approaches used by the authors and their sources. The common element seems to be analysis of particular kinds of parochial legalisms: a rather naive legalistic construal of analytical models (such as of matriliny) and Minangkabau models (e.g. adat and Islam), as well as equally naive associations of specific social forms and processes with these models. If adat is narrowly conceived as referring to "matrilineal law" and Islam is recoded as "patriarchal;" if Minangkabau land law is assimilated to Dutch legal conceptions, and practice is assumed to be in conformity with this law; if Dutch conceptions of official status are equated with Minangkabau conceptions of legitimate authority: in each case an illegitimate and parochial legalistic equation seems to have been made. It should be noted that the colonial literature on Minangkabau, and the evolutionist and (structural-) functionalist climate in which it was written, tended to give descriptive accounts of normative structures and institutions while offering little information on actual social experiences (for a wonderful exception see the classic paper, Korn 1941). Field experience in village life, allowing researchers to study normative structures and actual process at the same time and place, and to witness the relatively high negotiability of normative adat or religious ideas in social interaction, probably was as important as, and a condition for, the ability to expose such legalistic misconstruals. But if we are encouraged at being able to expose such misconstruals and to learn from having done so, we are at the same time cautioned; after all they are much more obvious in hindsight, and their prevalence in the past must give us pause to wonder about our own.

Acknowledgements. Christine Thomas and Jerry Moles provided help with Lynn Thomas´ travel arrangements for the Amsterdam symposium. Jean Russell typed intermediate drafts of several of the papers. Christine Thomas helped with the typing. The editors also thank Linda Talisman for her help with editing the volume. Financial assistance was provided by the William Kirk Fund. Help on the computer was provided by Pomona College students Jim Walnum and Ben Staat; Susan Eblen of XyQuest was also helpful. Three work-study students helped with the final typing and copyediting, Joyce Jones, Gabriela Pavlick, and Olivia Shores. William Frederick´s editorial advice was also most helpful.

THE RELEVANCE OF MINANGKABAU STUDIES FOR
ANTHROPOLOGICAL THEORY

P. E. de Josselin de Jong
Instituut voor Culturele Antropologie en Sociologie der Niet-
Westerse Volken

It may be fitting to [introduce the volume] with some
general remarks on the role of Minangkabau studies within
anthropology, before [readers] turn to...the papers on more
specific subjects.   I shall therefore now consider what the
study of Minangkabau culture can contribute to Indonesian and
general anthropology.

If I now try to set our particular regional specialization in a broader, more inclusive, framework, this does not
mean that I hold that this or any other similar specialization
is only justified if we treat it in this manner.   That is not
the case, and certainly not for Minangkabau.   Any anthropologist, philologist, linguist, or historian who concentrates his
or her efforts on describing and explaining this society is,
by that very fact, doing a worthwhile job, as the society with
which we are now concerned is such an important one.

It is important, in my opinion, because of its vitality.
We are dealing with a society which is well aware of its own
"distinctive features," and does not try to abolish or dis-
guise them for fear of being dubbed "primitive" or "backward."
Of course it is helped in this attitude by the fact that it
would be very hard for any critic to call the Minang "backward," in any respect. In short, we have a community which
for scores of years has been open to change—or rather, which
has been in the vanguard of economic and social change—but
which has not fallen into the trap of the false dichotomy
between, on the one hand, change, modernization, progress,
kamajuan, and, on the other, tradition, backwardness,
feudalism, et cetera.   The very fact that it has not unsuc-
cessfully achieved an integration of the new and the traditional, and is aware of the values of both, makes it interesting and important per se.   However, I shall not now speak of
Minangkabau per se, but as an anthropological "case" in the
Indonesian context. There are five aspects of such a study,
which, I believe, need our special attention.

(1)   In the first place, the very distinctiveness or

singularity of Minangkabau raises problems of considerable theoretical interest, particularly when we place this culture in the context of Indonesia as an Ethologisch Studieveld, or Field of Ethnological Study. You will recall that this concept (introduced 46 years ago, and a valuable research tool ever since) refers to an area

> with a population whose culture appears to be suffi-
> ciently homogeneous and unique to form a separate object
> of ethnological study, and which at the same time
> apparently reveals sufficient local shades of differ-
> ences to make internal comparative research worthwhile
> (J. P. B. de Josselin de Jong 1977[1935]:167, 168).

There are two characteristics of investigations of Indonesian cultures in the context of the Field of Ethnological Study (which we may abbreviate as F.E.S.) that should be mentioned. In the first place, such studies are often what might be called "mutually interpretative." What I mean by this term is that when an anthropologist has acquired a reasonable familiarity with a number of cultures within an F.E.S., the pattern that he or she begins to discern can be used to interpret elements in a particular culture that are not quite comprehensible and do not make sense when that culture is studied in isolation (P. E. de Josselin de Jong 1980a:320, 323). I shall not pursue this topic at present, but I will have to offer some comments on the second charac-teristic.

In the 1935 lecture from which I have already quoted, the speaker went on to specify what he considered to be the "structural core" common to "numerous...Indonesian cultures in many parts of the Archipelago," namely the four features of asymmetric connubium, double descent, a "socio-cosmic dual-ism," and the very special "reaction of indigenous culture to certain powerful cultural influences from without" (1977-[1935]:168, 170-174). Here, J.P.B. de Josselin de Jong not only summarized the conclusions to which his own studies had led him, but also set a program for his pupils and fellow-In-donesianists. As such, it has led to a respectable number of publications using the F.E.S. concept, but an important dif-ference is becoming apparent between the earlier studies—say, of the pre-war and early post-war years—and those of more recent date or at present still in progress.

In the first period (e.g. Van Wouden's Types of Social Structure in Eastern Indonesia) the tendency was to perceive the elements of the "structural core" in several societies, with the rider added that in particular cases they may appear in a "disrupted" or indistinct form, and the recognition that central Indonesia is puzzlingly distinct from the eastern and western flanks (e.g. Louis Berthe 1970). We are now moving from a search for similarities to an intra-Indonesian comparison which considers the individual cultures as transformations. By adopting this concept so successfully applied by Lévi-Strauss in his Mythologiques, we are just beginning, just beginning, to pass from a study of imperfect resemblances to one of individual cultures as variants on a common theme, linked together by transformations. In this effort, it is again Lévi-Strauss (1971:32) who provides us with a guiding maxim: "...we understand that resemblance as such does not exist: resemblance is only a special form of difference, namely one in which difference approaches zero."

This also brings us back to Minangkabau, and in particular to this society as a member of the Indonesian F.E.S. In this connection, there is an obvious need to investigate the structural core elements of asymmetric connubium associated with double descent, as transformed in our society. It is not our task to try to demonstrate that Minangkabau has, or had, asymmetric connubium as a functioning system; it is our task to investigate the position of the MBD [mother's brother's daughter] in a statistical and in a mechanical model of exchange relationships. The incidence of marriage with the matrilateral versus the patrilateral or second cousin is to be studied statistically. For the mechanical, now taken in the sense of the participants' normative model, arguments for and against MBD marriage are obviously important (e.g. Muhammad Radjab 1950:115; Schneider and Gough 1961:614, 620, 621; Umar Junus 1964:299-304, 311, 312; 1971:253; Kaba Cindua Mato; van der Toorn 1888:36).

As superiority of the bride-giving group soon came to be recognized as a feature of generalized exchange systems in Indonesia, it is of significance, when we follow the transformational approach, that this superiority is to be found in societies in our F.E.S. which have a cognatic kinship system, hence are without connubium in any form. Does it also occur in Minangkabau? The data are conflicting (see e.g. Korn 1941:308, 312, 323; Muhammad Radjab 1969:53; again, I only quote from the literature, and leave aside unpublished statements by Minangkabau informants), and one might conclude that here—and perhaps more generally in Indonesia—it is the indwelling spouse, the guest, who is treated with deference.

Double descent was also originally included in the "structural core," and here again we move from a search for similarities to a study of transformations: Indonesian societies have their own descent systems, which, as the case may be, can be of double descent type (as in South Sumatra), or patrilineal (as the Batak), matrilineal (as the Minang-

-21-

kabau), or cognatic (as in Java). We are not concerned to find double-descent, or traces of it, in societies of each type, or to explain its absence. Recognizing that, in comparative work, differences are as important as similarities, we consider each of the four types as being on an equal footing *sui juris*, but we also adopt the hypothesis that in each type in its own way account is taken of the inter-generational transmission of rights, duties, and qualities according to the two basic *principles*, the paternal and maternal.

For Minangkabau this means that an apposite theme of inquiry is this: to what extent does this matrilineal society conceptually recognize and/or apply the patrilineal principle? Several instances of this principle, as a not unimportant feature of Minangkabau culture, are known: the former Pagarruyung and present-day Sri Menanti royal dynasty, the patrilineal inheritance of certain *gelar*, the biological (as opposed to social) inheritance of certain aptitudes and characteristics. These, and others, are "known," but need further study. In the domain of property, the resemblance between the inheritance rule of Minangkabau and of cognatic Java has been noted (P.E. de Josselin de Jong 1970; 1980b:35-37, 44, 45). This may be cited as a specific, but minor, attempt to situate features of Minangkabau culture within the context of the Indonesian F.E.S. For a further study of property transmission, F. von Benda-Beckmann's book of 1979 and subsequent research will be indispensable.

A critical view of what was originally presented as the "structural core" of the F.E.S., that also needs to be further developed is Moyer's of "anti-exchange behavior." As opposed to the opinion that "matrilateral cross-cousin marriage and double descent...(represent) two aspects of the same general phenomenon," Moyer argues—so far, convincingly—that

> in a strongly unilineal system which has developed a double unilineal tendency the giving away of a person (in marriage) may be relatively easy because the givers can see that the given person is still related to them. But the problem develops when one takes the receiver's point of view. The receiver wishes to maintain his unilineal group but is faced with the problem of accepting an outsider with well recognized links to another group. Thus the receiver may behave in such a way as to deny the links or to virtually break the links that the outsider has with his or her natal group. Furthermore, this behavior may in fact take the form of a denial of exchange and any alliance creation. (Moyer 1976[1980]:2, 3)

This theory obviously needs further testing in the Minangkabau field; at present I only mention Cordonnier's (1972:10) remarks on men refusing to marry in order to avoid double responsibility toward their own and their wife's family's landed property.

(2) The second aspect of what I called the study of Minangkabau as a "case" in the Indonesian context is concerned with emigration. On the one hand, the Minang are almost as well known for the scale of their migrations as for their matrilineal institutions, and we owe an exceptionally detailed study of Minangkabau in the _rantau_ to Mochtar Naim (e.g. 1973). But it is a fact we all know, although we have not yet made any great use of it, that this society is by no means exceptional in this respect: I shall only mention the Aceh, Batak, Bugis, the inhabitants of Bawean, of Menado, and of Ambon as examples of ethnic groups with a long tradition of inter-island migration. (The Javanese transmigrations may fall into a different category, as they are much less voluntary in character.)

I really think that the main question for anthropologists concerned with _merantau_ is why certain Indonesian ethnic groups do _not_ habitually migrate. If we were better informed on the causes and effects of migration in what might prove to be the majority of cases, it should be possible to ascertain whether the causal factors are absent in the non-migrant societies. It will be satisfactory to realize that on this topic, at least, we are better informed on West Sumatra than on most other provinces—also, thanks to Nancy Tanner (1969), as regards such delicate and hard to study contributing factors as tensions and disputes within the family.

(3) So far I have been speaking of Minangkabau within the Indonesian F.E.S., but it is evident that there are specially close relations of similarity and difference between the societies of Sumatra: a region that could profitably be taken as a sub-field within which transformation studies are particularly feasible. As more attention is being paid to matrilineal features in the social organization of the extremely patrilineal Toba, we are gradually coming to see this relatively best known Batak society as a mirror image of the Minangkabau—rightly or wrongly, as further research will have to show.

A different situation appears when we turn from the northern to the southern and eastern neighbors of our society: we then, again tentatively, form a picture of a gradual merging of forms of social and other aspects of culture. The problem, in this case, is one of identity and of boundaries. For dealing with it, we owe much to the investigations that were being carried out by the late M. A. Jaspan in Rejang, or still are by Watson in Kerinci, and by Moyer on early Malay language sources from the Benkulen area. For the eastern marches, I owe to Khailan Syamsu Dt. Tumenggung the information that the inhabitants are so aware of being in an indeterminate situation that they say that if the trees they fell topple over westwards, they are Minangkabau; if the trees fall eastwards, Malays. This story—more than a mere anecdote, surely—may serve to illustrate my contention that besides the luak nan tigo it is also the vague periphery, this terra incognita, which deserves to be studied for its own reasons.

(4) There is also a linguistic side to this problem of how to delimit Minangkabau territorially. To the best of my knowledge we are totally ignorant of how the linguistic boundaries run, and of what is their nature. Let me take the case of Dutch to demonstrate the problem.

Westwards there is no problem, as the sea separates the Dutch from the English language areas. Eastwards this is quite different: dialects, considered to be dialects of Dutch, merge imperceptibly with dialects held to be German. The boundary between the two, in other words, is not linguistic but political, and because there is a Dutch and a German state there are two national languages which are taught as standard languages in schools to the west and to the east of the political state boundary respectively. I shall not deal with the problem that is the constant bugbear of our Belgian neighbors, the demarcation between Dutch- and French-speaking areas, but the Dutch-German contact zone may well be very similar to the areas where the Minangkabau language comes into contact with Malay, to the east, and the so-called Middle-Malay dialects southwards. Do they also merge? In that case, the research technique would be the tracing of isoglosses, a task for the linguist rather than the anthropologist.

As in the case of Dutch versus German, however, there is an additional factor which moves the whole question from dialect geography to socio-linguistic, namely the standard language and the national language. If we confront Minangkabau with Bahasa Indonesia, we are no longer dealing with territorial, but with social frontiers: in which circumstances do which people speak either language to which other people? Neither as a practical problem nor as a subject for sociolinguistic investigation is the relationship between the national language and one of the other languages in a multilingual state typical for Minangkabau, or even for Indonesian studies. It is one of crucial importance, and it is regrettable that so far it has been almost totally neglected. It is fundamentally very similar to a problem of no less importance, also for Minangkabau: national vis-a-vis local or regional law, but it may be more amenable to study because it is, I believe, rather less charged with emotion.

(5)   While there is not much to report on the socio-linguistic component of Minangkabau studies, the picture becomes brighter when we pass, in conclusion, from language to literature.   I am thinking now of those studies which study Minangkabau literary works as anthropological sources, that is, as I have attempted to indicate throughout this introductory paper, as sources for the study of Minangkabau culture within its wider, general Indonesian context.

If we begin with modern literature, the subject matter itself links up the society with which we are now concerned with the culture of the nation, as the so-called Minangkabau novel, from Marah Rusli onwards, is written in Indonesian and may be considered as the pace-maker for Indonesian literature in the 20th century.   Here it is a pleasure to be able to refer to on-going research by [authors of papers in this book] and others: Ok-Kyung Pak (1979); Postel-Coster (1977); Umar Junus (1976, 1977, 1980c), and others.

When it comes to the older works, including the classics of Minangkabau literature such as the <u>Kaba Cindua Mato</u>, I must once more begin with an appeal to linguists and philologists: can we <u>please</u> have proper, i.e. scholarly, editions of at least the principal <u>Kaba</u> and <u>Tambo</u>? This will then supply more and better tools for the outstanding pioneering ethno-historical interpretations of Taufik Abdullah (1970) and Umar Junus (1979), and for such efforts as my own (1980c) to build up a model of western Indonesian legitimacy beliefs by using such sources as the Malay Annals, the Malewar myth of Negri Sembilan and the truly Minangkabau <u>kaba</u>.

It is time to end this introduction, in which I have tried to outline the relevance of Minangkabau studies for the anthropological study of Indonesia as a Field of Ethnological Study. Did you perhaps find it stayed too much at the level of the anthropologist´s construct of the model, and gave insufficient attention to the empirically observable reality? If so, I shall only cite Gaston Bachelard for the defense: "Nothing is ´given,´ all is constructed" (<u>Rien n´est donné; tout est construit</u>), and leave it to [others] to fill in the gaps.

PART I: KINSHIP IN LOCAL AND SUPRA-LOCAL ORGANIZATION

MOTHER, MOTHER'S BROTHER, AND MODERNIZATION:
THE PROBLEMS AND PROSPECTS OF MINANGKABAU
MATRILINY IN A CHANGING WORLD

Joanne C. Prindiville
Memorial University of Newfoundland

It is the contention of this paper that discussions of
the persistence or disintegration of matrilineal systems must
be based on a revision of our notions of the structure and
operation of matriliny. On these grounds, this consideration
of changes in Minangkabau matriliny will begin by briefly
reviewing some key problems in the formulation of the theory
of matriliny. This critique will be followed by suggestions
for a revised interpretation of the Minangkabau case. Only
then will the possible implications of directed and undirected
change for Minangkabau matriliny be addressed.

The Theory of Matriliny

1. The Formulation

The anthropological literature displays considerable
consensus on the structure, operation, and inherent problems
of matriliny as conceptualized by, among others, Radcliffe-
Brown (1950), Richards (1934, 1950), Lévi-Strauss (1969),
Schneider (1961), Douglas (1969), and Fox (1967). The basic
model has gained wide acceptance, and current discussions are
focused on relatively minor issues, a matter of refinement
rather than drastic alteration or reformulation. Recently,
developments in the anthropological analysis of sex roles have
brought into question some fundamental anthropological truths,
precipitating the reevaluation of some of our fundamental
paradigms. Before proceeding to the issue of change in matrilineal systems it is essential to reexamine the conceptualization of matriliny and the assumptions underlying the current shape of its formulation. In assessing the state of the
art with regard to matrilineal theory, I will refer mainly to
the work of Schneider and Douglas. The intention here is not
to reject their analyses completely, but to expose some conceptual weaknesses and then qualify and expand them.
The general characteristics of matrilineal descent

groups are familiar and will not be outlined here. Anthropological interest in matrilineal systems focuses on what Richards designated "the matrilineal puzzle" (1950), that is, the lack of coincidence between the lines of descent traced through women and the lines of authority between males, creating a problem of control for men who must exercise authority within both the matrilineal descent group and the nuclear family. This problem is unique to matriliny. Richards´s analysis forms an important component of the subsequent formulations of Schneider and Douglas. In order to highlight the issues crucial to this paper I will not present the analyses of these authors in detail, but will deal instead with what I consider to be the four fundamental problems in the conceptualization of matriliny.

a. The primacy of patriliny

In contrast to the 19th century analysts who posited the evolutionary primacy of matriliny, current theorists, either implicitly or explicitly, assume the logical priority of patriliny over matriliny. Lévi-Strauss, for example, advises us to "consider the expedients that a matrilineal and matrilocal society, in the strictest sense, must employ so as to establish an order roughly equivalent to that of a patrilineal and patrilocal society" (1969:117). Discussions of matriliny, then, have a derivative quality. If patriliny is x, then matriliny is not-x, or, perhaps, x + y. Patriliny constitutes the standard measure, and matriliny is problematic insofar as it deviates from patriliny. Put bluntly, patriliny "makes sense"; matriliny does not. One is then compelled to discover how such a perverse system manages to function, and this has become the main theoretical issue in the consideration of matriliny.

Interestingly, the same roles for males (control) and females (biological reproduction) are postulated for both types of descent groups. In both cases, the focus of anthropological attention is on the male role, seen from the male perspective. This orientation generates two problems. First, the minimal definition of female roles effectively limits our understanding of the total system. At no point are we tempted, for instance, to consider the possibility of any form of the "patrilineal puzzle" visible from the female perspective. Second, the derivative quality of the analysis of matriliny impedes the positive, rather than residual, characterization of the form, and inhibits our anthroplogical imaginations from speculating on features radically different from those of patriliny. The parameters of our analysis are set by our notions of patriliny, and our vision of matriliny is thereby

limited. As it were, our image of the form is one reflected
in the looking glass of patriliny, and, at this juncture, we
must entertain the possibility that our vision of matriliny is
distorted.

b. The primacy of the nuclear family

One reason patriliny is seen as more "rational" is that
it simultaneously seems more "natural." That is, patriliny
coincides more neatly with our ideal of the nuclear family,
particularly in the roles assigned to males and females.
Since the nuclear family is widely considered to be the universal elementary kinship unit, this association reinforces
the logical primacy—patriliny is assumed to be somehow more
natural, more right. The assumption of the universal primacy
of the nuclear family, and the "natural" association of
father and child, render inevitable the structural tensions
within matriliny between men in their roles as father and
mother's brother, and between male affines and consanguines.
If, for instance, one were to assume that, on the contrary, the most elementary kin unit is that of mother and
child, the possible number of configurations would be broad-
ened. One might predict that the structural tensions within
matriliny would be possible, but not the inevitable outcome of
universal gender role ascriptions or of "natural" nuclear
family units.

c. The primacy of jural models

As James (1978) argues, unilineal descent systems have
been characterized largely in jural terms, that is, relative
to the differential distribution of rights, duties, and authority among male members pertaining to such domains as succession, property, and inheritance. A fundamental tenet of
anthropology underlying these analyses is that of universal
sexual asymmetry and the concomitant concentration of authority in male hands. As indicated above, the matrilineal puzzle
is posed in terms of the jural authority of males, who must
attempt to control those members of the unit responsible for
its continuity, females, while at the same time exercising
their "natural" authority within the nuclear family. This
male authority within the family and descent group parallels
their exclusive exercise of authority in society at large.
Both the orderly operation of the matrilineal descent group
and the interrelations of such groups are posed, therefore, as
political problems and are necessarily the concern only of
men. The universal attribution of authority to males, in
conjunction with the lack of congruence between spheres of

authority in matrilineal systems, is, then, the crux of the problem, variously experienced positively as dual loyalty (Douglas 1969) or negatively as dual responsibility (de Josselin de Jong 1980d) or conflict of interest (Richards 1950, Schneider 1961). Male/female relations, then, are reduced to the problem of control, and male/male relations are broadly defined in terms of cooperation (consanguines) or competition (affines). The attention to females is minimal and secondary; they exist in the theory as a problem of, and for, men. Thus, Schneider refers to the problem for brothers of controlling their sisters and preventing control by husbands, but does not speculate on the problem for mothers (or sisters) of controlling sons (or brothers) and preventing their control by daughters-in-law (or wives).

In such an analysis, women are reduced to the status of pawns in men's power plays. They do not appear as actors, except in their perverse ability to thwart men's, especially brothers', plans. Significantly, when Schneider considers alternatives to the authority structure he has proposed, the only solution which emerges is the possibility that male affines might somehow cooperate to control the group. Women's place in matrilineal descent groups is never elaborated beyond that of, minimally, the means of its replication, and, maximally, its symbols. They are accorded no active role in its orderly operation of intergroup relations. The problem of group structure and intergroup relations is posed and solved from the male perspective, relying on the elaboration of the mother's brother/sister's son relation within the group and the affinal relation between males of different groups.

In her critique of matrilineal theory, James asserts that "the association between the existence of a line of descent and the relative authority or power of the sexes is by no means a clear or simple one" (1978:143). She asks us to contemplate the possibility of a model of matriliny defined in other than jural terms. If this suggestion seems too radical, we might make a modest beginning by including women as social actors within the jural model of matriliny.

d. The primacy of males

Following from the preceding discussions, it should now be clear why matrilineal theory, as presently constituted, has only a limited place for females. Effectively, women are significant in two respects: (1) as the means of biological reproduction of the descent unit, and (2) as objects of control by men. Neither of these roles requires that women appear in the structure as actors. This conceptual invisibility is validated by the assumptions of universal male authority and female inactivity in the public domain. Women's role is logically both constant and limited to the domestic domain. Since the theoretical interest in matriliny lies precisely in its continued existence despite the ambiguous roles of men and the problematic relations between males of different descent groups, it is both unimportant and unenlightening to devote much attention to the place of females within or between units.

This view of female participation in matrilineal descent groups as essentially uninteresting should be reassessed in light of current challenges to the notion of universal sexual asymmetry and the utility of the domestic/public distinction, particularly as presently constituted. In reconsidering the "logic" of matriliny we should consider the probable impact of a number of propositions on the structure and functioning of matrilineal descent groups. These propositions are:

(1) that women, as well as men, may exercise authority; therefore, we must reevaluate the range and content of possible roles within matrilineal descent groups;

(2) that women may function as important actors in the public domain (insofar as the public/domestic distinction is a meaningful one within the particular society); therefore, we must consider women's active roles as mediators between descent units;

(3) that gender ascriptions are not naturally but socially assigned, and are not determinant factors in all roles or contexts; therefore, we should speculate on the circumstances under which the domestic-public opposition may be more significant in determining role content than the gender status of the actors; and

(4) that gender similarities are at least as significant and informative as gender differences; therefore, an important feature of our conception of matrilinal descent groups must be an analysis of those roles of males and females, e.g. mother's brother and mother, which may significantly overlap.

It is evident that our conception of matriliny is at best and at worst badly distorted. To provide a comprehensive image of the matrilineal structure we must include not only male–male relations and male–female relations seen from a male perspective, but also female–female relations and female–male relations. This project involves first, more thoroughly specifying the possible female roles within the structure, and second, exploring the nature of female relations between units. Such roles as mother-in-law, and the associated relations of mother-in-law/daughter-in-law and co-mothers-in-law would be a fruitful place to start. Putting together the complete picture including both males and females as social actors would require analyzing more closely the mother-in-law/son-in-law, mother/son, and father/daughter relations as well as reinterpreting the brother/sister relation.

Once the total configuration in all its variations has been defined we will be in a strong position to apply this more complex notion of matriliny to the problem of change in matrilineal systems.

2. The Issue of Change

The best way to present the contending viewpoints on the issue of change in matrilineal systems is to allow their proponents to speak for themselves. First, Gough, representing the disintegration hypothesis:

> Recent literature has accumulated evidence to show that under economic changes brought about by contact with Western industrial nations, matrilineal descent groups gradually disintegrate. In their place the elementary family eventually emerges as the key kinship group with respect to residence, economic cooperation, legal responsibility, and socialization, with a narrow range of kinship relations spreading out from it bilaterally and linking it to other elementary families (1961:631).

In response, Douglas, proposing the adaptability alternative:

> The general impression of these analyses is that among kinship systems matriliny is a cumbersome dinosaur. Its survival seems to be a matter for wonder. Underlying them all is the implicit assumption that the elementary family is the basic, universal unit of society (1969:-123).

The theorists predicting the demise of matriliny base their arguments on the notion that matriliny is an inherently fragile institution involving tensions between the roles of mother's brother and father, and lacking congruence between the two spheres of interest and authority, the matrilineal descent group and the nuclear family. The outcome of pressure from the West, then, is the gradual disappearance of the matrilineal descent group and the takeover of its functions by the "natural" unit, the nuclear family, and the concomitant enhancement of conjugal and paternal ties. This narrowing of relations and concentration of functions can be detected _via_ certain indicators, including a shift to neolocal residence, a redefinition of the domestic unit, decreasing cooperation in production, etc.—all demonstrating the loss of corporate identity of the matrilineal descent group and its decreasing ability to control its members.

The alternative hypothesis proposes that the ambiguity of male roles in matrilineal systems provides opportunities for individual initiative. Under certain conditions, namely those of an expanding economy, matriliny can actually prove advantageous. The operationalization of initiative by males under these conditions is enhanced, Douglas argues, by the fact that matriliny necessarily generates extensive inter-group ties for men.

These stances proposing either disintegration or adaptive value hold essentially the same model of matriliny in common and are open to the same three general criticisms. First, as Kahn (1976, 1980a) notes, the notion of "tradition" is a suspect one on two grounds: (1) it suggests a form not bound in time and space, an eternal configuration; and (2) it contrasts this configuration with the altered form, suggesting a linear progression from one to the other. Second, since the analysis begins with a definition of the logical structure and essential features of the form, explanations of change tend to be in terms of "function." As the two outlines above suggest, the relation between form and function is a problematic one. Third, discussions of change, as do discussions of structure, take the form of a consideration of the implications for male roles, viewed from a male perspective. Just as the maintenance of order within units and interrelations between units are conceptualized as male activities, so the problem of the demise of these units is a problem of and for males, and the opportunities for initiative are opportunities for males for new relations between males.

Within this jural, politico-economic model of matriliny in change there is only a residual place for women. Neither the breakdown of the unit nor its resilience and adaptability can be accounted for, evidently, even partially in terms of their positions, roles, or relations. The focus is once more on the roles of mothers' brothers and fathers. Even if one accepts the restricted notion of change offered by the authors, it should be possible to accommodate women within the model. For instance, if we anticipate breakdown, we could contemplate the possibility that the resulting minimal unit might be that of mother and children, rather than the nuclear family. Indeed, if we accept the notion of women as socially significant actors in both the domestic and the public domains, we should assess the continuity or change in such roles

as mother and sister and within such relations as mother-
daughter and sister-sister, as well as in the relations between female affines, males and female affines, and male and
female matrilineal descent group members. Changes in some
roles and relations may be accompanied by change or lack of
change in others. If these possibilities are not explored,
one is left with two equally unsatisfactory conclusions: (1)
no significant change has taken place; if there had been any,
it would have been discussed; or (2) any change is merely a
reflex of changes in the "important" roles, and its shape can
satisfactorily be understood by reference to the key roles.

The Minangkabau Case[1]

If we examine the manner in which Minangkabau matriliny
has been characterized and analyzed, we find that it at once
reflects and contradicts the assumptions of matrilineal theory
as it is formulated and applied. Before proceeding, it is
essential to note that the materials dealing with Minangkabau
matriliny deal with different periods and different regions:
some refer to concrete practice and others to folk models (cf.
Kahn 1980 on this problem). For the purposes of this paper
this variation will be reduced to a generalized configuration
of Minangkabau matriliny.[2] This exercise is a purely heuris-
tic one and is in no way intended to obscure the inherent
problems of such a procedure.

An analysis of the relative statuses and roles of men

---

[1] My field research in West Sumatra from 1975 to 1977 was
sponsored by LIPI and supported by the Canada Council (now the
Social Sciences and Humanities Research Council of Canada).
The assistance of both institutions is gratefully acknowledged.
[2] This ethnographic material and analysis is based on the following sources: Abdullah 1966, 1970, 1972; Bachtiar 1967; F.
von Benda-Beckmann 1980; K. von Benda-Beckmann 1980; K. and F.
von Benda-Beckmann 1978; Cooper-Cole 1936; Johns 1958; de
Josselin de Jong 1951, 1980d; Junus 1964, 1971; Kahn 1976,
1980a; Kato 1977, 1978; Naim 1973; Ng 1980; Prindiville n.d.,
1980; Radjab 1969; Schrijvers and Postel-Coster 1977; Tanner
1971, 1974; and Thomas 1977. The perspectives of these authors do not entirely coincide, of course, but in many respects
their conclusions are similar and very few of their views are
completely idiosyncratic. Where there is broad agreement on
data or analysis, individual authors are not cited.

and women must begin with a comprehensive understanding of
each. As Schrijvers and Postel-Coster (1977) note, the literature on Minangkabau deals nearly exclusively with the roles
of men. Major exceptions to this focus of research and analysis are the works of Abdullah, Johns, and Tanner, and recently, the research of Ng and Pak. Several authors, such as
Junus, Kato, and Thomas also present us with information on
the relative roles of women and men, but do not systematically
draw out the implications of their data. Nonetheless it is
possible to begin to glimpse the place of Minangkabau women
both within and between descent groups if we consider several
themes typically forming the focus for discussions of matrilineality, that is: (1) the composition of descent units and
their residence patterns, (2) the distribution and actualization of authority, (3) the degree of corporateness of these
units, and (4) the integrative mechanisms by which these
groups are related.

1. Group Composition and Residence

Analyses of matrilineal descent group composition highlight a number of key roles within these units, for males
those of mother's brother, and for females those of mother and
daughter. By and large, the discussions then proceed to
elaborate the definition and functions of male roles under
their various designations, such as mamak, tungganai, and
penghulu, with the female roles of mother, sister, and daughter and their implications for group identity and operation
being treated as self-evident, and of more symbolic than
pragmatic importance. The work of Tanner is particularly
useful here in demonstrating the structural centrality of
females, especially in their role as mother, and the importance of links between females in promoting the continuity of
the group. Elsewhere (Prindiville 1980), I have argued that
within the matrilineal descent group there is a considerable
overlap, in both image and function, between the roles of
males and females, and that, pace Tanner, both men and women
must be considered central to this unit. Both Kahn and Thomas
have pointed to the function of women in promoting lineage
solidarity. Schneider's (1961) comments regarding segmentation to the contrary, we must also consider the significance
of women, especially sisters, as the focus of group segmentation. The more or less exclusive concentration on males,
and especially on the mamak-kamanakan relation, obscures
another important relation, that of mother to son.
    Discussions of matrilineal descent group composition
invariably refer to their physical placement and to the
problems involved in conceptually segregating a unit which is

in many respects spatially and socially integrated with groups
defined by other principles of social organization. Thus,
although most authors agree the Minangkabau are uxorilocal,
there is less consensus on the definition and operation of the
household unit. The emphasis has been somewhat less on conjugal ties than on the father-child relation, and on the problems of urang sumando (in-marrying men) in their ambiguous
relation to the matrilineal descent group and the nuclear
family. I would suggest that we do not require the concept of
nuclear family to deal with the household unit in all its
aspects, and that a more useful notion is that of a ([mother-
child] + father unit), which may function in a variety of
fashions, only one of which is as a nuclear family unit in our
sense of the term, depending on the degree to and manner in
which the father is added. That is to say, I think we will
proceed further by considering the mother-child unit to be the
basic unit than by assuming a priori the presence of a nuclear
family unit on the basis of the residential coincidence of its
components. In attempting to attribute sufficient importance
to the roles of males as either non-resident insiders or as
resident outsiders, we have not clearly enough conceptualized
the roles of females as members of matrilineal descent groups
within the nagari and household and the relations by which
they contribute to both the orderly operation of and tensions
within the group.

2. Authority

Analyses of the distribution and exercise of authority
within the matrilineal descent group generally have focused on
decision-making and have tended to share with current theories
of matriliny the assumption that this is the province of
males, whose function is to control and order the relations
and activities of the group's members. The focus here has
been on the formal characteristics and structural importance
of the relation between mamak and kamanakan (assumed to be
male). The input of females to decision-making has been
variously assessed as ranging from a large degree of influence
on a sphere formally defined as male to control over decision-
making within the domestic unit. I am not aware of any
attempt to define the formal characteristics of this female
role in decision-making, and, indeed, most authors hesitate to
apply the authority to women's decision-making activities.
The consideration of authority within matrilineal descent
groups is generally divided into spheres, domestic and public.
Some authors (cf. e.g. Kato 1977, 1978) then willingly concede
the ordering and control of the domestic sphere to women,
while reserving the more important public sphere for men. I

have argued elsewhere (Prindiville n.d.) that the application of our notions of public and domestic to the Minangkabau case is not an informative exercise, and should, indeed, lead us to reevaluate the general utility of this dichotomy. Here I propose that we begin to examine and analyze the presence and character of both male and female participation in decision-making without resorting to an artificial bounding of these activities into domestic and public domains. In this enterprise K. von Benda-Beckmann's caution of the importance of distinguishing between rule and procedure, and of being conscious of the role of the procedural element, is of considerable analytic value. This distinction enables us to distinguish between the process of decision-making (involving both males and females), the process of decision affirmation and validation (a responsibility of males), and the process of implementation (largely, but by no means exclusively, the responsibility of females). The intent of the foregoing is to argue the importance of making visible and analyzing the management roles of both men and women, without prejudicing the outcome by the a priori assignment of tasks on the basis of gender status.

3. Corporateness

Analyses of the degree and nature of corporateness of the matrilineal descent group have focused on the related themes of communal activities and responsibilies, and on property and inheritance, the former receiving less attention than the latter. Although several authors (e.g. Kahn 1980a; Kato 1977, 1978) have commented on the frequency with which women work collectively, I know of no systematic analysis defining and comparing male-male, female-female, and male-female styles and patterns of cooperation and collective activity within the matrilineal descent group. Such an analysis is essential to our understanding of the definition and operation of such groups.

As noted above, the issues of (1) the legal definition of types of property, (2) the utilization of and control over property, and (3) the inheritance of property and their implications for matrilineal descent group definition, operation, and shape through time are much better represented in the literature. Analyses offered by Tanner and F. and K. von Benda-Beckmann are particularly illuminating in this regard. However, these analyses can be extended to include a thorough consideration of their implications for male and female roles and relations within matrilineal descent groups only in conjunction with a much more conscious and comprehensive exposure and analysis of these features of Minangkabau matriliny than is currently available.

4. Integration

If the roles and relations within matrilineal descent groups in Minangkabau have sometimes been analyzed with reference to both males and females, such is not the case with discussions of the mechanisms through which the integration of the units into larger social networks occurs. It is here that the assumed division of labor between males and females, whereby males are allocated to the public sphere and females to the domestic, becomes problematic. If females are from the outset excluded from analyses of inter-group relations, our ability to understand Minangkabau society is severely limited. In considering the interrelations of matrilineal descent groups within the nagari it is essential to analyze the roles of women as both representatives of and mediators between these units (Prindiville n.d., 1980). Data on the affinal roles of women is particularly crucial here, and thus far scant. Hopefully the current research of Ng and Pak will add to our more sophisticated appreciation of female-female and female-male intergroup relations.

In light of the concerns of matrilineal theory it is not surprising that there has been considerable attention devoted to the role of urang sumando and their relations with their wives' matrilineal kin. Not surprisingly, also, these relations have generally been conceptualized as male-male rather than male-male and male-female relations. If we acknowledge that women are actors in the public domain and begin to explore their activities as mediators and managers, the complete range of relations--male-male, male-female, and female-female--through which matrilineal descent groups are integrated into larger social networks will become visible. I would agree that the Minangkabau case can, in this regard, provide a corrective to the assumptions of current theories of matriliny which focus almost exclusively on male roles and male-male relations. This is only one way in which the Minangkabau case can stimulate the reformation of matrilineal theory.

A second contribution, related to the issue of public and private domains, is a reassessment of the tendency to allocate men to productive and women to reproductive roles (in the social as well as the biological sense). This assumption, within which framework the discussion of matriliny takes place, obscures the productive roles and relations of women and prevents a thorough analysis of women as producers.

A third contribution to the general theory of matriliny is a revision of our interpretation of the tension generated by the ambiguous role of men who are simultaneously mother's brothers and fathers. This tension has been treated as problematic. As Abdullah (1966) has noted, for Minangkabau, conflict and balance between opposing elements are normal features of the social and conceptual universe. The lesson for functional theories of matriliny is that structural tension is not necessarily pathological, that ambiguity can be a normal structural feature and does not necessarily require resolution. At least in part, the assumption that matrilineal descent groups are inherently fragile and must give way to more rational forms grows out of the notion that tensions strive toward resolution rather than balance.

Minangkabau Matriliny and Change

There has been much attention devoted to the issue of the survival of matriliny in Minangkabau, ranging from earlier assertions that its disintegration was already well advanced (Gough 1961; Maretin 1961; Schrieke 1955) to claims that it is in fact both vital and viable (F. von Benda-Beckmann 1980; Kahn 1980a; Kato 1977, 1978). These studies have made their predictions on the basis of indicators such as residence patterns, domestic group composition, inheritance, corporateness, patterns of land ownership and use, marriage patterns, Islam, and conjugal and paternal ties.

The above lengthy preamble should allow us to begin to imagine what shape a new analysis of changing Minangkabau matriliny might take. We are hampered in this exercise by the lack of what Kahn has called the historical baseline. To my knowledge, the historical data necessary to construct a historical sequence with regard to the factors, roles, and relations we wish to include with reference to men _and_ women simply does not exist. We shall have to content ourselves, in its absence, with the less appealing alternative of beginning with a conceptual baseline and proceeding to speculate on possible changes from this model.

One prediction we can make based on the above discussion is that rates and directions of change will most likely be different for men and women. We might also consider the possibility that directed and undirected change may have differential influences on the two.

The possibilities for analyses that start from a different notion of matriliny and include equally men and women can be suggested by briefly examining three areas in which change is currently apparent. Kahn has discussed at some length the relation of subsistence to commodity production in Sungai Puar, where the subsistence sector is defined by rice production. Given the involvement of women as matri-

lineal descent group members in rice cultivation, it is worthwhile to investigate the change from subsistence to commodity
production of rice in villages where rice cultivation forms a
much larger sector of the economy than in Sungai Puar.[3] In
doing so we can consider whether the relations of sisters, and
of brothers and sisters, are being transformed, to what degree, and in what direction.

Another observable change is the decline in _nagari_
endogamy. Given our emerging understanding of the depth and
complexity of women's roles and the style of their expression
(Ng 1980; Prindiville n.d.), and the _nagari_-bound nature of
its content, we should consider the consequences of this
decline for the nature and extent of women's roles in the
integration of descent units within the _nagari_. At least two
possibilities present themselves: (1) a loss of meaning of
the symbols by which this integration is achieved and expressed, and hence a loss of or decline in this role; and (2)
the development of new types of relations between female
affines of different _nagari_ and of new symbols to express
these relations. We must, of course, also consider how the
relations between male affines, and between male and female
affines, are being affected.[4]

Finally, we can speculate that the development of the
nuclear family is more apparent than real, and that the
elementary unit remains a matrilineally defined one, albeit in
its minimal mother-child form. I would suggest that the shift
from _biliak_ to _rumah_ does not necessarily imply marked intensification of paternal or conjugal ties. Much of the
evidence--residential proximity of female matrilineal kin, the
tenuousness of the rights of _urang sumando_ to the houses they
build, etc.--suggests that the assumption of a shift to
nuclear family units may be premature.

In conclusion, a word about directed change. As
Schrijvers and Postel-Coster have noted, inherent in develop-

---

[3] Thus, for instance, while Kahn (1980a) correctly asserts
that in Sungai Puar rice cultivation is part of the subsistence sector, this observation is not true for all Minangkabau
nagari. In other _nagari_ women are engaged in the production
of rice as a commodity.

[4] I have argued elsewhere (Prindiville n.d.) that the media of
communication of men and women, speeches and food respectively, are equally _nagari_-bound systems of meaning. It is therefore the case that men's symbols also experience a loss of
meaning as male affines from different villages attempt to
communicate.

ment programs are implicit assumptions about the natures and roles of males and females, and these assumptions are reflected in the types of programs directed toward men and women. To date, programs for women tend to be concerned with birth control, hygiene, and cooking. Programs concerned with agricultural development, on the other hand, tend to be directed toward men. Given the general pattern of rice cultivation by women on corporately held property, these programs appear to be directed toward the wrong audience. It is important to speculate on the ultimate influence of this policy on the roles of female and male matrilineal descent group members in both the subsistence and the commodity sectors.

Conclusion

This paper attempts to contribute to the ongoing discussion of matriliny by considering some conceptual problems in the theory of matriliny and their implications. The intention has been not to burden the reader with detail, but to highlight certain issues in the hope of stimulating further discussion and theoretical development.

RETHINKING MATRILINY: DECISION-MAKING AND SEX ROLES
IN MINANGKABAU

Nancy M. Tanner
University of California, Santa Cruz
and
Lynn L. Thomas
Pomona College, Claremont

If authority is not specified as allocated to male members, a wider number of possible arrangements is conceivable than can be dealt with here.--David M. Schneider 1961:27

In this essay we address aspects of matrilineal theory in relation to understandings about Minangkabau. In particular, we point out difficulties with assumptions on which David Schneider's classic 1961 article on matrilineal theory rests and present a different beginning point based on Minangkabau data. In 1961 Schneider indicated that he realized a different beginning point for reasoning about the structure and operation of matrilineal groups was possible, but chose not to look at it. However, time and additional research have shown the necessity of rethinking matriliny.

The Minangkabau are a large, well-known, matrilineal, Islamic people whose home area is the highlands of western Sumatra; many have migrated to Negeri Sembilan in Malaysia and large numbers now also live throughout urban Indonesia. Their matrilineal social system is made up of well-established, well-functioning, long-term decision-making units that control the basic commodities of land, houses, and subsistence. Women, as mothers, are central in basic cultural beliefs and in the day-to-day decision-making for the ongoing functioning of the matrikin unit; from time to time kin group men and husbands are active in consultation and group decision-making; and husbands begin their tenure as honored guests. Men have considerable freedom of movement; this has enabled them to have a wide variety of roles over the years in the islands of Indonesia--including activities as farmers, traders, politicians, authors, and professors. The Minangkabau social system is set up in such a way that a wide number of arrangements and opportunities are feasible for both sexes: a wider number of arrangements than can be understood within the limits of Schneider's kinship model. The case of Minangkabau requires a rethinking of matrilineal theory.

Introduction

Several assumptions form the inferential basis of David Schneider's 1961 paper, "The Distinctive Features of Matrilineal Descent Groups." First and most basic is that activities are seen from the perspective of a male ego; a male perspective is presumed throughout. Second, to quote, "Men by definition have authority over women and children" (1961:19). He does not say anything like: men are involved in kin group decision-making. Rather, men are simply presented unconditionally as having authority over women and children overall. In Minangkabau social life (some examples of which will be given later) this does not apply. Third, although Schneider does little to reason explicitly about or examine modes of descent group decision-making, the impression given is that he assumes that decisions are made by leaders exercising a hierarchical type of unshared authority or control. He states that the "minimal condition for such a structure is that authority be differentially distributed among the members of the group" (1961:4). Finally, he assumes that matrilineal descent groups are exogamous; and as a result, they have to contend with the out-marriage of men. Although Minangkabau kin groups are in fact exogamous, with women of one kin group marrying men of other kin groups, we must question the other assumptions on which his model rests.[1]

Schneider tries throughout his article to better understand matriliny by contrasting it with patriliny. The fundamental question in his paper is how order and coherence can be established in matrilineal descent groups given what he believes to be a "central discrepancy"--a "discrepancy" which is a consequence of the above suppositions. This "discrepancy" is that while "...in patrilineal descent groups the line of authority and the line of descent both run through men... [in] matrilineal descent groups...the line of authority also runs through men," but "group placement runs through the line of women. The lines of authority and group placement are thus

---

[1] In constructing this kinship model Schneider summarizes the "conditions which are by definition here, constant features of unilineal descent groups" in these terms: "...[W]omen are responsible for the care of children, ...adult men have authority over women and children, and ...descent group exogamy is required" (1961:5).

-46-

coordinate in males in patrilineal descent groups, but separated between males and females in matrilineal descent
groups" (1961:7). Schneider organizes his discussion of matriliny around the problems he thinks are presented by this
"central discrepancy," this separation of descent and authority. It is quite an awkward model to describe a system that
has been effective and useful to the energetic Minangkabau for
many years.

There is no reason to assume that there is only a male
ego, a male actor, or a male perspective in any society. This
is so obvious that it is absolutely amazing that such an extensive period of Western anthropology looked at the action of
only half the human species and tried to build behavioral
models on that basis. It makes a great deal of sense to study
both women and men, and much more can be understood about how
societies operate if analyses are from both male and female
perspectives. We will attempt this throughout.

Our major focus in this essay will be to examine the applicability of suppositions two and three—of unconditional
male authority over women and children in all spheres of activity, and of an unshared hierarchical control-type authority—in the case of the Minangkabau.[2] In other words, we
question the relevance of Schneider's assumptions about both
mode of decision-making and its sex role basis to the operation of Minangkabau matrilineal descent groups. Initially, we
present ethnographic and ceremonial information concerning sex
roles within and between Minangkabau descent groups. Next, we
examine five specific sets of observations: first, a dispute
which explicitly exemplifies aspects of male and female authority in conflict settlement in the descent sphere; second,
the kin group decision-making process per se; third, the question of "control" of and by males in matrilineal groups;
fourth, Minangkabau marital relationships and the relations of
men to their children and wives' kin groups; and fifth, the
question of asymmetries in Minangkabau address usages by husbands and wives. Finally, we discuss two traditional Minangkabau tales which indicate quite directly the nature of the
basic difficulty in Schneider's suppositions regarding both
"male authority" and "mode of authority" and therefore of his

---

[2] As Franz von Benda-Beckmann has noted (pers. comm.),
authority can be differentiated according to cultural (and
especially ideological) conceptions, authority invested in
particular positions, and actual exercises of authority.
These forms of authority are related, but their relative
importance and the ways they interplay can vary contextually.

"central discrepancy." We find his basic definition regarding "male authority" and underlying assumption regarding "mode of authority" in matrilineal societies problematic and, if applied to Minangkabau matriliny, conducive to erroneous interpretations of Minangkabau social life. Therefore, we suggest an alternative approach.

Ethnographic and Ceremonial Data on Minangkabau Sex Roles Within and Between Lineages

To analyze the operation of Minangkabau kinship one must begin anew, looking first at the rich data that have begun to accumulate, and then from that information begin to reformulate a model of matrilineality.

In the early part of this century Willinck noted the relative authority of the senior woman (a mother or grandmother) and implied that she and the mamak (Mkb., a mother's brother) shared authority when he stated that "in the Minangkabau family circle the oldest common ancestress, if still alive, stood actually above the mamak" (1909:391).[3]

More recently, both Joanne Prindiville (1980) and Ok-Kyung Pak (1980) have noted women's public, economic, and ceremonial roles. Perhaps in the simplest and most basic sense, "houses are identified by the name of the most senior resident woman" (Prindiville 1980:5). Women have a central economic responsibility in providing for their children's and husband's food and their children's education from as many sources as they can put together: deriving from their use-rights over lineage harato pusako (Mkb., ancestral lands) and produce, home industries, market work, jobs, and whatever they obtain from husbands, brothers, and sons (Ok-Kyung Pak 1980; Prindiville 1980). Minangkabau homes are matrilocal from the perspective of daughters and uxorilocal from the perspective of males, and are matrifocal in both organization and values (Tanner 1974, 1976).

Women in the ordinary course of affairs control the day-to-day usage of most of the ancestral rice land (harato pusako), its harvest, the money they earn from that land, and the money they earn from other economic activities such as marketing and/or home industries (Schrijvers and Postel-Coster 1977; Tanner 1971). Thus authority, in the sense of economic

---

[3] Von Benda-Beckmann has stressed that the group within which central decisions pertaining to property are made is demarcated with reference to the apical ancestress (1979a:160).

control over property or individual autonomous decisions concerning both personal and lineage economic resources, regularly involves the lineage women.[4] The centrality and authority of a woman's role within the matrilocal extended family increases with age.

With regard to descent group ceremonial affairs, Ok-Kyung Pak observed and described a week-long wedding ceremony in one area (1980:15-20).[5] She points out that much of the organization of the wedding and the expense for it were managed by women. Ceremonially--and symbolically--both women and men have important roles to play: the groom was accompanied to the bride's house twice by male friends, but on the afternoon that he was seated next to the bride he was delivered by his mother and about ten other women; a rice exchange occurred between the women of the two families; and very special adat (Ind., customary)[6] clothing was worn by women in particular kinship roles on various occasions. She observed an exchange of formal speeches by male penghulu (Ind., kin "headmen")[7] and an exchange of formal speeches by male professional speakers from both the bride's and groom's side. At another time a woman from the bride's house stood up and called out the names of women from a variety of kin groups linked to her own matrilineal kin group who had to be acknowledged: women married to men of the bride's house; women of the bride's father's house; the mother of the groom; women of the groom's father's house.[8] Here, then, is activity in the ceremonial realm by both women and men; both have a variety of significant roles to play.

In kin ceremonial behavior, day-to-day economic activities, house identification, household management, and land-use rights, women occupy central positions in Minangkabau kin groups. Assumption number two, authority held exclusively by men, simply does not bear up if one starts from an ethnographic description of Minangkabau society.

---

[4] Von Benda-Beckmann discusses the authority vested in women as not limited to the domestic sphere only (1979a:81ff); he also discusses the significant role women play in lineage decision-making (1979a:93), and in a history of a lineage, he gives a number of useful empirical illustrations (1979a:218-225).
[5] Kota nan Gadang, Pajakumbuh, 50 Kota.
[6] Mkb., adaik.
[7] Mkb., panghulu.
[8] Each then came up and put pounded flower petal on a fingernail of bride and of groom.

A Conflict Over Lineage Property

Women have been seen to be often directly involved in
disputes about kin property (harato pusako) and in the settlement of disputes about this land (Tanner 1971, 1982). For
example, one dispute illustrates (1) day-to-day control of
land by a village woman, (2) a male kinsman's objection to how
she controlled the harvest and earnings from the land, and (3)
the involvement of both a penghulu (lineage head) and a senior
lineage woman in the settlement after the mamak (Mkb., mother's brother; a senior male minor lineage member) had been unable to resolve the matter (Tanner 1969:44-46).

In this dispute within a minor lineage group, a male
plaintiff objected to a woman's use of all the descent group
land, and especially to her further borrowing of rice for
financing her husband's political activities. The parties
involved were the mother's sister's son versus the mother's
sister's daughter. The mamak attempted to settle the dispute,
but was unsuccessful in ending it. The dispute was then
taken to the lineage penghulu. He asked that the senior
living woman of their minor lineage (the disputants' mothers'
mother's sister), who was involved economically, be asked to
return home from Jakarta for consultation on the matter. Upon
her return there was a meeting between her, the penghulu, and
the disputants. The senior woman first stated her right to
decide "by adat and agama," i.e. by matrilineal custom and
Islam. The plaintiff did not agree with the interpretation
that Islam substantiated her right of decision. Then the
senior woman went on to point out that it was, in any case,
she who had bought or reclaimed most of the ancestral sawah
(rice land) they were fighting about. After this, she and the
penghulu conferred and decided that the rice harvest should be
divided 50:50, but the land itself not be divided. Thus,
there was a compromise on the use-rights, but the integrity of
the ancestral land was maintained as the senior woman
preferred. It was decided that half of the harvest was to be
for the female defendant and half for the minor lineage as a
whole, with joint decisions each season over the communal
half's use. The following season the plaintiff was allowed to
buy a cow with the half of the harvest allocated to the
lineage as a whole.

Here we see the active and important roles of both women
and men, in this instance not only in disputing but also in
settling the dispute. The day-to-day authority over the land
was in the hands of the minor lineage woman residing in the
village until a male minor lineage member also residing in the
village (her mother's sister's son) felt she misused this

authority. But he was unable to obtain control over the land himself by appealing to his and her mothers´ brother (the mamak of that minor lineage) or to a penghulu (from another part of the lineage). The dispute was not settled until the senior female who had redeemed the land for that minor lineage was called home from Jakarta. Even then the final decision allowed the younger village woman´s authority over the land to be limited but not lost, with 50% of the harvest to be decided upon by the minor lineage as a group.

Initially, the dispute appears in important respects to be quite consistent with Schneider´s point of view. One can grant generally the point that in Minangkabau the positions of mamak and penghulu are prototypically male. These two positions are, moreover, generally arranged hierarchically in the order in which they were brought into the dispute. First, the "lower ranking" genealogically nearer mamak was brought in, and then, when he failed to resolve the dispute, "higher" authority was sought. But it is also clear from the events of the dispute that senior women with economic power have definite positions of authority. Recall that Willinck noted the shared authority of the senior woman (a mother or grandmother) and mamak early in this century when he stated that "in the family circle the oldest common ancestress, if still alive, stood actually above the mamak" (1909:391). Willinck´s observation of the senior woman of the lineage "actually" standing above the mamak is substantiated in this instance. Indeed, here, her practical authority over her branch of the lineage seems at least equal to that of the penghulu, the titled "head" of the larger unit.

The Kin Group Decision-Making Process: Mupakaik

It is also important to examine the nature of "authority" itself within Minangkabau descent groups. Although Schneider does not preclude other modes of authority, he gives the impression of command decisions made in the context of a hierarchical chain of positions. But in Minangkabau many decisions are made in consensual modes termed mupakaik (Mkb.), shared consultation by group members. Titled or "authority" positions are often more used to influence the manner of decision-making than to make command decisions. Minangkabau individuals themselves are not romantics when they note that discussion and consensus must at least be given attention, and perhaps typically, are one of the foci of attention in dispute settlement, resource allocation, and other kinds of kin group decision-making.

In the dispute described above, the lack of success of

-51-

the __mamak__ in his initial attempt at resolution serves as a reminder of the constraints to which he is subjected in his exercise of authority. __Mamak__, in general, cannot force decisions. Neither can __penghulu__. So far as we are aware, neither can a senior woman--although, in the exercise of assertive speech and in "laying out the facts" she comes closest to being the one to do so in the dispute just described.

But insofar as women tend to have great responsibilities for the day-to-day management of lineage affairs, among which are difficult and continuous work obligations, women's investments and immersion in the details of local kin affairs can have among their limits the possibility of parochiality or partiality; this possibility, in itself, might reinforce the tradition of discussion, consultation, and group decision-making.

In many respects, kin "authority" in Minangkabau--especially when it brings in the men for aspects other than the women's day-to-day decision-making in the exercise of ongoing activities--rests on group-decision making, not command. Group decision-making has its own refined, very polite, sometimes almost poetic, verbal style of consultation called __pasambahan__ (Mkb.) which is used in formal meetings. In such formal meetings in a matrilineal household this refined verbal style is used by men whereas the women succinctly and directly put forth their points of view in everyday speech.

For example, a group of men can be brought into a matrilineal long house for special consultation. One manner involves use of the __pasambahan__ speech style by men, wearing black, rather formal clothing, sitting on the floor up and down the long front room of the house in formal body positions talking with each other. In contrast, a few women of the household sit casually by, not in the men's rows, clustered somewhat together and not wearing their elegant ceremonial clothing but rather dressed as if this were an ordinary matter. A woman may sit with a leg stretched out comfortably, unlike the men, whose legs are carefully folded. On such an occasion, a woman does not participate in the long poetic interchange of __pasambahan__ speech itself, but simply puts forward her opinion or a pertinent fact in daily speech when she thinks it needs discussion.

Adjudicatory, advisory, conciliatory, legitimizing, and expressive aspects are more important functions of "authority" in such Minangkabau kin group settings than command. Negotiation is basic, and compromise decisions are not unusual. Male and female "authoritative" styles differ, but both men and women are involved as integral participants in the processes.

Schneider and "Control": Of and By Males?

Schneider's discussion of male descent group "control" systematically confuses male "control" <u>by</u> their descent group with male "control" <u>over</u> the other descent members.

In terms of kin group constitution, Minangkabau "control" over male and female members is in one respect quite unproblematic: men and women are members in perpetuity of the lineage of their mother and through their mother's kin group are also members of the higher-order descent groups in which the mother's kin unit is nested.[9]

On the other hand, we should not be understood to be suggesting that a relative unimportance of a problem of the constitution of descent groups necessarily implies the absence of problems of engaging members in group activities and responsibilities or of effective "control" of particular persons or positions within the confines of that group. It is in this context especially, that the matters of lack of unconditional male headship and authority, and presence of decentralized day-to-day decision-making, combined with consultation in lar-

---

[9] Conceivably, Schneider might have had the implicit proposition that constitutional matters such as this have to be negotiated (or otherwise worked out) in terms of daily conduct anyway, and that it is his purpose to describe some of the potential limits of matriliny in relation to patterns of behavior that could subvert it. Such would be taking a long view of matters, one in which constitutional norms are seen as being insufficient by themselves to prevent the subversion of the system. This point of view has considerable appeal, but it raises questions of the boundaries between modes of conduct of affairs and the defining terms of such conduct which are beyond the scope of this paper. We cannot here do more than indicate one possibly relevant bit of speculation on the matter of control of male members of matrilineal descent groups. Consider then, the possibility that if membership control were quite problematic, there would be numerous ambiguities and qualifications placed upon it, especially for males. But membership is unambiguous and unqualified (save for crimes and migrations of descent groups). If men's involvements away from their matrilineal descent groups and in the descent groups of their wives were problematic in the way Schneider's proposition seems to imply, then the problems are strangely unrecognized among Minangkabau. Schneider himself, at several points in his paper, shows his awareness of a general unequivocalness of matrilineal descent group membership.

ger scale decision-making both among males and between males and females, become so important. The matter of "control"—either of males or by males—is less difficult or important than is implied by Schneider, given these Minangkabau forms of group kin decision-making, the matrilineal constitution of lineages, and of both cultural, idealized matrifocality and of practical, daily matrifocality in decision-making in at least the matrilineally extended family and the minor lineage branch.

In order to give an idea of the kind of practical day-by-day matrifocality in decision-making that we perceive to be a part of Minangkabau matriliny, we will comment on the first of Schneider's propositions:

> (1) Matrilineal descent groups depend for their continuity and operation on retaining control over both male and female members (1961:8).

Most of Schneider's discussion of this proposition relates to his assumption that male authority implies descent group control over male members. "If males are required for authority roles then they, too, cannot be relinquished by or alienated from the group" (1961:8). But, in Minangkabau matriliny, male authority is set beside, or replaced with, female (e.g. motherly and sisterly) cultural authoritativeness (which need not entail matriarchy in the sense of unconditional female control). The mode of decision-making values maturity and practicality, and involves day-to-day decisions largely by women along with consultation and group discussion and consensus. In this form of matriliny, the question of retaining control of male members has to be seen in a different light.

Note that many Minangkabau lineages function quite well in spite of the absence of many male members, who are away on merantau (Mochtar Naim, this volume). Many Minangkabau women are in charge on a daily basis and make the decisions of greater or less consequence for the well-being of the lineage. It is not quite that men in Minangkabau are released to the matrilineages of their wives, as women of Schneider's patrilineal descent groups are said to be incorporated into their husbands' groups, but it is the case that keeping control of men as prime decision-makers is less problematic among Minangkabau than in Schneider's picture. In part this is because the central cultural authority of women is translatable, depending on circumstances (which certainly include the presence of men of the lineage and/or in-marrying men), into real power regarding decisions; in part this is because of the relative decentralization of much decision-making; and in part it is because of an ideology of group mupakaik in the decision-making process itself.

It is an aspect of the normal functioning of Minangkabau matriliny that many men are absent from the group's immediate "control" for extended periods of time, not to be incorporated into the group of their wives but to engage in activities not in the purview of the descent groups. Many men often are not even in West Sumatra, the area of Indonesia in which lands are owned by Minangkabau matrilineages.

This custom of "going out" from West Sumatra, or meran-tau, makes it possible for men often to bring something of value to both their ancestral descent group and the descent group(s) into which they marry. In such merantau, a Minang-kabau man may acquire respect, influence, and financial success; increase sophistication, knowledge, cross-cultural capabilities, and wit; become a good candidate for marriage; or sometimes even escape what are usually viewed as reasonable responsibilities.

This is not just a matter of losing redundant men, since men who are potential successors to titles can be absent as well. Rather it is a matter of protecting the lineages' next generations through the use-rights for homes and farms residing with the mothers and of providing considerable freedom of movement for the men.

Minangkabau Men's Relationship to their Wives' Descent Groups

The relationship of Minangkabau men to their wives' descent groups also takes a different form than Schneider gives it. To see this point, note two others of Schneider's propositions:

> (4) The institutionalization of very strong, lasting, or intense solidarities between husband and wife is not compatible with maintenance of matrilineal descent groups (1961:16).

> (4a) Matrilineal descent groups require the institutionalization of special limits on the authority of husbands over wives (1961:19).

This is supposed to be because, as figures of authority, in-married men present a threat to the descent group's authority over women and children; and therefore those in-married men are denied close ties with their wives, for the wives' loyalties could then be pulled away from the lineage.

However, in observing Minangkabau marriages, one notes several contingencies: marriages are arranged by the descent

-55-

groups, especially first marriages; there is a high divorce rate; a very real closeness exists in most marriages that do continue since marriages generally do not need to continue if they do not work out; and there is (in recent times at least) an ideal of romantic love, particularly exemplified in Minangkabau literature (Tanner 1982). In contrast to Schneider, we reason that if the husband's authority over his wife is sufficiently limited, the effect of authority in decreasing intimacy is likely to be correspondingly limited.

It is true that in Minangkabau a husband's authority over his wife and children is sharply limited and demarcated. However, we can think of sources of the limits other than Schneider's: first, it is because the husband is entering an established unit of well-functioning organization from the outside. His authority is limited because of his standing as an outsider to the matrilineage and because the lineage's members are already established there and not apt to give up their rights or position to an outsider. His wife has a well-established source of solidarity there, with a definite role in decision-making in the lineage and a position of authority, especially with respect to her prospective children and daughter's children. It is not so much, however, that a husband is "kept out" of lineage business as that his participation in that business has to be seen in the context of the pre-existence and continuing functioning of the lineage. But there is a rider that we think needs to be attached to these interpretations that was surprisingly missed by Schneider. Either as an outsider in general, or as a person who has had long-term partial involvements with the lineage as in the case of an older in-married man, an in-married man may become a special source of influence in his wife's lineage. Such a man may have just enough distance from personal interestedness in some lineage affairs that he may provide a broad perspective on those affairs. If he learns them intimately enough--as he has ample opportunity to do in many cases--then he may be able by virtue of a combination of distance and involvement to mediate in disputes or give advice. Note well that insofar as an in-married man is successful at mediating in the way suggested, however, he would be unlikely to be the sort of man, or to be in the sort of position, that would enable him to use his influence systematically in ways that would "subvert" his wife's lineage interest in his own personal or lineage interest.[10]

---

[10] This is, by the same token, not to suggest that Minangkabau men as affines and husbands are apt to be saintly. There is great ambiguity in the folklore about urang sumando (Mkb., in-

-56-

We should also point out that in Minangkabau the demarcations of descent and domestic spheres are constructed in a way which is pertinent to our discussion. We take the basic constitutional relation of Minangkabau kin groups to be recursive mother-child relations. The mother-child unit in particular is both a domestic and a descent unit, by which we mean that it can be pictured in terms of not only its close family nurturance but also of its connections and wider relations with the groups within which it is nested. Some of these wider relations involve strictly matrilineal ties with higher order or coordinate lineages; some of them involve the political groups and relations among them in the context of life in a part of the village or in the village as a corporate unit. Or, correspondingly, the mother-child unit can be seen as the beginning of a long line, for it is with it that a new lineage segment can begin. Husbands are parts of close domestic units, or at least they have or have had some close and marked relation with a woman of some such unit. The husband, of course, is not himself part of his wife's or wives' and children's larger matrikin descent unit(s).

What this means is that a husband's "domestic sphere" is nested in a wife's most immediate descent sphere: the nuclear family is thus nested within the matrilineal extended family. One indication of this nesting of "domestic sphere" in "descent sphere" as it relates to the husband's "authority" is the following observation.

> Generally a man will not need to discipline his sister's children. But when I asked on one occasion what the children's father would do should their mother's brother see a need for disciplining them, my informant...sat back in his chair, folded his arms resolutely, put on a blank expression, and said nothing—he was acting out the behavior appropriate to the father in such a case. The father [he said] is <u>diam saja</u> "quiet"; he does not interfere with the mother's brother's prerogative (Thomas 1977:119).

At the same time it seems reasonably clear (in some Minangkabau villages at any rate) that a man will often devote himself more fully to his wife's "domestic family," which for her may

---

married men), ranging from denigration of their unreliability to respect for their role in lineage affairs (de Josselin de Jong 1980b). The folklore is wonderfully consistent with the points we are trying to establish.

be her nuclear family or matrilineally extended family, than to his own lineage (Korn 1941:305).[11] In either case the members of any nuclear or extended family, save for their husbands, are members of their immediate minor lineage. The placements of women in intersections of descent and domestic spheres tend to give them secure sources of influence and reinforce the image of their central cultural authoritativeness, particularly as mothers. The in-married men who are already fathers sometimes make special efforts to care for their children in ways that are apt to preclude the children's lineage mates from taking undue advantage. What this may mean, for example, is the provision of a gift from a man to his children, say a small holding of cinnamon trees, it being made clear that the gift is to the children, not the children's mother. Then, in case of a divorce, which can lead to a marked decrease of a man's contact with his children, the children and not the mother's lineage in general, benefit. One sometimes hears men express the sentiment that a woman's lineage is supposed to care for the woman, and so her husband should take more care (in cases of limited resources) to provide for the children. This could help provide an economic foundation for segmentation of their lineage, and the formation of a new matriline if some intra-lineage conflict were to subsequently occur.

In short, the roles of men and women regarding the relations between domestic and descent spheres are considerably more complex, yet less problematic, than Schneider's paper would have led one to expect.

Husband-Wife Asymmetries?

In the Minangkabau language, as in the national language Indonesian, third person terms are not marked for gender, as they are in English by "he" and "she." Inyo (Mkb.), and ia (Ind.), each refer to either he or she and, roughly speaking, can be translated as "that individual." With third person terms not marked for sex there is, of course, also no elevation of a term for one sex to refer to people in general as occurs in the English usage of "Man." Minangkabau and Indonesian have their own terms--not gender marked--for "human," and "people": urang (Mkb.) and orang (Ind.).

---

[11] To be sure, in cases of potential conflict between the two spheres, a man is loath to abrogate responsibilities and ties to his own lineage.

However, in some Minangkabau villages, perhaps generally, there is something of an apparently gender related asymmetry in the ways wives and husbands address or refer to one
another in public contexts. The usage is asymmetrical in that
while a husband may address his wife by name, she does not
usually reciprocate with her husband's name. A woman may use
her husband's title[12] in speaking to or about her husband.
Since women do not have <u>adat</u> titles (Mkb., <u>gala</u>)[13] they are
not ordinarily addressed by title. She may also use the terms
<u>laki</u> or <u>suami</u> (Mkb. and Ind., "husband" in both cases). A wife
also may be addressed as <u>adiek</u> (Mkb., "younger sibling"), or
as <u>bini</u> or <u>isteri</u> (Mkb. and Ind. for "wife").

It might be tempting to assimilate the asymmetry in husband-wife usage to an assumption of a general system of as-
cription of rank in male-female relations and to view it as an
instance of Schneider's generalization that in matrilineal
kinship systems men as a rule have authority over women. One
might presume that the asymmetry of husband-wife nomenclature
has its source in a domestic asymmetry of men as husbands and
fathers over women as wives and mothers.[14]

However, this wife-husband address asymmetry parallels a
general asymmetry in the use of kin terms and titles versus
names according to age or seniority. The general rule is that
while non-adults use title or kin terms for adults, male or
female, and not names (at least not names alone), adults speak
to, or of, non-adults by name. Similarly an adult sometimes
will speak of another adult (who is younger or lower in social
standing) by name.[15] Wives as a rule tend to be younger than

---

[12] A title is generally given to men at marriage or before;
titles are also parts of <u>penghuluships</u>.

[13] <u>Adat</u> ("customary") kin titles are not held by women, but in
some cases women do have other kinds of titles, such as <u>haji</u>
for a woman who has been to Mecca, or <u>Dra</u>., for a masters'
degree.

[14] One could also imagine that the usage might be involved in
the demarcation of boundaries between domestic and descent
spheres. Schneider's picture of limitation of the husbands's
authority to the domestic sphere and of the matrilineage's
authority outside that sphere would be broadly consistent with
the asymmetry, as well as being consistent with the fact that
the husband-wife asymmetry does not have usage entailments for
the ways in which a woman's matrikin speak of her husband or
he them. Finally, one might even imagine invoking his
hypothesis of an inverse relationship between closeness and
authority. Compare with Peletz, this volume.

husbands. Traditionally, a husband was provided for a woman by her kin group about when she reached sexual maturity in early adolescence.[16]

Although young women are ordinarily provided husbands, a man must wait to be invited; and the best way to ensure an invitation is for him to exhibit something desirable, usually in terms of skills, finances, or status. Minangkabau have a rough rule of thumb that it is appropriate for a husband to come from a group of higher standing than that of the wife.[17] The household tries to bring in a man who has something to offer: educational, professional, or business proficiency, and/or status of some type—his lineage's status or his titled status within that lineage. There is, in fact, a "groom price" offered in some communities and it may vary according to the man's "value." The members of the minor lineage who are inviting in a husband tend to invite those men who can benefit the kin group either economically or through increased status.

Further, the use of titles regarding Minangkabau men and the general non-use of titles for Minangkabau women may have little to do with matriliny as a form of kinship organization. Rather, it may relate more to concepts and customs in the societies from which the Minangkabau borrowed political ideas as they organized their communities politically and constructed the Old Kingdom. In other words titles may relate to conceptualizations of leadership attendant upon political expansion,[18] and may have been adopted from those of other large-

---

[15] Use of personal pronouns parallels the kin term-or-title versus name usage: all personal pronouns are marked for seniority or social rank such that a term used in speaking to a person of junior rank (say a youngster) will be reciprocated with a pronoun (or kin term or title) appropriate for speaking to higher ranked or older people.

[16] Today, in some villages, many women marry later (eighteen or older), often because of involvement in education and professional training.

[17] The pattern of marriage by lineage rank is one which has numerous exceptions in practice; men do fairly often marry women whose lineages have higher social standing than their own lineages. In those cases, other things being the same (in particular that a woman is younger than her husband), the same nomenclatural usage will occur.

[18] Politics to relate kin groups within communities and in inter-community relations could have been involved. The politics of the Old Kingdom of Minangkabau also may have been

scale societies, such as India, with whom they have had historical contact.

Overall, an initial asymmetry in age and achievement or rank is not uncommon between brides and grooms, particularly for first marriages arranged by kin groups, and the forms of address and reference follow general usage regarding rank and age. With increasing maturity a woman's status within her matrilineal kin group increases, as does her economic self-reliance. Economically, her position usually becomes increasingly solid through use of kin property and other economic activities such as market sale of garden products or of her own home industry produce; she compiles funds from her own earnings and those of other family members (such as husband, brothers, and sons) to educate children, hold ceremonies, build a house, redeem lineage property, etc., and may increase or obtain personal property such as beautiful hand-crafted gold jewelry or jewelry made of gold coins that can act as "savings" and have direct economic value. Generally she continues to exhibit public politeness to her husband in terms of address and reference. However, she also becomes increasingly capable of managing her own household should she divorce him.

Is asymmetry in address usage associated with a general notion of husbands having authority over wives? This appears unlikely: a woman operates on a day-to-day basis the lineage properties for which she has use-rights; the home is known by

---

involved. Growth in Minangkabau political organization may have included titles for lineage "headmen", who came to function in the village councils in addition to within their own lineages at the village level, and titles for "royalty" in the Old Kingdom. Both these types of political roles have existed among the Minangkabau for at least several hundred years and have been largely inhabited by titled men during Minangkabau history. Yet, in some more forested parts of Sumatra there are societies which are far smaller and less politically organized than the Minangkabau—for example the Talang Mamak, who Minangkabau say are related to them but "ran to the forest" when Minangkabau accepted Islam. Long-term villages in lasting locales relying on wet-rice agriculture or political institutions such as kerajaan (Ind., kingdoms; Mkb., karajaan) made up of long-term villages do not even now exist in these jungle regions. So too, the political roles specific to these institutions do not yet exist in such nearby forested parts of Sumatra. Some of the specific Minangkabau concepts regarding titled roles appear to have been relevant to Minangkabau political structure.

her name; and a wife can readily tell her husband to leave or "put his shoes outside the door" if she feels it is necessary to do so. A female's role changes and status increases with motherhood and age--as she ceases to be a juvenile and becomes a woman--although she continues to address and refer to her older husband, who in many respects is treated as an honored guest in her home, by "older brother," "husband," or his title.

Our examination has suggested that the interpretation of the nature of any husband-wife asymmetry in address is in some doubt, on the simple grounds that it could as well involve an age asymmetry, an asymmetry of relations by marriage among descent groups, or a straightforward effort to offer respect to a husband who exercises little power or control, but who can make a real contribution to the mother-child unit.

Two Minangkabau Tales

In Minangkabau culture there is a traditional tale, <u>Kaba Rantjak diLabueh</u>, translated into English by Anthony Johns (1958), which offers some insights into the ideal functioning of male and female roles in the matrikin group. The main characters in this <u>kaba</u> (Mkb., tale) are Siti Djuhari, the mother, her daughter Siti Budiman, and her son Rantjak diLa-bueh--who is later given the title Sutan Sampurna (Mkb., Sam-parono) and later yet, after his marriage, becomes a <u>penghulu</u>. The story supposedly is told by the son who had once been called Rantjak diLabueh, an appelation meaning "Good-looking in the Village Square." He begins by saying, "I tell you the story of my mother, a story in which you see my part" (1958:2).

Siti Djuhari, the mother, is the one who is the source of family wisdom in this tale, and it is she who teaches her son and daughter their adult kin roles. According to this traditional <u>kaba</u>, the mother "was clever and eager to learn...a store-house of sense, a sea of sound discourse...able to see what was useful and what waste" (1958:6). In contrast, her son, Rantjak diLabueh, was "only happy to amuse himself, heedless of profit or loss. While others worked he played" (1958:6), and "when it was past noon back he went to his mother's house to ask for food and drink" (1958:8). He bought gorgeous clothes, and to get the money he pawned rice fields. Siti Djuhari put forward instructions about many things--she told him that he should not act in that way, informed him that she worked hard and that sort of

behavior was injurious to her, told him how he should
not dress fine without working, and warned him that
later he would "feel the consequences of ignoring your
mother's advice" (1958:18). Later he ran out of money
and asked her to pay his debts. She said "if you will
really obey and accept my teaching, then I will pay your
debts" (1958:22). He replied "Neither now, nor in the
future will I ever disobey you" (1958:24).

Rantjak diLabueh did indeed reform. He began working
seriously, and "all that he earned he gave to his dear
mother" (1958:26). One day she said, "Let us arrange a
feast and change your title" (1958:30). She gave him
money to buy things and pay his debts. She then taught
him specifically how to act properly: how to sit correctly, what way to eat, to love the young, to respect
the old. And he followed her advice. She then went on
to initiate the feast for their kin, also with the village and district penghulu. At the feast she announced
she wanted to change his title. It was all discussed,
all agreed that it was a good idea, and his title was
changed from Rantjak diLabueh to Sutan Sampurna ("Sutan
Perfect"). Afterwards, his behavior had changed; he
followed his mother's teaching in entirety. People all
over the district were well-disposed towards him; and
many began to invite him as a husband.

Siti Djuhari then brought him to her and suggested his
sister was ready to marry and that he should begin looking at other young men; and she said if he found someone
suitable "to come quickly and tell me: so I can see
what your judgment is like and if you remember what I
have taught you" (1958:42). Siti Djuhari then taught
her daughter, Siti Budiman ("Siti Sensible and Wise")
how to be a good wife. The kaba goes on to give an
example of how her son, now titled as Sutan Sampurna,
was invited to become a husband. For this, it was a
woman who came to visit Siti Djuhari, to ask for her
son. The woman said: "we are all agreed on what I have
come for: to ask hoping you will give, to buy, hoping
you will sell...it is to invite your son...to be husband
of our young daughter" (1958:72). When Siti Djuhari
told her son about it she said, "it is right for you to
belong there" (1958:76). He agreed to obey her on this
and was married. Then, he asked his mother to go see
the father of the young man they were thinking of as a
groom for his sister, Siti Budiman. The mother agreed
to go and to make the arrangements herself. When she

went, she asked for a decision—a consultation among them—right there while she waited, and an exchange of tokens that they had made an agreement.

The mother also teaches her son how to be a good husband, as she had taught her daughter how to be a good wife; and he goes to live in his wife's house. Subsequently, she teaches him what he would need to know to be a penghulu, first giving examples of what not to be by making illustrations from several amusing types of penghulu.[19] For example, she says:

> The meaning of Penghulu Ajam Gadang ("Panghulu Big
>   Chicken")...
> There's a lot of clucking, but no egg,
> a fine parcel, but no contents,
> a beautiful package but not enough string.
>
> The meaning of Penghulu Bulueh Bambu ("Panghulu
>   Bamboo")
> his outside looks solid enough
> but within he is hollow (1958:100).

Then she goes on to teach him further about adat (Minangkabau custom or customary law), presents the importance of knowledge, tells how confidence can be gained from travel, emphasizes that the penghulu and other guests must respect those, women, who put on the feasts, and teaches him to speak humbly and to live by his principles.

The son mentions to his mother when the time has come that she had promised his sister's wedding. His mother wants to make him a penghulu and she decides it will be more practical to do so at the same ceremony when her daughter is married. At that ceremony a title for penghulu from her line is put in effect.

After his important elevation to Penghulu, his mother thinks further and tells him "now you are an elder, people speak of you as Penghulu—be sure you gather up very carefully all that I let drop to you" (1958:124). He responds, "Since you have said this I will hold on to

---

[19] See Abdullah 1976 on the status and function of penghulu during Dutch rule.

it firmly, grasp it as tightly as I can" (1958:124).
The kaba then goes on to describe that he, now Datuek
Naratjo ("Dt. Weight"), "turned as if to bow to his
mother. As for Siti Djuhari, she turned herself to her
son, stretched out one leg, and continued speaking"
(1958:124). The kaba thus, by describing Minangkabau
nonverbal communication, tells us how respectful he--now
a penghulu or datuek (Mkb.) with a title--is to his
mother as he listens carefully to her advice. She on the
other hand [probably wearing a long sarong and sitting
on a mat on the floor], casually stretches out one leg
as she continues teaching him.

Later, the kaba tells of the mother teaching both her
children further, saying she had mentioned the wretched
types of young people, then describing to them the
wretched types of old people. So, it seems, the wisdom
and teaching of the Minangkabau mother are not only for
young children, but also for them as they grow older.

How can we summarize the teachings of this kaba? And how does
it relate to formulating a model of Minangkabau matriliny, one
that is more appropriate for the Minangkabau than Schneider's
model? Recall that Schneider's model of matriliny was based
on male authority and on a concept of authority that was non-
shared and hierarchical--in other words, a concept more like
command than group decision-making or consultation. In this
tale, Kaba Rantjak diLabueh, the mother, Siti Djuhari, is both
a teacher and an actor. She recommends aspects of both her
daughter's and son's general behavior and initiates specific
matters, such as searching for a good man to become her
daughter's husband, that she asks her son to carry out. In
certain instances, he thinks it is better that she carry out
important inter-kin group negotiations, such as those regarding her daughter's marriage, than that he carry them out, and
she agrees to his recommendation and does so. In other instances she initiates action such as the change of her son's
title and, later, his elevation to penghulu by holding a feast
for his penghuluship and the prior feast where the matter of
his initial title change to Sutan Sampurna could be discussed
and agreement reached.
    There are two images of consultation here: (1) between
a senior woman and a penghulu who is her son, a son who has
promised to obey his mother, and a mother who listens to her
son's recommendations; and (2) between a senior woman, kin
group, broader community, and many penghulu who discuss her
proposals at feasts she holds. Decisions and actions are
shared between male and female: by the mother and her son;

and by the senior woman and a variety of _penghulu_, kinspeople, and community members.

Interestingly, a Minangkabau scholar, Taufik Abdullah, also writes concerning the image of decision-making given in a traditional tale in his article, "Some Notes on the Kaba Tjindua Mato: An Example of Minangkabau Traditional Literature" (1970). This is a famous epic about Minangkabau royalty which has as two of its primary characters a "queen-mother," Bundo Kanduang and her son, Dang Tuanku. The mother in this tale, Bundo Kanduang, here too is presented as wise, and she has definite opinions which she puts forth emphatically. She consults with both the "Council of Ministers" (Mkb., _Basa Ampek Balai_) and with her son, who counsels temperance before action (1970:5): "Again and again Dang Tuanku reminds his mother, Bundo Kanduang, about her own advice to use akal [the ability to reason] in directing nafsu [impulse]" (1970:15-16). At one point in the _kaba_, "Bundo Kanduang with her strong sense of justice almost followed her nafsu and punished Tjindua Mato. Again Dang Tuanku proposed that she use akal to consider the matter more thoroughly" (1970:16). In this _kaba_, like the previous one, an important male-female kin role pictured is also that of mother-son; and consultation, not only between mother and son but with a council too—here, a council of the Kingdom—is considered important.

In both of these traditional tales, the ideal cultural images are extremely different from those assumptions, based (selectively) on Western culture, which David Schneider used to build a model of matriliny. In these two _kaba_, both mother and son are especially significant, in action and in consultation with each other. Other consultation is also important in both _kaba_, often initiated by a mother and bringing in important men. Here, then, is a possible beginning for building a more reasonable understanding of matriliny, for the Minangkabau at least. It is one in which both men and women are basic, in which the mother-son relationship is especially significant—as well as the mother's and mother's brother's roles, which are more frequently noted in descriptions of matrilineal kinship—and in which consultation even beyond that of mother and son plays an important part.

Kaba Rantjak diLabueh depicts realistic scenes of Minangkabau daily life, for instance scenes of a senior woman's casual sitting style even when putting forward important ideas, of a senior woman's initiation of political and ceremonial action, of the convergence of the senior woman and "Mother" role, of the valuation of financial practicality as in Siti Djuhari's holding one feast for two affairs—her daughter's marriage and her son's elevation to _penghulu_. At the same time, the story is probably idealized. The portray-

als of mother and of mother-son relations are in some ways
"almost too good to be true." Nonetheless the tale points to
a central cultural importance of the mother's role, and to an
authoritativeness of motherly strengths. As in Biblical tales
in Western culture, the very discrepancies between Minangkabau
idealizations and people's daily lives are of the sort that
enable this kaba to be the kind of idealization which people
want to better realize. Specifically, this kaba generates expectations regarding kin roles the Minangkabau people want to
meet and to have met.

It is very difficult to compare the other traditional
tale, Kaba Tjindua Mato, with historical politics of the
Kerajaan Minangkabau (Minangkabau "Kingdom"), or with more
recent Minangkabau social organization beyond the nagari
(Mkb., village). This is because very little pre-colonial
historical information is available on the functioning of the
Kerajaan Minangkabau, and neither women's traditional nor contemporary political roles beyond kin groups have been re-
searched. In the ordinary day-to-day political life of the
Kerajaan as well as in Kaba Tjindua Mato, was there a Bundo
Kanduang ("Queen Mother"), and if so, what was her role?
Similarly, how did the Basa Ampek Balai ("Council of Ministers") function? Since descendants of the Basa Ampek Balai
may still live in West Sumatra, such a study might be feasible
and would certainly be fascinating. The Dutch controlled Minangkabau for only a little over a century. They came in at
the time of a revolution of Minangkabau Islamic leaders versus
adat leadership, the "Parang Hitam Putieh", and the Dutch
retained control only until the second World War.

Both kaba--whether regarding a Mother-as-Senior-Woman in
a matrilineal kin unit or a Woman-as-Queen-Mother in the Kerajaan Minangkabau--stress motherly wisdom, initiative, assert-
iveness, stability, integrity, and practicality. In both
kaba the Mother is central, with men important too, and in
both tales discussions are of basic significance in decision-
making.

Schneider would probably agree that it is consistent
with his picture of matriliny that mothers have a measure of
authority over their children. However, we suggest that in
the course of his discussion, motherly authority was systematically stripped away in the overriding focus of attention on
male authority. In assuming a "control" type of authority by
males, the nature of male roles became confused and female
roles in decision-making were not even noted. Women in
Minangkabau as lineage members, mothers, wives, and sisters
are subject to pushes and pulls of various conflicts of
purpose in their different spheres of daily life. We would
stress, however, that the picture presented in these two kaba

-67-

does not _only_ represent Minangkabau ideals. It is also realistic in at least three important respects: (1) in the specification of the central cultural authority of mothers—especially those who have become senior women in the kin group—in a wide variety of intra-kin group matters within and beyond the domestic unit, including instruction, dispute settlement, and the initiation of many activities such as choice of _penghulu_; (2) in their even more public roles in inter-kin group junctures, especially regarding marriage and ceremony;[20] and (3) in the cultural and practical importance of consultation and discussion in kin group decision-making. We would note moreover that, although the significance of Senior Woman in the kin group is related to maternal centrality, it is not restricted to child rearing[21] even though child rearing is central to its symbolization in tales such as _Kaba Rantjak diLabueh_ and _Kaba Tjindua Mato_.

Conclusion

Schneider's model of matriliny, seen from the vantage point of our interpretations of Minangkabau, was partial in ways that made it misleading. In particular, the picture of unconditional male authority and the impression presented of hierarchical command-type authority are inaccurate for Minangkabau. These assumptions should also be questioned for other matrilineal groups as well.

Mother-child relations are central to the cultural constitution of Minangkabau matriliny in ways that escaped Schneider's formulation. Mother-child relations are centered in conjoined descent and domestic spheres, with the nuclear

---

[20] The political realm for senior women—beyond that _within_ a kin group—still requires much study. In marriage negotiations _between_ kin groups senior women play a major role. So too do they play very important ceremonial roles. There is also symbolic centrality both within the kin group and at the _kerajaan_ level far beyond the village. However, what historical and present day roles do and did senior women have regarding matters such as village council meetings, Islamic organizations, the past Minangkabau _kerajaan_, or contemporary village, city, provincial, and national politics? Much further study is needed.

[21] See the earlier example of "A Conflict Over Lineage Property" where the Senior Woman involved is the disputants' mothers' mother's sister.

family nested within the matrilineal unit.[22] Men's placements in their own and wives' groups give them partial involvements and cross-cutting interests; it is the great merit of Schneider's paper that he noted important aspects of this matter so clearly. But the limits thereby placed on men's cultural centrality and on the feasibility of their enacting what is often thought of as "authority" in western societies were given inadequate attention by Schneider.

In particular, the questions whether another cultural centrality was possible and another decision-making mode was feasible were not asked. For Minangkabau, the fact is that another cultural centrality (involving mothers and sisters) and other effective modes of decision-making and action do exist.

Schneider wrote:

> The problem is to put forward theoretical statements, not empirical generalizations. That is, I am concerned with some of the logical implications of a set of definitions, and the task is to show how the implications follow from the definitions so that they may have both predictive and analytical utility (1961:1).

The basic difficulty to which we wish to draw attention is that in examining our case in point we constantly find ourselves having to refer back to his definition that only men have authority. This simply is not the case.

The other major problem Schneider faced was in not realizing that "authority" need not be control by hierarchical command. In fact, the type of mupakaik (consultation and group decision-making) practiced by the Minangkabau tends both to maintain matriliny as an integrated system while also providing an ongoing sophistication regarding the "outside world." It clearly limits any likelihood of resentment or any feeling of being excluded from the decision-making process. The Minangkabau system of women within matrilineal/matrifocal groups making most of the day-to-day decisions regarding many practical matters, yet with fairly frequent group consultation regarding particulars such as ceremonies to be held or disputes to be settled, makes for a well-functioning group for many purposes with no need for male "control."

Each coming generation is protected by house and land

---

[22] Sister-sister and sister-brother relations are also centered within both domestic and descent units and, although not discussed here, are also of real importance to Minangkabau.

use-rights being in the hands of mothers, with mothers also having financial and other assistance available from husbands, sons, and brothers, and considerable financial protection is provided to children by their fathers. The men have relative freedom to come and go, facilitating their becoming merchants, craftsmen, traders, scholars, writers, politicians, and professors. The system seems reasonably successful in its practice. These facts force us to entertain doubts about the analytical utility of Schneider's suppositions and therefore their "predictive utility" even in some less ethnography-bound interpretation than ours here.[23]

We observe far more centrality and authority for women, specifically as mother and senior woman, in Minangkabau than hinted by Schneider's model. However, we have also recognized respects in which men do have a privileged place in the society. As noted, men do hold high positions of descent group responsibility, status, and influence as mamak and as penghulu; and the tendency is real for husbands to be considered honored guests in their wives' descent units. But a man's involvement in his own and in his wife's lineage and domestic group gives him a peripherality in both which decreases his "authority" if conceptualized as rule or control—yet provides a context for effective male roles as moderator, mediator, consultant, and representative. At the same time, a man is given opportunity to find positions outside the descent group, village, or homeland. This migration is valued for both learning and earning; although mostly by men, it is not carried out by all men or only by men.[24]

In conclusion, then, we see four central aspects of this form of matriliny constituted in Minangkabau practices: (1) cultural and social structural centrality of the mother role; (2) the practicality of a major proportion of ongoing day-to-day kin-related decisions being made within moderately sized kin groups by women exercising this matrifocal role[25]; (3) the

---

[23] Questions about the role of predictive utility, and the relations between prediction and explanation are too much neglected in anthropology; cf. Hollis and Nell 1979; Hesse 1980.

[24] Minangkabau merantau has historically been far commoner among men than women. Women—as students, wives, divorcees with children, senior members of extended families, and as traders or employees—now go to the rantau (Mkb., migration areas) considerably more often than at earlier times.

[25] Day-by-day kin-related decision-making is generally within the Minangkabau co-residential matrilineal, matrifocal extend-

significance and regular practice of discussion and consultation as the mode of decision-making for matters involving larger kin groups; and (4) the participation of women as well as men in kin and inter-kin group affairs, with mothers active in arrangement of marriages and having significant ceremonial roles.

---

ed family. This kin unit is larger than the western co-residential nuclear family, but may be smaller than the co-residential lineal kin units of some societies. In Minangkabau, house style is changing from the traditional long house to smaller styles. Both generally house a matrilineal extended family, although it seems probable that historically the long house held an even larger extended family than either do now.

SIBLINGSHIP AND SOCIAL STRUCTURE IN NEGERI SEMBILAN:
PERSPECTIVES FROM MYTH, HISTORY, AND THE PRESENT

Michael G. Peletz
Colgate University

The social institutions of the Malays residing in the
state of Negeri Sembilan (West Malaysia) have been of considerable interest to outside observers ever since the early
decades of the nineteenth century. The period of British
colonial rule (1874-1957) in particular saw the appearance of
numerous topically oriented essays devoted to Negeri Sembilan's pre-colonial polities, and the nature of clanship, inheritance, marriage, and the like (cf. Hervey 1884; Lister
1887, 1890; Hale 1898; Parr and Mackray 1910; Wilkinson 1911;
Winstedt 1920; Taylor 1929, 1948; DeMoubray 1931; Gullick
1949; de Josselin de Jong 1951). The post-Independence years
have witnessed a continuation of interest in many of these
areas, especially on the part of fieldworkers schooled in the
theories and methods of modern anthropology (e.g., de Josselin
de Jong 1960; Lewis 1962; Abdul Kahar bin Bador 1963; Swift
1965; A. Wahab Alwee 1967; Khadijah binte Haji Muhamed 1978).
One consequence of this latter fact appears in the laying to
rest of a good number of speculative hypotheses advanced by
early colonial-era scholars and their predecessors: for
example, that the social organization of Negeri Sembilan
Malays was once matriarchal in design and characterized as
well by various elements of "primitive communism." Despite
the debunking of such myths, however, certain implicit biases
still permeate the literature owing to a long-standing preoccupation with the entailments of descent and varied dimensions
of unilineally bounded groups (e.g., their internal composition, external linkages, and social reproduction). These
latter themes have received divergent treatment over the
years, particularly in light of de Josselin de Jong's (1951)
pioneering exegesis on the structural significance of affinal
exchange and alliance. The fact remains, though, that anthropological treatises on alliance are no less wedded to group-
level analyses than are those that focus largely on descent.
In either instance descent-based social units constitute the
point of departure and ultimate loci of one's investigation.
More to the point is that in either case relatively little

attention is devoted to other structural principles[1] such as siblingship, which may have highly variable implications for the presence or absence of bounded groups per se but may nonetheless serve to inform a broad array of social relations and many domains of cultural order as well. As a result, certain fields of kinship and social relations in contemporary Negeri Sembilan have been seen as unordered, and we have been told that the overall social system is "not highly structured" (see Swift 1965:167-174).

I hope to demonstrate that an understanding of kinship and socio-political relations in nineteenth-century Negeri Sembilan fully requires that we range beyond discussions of descent and alliance, and that we devote sustained analytic scrutiny to the social and cultural relevance of principles and idioms of siblingship. Following the theoretical leads of Kelly (1977), it shall be argued that principles of siblingship cannot be subsumed under the rubric of descent and may in fact enjoin behaviors and social linkages that are at sharp variance with a descent-based logic (as occurs at times when the calculation of structural distance proceeds through ties between cross-sex siblings rather than those of the same sex). I hope to show as well that the connective and overall ideological scope of siblingship was of comparable if not greater relevance in myriad domains of pre-colonial society and culture than were norms and values keyed to descent (and/or alliance). _Inter alia_, the data adduced to support these contentions suggest the need for a critical reappraisal of received wisdom, which has it that the limited scope and force of descent-based values and norms in present-day Negeri Sembilan is primarily a function of the combined impact of colonialism, modern market forces, and other individualizing and socially divisive developments (cf. de Josselin de Jong 1951, 1956; Lewis 1962; Swift 1965; A. Wahab Alwee 1967).

---

[1] According to the perspective employed in this essay, social structural principles delineate relationships (alignments, connections, etc.) among individuals, dispersed social units, categories of property rights, and other socially relevant taxa. Principles of descent, alliance, siblingship and the like are also included under the rubric of cultural concepts, as are attendant constructs of greater or lesser specificity (ranging from context-specific behavioral ideals to more abstract notions keyed to the nature of sociability).

Background Sketch

The Malays of Negeri Sembilan trace their descent from Minangkabau immigrants who established permanent, agriculturally based settlements in various areas of the state beginning in the 1500s (if not somewhat earlier). The circumstances of the Minangkabau's immigration and ensuing interactions with aboriginal horticulturalists and others of non-Minangkabau ancestry occasioned numerous structural innovations, certain of which appear in the subsequently considered realms of clan recruitment and political succession. A good many developments and divergences of an analogous nature have been noted elsewhere (de Josselin de Jong 1951) and require no further comment here aside from the caveat that they militate against facile generalizations encompassing the Sumatran Minangkabau and the Malays of Negeri Sembilan (cf. Abdul Kahar bin Bador 1963:8-9; Peletz 1983:77-78).

It is nonetheless true that the Negeri Sembilan communities with which we are concerned have always had much in common with those of the Minangkabau, including, most obviously, an identification both with the Shafite branch of Sunni Islam and with the analytically distinct though culturally interlocked models of and for behavior that were (and continue to be) subsumed under the rubric of adat (perpateh). Of more immediate relevance is that kin and social relations in nineteenth-century Negeri Sembilan were ordered in accordance with principles of siblingship and matrilineal descent, as were critical features of the political system. A thumbnail sketch of selected elements of the social organization characteristic of the Rembau district[2] during the 1800s will serve to sub-

---

[2] Prior to British intervention in the late 1800s, Rembau boasted a largely autonomous chiefdom structured along lines quite similar to those found elsewhere in Negeri Sembilan (e.g., in the region of Sungei Ujong). Throughout much of its pre-colonial history, the chiefdom of Rembau embraced a territorial domain greatly in excess of the approximately 167 square miles included within present-day Rembau (defined as one of the six principle administrative units or jajahan of Negeri Sembilan). Official census figures for 1970 indicated a population of 30,240 Malays, and 9,602 Chinese, Indians, and others (see 1970 Population and Housing Census of Malaysia, Vol. I, Part IV, p. 63). Since this essay is not concerned with the non-Malay residents of Rembau (or Negeri Sembilan more generally), all references to Rembau (and Negeri Sembi-

stantiate these latter generalizations, and will also provide
the requisite background for ensuing discussions given over to
a more in-depth treatment of clanship, territorial alignment,
and political succession.

Written sources, myths, and contemporary villagers
indicate that dispersed matriclans (<u>suku</u>) have existed in
Rembau ever since the 1500s. Each of these dispersed units
consisted of a variable number of localized clan segments
(also known as <u>suku</u>). In addition, they were (and still are)
divided into residentially aggregated components such as
lineages (<u>perut</u>), lineage branches (<u>satu pangkal</u>), and the
less inclusive groupings defined in relation to a married (or
formerly wed) woman, her adult daughters, and their household
plot(s) (or <u>kampong</u>). Both dispersed and localized clans were
named and further differentiated from other units of like
order not only by pedigree but also by virtue of their
generally exclusive rights to ritual prerogatives, territorial
domains, and certain political offices. Individual lineages
were also conceptualized as having mutually exclusive (or
equivalent) rights to one or more political titles, and they
too had distinctive names. Features of this sort served to
distinguish clans and lineages from smaller genealogical
groupings in the form of lineage branches. The latter, by
definition, embraced only those individuals with whom one
could actually specify enatic (i.e., matrilineal) linkages.[3]

Twentieth-century data reveal that the horizontal
boundaries of lineage branches do not range beyond the third
degree of collaterality, and there is no evidence to imply
that this situation was any different during the 1800s. This
degree of horizontal spread is a product of teknonymous
practices in conjunction with a broadly classificatory scheme
of reference and address terminology as well as a sanctified
prohibition on addressing by name anyone of senior age or generational standing. Such combinations of kin designations undoubtedly fostered a variant of genealogical amnesia as
suggested by the fact that present-day villagers are typically
unable to produce the names of their great-grandparents, and
are likewise usually incapable of precisely defining the
latters' relationships with others of the same generation.
Thus, whereas persons standing as third cousins through the

---

lan) are meant to apply only to the Malay inhabitants.
[3] As suggested in the text, the term <u>enatic</u> is used as a gloss
for all relationships through the matriline. Enatically related individuals (e.g., members of the same clan) are also
referred to as enates.

matriline are typically included in an individual's lineage
branch, fourth cousins are simply of the same lineage. In
either instance, however, kin ties among collateral enates of
the same generation are reckoned in terms of actual or classificatory sibling bonds among enatic relatives of one or
another antecedent generation, such that the conceptual
emphasis rests on siblingship linkages rather than descent
from a common ancestress (cf. Lewis 1962:125-127; Peletz
1983:85-100, 356-358).[4] As will be explained in due course,
all of this is wholly consistent with the cultural construction of relationships both among lineage branches and among
lineages of the same clan, and as regards the linkages

---

[4] I might stress here that Lewis' (1962) study of the Inas
district does devote considerable attention to the connective
and ideological significance of siblingship (and idioms of
sisterhood in particular) as regards social relations within
lineage branches and lineages as a whole. The perspective
informing this essay differs from that found in Lewis' work in
a number of areas, two of which merit special emphasis.
First, I do not derive siblingship from the domestic realm or
the sphere of clanship more generally. And second, I aim to
highlight certain of the more abstract structural features
common to all relationships framed in terms of siblingship
(whether or not they are grounded in the fact or fiction of
genealogical relatedness) (cf. McKinley 1975). Perspectives
of this nature facilitate recognition of the conceptual and
behavioral domains in which principles and idioms of siblingship supplanted or effectively overrode those of descent.
As previously noted, they also encourage us to reassess the
degree to which the limited scope and force of descent-based
values and norms in present-day Negeri Sembilan can be taken
as evidence of historical disjunctions vis-a-vis the system
that prevailed during one or another phase of the nineteenth
century. None of this is to deny the significance of the
social, economic, and political transformations that were set
in motion by mining and other commercial developments during
the half-century or so prior to direct British intervention
and further reinforced by the circumstances and objectives of
colonial rule (see Peletz 1983). An understanding of the
characteristics and outcome of these processes is clearly of
critical importance. Nevertheless, my primary concern in this
paper lies in elucidating certain historical continuities in
the structure of social relations and siblingship especially,
particularly since a good number of these continuities have
eluded previous observers.

connecting certain dispersed clans in their entirety (despite an explicit recognition of their disparate enatic origins).

Post-marital residence patterns of the nineteenth century were both derivative from and generally congruent with codes governing the intergenerational transmission of rights over property in the form of houses and land. By and large, all such rights were vested in females (just as rights to political titles, weaponry, and livestock typically devolved upon males[5]) (Lister 1887:39, 45, 1890:316; Hale 1898:48). These rights were provisional, however, and a female proprietor's enatic kin retained residual claims with respect to the same property and could thus exercise liens thereover and otherwise help insure its conservation within the clan and less inclusive components thereof (Parr and Mackray 1910:27, 65). This favoring of female heirs worked to insure a pattern of uxorilocal residence (Lister 1890:316; Hale 1898:54). For a woman's rights to houses, homestead plots, and wet-rice acreage derived mostly from her mother and centered quite literally upon her natal compound. Access to property of this sort on the part of an adult male, on the other hand, came almost invariably through wedlock and the establishment and continued maintenance of a conjugal household within or in immediate proximity to his wife's natal compound (see Peletz 1983:80-130). This was so despite the fact that a married man retained certain proprietary interests in his sisters' holdings, and might also claim a share of the harvest if he had contributed to the process of production (the bulk of which was shouldered by women [Gullick 1951:47]).

Residential patterns flowing from the property and inheritance codes alluded to above are also profitably viewed against the types of relationships that obtained among sisters (as opposed to brothers and cross-sex siblings). More precisely, the spatial aggregation of domestic units defined in relation to enatically connected women contributed to the proliferation of widely ramifying webs of interdependence both among women linked as natural or classificatory sisters, and among their respective households. These bonds of interdependence received expression in a multitude of ceremonial exchanges and labor arrangements, although they were perhaps

---

[5] In certain of the eastern districts of Negeri Sembilan, however, women also held political office (cf. Lister 1887:88). Interestingly, Lewis (1962:43-44) reports that titled females in Inas were held to be much "like sisters" in relation to men occupying complementary political positions (e.g., at the head of a localized clan).

-78-

most critical in the context of wet-rice agriculture. It was not merely the case that the successful completion of the most labor-intensive phases of the production process presupposed a reliance on extra-domestic labor. Rather, and of greater significance, the entailments of production encouraged cultivators to seek such assistance from their closest female kin, even if only for the sake of convenience. In brief, the cumulative effect of partible inheritance practices helped insure that a woman's sisters and enatic cousins would be vested with rights over plots that were contiguous or otherwise proximate to her own, and thus ideally situated for the tasks at hand.

To generalize from the foregoing, we might simply emphasize that various features of proprietorship, inheritance, and residence helped to produce in the interrelationship of sisters what could well be judged the primary structural bond within the domestic realm as well as in local society as a whole (cf. Lewis 1962:79-80, 124-127). But this is not to imply that ties of sisterhood were free of ambivalence or petty rivalries, or unencumbered by sentimental configurations comparable to what we might gloss "hostile dependence." Similarly, I would caution against the view that the conceptual and ideational dimensions of female siblingship (including its classificatory meanings) were an inevitable outgrowth of primordial sentiments or norms flowing from or otherwise keyed to commonality in residence, socialization, and/or shared property rights coupled with a system of reckoning descent through the matriline. All of this is to suggest that female siblingship, although perhaps the most critical variant and expression of more general phenomenon of siblingship, must be assessed in terms of that more inclusive category of relationship.

Property, inheritance, and residential arrangements of the nineteenth century also served to disperse actual and classificatory brothers and enatically related males on the whole. (As such, these arrangements assumed considerable importance with respect to the content, though not the structure, of the bonds linking brothers as well as cross-sex siblings.) This dispersal of male kin was further accentuated by exogamous principles, which typically enjoined marriage outside the lineage at the least and occasionally required looking beyond the boundaries of a non-localized clan (cf. Parr and Mackray 1910:120-141). (These principles varied in scope according to mythic encapsulations of the developmental relationships among particular clans and their internal components.) Male enates were thus scattered about a number of different communities in consequence of their marriages, particularly since there seems not to have been any explicit preference for, or prescription relating to, village endogamy.

Also relevant here are the cultural values that pertained to the formation of conjugal bonds as well as affinal exchange and alliance. On the one hand, these values did place a premium on cross-cousin marriage and the perpetuation and consolidation of extant affinal linkages. At the same time, one can discern analytically distinct cultural ideals that encouraged localized clans, lineages, and lineage branches especially to disperse their affinal alliances as widely as possible, rather than simply maintain or reduplicate affinal ties created in previous generations.[6] Conjugal bonds effected in accordance with these latter ideals clearly engendered a further dispersal of male kin. Additionally, they certainly reduced the likelihood that adult males defined as enatically related brothers would find themselves interacting with one another on a daily basis, let alone engaging in exchange relations or cooperative endeavors other than those involving formal political representation of a lineage or clan.

The content (though not the structure) of relationships among brothers thus differed quite markedly from the content of the bonds that obtained among sisters. In both instances, however, we are dealing with cultural constructions of parallel-sex siblingship that had the effect of defining siblings of the same sex as more or less equivalent in terms of their property rights and jural statuses as well as their overall social roles and identities. It may be noted further that the generalized equivalence at issue here presupposed an idealized intimacy based in part on interests and loyalties

---

[6] Support for this position derives in part from Parr and Mackray (1910:78), who noted that a divorced individual could not seek a marriage partner from the clan to which his or her former spouse belonged. More generally, villagers seemed always to have viewed it as "wasteful" for same-generation collaterals of a single lineage branch or lineage to marry in such a way as to effect more than one set of affinal ties with any particular unit of like order. A comprehensive assessment of the structural implications of these facts and divorce rates in particular appears in Peletz (1983:131-164, 390-450). There I suggest that the formation of conjugal bonds entailed a transfer of jural rights and responsibilities with respect to males (rather than females), and that the principal units linked through these and subsequent affinal exchanges were most likely lineage branches (or lineages), as opposed to localized, let alone dispersed, clans.

that were shared (in theory if not in fact) by persons classed as same-sex siblings. The ultimate irony (and problem), though, was that the social intimacy ideally characteristic of such relations appears always to have been grounded in a prescriptive amity that imposed ritually sanctified and potentially burdensome moral obligations—to cooperate, share, and/or exchange—on the very same individuals who found themselves competing with one another for the same (limited) property rights and other emblems of prestige and social capital. On a more general note, I would contend that ties of kinship and siblingship in particular have always cut both ways. Inter alia, this is to say that the deep-rooted ambivalences underlying contemporary villagers´ attitudes toward, and interactions with, kin do not constitute "a breakdown of the system," but testify instead to a very basic thread of historical continuity within the field of social relations.

We need also consider certain features of cross-sex sibling ties so as to highlight the scope and variable nature of relationships cast in idioms of siblingship. Especially worthy of note is the degree to which notions of cross-sex siblingship informed and were themselves partially derivative from constructs of gender, and likewise conduced toward a conceptual linkage between males and externality (and a corresponding association between females and centrality). Constructs of this latter sort received expression in male predominance both in the public realm of politics and in the collection of forest produce, extra-local trade, and voluntary out-migration (merantau) more generally (cf. Lewis 1962:290, 329); and in the fact that females were central to the maintenance and reproduction of households (and more encompassing social units), and also tended to remain in their natal compounds and communities throughout much of their entire lives. Further, constructs of gender and cross-sex siblingship served to foster considerable respect and social distance between females and their (natural as well as classificatory) brothers, and to define sexual activities (and all physical intimacy) between enatic siblings as a form of cannibalism as well as treason (Lister 1887:49, 1891:143-144; Peletz 1983:96-100, 131-134).

The maintenance of social distance between cross-sex siblings hinged in no small measure on the reproduction of various conventions insuring that the property rights, occupational tasks, and basic social roles of sisters and brothers were somewhat separate and distinct though mutually complementary (rather than strictly equivalent, as in the case of same-sex siblings). Such complementarity was essential to the stability and viability of virtually all social units. It helped minimize the likelihood of potentially divisive rivalries and antagonisms that obtained among siblings of the same sex, who, as already noted, were bound to one another through heavy moral obligations to cooperate, share, and/or exchange, but also found themselves in sharp competition with one another for the same property rights and other social capital.

Especially significant too is that the structural complementarity underlying sisters' ties with their brothers also provided the model for relationships between women and their husbands, who did in fact address and refer to one another with terms used by siblings (standing as older brother and younger sibling of unspecified gender, i.e., abang and adik respectively). Facts of this nature, along with others to be considered in due course, point to the widely redounding connective and overall ideological scope of principles and idioms of siblingship. No less germane, as we shall see, is the implicit suggestion that relationships informed either wholly or in part by idioms of siblingship were by no means limited to those grounded in the fact or fiction of shared parentage, common descent, or genealogical connections of any other sort.

Clan Recruitment and Alignment

Membership in one or another clan was an essential prerequisite for permanent residence among Malays and most everywhere else in Rembau prior to the twentieth century (Newbold 1839 II:123; Parr and Mackray 1910:5, 26). A widely known customary saying, though referring immediately to itinerants or immigrants of one sort or another, sums up the issue quite nicely: "the stranger seeks a place (or clan) as the boat requires anchorage" (dagang bertepatan, perahu bertambatan [cf. Hale 1898:53-54; Parr and Mackray 1910:981]). The notion of anchorage or mooring is especially relevant here since at the most fundamental level this is what clanship—and kinship more generally—was all about. The same could of course be said of adat in its entirety, for just as kin and social relations ordered in accordance with adat presupposed affiliation with one or another clan, so too did the overall corpus of symbols and idioms defined in relation to adat provide models of and for behavior in virtually all domains of existence.[7]

---

[7] This latter point receives clear expression in another customary saying often encountered in the literature and in

To say that clan affiliation was a <u>sine qua non</u> for membership and social placement within Rembau villages of the nineteenth century is also to point up that idioms of clanship provided certain of the hegemonic constructs in terms of which individuals and social units both defined and oriented themselves in relation to one another. Persons of a single (and especially localized) clan, for instance, were generally held to have more in common than individuals associated with different clans (even if only by virtue of shared obligations to the same political leaders), and in any event were subject to heavier moral constraints as regards the conduct of their interrelations. Hence, whereas it was certainly reprehensible to strike let alone kill someone of another clan, aggression of this nature was deemed far more criminal if directed toward a member of the same clan (and likewise called for heavier atonement and retribution on the part of the aggressor and/or his enatic kin). The same pertained to theft and property destruction as well as sexual impropriety (even when infractions of incest taboos did not figure into the picture).

Contemporary elders' delineation of recruitment policies characteristic of the pre-colonial era (and Rembau's initial settlement especially) suggest that residential, defense, and other essentially political considerations commonly overrode those based upon matrifiliation <u>per se</u> (even while an all-encompassing matrilineal ideology served in the long run to reorder and contain all such "ground-level noise"). One should bear in mind that the centuries preceding the imposi-

---

present-day villages: "The living are moored and guided in all of their actions by <u>adat</u>, just as the dead are surrounded and held in place by the earth of the grave" (<u>hidup di kandung adat</u>, <u>mati di kandung tanah</u>). It may be noted in addition that the ideology of Islam boasts an equally comprehensive moral and sociological relevance. Likewise, it also places great emphasis on non-genealogically based bonds of siblingship: namely, those that obtain among all Muslims by virtue of their identical standing in the eyes and codes of Allah (cf. al-Ghazali 1979). The conceptual and sociological implications of the resultant deemphasis of categories of kinship delineated in terms of shared bodily substances or other local cultural criteria merit far greater attention than is indicated by the literature on Negeri Sembilan, which concentrates heavily on what are referred to as Islam's "patrilineal biases" (e.g., in inheritance codes). Unfortunately, an adequate treatment of such issues is well beyond the scope of this essay.

tion of British colonial rule witnessed considerable movement
of population throughout Negeri Sembilan, and in most other
areas of the Malayo-Indonesian world where local groups found
themselves susceptible to or otherwise implicated in the
shifting political fortunes of regionally dominant powers, be
they Johorese, Buginese, Achehnese, Minangkabau, or Europeans
(O'Brien 1884:342; Wilkinson 1911:309; Gullick 1958; Andaya
1971). In the case at hand, then, it was not altogether in-
conceivable for individuals or entire communities to choose or
find themselves forced by feuding or warfare to resettle
within the territorial domain controlled by a clan other than
their own. In some such situations, peaceful resettlement
hinged firstly upon successful negotiations with the leaders
of established communities, who might agree to accept the
newcomers into a local clan in exchange for their pledges of
loyalty and support. Additionally, it appears to have been
necessary for an outsider to find an older woman of the host
community willing to stand as his or her adoptive mother, one
consequence of which lay in maintaining at least the fiction
of recruitment via matrifiliation (DeMoubray 1931:172-190).
In the instance of a married couple seeking to affiliate
themselves in this way, however, one adoptive mother would
suffice for the two of them and would likely define only the
woman as her adoptee such that the man would be ascribed the
status of son-in-law and in-marrying male, rather than enate
per se (DeMoubray 1931:178-179). This served to reproduce the
basic structure of filiation and descent inasmuch as the
adoptive mother would thus share the same descent affiliation
as both her adopted daughter and all children born to that
woman.

Also of considerable importance is that emigration from
the Minangkabau area, as well as from Acheh, Jambi, Kampar,
and even southern Thailand, continued over many centuries, as
did overland migration from the neighboring regions of Sungei
Ujong, Malacca, and Pahang. Given the military and other
advantages of augmenting one's clan through the adoption of
new members, and the absence of unilineal descent reckoning in
many of the areas from which sojourners hailed, it became
necessary (or at least highly advantageous and convenient) to
group individuals into one Rembau clan as opposed to another
(or even two different clans) on the basis of regional or
ethnic origins (Parr and Mackray 1910:5; Wilkinson 1911:315-
316; de Josselin de Jong 1951:138). There is no way of ascer-
taining even a general date for the emergence and spread of
this classificatory scheme, but village elders in the fieldwork site of Bogang could well stand on firm ground in asserting that its appearance coincided with one of the earliest
waves of emigration from Sumatra. Be that as it may, persons

from the Payah Kumboh region of Minangkabau, for example,
whether or not related to one another or associated in any way
with the descent unit of that name in their homeland, were
deemed to be members of Rembau's Payah Kumboh clan. Similarly, pioneers from the Minangkabau area of Batu Hampar—however
related—came to share membership in the Rembau clan given
that same name. Those claiming other than Minangkabau ancestry were classified in similar fashion such that Malaccans,
Achehnese, and Buginese, for instance, each tended toward affiliation with a particular clan. Some of the clans in which
these individuals were ascribed membership continue to bear
names denoting their non-Minangkabau origins (e.g. Anak Melaka
and Anak Acheh). It is especially significant too that
Hervey's (1884:259) enumeration of Rembau's principal descent
units includes separate entries for the "nationality" of each
clan.

From the outset, then, disjunctions clearly characterized the relationship between the matrilineal ideology of
clan recruitment and the actual composition of dispersed as
well as localized clans. Though quite marked with respect to
commoner groups, disjunctions of this sort also existed in the
case of Rembau's two gentry clans, Lelahmaharaja and Sediaraja. The larger issue, however, is that relationships among
clanmates, including persons recognized as having territorially or ethnically diverse origins, were both cloaked in and
partially informed by the symbols, idioms, and constraints
associated with common matrilineal ancestry. This entailed
shared responsibilities toward the clan's estate of residential and agricultural acreage, unexploited tracts of forest
lands (and certain political titles), particularly since the
bestowal of rights guaranteeing eventual access to these
estates typically accompanied most modes of recruitment to the
clan. The activation of such shared rights in the course of
production served as a critical material referent of matrilineal kinship and classificatory siblingship more specifically, regardless of whether the bonds in question were
biologically grounded or simply imputed on the assumption or
fiction of common descent from the same ancestral set of
female siblings. Moreover, joint claims to an estate vested
in a localized clan or lineage undoubtedly fostered genealogical revision in the direction of matrilineal consistency among
individuals unable to demonstrate shared descent through the
female line. Indeed, even today, if villagers are at a loss
to explain the details of kin connections among individuals
classed as collateral relatives within the matriline, they
frequently invoke the issue of shared property rights as
evidence, or at least a good indication, of common matrilineal
ancestry. This fact alone suggests quite clearly that gen-

ealogical connections were not the sole or even the most important criteria of relatedness among persons associated with the same clan.[8]

It remains to consider certain aspects of clan affiliation via formal adoption so as to underscore that the kinship ties thus created were conceptualized primarily in terms of siblingship rather than descent. The distinction merits special emphasis in light of the more general point that constructs of siblingship seem always to have been hegemonic both in terms of defining relatedness within descent units of various degrees of inclusiveness and as regards the linkages among such units.

Throughout most if not all of the pre-colonial period, a female of any age could obtain formal affiliation with a clan other than that with which she stood associated by birth. This might occur in the case of a relatively poor individual seeking to avail herself of access to productive acreage vested in a daughterless old woman of another local clan, and would thus entail assuming responsibilities for the adoptive mother's overall welfare in exchange for rights of proprietorship over her residential and other acreage as well as the house in which she lived. Adoption of this nature bears certain structural similarities to the other instances of formal adoption referred to earlier, although we are dealing here with isolated cases involving individual adoptees rather than entire households or larger groupings seeking acceptance within an established community. All such adoptions are also to be distinguished from informal child transfers which usually occur at present among women belonging to the same lineage and lineage branch in particular (Peletz 1983:364-370).

---

[8] Although we have emphasized here that an individual's affiliation with one or another clan might well hinge on political and/or residential considerations, one should bear in mind that most inhabitants of pre-colonial Rembau were recruited into a particular clan at birth and retained membership therein throughout the course of their entire lives. Stated somewhat differently, by drawing attention to the fact that clans could, and in some instances clearly did, obtain new members whose mothers had been associated with separate descent units (let alone distinct territorial or ethnic origins), we are not suggesting that these units tended to reproduce themselves over time primarily through ties other than those of matrifiliation. In the long run, in other words, recruitment clearly presupposed ties of this latter nature.

In any event, reaffiliation of the sort with which we are most directly concerned presupposed public proceedings in the form of ritual animal slaughter and feasting, symbolizing the severance of an adoptee's links with her original enates on the one hand and the creation of new ties of enation on the other (Parr and Mackray 1910:26-27; DeMoubray 1931:182-188). While analogous proceedings could also effect formal reaffiliation at the level of lineage, one of the most salient features of all such phenomena emerges from their designation as <u>kadimkan</u> (or <u>berkadim</u>). This term denotes the process of becoming siblings, and sisters in particular, and clearly suggests a cultural emphasis on the creation of (enatic) siblingship rather than common descent <u>per se</u> (cf. Lewis 1962:137-138). This is wholly consistent with (though by no means derivative from or confined to) the conceptualization of relations among persons affiliated (by whatever means) with the same descent unit, be it a dispersed or localized clan, a lineage, or a less inclusive segment thereof. In sum, just as such individuals think of their relatedness primarily in terms of siblingship, so too is it the case that the conceptual scope of siblingship seems always to have ranged well beyond that of descent.

We have already suggested that constructs of siblingship also provided the hegemonic idioms in terms of which clans and less encompassing components thereof were held to be related to units of like order. We may thus proceed to an analysis of mythic accounts pertaining to the scheme of clan ranking that had emerged in Rembau by the early 1800s (see Newbold 1839 II:121-123; cf. Hervey 1884:259), and is probably of much greater antiquity. The more encompassing domain of inquiry here is that of the structure of alignment among Rembau's dispersed clans, mythical explications for which afford additional insights into the previously outlined sphere of clan recruitment.

Local myths contain no mention of a Minangkabau clan hierarchy prior to or at the time of the arrival in Rembau of the first immigrant settlers, but a system of clan ranking did emerge within Rembau, and presumably this occurred during the earliest decades of its foreign occupation (see Figure 1, next page). This hierarchical scheme of descent-unit ranking had its mythical origins in the union of a Minangkabau chief, To Lela Balang, and an aboriginal woman of Jakun stock, To Bungkal, which ultimately gave rise to three female offspring, and a son known as Seri Rama. The latter, basing his claims upon ties of matrilateral filiation with To Bungkal, whose tribesmen were the original "heirs of the soil" (<u>waris</u>), emerged as the acknowledged head of a newly constituted gentry clan thereafter styled Waris Jakun. Some myths suggest as well

```
------------------ Biduanda------------------:---Suku Sebelas------
Waris, Biduanda Waris:    Client or      :"The Eleven Clans"
   (Gentry Clans)      :Satellite of Waris: (Commoner Clans)
------------------------:-------------------:----------------------
   1 Lelahmaharaja      : 3 Biduanda Dagang:  4 Batu Hampar
     (Waris Jakun)      :                  :  5 Payah Kumboh
                        :                  :  6 Mungkar
   2 Sediaraja          :                  :  7 Tiga Nenek
     (Waris Jawa)       :                  :  8 Tanah Datar
                        :                  :  9 Seri Lemak
                        :                  : 10 Batu Balang
                        :                  : 11 Tiga Batu
                        :                  : 12 Seri Melenggang
                        :                  : 13 Anak Acheh
                        :                  : 14 Anak Melaka
```

Figure 1: Rembau's Clans During the Nineteenth Century
Source: Hervey (1884:259). Cf. Newbold (1839 II:121-123).

that Seri Rama became the first territorial chief and Supreme
Law Giver of Rembau, i.e., the <u>Undang</u>,[9] and that his candidacy
for the office and his title--Dato Lelahmaharaja--had been approved by the Sultan of Malacca (Parr and Mackray 1910:4).
Far more certain is that the designation Lelahmaharaja has
long stood as a common synonym for the clan first known as
Waris Jakun (Hervey 1884:243).

The only other clan claiming the prerogatives and status
of gentry traces its origin to To Laut Dalam, who was a con-

---

[9] As noted elsewhere (Peletz 1981:9), the precise date of the
creation of this office remains rather elusive. Parr and Mackray (1910:12) assert that it was established circa 1540, as
does Abdul Samad bin Idris (1968:191), who seems to rest his
claim on the authority of Parr and Mackray. Both the former
and the current <u>Undang</u> of Rembau concur with this view, as is
indicated by official documents housed in the <u>Balai Undang
Rembau</u> (BUR M 1962 53/62). Wilkinson (1911:280-289), however,
disputes such positions and argues from the genealogical and
chronological information contained in the Malay Annals
(<u>Sejarah Melayu</u>) that the first <u>Undang</u> of Rembau "flourished"
between 1600 and 1640.

temporary and a "brother chief" of To Lela Balang, and quite
possibly his patrilateral half-sibling by virtue of a common
father (or other male ancestor) and different mothers (the
latter of whom belonged to wholly separate Minangkabau
clans).[10] To Laut Dalam had once been married to a woman who
bore him four daughters (the eldest of which, Siti Hawa,
married the above mentioned Seri Rama). But as his former
wife hailed from Java, none of their children had any grounds
upon which to assert matrilineal ties to the aboriginal Jakun,
the group from whom members of the Lelamaharaja clan could
trace the pedigree which validated their status as "heirs of
the soil." Nonetheless, To Laut Dalam's apparent envy over
his chiefly brother's success in gaining political recognition
and privileges for his son motivated him to persuade the
Sultan to agree to a provision whereby the office of Undang
would rotate between the brother's descendants and his own.
In consequence of having secured this guarantee, To Laut Dalam
and his progeny assumed prominence as the effective origin
point of the gentry clan known from that time onwards as Waris
Jawa (the latter being the local term for Java or Javanese),
or alternatively as Sediaraja (from the title granted to the
first Undang chosen from their clan, namely, the son of Siti
Hawa and Seri Rama) (Parr and Mackray 1910:4-5).

---

[10] In discussing myths pertaining to Rembau's origins, Parr
and Mackray (1910:3-4) refer to To Laut Dalam and To Lela
Balang as "brother chiefs." So too does Dato (Sediaraja)
Abdullah, the Rembau Undang who reigned during the period
1922-1938 (NSSSF 1924 920/24). Similarly, Abdul Samad bin
Idris (1968:167-173) uses the Malay terms for elder brother
(abang) and younger sibling of unspecified gender (adik) to
describe their relationship. In the same discussion he indicates their social tie to be one of bersaudara, which denotes
kin connectedness in general and siblingship in particular.
It is not clear, though, if these details of the Rembau myths
appearing in Abdul Samad bin Idris derive wholly from the Parr
and Mackray volume, which is cited as a major source, particularly for the section on Rembau. In any event, To Laut
Dalam and To Lela Balang did belong to different clans and
thus could not be of the same mother or even born of different
women belonging to the same clan. The aforementioned
references would suggest, then, that they might well have been
(actual or classificatory) half-brothers, either by virtue of
having the same father or else owing to their common descent
from a single male ancestor in one or another antecedent
generation.

Referred to collectively as Biduanda Waris or simply Waris, the Lelahmaharaja and Sediaraja clans together occupied the highest rung of Rembau's clan hierarchy (Newbold 1839 II:120-123). Of far broader significance in light of our concerns with clan alignment is that these two clans are currently held to be related to one another as siblings (adik-beradik), and were presumably always regarded as such. This is so despite the profound ethnic differences between their respective apical ancestresses, and their wholly disparate enatic origins. It may be noted as well that the tie of chiefly siblingship, which emerges from the preceding myths as the initial genealogically framed bond between these two clans, is not widely recognized in otherwise comparable mythic texts encountered in contemporary Bogang. Nonetheless, the generalized siblingship linking the two clans is most emphatically maintained at the cultural level. I would thus propose that the construction of this linkage in terms of siblingship testifies to the continuity of an extremely pervasive tendency to define individuals and social units as related like (or as) siblings whenever they share equivalent, parallel, or essentially complementary rights, obligations, or experiences with respect to a particular political office, territorial domain, or other mediating element (cf. Kelly 1977; McKinley 1975; Marshall 1981; Smith 1983).

The sibling equivalence obtaining between these two clans was manifest in the fact that neither of them was ever able to exercise any appreciable precedence over the other as regards political authority or privileges of any other sort (Parr and Mackray 1910:5). Indeed, as noted above, rights to the office of Undang rotated in theory between these two clans such that each took its turn in providing a candidate for this position. The same situation prevailed with respect to the office associated with the title of Dato Perba, the occupant of which was second only to the Undang as the highest ranking leader of all persons affiliated with these clans. Additionally, the marriage payments due their women were equivalent in value and larger than those received by women of all other clans (Parr and Mackray 1910:52) and intermarriage between the two groups seems to have been the ideal, as would be expected in light of analytically distinct (though mutually reinforcing) considerations of status endogamy.[11]

---

[11] Cross-cousin marriage appears always to have been the ideal, although I find no historic or contemporary ethnographic data to indicate a clear preference for (or more positive weighting of) any particular variant of this type of

The historical preeminence of the two gentry groups vis-a-vis the catch-all category of non-gentry clans received political expression primarily in the former's sanctified monopoly on furnishing candidates for offices whose jural domains were of district-wide significance, as in the case of the four posts comprising the <u>Undang</u>'s Privy Council (<u>Orang Besar Undang</u>) and of course the position of <u>Undang</u> itself. Members of these two clans also enjoyed the right to demand relatively higher retributions for the murder of their kin, although most of their other privileges surfaced only in ritual contexts.

In proceeding to an assessment of the structural bonds linking gentry clans with their non-gentry counterparts, we might first consider certain additional implications of the culturally defined siblingship that united the two gentry units. Perhaps the most important of these is the exclusivistic nature of this particular tie, specifically, that the siblingship at issue linked only two clans and did not extend to any of the others, which were therefore defined as nonsiblings in relation to gentry clans or in any event "much less like siblings." This despite the fact that the apical ancestors of the two gentry clans were themselves affiliated by descent with clans of Minangkabau origin that were eventually accorded commoner status within the context of Negeri Sembilan.

A rationale phrased partly in terms of historical precedence or "origin point" ascribes commoner status to Rembau's non-Waris clans, for according to most mythical explications of the basis of clan ranking, their forefathers were not the leaders and in some cases were not even members of the original expedition to arrive in Rembau. Consequently, permission to clear land, set up villages, and wield legitimate political power derived neither from the autochthonous aborigines nor from the aforementioned Sultan. Rather these privileges were granted them (in exchange for token payments, or the promise of such) by the representatives of the Lelahmaharaja and Sediaraja clans, who thus stood, if only on that account, as their benefactors. This patronage relationship appears to have been most explicit, albeit primarily at the level of ideology, in the case of the client-like Biduanda Dagang clan, which contemporary villagers regard as the lowest ranked of all Rembau descent units. Persons affiliated with this clan are held to be descendants of the most recent arrivals in Rembau, many of whom fled their natal homelands as a result of

_____

union (e.g., a male marrying his natural or classificatory mother's brother's daughter).

famine or warfare or else were simply itinerants or foreigners (as suggested by the term dagang). Those who attained Biduanda Dagang standing in the past purportedly did so owing to the benevolence of Lelamaharaja and Sediaraja leaders who not only agreed to accept their presence within or in proximity to their own settlements, but also consented to extend them the protection and representation provided by their own clan chief (while at the same time granting them a number of less prestigious political titles).[12]

Not much is known about the nineteenth-century construction of linkages between or among commoner clans. Information collected around the turn of the century, however, reveals that the members of certain of these descent units could not intermarry owing to ties of patrilateral half-siblingship

---

[12] For reasons such as these, the Biduanda Dagang clan seems always to have had a rather unique and structurally ambiguous relationship vis-a-vis the Lelahmaharaja and Sediaraja clans. All three clans, after all, could be referred to by the short-hand gloss Biduanda, and, as noted, all three of them owed their allegiance to the same clan chief. And yet in terms of numerous expressions of power, status, and genealogical purity, Lelahmaharaja and Sediaraja occupied the uppermost niche of the descent-based hierarchy whereas Biduanda Dagang fell at the other extreme of the continuum. Even at present, and despite the radically egalitarian thrust of Islamic doctrines, those identified as Biduanda Dagang continue to bear the burden of an ancestral stigma (as reflected in the gentry's reluctance to seek them out as potential marriage partners, and sotto voce references to their tainted pedigrees). Significantly, none of this precludes Biduanda Dagang individuals from being regarded as (classificatory) siblings (saudara) in relation to members of one of Bogang's gentry clans. Indeed, in some instances siblingship of this nature is readily acknowledged by gentry women whose rights over land include claims to acreage that was first cleared or otherwise made available through the efforts of a renowned nineteenth-century Undang who also boasted a number of Biduanda Dagang individuals as his servants or slaves (hamba). The Undang in question eventually granted these people their freedom along with rights to certain plots of village land. The holdings of their contemporary descendants thus derive in part from the same luminary credited with augmenting the estate of one of the local gentry clans. In short, the bonds of siblingship at issue here testify to certain commonalities in each clan-segment's relationship vis-a-vis a third mediating element.

between their apical ancestors (Parr and Mackray 1910:77). This suggests a cultural recognition of brotherhood that was altogether separate from enatic calculations of relatedness, just as it lends further testimony to the relevance of siblingship as a connective (and potentially disjunctive) principle at the level of clan. Stated somewhat differently, even though the relatedness at issue here appears in the guise of a particular variant of genealogical intimacy expressed as siblingship, it is no less significant for enjoining a measure of social distance between individuals and social units thus linked. Explanations for this may lie in part with indigenous notions pertaining to the transmission of biogenetic essences from fathers to their children, but must in any event be viewed in light of the more general aversion to sexual activity and marriage between those categories of siblings defined as "too close" for sexual union or marriage by virtue or presumption of shared bodily substances.[13]

---

[13] Contemporary village notions of procreation and reproduction undoubtedly differ from their counterparts of earlier centuries, but it has long been recognized that conception presupposes biogenetic contributions from genitor and genetrix alike. Villagers in present-day Bogang view an individual's flesh (daging) and bones (tulang) as the product or manifestation of essences derived from the natural mother, thus shared by, and prohibiting physical intimacy and marriage among, matrilateral half-siblings and all other enatically related kin. Physical contributions from the father, on the other hand, inform one's blood (darah), and they too figure into a social calculus discouraging sexual activity and wedlock between certain individuals, e.g., patrilateral half-siblings and those related as (actual or classificatory) patrilateral parallel-cousins. It may by emphasized here that neither the conveyance of biogenetic substances (or property rights) via links of patrifiliation, nor the patterned aversion to marriage with patrilateral parallel-cousins should be taken as evidence of "double descent" (as occurs in de Josselin de Jong 1951). More generally, the full range of unions viewed as inappropriate is best analyzed by taking as one's point of departure the cultural construction (and sociological entailments) of various categories of siblingship (cf. Peletz 1983:131-164, 390-450). Such a perspective can accommodate local injunctions on unions involving persons of the same clan as well as individuals of different clans who are known or presumed to have had a common male ancestor in one or another antecedent generation. In addition, it can account for other,

Territorial Alignment

In shifting our focus from certain of the formal properties of clans to the nature of territorial alignment, we find that principles of siblingship were accorded far greater centrality than those of descent and did in fact provide the hegemonic idioms underlying both the conceptualization and actual organization of a broad range of relationships and activities. To substantiate these contentions, we shall examine various levels of such alignment and proceed from the most inclusive territorial domains to those of progressively restricted scope.

Perhaps the most fundamental of all territorial distinctions ever recognized by Malays in Rembau or other districts of the state was that between their homeland of Negeri Sembilan on the one hand and all other regions of the Peninsula on the other (Parr and Mackray 1910:26-27; DeMoubray 1931:182-188). While many of the less encompassing territorial divisions found in Negeri Sembilan were probably conceptualized in terms of social or cultural divergence as well (cf. Gullick 1958:25-26, 37-43), this particular distinction symbolized the most basic level of social and cultural variation found among Malays anywhere in the Peninsula. As we have already seen, the Malays of Negeri Sembilan appear always to have ordered their relations along lines set out in the codes of _adat perpateh_, and have been associated throughout history with a social organization characterized by descent units of matrilineal design. Most Malays outside of Negeri Sembilan, in contrast, have long, and quite possible always, ordered their kin and social relations in accordance with a body of cultural codes glossed _adat temenggong_, one manifestation of which appears in the cognatic thrust of their social institutions both historically and at present. In sum, the territorial distinction encodes significant cultural and especially social variation, and the question thus becomes one of discerning the cultural construction of the relationships at issue.

As expressed in numerous mythic portrayals of Negeri Sembilan's cultural origins, the relationship between the

---

analytically distinct prohibitions, such as those that apply to persons of wholly disparate ancestry who happen to have been breast fed by the same woman (and are therefore regarded as "milk siblings" or _saudara sesusu_).

Malays of Negeri Sembilan and those residing elsewhere in the Peninsula is ultimately one of siblingship inasmuch as the two ancestral figures associated with the genesis of cultural divergence are held to be related as brothers. It is not clear from any of the accounts with which I am familiar if these two culture heroes, Dato Perpateh Nan Sebatang and Dato Temenggong, were actually full brothers, or were instead half-brothers (or, for that matter, classificatory brothers of one sort or another). As suggested by their titles, though, the former was responsible for conceptualizing and establishing the framework of adat perpateh institutions, while the latter either founded or simply continued to support that body of tradition known as adat temenggong. Judging from Negeri Sembilan accounts, their divergent opinions concerning the status and rights of women in inheritance, and the ideal organization of their respective (and all future) communities, laid the foundations for the earliest cultural distinctions among the Minangkabau. More importantly, given the Negeri Sembilan perception that most if not all Malays are ultimately of Minangkabau ancestry, their lack of consensus in these areas gave rise to the dominant cultural marker serving throughout history to distinguish Negeri Sembilan Malays from all others. Here then, the principle of siblingship structures a critically important nexus of relationships embracing mythical culture heroes, the origins of ancestral social and cultural diversity, and all subsequent expressions thereof.

Within Negeri Sembilan, moreover, a focus on (classificatory) siblingship rather than on the fact or fiction of common matrilineal ancestry appears in the reckoning of relationships among the Undang of Rembau and the leaders of the three other polities within Negeri Sembilan (Sungei Ujong, Johol, and Jelebu) who formed an unprecedented but largely ineffectual politico-military union in the 1770s.[14] Ever since that time, both the four Undang and their respective territories (luak) have been regarded as related to one another "like brothers" (cf. Newbold 1839 II:93). Their siblingship and birth-order relations continue to receive

---

[14] Local reports are not entirely consistent as to the initial locus of the fourth polity in this union. Most villagers claim that it has always been centered in Jelebu. There are some elders, however, who assert that it was originally defined in relation to the adjacent territory of Muar. Similar ambiguities appear in recently authored accounts bearing on the latter part of the eighteenth century (cf. Hooker 1969:161, 1971:105).

elaborate symbolic expression in installation and other state-level rituals involving the participation of the four <u>Undang</u>. Worthy of remark too is that the construction of these relationships in terms of siblingship reflects a situation wherein each of the leaders in question stood (and remains) more or less identically situated vis-a-vis the titular head of the union, styled <u>Yang diPertuan Besar</u>, who hailed initially from outside of Negeri Sembilan and in any event has long been associated by birth with a royal dynasty of Minangkabau origin. Interestingly, the politico-military pact at issue was formed with an eye toward checking the incidence and scope of strife and warfare in Negeri Sembilan. It contributed instead, however, to the intensification of hostilities throughout the area owing in no small measure to the emergence of a notoriously self-interested and highly autonomous dynasty that centered on the office of <u>Yang diPertuan Besar</u> (Newbold 1839 II:87-92, 149-150; Parr and Mackray 1910:19-23; Wilkinson 1911:296-310).

Of far greater significance is that many of the military and other altercations characteristic of the ensuing century revolved around direct and frequently highly sanguine confrontations between the principal chiefs of Rembau and their supporters on the one side, and those of Sungei Ujong on the other (Newbold 1839 II:97, 105, 111-112). A good number of these conflagrations did in fact entail one or another variant of fratricide. More broadly, whether or not the cloaking of all such potentially bellicose relations in idioms of siblingship served to endow them with a modicum of cordiality (to say nothing of amity), the fact remains that competition, petty rivalries, and overt antagonisms among titled males and political aspirants defined as brothers constitutes one of the most pervasive themes running throughout Negeri Sembilan's history (cf. Hooker 1972:22-23; Khoo 1972; Andaya 1971).

There also exists strong evidence that siblingship figured into the cultural representation of the dualistic and earliest known political division within the district of Rembau. This despite the analytic relevance of somewhat separate constructs embracing temporal precedence in addition to culturo-geographic roots--all of which may be subsumed under the rubric of origin point. Here we might simply consider the mythic genesis of these divisions along with an attenuated cultural explanation as to why clan leaders within the first of the two regions settled--Lowland Rembau--enjoyed certain ritual and political prerogatives not extended to their chiefly compatriots in Rembau's Upland territory (Parr and Mackray 1910:3).

Stated briefly, To Lela Balang and To Laut Dalam founded Rembau's first two villages, and these were in the Lowland

district (Rembau Baroh) (Parr and Mackray 1910:3). Affiliated
with the Batu Hampar and Payah Kumboh clans respectively,
these chiefs were accompanied in their emigration by others of
these descent units and by members (including leaders) of the
Mungkal and Tiga Nenek clans loyal to one or another of them.
Together, but presumably after the Upland area (Rembau Darat)
was settled, these four clans forged the earliest formal politico-military pact within Rembau. Known as the (Lowland)
League of the Four (Yang Empat or Yang Empat Sebelah Baroh),
this council or federation stood as the most highly esteemed
and powerful political body throughout all of Rembau's pre-
colonial history (Parr and Mackray 1910:7, 42-43). Indeed,
even after 1831, at which point the council was expanded to
include four leaders from Rembau's Upland district and renamed
the League of Eight (Yang Delapan), the chiefs of the original
federation continued to exercise many of their earlier privileges and likewise played a pivotal role both with respect
to political developments within Rembau and in terms of Rembau's relations with neighboring and other foreign polities.

The colonization of the Upland district may have taken
place shortly after Lowland Rembau was opened up by To Lela
Balang and To Laut Dalam. Judging from myths presented in
Hervey (1884:253-255) and Parr and Mackray (1910:8), it was
settled within the lifetime of (and in part by) To Laut Dalam
and his contemporaries within the Payah Kumboh clan, along
with persons affiliated with one or another of the three clans
of Seri Lemak, Batu Balang, and Seri Melenggang. Each of
these clans staked out a specific locale of its own, and each
of the clan leaders claimed jurisdiction over the territory
occupied by his own kin and all subsequent arrivals. These
chiefs in turn forged a political counterpart to the Lowland
League of Four, designating it the Upland League of Four (Yang
Empat Sebelah Darat). This body also assumed a position of
centrality in Rembau's pre-colonial polity even though its
more recent emergence (hence less prestigious origin point)
resulted in its being endowed with lower status and fewer
ritual and political prerogatives than its predecessor.
Noteworthy too is that in this instance the notion of origin
point receives congruent expression in birth-order relations
inasmuch as the younger of the two brother chiefs appears in
myth as the more directly responsible for the founding of the
lower ranking federation.

Significantly, one also encounters scattered mythical
references to a tie of patrilateral half-siblingship between
To Laut Dalam and the apical ancestor of the Tiga Nenek clan
(Parr and Mackray 1910:77). Hence, of the original four clans
to settle within Rembau (Batu Hampar, Payah Kumboh, Tiga
Nenek, and Mungkal), three were linked through a particular

variant of siblingship that also emerges as the earliest (and for some time the sole) genealogically-framed connection between the Lowland League of Four and the Upland League of Four, and between the entire Lowland and Upland divisions within Rembau.

These two federations bore some of the trappings of strictly matrilineally constituted alliances, but were essentially territorially based defense organizations whose structure and operations were simply couched in idioms of matriliny and siblingship. This situation obtained as well with respect to subsequently formed political alliances, the most recent of which arose during the period 1795-1820, operated in Rembau's Lowland district, and took as its name the League of the Five (owing to its being comprised of five different clan chiefs and their adherents). The origins of this latter league are quite instructive (cf. Hervey 1884:253), especially in view of the ritual blood pact that was effected by the five leaders and appears more or less identical in overall design to the traditional symbolization of siblingship between clanmates on the one hand, and those formally adopted (berkadim) into the clan on the other.

The foregoing indicates that formal political alliance at the clan level presumed neither the existence nor the fiction of matrilineal ties among the constituent descent units. The criteria for the inclusion of one or more of these units within an established or proposed clan federation did not necessarily rest on genealogical proximity or distance measured through the matriline, or through kin ties or categories of any other sort. Rather, territorial, demographic, and political factors were undoubtedly the effective prime movers in these matters even though the cultural expression of all such material realities was commonly framed instead in the imagery of kinship—and of siblingship, in particular.[15]

There are various other levels at which the alignment of territories defined by, or simply identified with, discrete and theoretically exclusive social units appear both cloaked in and consistently informed by idioms of siblingship. To

---

[15] It is quite possible, nonetheless, that certain ties of kinship among some of the chiefs (e.g. affinal bonds, relations through adoption or patrilateral half-siblingship) led on occasion to mutually acceptable decisions regarding the advantages of joint emigration, internal migration, proximate settlement, military cooperation and the like. This might have occurred in the last example cited above and also in the instance of To Laut Dalam and To Lela Balang.

illustrate, we may examine the mythically encoded structural alignments of settlements associated with Rembau's gentry clans.

Returning once again to the mythical account of the origins of the Lelahmaharaja and Sediaraja clans (see Figure 2, next page), we see that To Laut Dalam (who was the founder of the Lowland village of Padang Lekoh) had four daughters by his marriage with the unnamed Javanese woman said to be the apical ancestress of the Sediaraja clan. By her marriage with Seri Rama, To Laut Dalam's eldest daughter (Siti Hawa) gave birth to a male child who is considered to have been the first member of the Sediaraja clan and to have eventually resettled and established the Lowland village known as Kampong Tengah. Likewise, the descendants of Siti Hawah's three sisters opened up three new communities (also in Lowland Rembau), each tracing its origin to a different sister. In sum, the progeny of To Laut Dalam's four daughters succeeded in founding four distinct villages regarded throughout history as the most senior of the Sediaraja settlements.

At the apex of their mythical genealogy, and in the final analysis, each of these four villages stands connected to the other three by virtue of the fact that Siti Hawah, Melidi, Norimah, and Shamsiah were sisters. Note, however, that since none of these women actually belonged to the Sediaraja clan founded by the son of Siti Hawah, or to any other descent units, it makes little sense in terms of an exclusively matrilineal transmission of descent-unit membership and status that the progeny and settlements associated with Melidi, Norimah, and Shamsiah stand on a par with those of Siti Hawah's son. Rather, this parity exists owing to the sibling bond that not only links the four women in question and renders them more or less structurally equivalent, but also dictates a de facto mythical extension of Sediaraja status from Siti Hawah's son (who is thus treated as a female) to the offspring of his mother's sisters.

A fairly similar pattern of territorial expansion and alignment appears in the case of the Lelahmaharaja clan, which, as discussed earlier, traces its origins to the union of To Bungkal and To Lela Balang, the latter being the founder of the Lowland village of Kota. None of the four offspring of these luminary figures are linked in any direct way with the establishment of new settlements. Even so, one of the female children (To Lijah) did give birth to two women, each known curiously as Tiaman, who appear to have been responsible for the initial occupation of the Lowland villages of Chengkau and Chembong. In turn, their brother (Dato Uban Puteh Kepala)

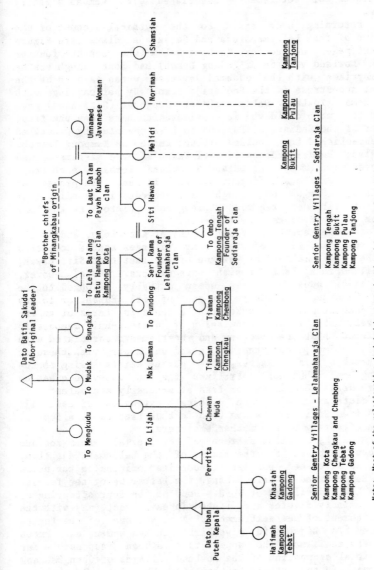

Figure 2: Mythic Genealogy of Relations Among Founders of Rembau's Gentry Clans and Senior Gentry Settlements

fathered two daughters, Halimah and Khasiah, who rank as the founders of two additional villages (Tebat in Upland Rembau and Gadong in Lowland Rembau respectively). During the lifetime of To Lela Balang's great-grandchildren, then, the Lelahmaharaja clan's territorial domain embraced five distinct settlements or senior gentry villages (Kota, Chengkau, Chembong, Tebat, and Gadong), and by that point had also come to include a colony within Upland Rembau.

The structure of genealogical connections among these senior gentry villages is analogous to, though somewhat more complex than, that of the Sediaraja case. Strictly speaking, there are five of these Lelamaharaja villages, although two of them (Chengkau and Chembong) occupy a single politico-jural status. Thus, myths, written sources, and contemporary elders tend to speak of Lelahmaharaja's four (as opposed to five) senior gentry communities, even while they recognize that Chengkau and its apparent offshoot Chembong are wholly separate settlements located at some distance from one another. In any event, the structure of ties among these villages is also patterned on siblingship rather than descent. Here too, in other words, myths effect an extension of descent unit affiliation from a male clan founder (Seri Rama) to his otherwise unaffiliated sisters (To Pundong, Mak Daman, and To Lijah). In so doing, these myths underscore the equivalence of siblings and the connective or relational significance of the siblingship principle. More specifically, they serve to generate a linkage conceptualized in terms of siblingship between Seri Rama's village (Kota) and those founded by the descendants of his sisters' daughters, namely, the settlements of Chengkau and Chembong.

The structural relevance of siblingship in terms of village and descent unit alignment is manifest as well in the relationship between these latter three villages on the one hand, and the communities of Tebat and Gadong on the other. Tebat and Gadong, for example, were originally connected to one another through bonds of patrilateral siblingship and possibly (though not for certain, since the myth is silent on this point) by virtue of common ties of matrifiliation. They were established by the two daughters (Halimah and Khasiah respectively) of the brother (Dato Uban Puteh Kepala) of the founders of Chengkau and Chembong. Interestingly, Halimah and Khasiah share their father's descent group membership. This could possibly indicate an incestuous union on the part of the father, but is more likely yet another mythical expression of the structural equivalence of siblings (i.e., Dato Uban Puteh Kepala and his sisters). In short, the descendants of Halimah, Khasiah, and the two Tiamans do not stand related to one another through an unbroken succession of matrilineal links.

Rather, the consistent structural logic connecting these groups and their associated villages derives from the principle of siblingship, as reflected in the fact that Dato Uban Puteh Kepala and the two Tiamans were all siblings. We might emphasize here that there are no principles of descent (and/or affinal alliance) that can accommodate these mythic representations.

The relations of equivalence suggested by the mythic siblingship linkages among the senior settlements of each gentry clan received congruent expression in the principles governing the devolution of rights to gentry political offices, and were therefore of far greater structural significance than data derived from myth alone might lead one to assume. Our analysis of the logic underlying political succession will serve to substantiate this contention. Additionally, it will shed light on the structure of genealogical relations among the founding settlements of individual commoner clans insofar as an identical set of principles appears to have prevailed in the case of commoner titles and would seem to point up the hegemony of siblingship in these latter instances of alignment as well.

Political Succession

Rembau's indigenous office system served in certain respects to encode a model of "pure matriliny," and yet it did so in a larger context of territorial and descent-unit alignment where organizational idioms drawn from concepts of matrilineal relatedness provided but one component of the relevant structure (and thus only a partial explanation for its expression "on the ground"). The other nexus of idioms at issue here, and in virtually all other realms of indigenous social theory and practice, were constructed on notions of siblingship, the entailments of which were contextually variable but nonetheless capable of being wholly inconsistent with those based on matrilineal descent. Elsewhere I have proposed that an understanding of the interplay of such analytically distinct principles provides a critical window on the dynamics of the traditional political system, and on critical themes in Rembau's social history more generally (Peletz 1983). Here we will simply examine the office system from certain of the aforementioned perspectives and consider first of all the model of "pure matriliny" referred to earlier.

By and large, rights to any particular political title were vested in a single dispersed clan (or territorially defined segment thereof), with the partial exceptions repre-

sented by the title of <u>Undang</u> and a few others also monopo-
lized by the two gentry clans. Disregarding these cases, it
can be said that each title was held to be the property of one
specific social unit, membership in which was frequently
expressed in terms of common matrilineal relatedness and
typically ascribed at birth by virtue of ties of matrifiliation with a woman belonging to that same category (or, alter-
nately, by adoption). As in most ethnographic instances of
such estates, rights to any given political office were wholly
concentrated among the members of one or another clan (or
segment thereof), and could not devolve upon persons or col-
lectivities defined as external to the relevant category.
Viewed from the other side, an appropriate descent affiliation
was the <u>sine qua non</u> with respect to political succession,
even while a multitude of other considerations (such as moral
character, verbal skills and charisma, physical well being,
and patrilateral connections) also figured into the picture.

Further testifying to the idiom of descent underlying
the structure of the office system was the convention whereby
the term used to designate enatically related kin of junior
generational standing (i.e. <u>anak buah</u>) was also employed by
political leaders in referring to their adherents. Just as a
man's sisters' children stood as his <u>anak buah</u>, to take the
most relevant example, so too did everyone within Rembau share
that designation in relation to the <u>Undang</u>. More generally,
all titled males were in effect defined as mother's brothers
vis-à-vis their charges.

Other data could be marshalled to provide additional
insights into the prevalence of matrilineal idioms within the
system of offices, but the foregoing should suffice for our
present purposes. At this point I am more concerned to
suggest that a closer focus on the logic informing the
devolution of rights to political office reveals the hegemony
of siblingship as a basic ordering (and fundamentally disjunctive) principle within that same system.

We may first examine the devolution of rights to offices
vested in a localized clan through an example drawn from contemporary Bogang. The principles of relevance here dominate
ancient as well as recent mythic accounts pertaining to
political succession at all levels of the indigenous hierarchy. At issue is the Lelahmaharaja clan, which is represented throughout Rembau and comprised of three named lineages
in the case of Bogang. This clan holds exclusive rights over
four political titles. One of these is that of clan sub-chief
(<u>buapak</u>), the other three are those of lower standing, "big
men among the kin" (<u>orang besar dalam anak buah</u>), or what I
refer to as lineage heads. The most significant structural
feature informing access to these offices emerges from the

-103-

fact that rights over each of them pass from one lineage to the next in a set sequence. Thus when any one of these political figures dies, the title currently vested in him will be bestowed upon a member of the lineage next in line for that particular title. (This despite the fact that all four of the titles could conceivably accumulate within two or even one of the lineages at any point in time.) Stated somewhat differently, even though rights to these titles never pass out of the localized clan, neither do they devolve from mother's brother to sister's son, as occurs in many other political systems associated with matrilineal descent. Rather they pass among structurally equivalent social units (lineages) held to be related to one another "like sisters."

An analogous logic governed access to the title of Undang, which has been defined as the "ancestral property" (harta pesaka) of Rembau's two gentry clans ever since its inception (circa 1540-1640). Especially worthy of recall is that the mythical genealogies of these clans portray their respective apical ancestresses as wholly unrelated to one another except for the fact that their husbands stood linked as "brother chiefs." In brief, while these two men belonged to entirely separate clans, and were thus structurally distant in terms of matrilineal calculations, their relationship of chiefly brotherhood provided the primary linkage not only between their wives but also between the latter's respective enatic descendants (who were associated with Lelahmaharaja or Sediaraja). It remains to emphasize that rights to the office of Undang have always rotated in theory between Lelahmaharaja and Sediaraja (Parr and Mackray 1910:48-49), and that such rotation implies the same structural equivalence of these two units that appears in myth as grounded in a particular variant of non-enatic siblingship. Further, just as villagers of the present-day conceptualize the relationship between the two in terms of siblingship (adik-beradik), so too do long-standing marriage ideals enjoining conjugal and affinal linkages between them point to a cultural recognition of the non-enatic nature of this tie.

To point out that rights to the office of Undang rotated between Lelahmaharaja and Sediaraja is to draw attention to but a single dimension of the devolution in question. For it was also the case that rights to provide a candidate for this office passed among each of the senior settlements associated with these clans. For example, when an Undang of the Lelahmaharaja clan died (or else vacated office owing to impeachment or infirmity), the title passed to one of the Sediaraja communities which was not only endowed with senior standing but also held to be next in line for candidacy vis-a-vis the other three Sediaraja villages of equivalent status (Parr and

-104-

Mackray 1910:8-9). There was in short a second circuit
involved here inasmuch as access to the title passed between
the two clans on the one hand, and among each of their senior
settlements on the other. As we have already seen that the
genealogical bonds among the senior villages of each clan
receive mythical expression in terms of sibling ties, this
level of rotation provides additional justification for regarding siblingship as the hegemonic idiom informing the
devolution of rights over the office of Undang. So too does
the fact that there existed one further circuit in all of this
insofar as the residentially localized lineages within each of
these settlements also took turns in furnishing nominees whenever their village was deemed eligible for candidacy. Unfortunately, we do not know for certain how such lineages were
held to be connected to one another during the nineteenth
century. Present-day residents of Bogang do view them, however, as related like siblings, and, in particular, like
sisters; and I suspect that this situation has always
obtained.

     We may generalize from the foregoing and reiterate that
all social and territorial units associated with the founding
settlements of gentry clans and vested with equivalent, parallel, or essentially complementary rights to the same political
title(s) were held to be related as (or like) siblings by virtue of their common relationships to the office(s) in question. We might underscore, in addition, that the same rules of
political succession from which these generalizations were
deduced can be discerned in the case of founding settlements
associated with individual commoner clans (see Parr and Mackray 1910:120-141). In a word, an identical logic grounded in
siblingship seems to have prevailed in these instances of territorial alignment as well.

     One final point concerning the devolution of rights over
political titles is that there appears not to have been any
explicit notion of structural precedence owing to which
certain adult males within a sibling set, lineage branch, or
lineage would merit preferential or exclusive consideration
when their lineage received its turn to provide a candidate
for office. That is, while the schemes of rotation sketched
out earlier enjoined serial succession at the levels of
dispersed and aggregated clan as well as lineage, they seem
not to have ranged beyond these units, e.g., by specifying a
variant of primo- (or ultimo-) geniture. One might well
perceive in this a mechanism geared toward fostering intralineage equality since there existed no explicit differentiation in terms of distance from a founding line or apical
sibling set, and candidates could thus be selected instead on
grounds of "paternal luster" or some combination of learned

skills or other achievements. The problem, however, was that this might also pave the way for the emergence of invidious intralineage distinctions, based on potential military prowess or acquired competence of one sort or another, which could effectively negate the structural equivalence ideally characteristic of relations among adult male enates (particularly those of the same relative generation). Further, this necessarily meant that all males within a particular sibling set, lineage branch, and entire lineage might well be vying for the same political stakes. Hence their competition for a post that entailed representing a descent unit of one or another order of inclusiveness vis-a-vis other units of like order could well engender divisiveness within the very unit they sought to represent. Indeed, in light of the pronounced cultural emphasis on the equivalence of same-sex siblings, one would certainly expect a man to harbor profound resentment toward a brother who attained political office while he himself simply muddled along as a "mere villager." More to the point, perhaps, is that structurally induced sentiments of this nature continue to provide a context for the florescence of myriad variants of fraternal strife and do in fact inform widely redounding social schisms (Peletz 1983:506-527).

Negeri Sembilan and Beyond

In this concluding section I should like first to consider the implications of Kelly's (1977) illustration that the traditional anthropological concept of descent subsumes two analytically distinct phenomena: the alignment of descent units on the one hand, and recruitment to these units on the other. The extent to which the alignment of descent units and groups conforms (even conceptually) to a unilineal logic and ideology is essentially an empirical question quite separate from the issue of clan and lineage recruitment. Kelly's (1977) interpretation of Etoro material points this up quite nicely, as does the accompanying resolution of those "structural anomalies" discussed in Evans-Pritchard's (1940, 1951) work on the Nuer (and since dubbed "the Nuer paradox" [cf. Schneider 1965; Buchler and Selby 1968]). Analyses of these two societies reveal that principles of siblingship may serve to link and equate parallel- as well as cross-sex siblings and thus inform or even dictate structural relations among descent units or territorial segments of varying levels of inclusiveness. Such principles can also entail contradictions with respect to a unilineal logic (which measures structural equivalence and distance through persons of a single gender), for relationships, activities, or domains of behavior ordered in accordance with the former may be incompatible with the latter (and vice versa). Incompatibilities of this sort have often been construed as evidence of a "loosely structured social system" (cf. Embree 1950; Barnes 1962; Swift 1965:167-174); in other words, a society with regard to which it is claimed that relationships and/or activities lack regularity, are ambiguously patterned, or are organized in such a way as to be inconsistent with espoused ideals and/or structural principles. But to invoke the notion of "loose structure" would be to miss the point; indeed, there is nothing necessarily "loose," "unstructured," or ambiguous in a social system characterized by structural principles (or cultural categories) among which there are relationships of mutual incompatibility or contradiction. In the final analysis one would be extremely hard pressed to demonstrate for any social system that all of its internal relationships and constituent elements are (or were ever) wholly consistent with one another.

The relevance of all such insights to data from precolonial Rembau should be obvious. For in the case of Rembau, we are not dealing with a situation wherein principles, idioms and values keyed to one or another facet of descent were simply so pronounced that they allowed for and simultaneously served to contain myriad deviations from a descent-based logic. (This was Evans-Pritchard's explanation for inconsistencies between the formal ideology of Nuer descent on the one hand, and various structural relationships and "on the ground" activities on the other.) To phrase the issue more positively, principles and idioms of siblingship provided the hegemonic constructs informing the conceptualization and realization of relationships and activities in a wide variety of analytically distinct organizational domains. Viewed collectively, these domains encompassed bonds among collateral enates, ties among otherwise wholly unrelated individuals connected to one another through mechanisms of formal adoption, in addition to linkages among lineage branches and lineages of the same clan as well as certain non-aggregated clans of disparate enatic ancestry. They also subsumed relationships both among territorially defined units of various degrees of inclusiveness, and among the analytically discrete (though culturally interlocked) components of the office system. One might recall, further, that notions of siblingship figured into the conceptualization and content of conjugal bonds (and were likewise keyed to constructs of gender). In sum, there exists a good deal of evidence to support our contentions that siblingship served as a major source of uniform (and unifying) idioms for a broad range of organizational domains; and, perhaps more importantly, that it provided the template for an ideological framework that effectively interrelated and overlay all such domains (despite the fact that many of the latter were also

-107-

partially structured in accordance with altogether separate and mutually incompatible principles that varied considerably from one case to the next).

The ethnographic and theoretical issues emphasized here suggest that one of the very first tasks facing the historically oriented anthropologist of the present is to discern the specific pre-colonial contexts in which principles of siblingship, those of descent, or some combination or interaction of these or other constructs (e.g., patrifiliation), assumed a dominant role whether in terms of ideology or the actual organization of activity. Only after we have adequately specified the full scope and force of principles informing behavior or linkages associated with one or another domain of activity or cultural order can we begin to reconstruct the dynamics, cleavages, and tensions that existed within the system during one or another period of the nineteenth century. Of comparable if not greater significance is the related point that a thorough assessment of such phenomena would seem to constitute an essential prerequisite for any comprehensive discussion aimed at elucidating which elements or components of the system have been reproduced or transformed since that time.

More generally, especially illuminating contributions to our knowledge of tribal and peasant societies elsewhere in the Malayo-Indonesian world and beyond might well come from diachronic analyses of the shifting entailments of various categories of siblingship and other forms of social relatedness, particularly those grounded in an awareness that the conceptual, moral, and political economy dimensions of descent (and/or alliance) are far less critical in many "traditional" and modernizing systems than once thought. Such analyses will undoubtedly reveal as well that kinship always cuts both ways; and that relationships cast in idioms of siblingship are especially conducive to the expression of ambivalence, discord, and divisiveness, if only on account of the burdens and invariably incomplete social realization of the prescriptive amity that is their most culturally elaborated hallmark. I also suspect that future inquiries along these lines will afford more powerful insights than those concluding in effect that the combined impact of centralized state rule, modern market forces and the like has engendered "loose structure" or simply brought about a situation wherein "the system has broken down" (or is well along the road to decay). Moreover, they should yield extremely valuable perspectives on the highly selective nature of social process. As such, these types of investigations might also provide additional impetus for the development of an historical anthropology (cf. Sahlins 1981:8) that is geared toward elucidating the myriad ways in which structural principles and attendant constructs may not only serve to channel and otherwise constrain the local-level cultural realization of exogenous forces of social change, but may also come to be reconstituted as a result.

Acknowledgements. This essay constitutes a revised version of certain sections of my doctoral dissertation (Peletz 1983), which was based on 16 months of field research (during the period December 1978 to May 1980) and subsequent archival study in Kuala Lumpur and England. Support for the project was obtained from the National Science Foundation (under Grant No. BNS-7812499), the Center for South and Southeast Asian Studies of the University of Michigan, and the University of Michigan's Horace Rackham School of Graduate Studies. In addition to thanking these institutions for their generous financial backing, I would like to acknowledge my profound debts both to Ellen Peletz, who provided much appreciated support during all phases of the project, and to the inhabitants of the Rembau village herein referred to as Bogang (a pseudonym). Raymond Kelly, Sherry Ortner, and Aram Yengoyan offered valuable comments on earlier formulations of themes addressed in this paper. The reader will also recognize my intellectual debts to K.O. Burridge whose (1959) essay on siblingship in Tangu inspired many of the arguments set forth here. I alone am responsible for any inaccuracies and shortcomings.

IMPLICATIONS OF MERANTAU
FOR SOCIAL ORGANIZATION IN MINANGKABAU

Mochtar Naim
Andalas University

Voluntary migration with the clear intention of eventually returning home is not unique to Minangkabau. Reports
by Freeman (1955) on the tradition of "bejalai" (Ind.: ber-
jalan, going away from home) among the Iban of Sarawak, and by
Cunningham (1958) on the tradition of "marjajo" (wanderings)
among the Batak, show that institutionalized voluntary migration can and does occur in bilateral and patrilineal societies as well as in matrilineal ones. Voluntary migration is
found in a less institutionalized form among, for instance,
the Buginese, Banjarese, and even the Javanese and Sundanese.

Merantau in Minangkabau, as in some other societies, involves a departure from home for a certain period of time in
search of wealth, knowldege, or experience. In some societies, as in Minangkabau, it has become essentially a rite of
passage to adulthood for men. Attempts to generalize cross-
culturally about merantau might involve questions of whether
or not merantau is more often or more deeply associated with
societies of differing social organization. Obviously, full
answers to such questions require extensive and controlled
comparative study, requiring in turn attention to specific
cases. Accordingly, in order to better understand the roles
of merantau in one society and as a step toward comparative
study, this paper will survey specific structural linkages
between merantau and matriliny in Minangkabau.

Naim (1973) and Kato (1977) have suggested that merantau and matriliny are historically related in Minangkabau;
perhaps in the earlier history of the society, men were required to leave their homes to look for new settlements or new
ventures, or simply to undergo initiation into adulthood.
Such a custom might have been a manifestation of the peripheral role of the male in matrilineages. Merantau may also
have been an integral part of processes of village and lineage
segmentation.

Whether matriliny and merantau have historically perpetuated and mutually reinforced one another is something
which has begun to be explored (Abdullah 1967; Naim 1973; Kato

1977) though there is still a need for vigorous and in-depth research to substantiate the hypothesis.

Nowadays the tendency is toward a longer, if not permanent, period of residence in the rantau area, which is popularly called "merantau Cino" following the more permanent Chinese migration pattern. The question of mutual reinforcement versus mutual antagonism between matriliny and merantau becomes even more challenging. It is easy to see how some structural linkages function in the lifetime of an actual actor who experiences the more traditional (circulatory) pattern of merantau, encompassing smaller units of time and distance, which is popularly known as "merantau pipit" (lit.: sparrow style merantau). The migrant himself would link the home and the rantau and among his concerns would be the preparation of a better home to which to return. It is more difficult to see how a "reinforcing" linkage is functioning if the actor remains in the rantau permanently. The problem is further complicated in the case of his offspring who were born and raised in the rantau and know little of their parents' homeland, especially if the parents were the result of a mixed marriage, themselves products of the modern multi-ethnic, heterogeneous and urban rantau.

As I argued previously (1973), knowledge of the actor's intentions before he embarks for the rantau is pivotal in attempting to answer such important questions. For example, is the act of migration voluntary or forced by circumstances? Does the actor plan to reside in the rantau on a temporary or permanent basis? It is, of course, easy to hypothesize that the linkage will be eventually terminated if the intention is to outmigrate permanently, or in circumstances in which departure from the village is forced by uses of adat, for example, sanctioning for violation of social taboos. However, such instances, to the best of my knowledge, are relatively rare. Despite exposure to outside influences, very few Minangkabau leave home with the clear idea of never returning, or of disengaging themselves from family or village ties. By definition, migration that is intentionally permanent or is forced by external factors would no longer be considered "merantau." This is simply "berpindah" or permanent migration.

Conceptually it is therefore important to restrict usage of the term merantau to those cases in which the person departing intends to return. The intention of the person at the time of departure regarding return to the home area is crucial in determining whether the move is merantau or berpindah.

Limitation as to the reference of distance seems to have been spiralling over time. The ever-widening socio-cultural boundaries between "us" and "them" appear to be decisive in

determining whether the actor considers himself to be merantau. Thus far, there has been a general agreement that only
by leaving the Minangkabau area would one be considered
merantau, since in that case the perantau no longer interacts
socially with people of the same ethnic and socio-cultural
background exclusively, but with others as well. The perception of socio-cultural boundaries between "us" and "them" may,
however, differ by social class membership. Perhaps among
more mobile, higher class Minangkabau there are those who do
not consider their departure to be merantau if they only move
to other parts of Sumatra or even Indonesia, while those at
lower social levels may still feel that they go merantau if
they move only to a nearby town or some other part of West
Sumatra.

But regardless of the spatial boundaries involved, what
is crucial to the definition of merantau is the experience of
social interactions with persons dissimilar to the migrant in
their ethnic or socio-cultural background, as well as the
constant awareness of being in rantau away from home.

With these conceptual definitions in mind, both the home
and the rantau areas have to be observed to determine the
extent to which merantau affects and is affected by the social
organization in the respective areas.

First we will examine the rantau area. With the exception of the earlier pioneering migration to acquire new lands,
Minangkabau merantau has always been innovative in that perantau (migrants) do not engage in the same occupations in the
rantau as they did at home. They become traders, artisans,
students, teachers, religious leaders, or white collar workers; they shun menial, low respect, subservient positions,
including those of lower rank in military and police services.
The occupational preference as such and the fact that they
choose to stay in urban centers rather than in rural areas is
enough to form a type of social organization in the rantau
that is distinct from that at home. With no agricultural
base, the need for an extended family system is consciously
avoided by the average Minangkabau family in the rantau,
ostensibly to minimize family entanglements that frequently
occur back home. The family system adopted in the rantau is
therefore purely conjugal, suggesting that the system is meant
to be temporary. Those who are well established in the rantau
and appear to have no intention of returning home often adopt
the nuclear family residence pattern permanently. Tracing
descent through the maternal line for various purposes (such
as to identify appropriate marital candidates) is still
largely operative and may go on for a few generations until

the families are fully absorbed into the <u>rantau</u> system.

The above fact, however, does not imply that Minangkabau families in the <u>rantau</u> are less accommodative to kin members of both sides. Field observations have shown (Naim 1973) that they are even more hospitable, giving shelter or assistance when necessary, not only to immediate kin members, but also to distant relatives or even unrelated villagers. Such social obligation is a norm and it is considered a virtue to show ethnic solidarity in the <u>rantau</u>. At any rate, the husband tends to be the family head and major breadwinner. This is, of course, in complete contrast with the titular position as <u>samando</u> back home in his wife's corporate house in which his main duty in the traditional sense is as guest of honor for procreational purposes.

The presence of maternal uncles (<u>mamak</u>) or brothers of the wife in the same <u>rantau</u> (or even staying in the same house), if such a situation occurs, does not affect the efficacy of the husband's authority, which is fully accepted and recognized by the family. Consequently, the traditional responsibility of maternal uncles as guardians to their nephews and nieces becomes only nominal in the <u>rantau</u>. In practice, the husband assumes full responsibility for the care and raising of his children.

On the other hand, since the <u>rantau</u> life is only temporary (at least in the <u>perantau</u>'s mind) and is essentially meant to enrich or support the life at home in the village, the <u>perantau</u> have moral and social obligations of caring for the welfare of extended family members back home. In fact, success of a <u>perantau</u> is often judged in terms of the amount of care and attention he gives to his people who remain in the village while he is in the <u>rantau</u>. The results can indeed be seen, especially in the areas most heavily affected by <u>merantau</u>, from the number of new houses and even schools or mosques built with the money sent from the <u>rantau</u>, and in the large number of children that are sent to schools with <u>rantau</u> funds.

This pattern may distinguish the Minangkabau <u>merantau</u> from that of other societies. Departure to the <u>rantau</u> does not necessarily cancel social obligations back in the village. The <u>perantau</u> often moves back and forth between home and the <u>rantau</u>.

At this point it will be useful to examine the home life of the Minangkabau. Many changes have taken place in West Sumatra over the last several decades and especially after achieving independence. It is significant that West Sumatra, the home of the Minangkabau, is now only a province in the Indonesian nation. The notion of <u>alam</u> (world) which once was

restricted only to Minangkabau (Abdullah 1972) now encompasses
the wider home of the Minangkabau: all of Indonesia. The
changes that appeared to be only political and administrative
in the beginning brought with them far-reaching socio-cultural
consequences. Values, norms, modes and even styles of life
are now more heterogeneous as a result of conscious efforts to
mold a national identity. It is now difficult to distinguish
Minangkabau cultural traits from Indonesian elements; and this
applies to almost all aspects of life.

If one were to travel extensively through West Sumatra,
one would hardly find anything economic, political, educational, social or cultural that is distinctively Minangkabau.
Everything is integrated into a streamlined, homogeneous,
hierarchical national system that tends to obscure regional
and cultural differences. Above all, improvements in communication and transportation whet the desires of many Minangkabau to travel and go merantau. This became particularly
evident in the early nineteen-fifties when the fight for independence was over and avenues to the rantau were again open.

While efforts at national integration may have produced
a modern bureaucratic administrative structure, the more profound social foundations of Minangkabau culture remain, however, relatively unchanged. The matrilineal kinship system in
particular remains entrenched. The suggestion that patriclan
organization as construed by Maretin (1961) and others is
replacing matriclan organization is only circumstantial and in
large part pertains to surface socio-cultural phenomena. No
research has thus far discovered a lineage household that has
moved away from the traditional pattern to the extent that it
is no longer matrilineal but patrilineal or purely bilateral.

It is true that fewer lineage houses are now built in
the form of the traditional rumah gadang. The extended family
unit (paruik) that once lived under one roof is now branched
out in more independent sub-units centering normally around a
mother instead of a grandmother as in the old rumah gadang.
The sub-unit houses normally are built adjacent to each other
in the same kaum or suku [clan] land. The samando who used to
be a mere guest of honor with little responsibility now plays
a more active role as father and husband. In socio-economic
terms he now actually heads the nuclear unit and is thus
responsible for the care and raising of his children. The
maternal uncle who used to be responsible for the welfare of
the extended unit now plays a more supervisory and ceremonial
role, which in turn means he plays a more active role as
samando in his wife's lineage house.

The shift to the more active role of the samando as
breadwinner for his wife and children cannot, however, be interpreted to mean that the lineage system is now swaying to

-115-

the more bilateral or even patrilineal side, as some have argued. Strictly in terms of the lineage system, not even those who stay in towns or in the _rantau_ have turned away from the traditional matrilineal system. What seems to have been occurring is a trend toward a nucleated residence pattern while preserving the matrilineal kinship system, as has generally been the case in the lowland _rantau_ of West Sumatra.

Demographic and socio-economic variables, in addition to the above-mentioned socio-political factors, may have played a considerable role in reshaping the social organization in West Sumatra, and within this framework the institution of _merantau_ takes an active part.

There was a time when the available land was capable of supporting the existing agrarian population. However it is becoming difficult for an increasing number of people to subsist solely by agricultural means. Some, especially among the more active and economically productive age groups, withdraw and look for other income-producing activities. These are the people who migrate to urban centers in West Sumatra and elsewhere, and thus engage in _merantau_. As Kato (1977) and others argue, it is the draining off of excess population through _merantau_ that helps maintain matriliny and the relative stability of village life.

In areas of greatest _merantau_, the situation is such that the role of women in the household is next to "matriarchy" since there are no longer enough men to work in the fields or houses. Often women are forced to make decisions without consulting the men. In addition, the cherished work of _gotong-royong_ (mutual help) begins to disappear, to be substituted by wage labor. Therefore, the process of individualization, motivated also by other factors, cannot be avoided. The fragmentation of the once closely knit extended kinship system to more nucleated sub-systems, as described above, can be seen also in this light. The once abundant communal land has been divided into smaller portions as extended family members have continued to proliferate. This process continues until they can no longer subsist merely from farming their land.

Here lies the essence of the institutional function of _merantau_ that acts as a valve to siphon off excess population. The amount of land available is enough to feed only a certain number of people; the remainder must seek other professions or go elsewhere. This leveling mechanism helps to stabilize village life, although it may also work to the disadvantage of village growth and create other problems. Excess people who are unable to go _merantau_ are not only those in the productive ages group, but also young, energetic and better educated people. _Merantau_ is also involved in a sort of "natural selection," in that it is only those who have courage to gamble with the uncertain life in _rantau_ who leave the village. _Merantau_ to them is a calculated risk, requiring not only courage but also vision and far-sightedness.

The fact that the communal land is continuously diminishing with the constant increase of population creates at least two additional effects: the departure of wives and children to join the husbands in the _rantau_ and the growing trend toward more permanent residence of members of the nuclear unit together in _rantau_. The occupational variable in the _rantau_ may finally determine whether the intentions to eventually return home are still viable or subsiding.

Two distinct patterns appear to have emerged as a result: one in which the _perantau_ remains in the _rantau_ permanently; the other in which he eventually returns home. The first pertains especially to the so called _rantau pegawai_, whose good position, guaranteed salary, and old age pension give them more security in the urban _rantau_. Returning home would only mean _merantau_ for the second time as they would have to readjust and reorient themselves to the simple village life that they have left for so long.

The second pattern pertains to the so called _rantau pedagang_ who, after some time, may decide whether to stay or return home. Petty traders especially, who are the majority of the Minangkabau _perantau_, know that there is a limit to their occupational mobility in the _rantau_. Normally, the desire to return to his village of a _rantau pedagang_ who has not fared extremely well in his new life may become relatively strong as he advances in age. Such a person would send money to the village to build or repair homes, buy new lands, or expand properties, because he knows for sure that no pension will be available to support him in his old age.

There are other factors such as the need for better education, the strong attraction to urban centers, regional revolts, and political unrest, which motivate people to migrate. All of these factors affect the Minangkabau decisions to go _merantau_ (Naim 1973: esp. Ch. VI). One can therefore conceive that as a result of all these factors, substantial changes have taken place. The importance of _merantau_ in Minangkabau life can be judged from the fact that it is difficult to find villagers who have not had any such experience. Yet, despite all of these facts, it is also true that the underlying social structure and social organization remain entrenched in the matrilineal system. As has been described above, _merantau_ has been instrumental in maintaining this matrilineal system.

PART II: THE RANTAU, ISLAM, POLITICAL HISTORY, AND IDEOLOGY

MYTH AND REALITY: MINANGKABAU
INSTITUTIONAL TRADITIONS IN THE RANTAU

J. Kathirithamby-Wells
University of Malaya

Largely due to its inaccessibility in the heartland of
Bukit Barisan, the history and institutional traditions of the
core-region or darat of Minangkabau have been little known to
the outsider. The earliest historical reference we have to
the Raja Nan Tiga Sila (the Kings of the Three Seats) is from
the account of Tomé Pires in the early sixteenth century (Cortesão 1944:164). After a considerable lapse of time, Thomas
Dias from Melaka recorded his visit in 1684 via the east coast
to Bua, the seat of Raja Adat (Haan 1897:327-66). The western
rantau provided easier access to the Minangkabau interior, but
for well over half the seventeenth century Tanah Datar, the
"administrative capital" of the Raja Nan Tiga Sila, was cut
off from contacts with the area by Acehnese occupation. It
was not until Dutch settlement of the west coast and the treaty which they made in 1668 with Raja Alam at Pagarruyung that
relations between him and the west coast were restored,
though, even then, not very effectively (Kathirithamby-Wells
1969:458-9).

The exchange of letters from time to time between the
Dutch and English west coast settlements and Pagarruyung provides ample evidence of the grandiose and pretentious claims
of the Minangkabau rulers but insufficient information on the
mechanics of the kingdom (Marsden 1811:388; Kathirithamby -
Wells 1970:53-63). In their contacts with Pagarruyung, the
Dutch, who confined their activities to the rantau, preferred
to use the coastal rajas as their emissaries. They had no
clear idea, for example, of the details and issues pertaining
to the political upheavals in Tanah Datar following the death
in 1674 of Raja Alam, Ahmad Syah (Andaya 1972-73:99-101).

Raffles, who made his journey into Minangkabau in 1818,
was aware that "the respect still paid to its princes by all
ranks, amounts almost to veneration," but there is no enuncia-
tion of the concept of kingship in his description of the
kingdom (Raffles 1935 I:432-33). Aspects of the composite
structure of the Alam Minangkabau (the Minangkabau world)
constituting the conceptual conflicts and balances between the
darat and rantau, ruler and nagari, adat, and Islam,

matrilineal and patrilineal, and the adat systems of Koto
Piliang and Bodi Caniago, remained largely unknown. It was
only with the slow progress of the Padri War and Dutch
attempts to find economic and political solutions that the
complexities of the socio-political structure became clear,
though conceptual explanations for them were not offered until
the early part of this century.[1]

While bringing earlier accounts together in his description of the Minangkabau socio-political system, Professor de
Josselin de Jong drew attention to the significance of Minangkabau legends in general and the Kaba Cindua Mato, in particular, for a definition of the role of the Minangkabau rajas
and great chiefs in Tanah Datar (de Josselin de Jong 1952:101-
5). In a more detailed and critical examination of the same
kaba, Taufik Abdullah has pronounced it "a state myth par
excellence and a standard reference work for Minangkabau adat
theoreticians and guardians" (Taufik Abdullah 1970:3).
Although it is difficult to establish the historicity of the
Kaba Cindua Mato it was not so much its accuracy as its
didactic role which is important. The Kaba Cindua Mato
"describes an orderly, balanced world where every aspect of
life is arranged according to certain principles. Tragedy
occurred because the protagonist ignored these principles...."
(Taufik Abdullah 1970:13).

At the head of the structured world of Minangkabau was
the Tuanku or Raja Alam at Pagarruyung; but what was the
actual substance of his authority? The central authority of
Minangkabau was withdrawn from the coastal areas during the
period of Acehnese influence and, even after the nominal
restoration of its power after the 1668 treaty with the Dutch,
it was apparently non-effectual. The coastal nagari which had
allied with the Dutch in revolt against the vexations and
burdens of the Acehnese representatives with the title of
panglima earned little respite under the new regime. They
soon found they had merely exchanged one external authority
for another. In January 1667 the Raja Alam sent representatives to Salida, Inderapura, Padang, and Kota Tengah demand-
ing the customary tribute (ruba-ruba), which was a nominal
acknowledgement of his sovereignty, without his interference
in the internal administration of the rantau (Kroeskamp
1931:65-7). Nonetheless, the Raja Alam was active in the

---

[1] The important works which may be cited here for early descriptive accounts are Hollander 1847; Van der Linden 1855;
and Nahuijs 1826. For more analytical descriptions, Leyds
1926; Schafer 1938; Willinck 1909; and Westenek 1918a.

performance of other functions such as seeking protection for Minangkabau sailors and vessels (Kroeskamp 1931:55, 77) and even for those Minangkabaus resident outside, such as the pepper cultivators in Palembang (Andaya 1975:135). Though exercising no effective political force, the Raja Alam continued to function as an arbitrator and supreme adjudicator in affairs affecting his subjects which were beyond the jurisdiction of the _nagari_. What might seem the residual functions of the Raja Alam at a period of political ebb would appear to have been also his crucial and basic functions within the Minangkabau world.

There is nothing in Minangkabau history or legend purporting to the might and physical force of the ruler to match that of the conventional Hindu, Christian, or Muslim monarch. The latter was constantly under pressure to actualize his claims through demonstration of military power, particularly in the peripheral areas of his realm. The Minangkabau sovereign was singularly exempted from such a military role and his credibility determined solely by his conformity with institutional prescriptions. The Minangkabau political system was unique in that, despite the shadow figure of the ruler, the Alam Minangkabau was indestructible so long as the institutional traditions were maintained and for the very preservation of which he existed. The glorification of Minangkabau's first and most celebrated ruler, Adityavarman, rested not on his military role but on his endowment of the sterner and more autocratic laws of Koto Piliang, in addition to the already existing more egalitarian laws of the Bodi Caniago (Mansoer 1976:58-60). He, thus introduced the eternal conflict aimed at achieving the ideal balance by setting opposite forces in motion (de Josselin de Jong 1952:112-15).

The significance of the Minangkabau political and administrative philosophy and its astonishing endurance is convincingly demonstrated in its actual functioning as an indestructible political ferment in the _rantau_. In the case of the Minangkabau coastal centers of Tiku, Pariaman, Passaman, and Padang, Acehnese influence for more than a century left _adat_ political traditions unaltered. The acceptance of Dutch protection brought about the total overthrow of the Acehnese _panglima_[2] and, in Padang, he was

---

[2] In 1664 the Acehnese _panglima_ on the west coast included:
The Maharaja Indra (Pariaman)
Sri Bijendara (Bandar Khalipah)
Orang Kaya Sri Indra Palawan (Panglima Padang)
Orang Kaya Sri Raja (Batang Kapas)

replaced by a local chief, Orang Kaya Kecil, who was assisted by a Bendahara and eleven penghulu (Daghregister 3, Nov. 1666:175). Within the council of chiefs a balanced representation from the two adat groups (laras), the Koto Piliang and Bodi Caniago, was of paramount importance. In 1730 the Panglima Sutan Amas and the Bendahara belonged to the same laras, possibly the Koto Piliang, while all the penghulu came from the other (Kielstra 1887:530-1). This arrangement was altered during the next century when the panglima and Bendahara were appointed from separate laras, the former preferably from the more dominant Koto Piliang. Latent tensions between the Minangkabaus of Padang and those of Pau and Kota Tengah were, apparently, held in check by adherence to this principle. Departure from it, in 1783, precipitated in open enmity among the nagari (Netscher, VBG, XLI, 12; Kathirithamby-Wells 1977:172-3 n.102).

Adherence to Minangkabau political philosophy and adat prescriptions was a pre-requisite for equilibrium and peace even within the rantau areas as far as the Sultanates of Inderapura and Anak Sungai (Mukomuko). How was the indestructible link of Minangkabau institutions perpetuated in the peripheral zone of the Alam notwithstanding the distance and lack of immediate contact with the Minangkabau kernel?

In the Kaba Cindua Mato, whose role in these regions is unclear, conceptual and moral messages are attractively garbed in colorful romance. More specifically, in the Sultanate of Anak Sungai, originally part of the Inderapura kingdom (see Kathirithamby-Wells 1976:81-4), the vital institutional prescriptions were contained in the stern laws of the Undang Undang Muko Muko, committed to memory and preserved through oral tradition (see Appendix).

Because of its importance, the preservation of the Undang Undang Muko Muko (UUMM) was entrusted to the eldest and most senior menteri among the Menteri Empat Belas of MukoMuko. Singa Maharaja, otherwise known as Singa Diraja, was the incumbent of this prestigeous office at the time the UUMM was written, a translation of which was published in 1822 in the Malayan Miscellanies by the Baptist Missionary Society in Benkulen. I have so far been unable to locate the original Malay version from which the translation was made. But the introduction to the translation, for which the authorship is unknown,[3] states that it was "composed in a kind of measured

---

Orang Kaya Sriguna Diraja (Salida)
Daghregister, 17 March 1664:74
[3] The author was incorrectly identified by me earlier (see

prose broken into stanzas, and it is recited in the manner of a verse, by which it was no doubt better impressed upon the memory" (UUMM 1822:1). However, we learn from the Syair MukoMuko that the adat was recited by Singa Diraja in the syair form.

> Singa Diraja the pious menteri
> spoke with much thought
> reciting the adat in the manner of the syair
> and as ordained by God.[4]

It is interesting how the UUMM agrees totally with the Minangkabau precepts contained in the Kaba Cindua Mato and how the "state myth" embodied in the Kaba is translated into the realities of practical laws in the UUMM.

It is evident from the UUMM that as a basic principle the effectiveness of Minangkabau authority was not dependent upon the personal force of the ruling authority but upon the adherence both by him and his subjects to the detailed prescriptions of the law. Accordingly, the boundaries of the kingdom were not subject to the fluctuations of personal authority and were more permanently determined by the limits of those resident under Minangkabau laws. It included the territories from Air Bangis in the north to Air Hitam (near Benkulen) in the south, and as far east as Nibong on the upper reaches of Jambi, the country of Tuanku Imbang Jaya (UUMM 1822:5-6).

The UUMM describes the two law traditions or "usages" of the legendary adat-law givers, Datuk Ketemanggungan (Koto Piliang) and Datuk Perpatih Nan Sebatang (Bodi Caniago) and, interestingly, lists the customs observed towards the "Tuanku," or sovereign, as a third tradition. The ruler or raja in the rantau was viewed as the true representative of the Tuanku at Pagarruyung in functioning as the supreme arbitrator. The first raja at Inderapura, in fact, is believed to have been Tuanku Darah Putih, the eldest son of Cindua Mato, the legendary first Yang Dipertuan.[5] He leaned equally to the adat

---

Kathirithamby-Wells 1976:66, n.4) as Richard Farmer, Governor of Benkulen (1717-18).

[4] Singa Diraja menteri yang fakir
mengeluarkan kata dengan difikir
membilang adat seperti bersair
sekeliannya itu dengan takdir
    --Syair Mukomuko, vs. 160.

[5] See Appendix, "Origin and descent of the Rajahs of Indrapura

and to Islam, observing impartiality and fairness in his judgements which were, therefore, to be accepted without question.[6] The ruler was, in turn, accorded due ceremonies such as the salute of a single gun, the use of the umbrella, and homage at his residence--customs which were faithfully adhered to in the Sultanate of Mukomuko (Syair Mukomuko vs. 14, 15, 78, 94).

The Tuanku, or ruler, was believed to be endowed with special talents and supernatural powers, blended with knowledge, wisdom, and sagacity. With these attributes he could "overawe the children of men." In a system of government where the two opposing law traditions were continually in conflict, the fair and tactful arbitration of the ruler was particularly important. Thus, the credibility of his final judgement rested on his supernatural talents and moral superiority. He could "counteract the effect of spells" and was "sagacious in comprehending the real object of all that is said." Sultan Khalifatullah Inayat Syah (1789-1816), one of the most popular and successful rulers of Anak Sungai, is praised in the Syair Mukomuko for displaying some of these characteristics.

> This ruler of distinguished descent,
> achieved good work with extreme patience.
> He was just in the maintenance of law and
> order such that his fame spread.[7]

On the side of the people they were obliged to comply with the laws of justice and settle due payments in court-fees, fines, anchorage duties (ubar ubar) and blood-money (bangun) for high crimes. Their reward was the freedom to cock-fight, "make salt at appropriate places," fish, own vessels, and conduct trade. (UUMM 1822:7). British interference with and restriction of some of these privileges, such as salt-making and

---

and Moco Moco".

[6] Bagindalah raja yang usali
dari Paggaruyung asal terjali
hukumnya adil segenap hari
segala rakyat sakeliannya nagari
　　　--Syair Mukomuko, vs. 26.

[7] Bagindalah raja yang berasal
mengerajakan amal terlalu sabar
mehukumkan rakyat dengan sebenar
segenap nagari terdengar khabar.
　　　--Syair Mukomuko, vs. 68.

cock-fighting, was tantamount to a breach of natural rights and constituted serious grievances against their administration (Kathirithamby-Wells 1977:95, 119, 151, 212-3).

In similar recognition of the sovereignty and authority of the Tuanku by the Great Chiefs, the Besar Ampat Balai offered him tribute in token of submission and allegiance (UUMM 1822:8). Since the nature and the amount of the material token payable in tribute receives no mention it was, presumably, the ceremony itself which was significant. According to Minangkabau philosophy, relationships between the ruler, chiefs, and people were, thus, reciprocal and did not rest on force.

When the "usages of the Darat descended along the rivers," down to the coast of Tiku, Pariaman, Pau, Padang, Kota Tengah, Bayang, Trusan, Sepuluh Bua Bandar, and as far as Inderapura and Anak Sungai, the governmental forms established here drew their basic characteristics from the constitution at Paggarruyung (UUMM 1822:8-9). Ideally, the sovereign authority of the Tuanku, the supreme guardian of the Minangkabau constitution, was represented by the raja who acted as primus inter pares among the heads of the kota or laras of that particular nagari grouping or federation. Below this level authority rested with the penghulu ke ampe suku (heads of four clans) who formed the rapat penghulu (council of penghulu) and, at the lowest level, with the penghulu kampung (Loeb 1935:105; Kathirithamby-Wells 1976:66).

While the Minangkabau adat and the village administration was preserved more or less in pristine form, the proximity of the western rantau to external contacts had rendered the supra-village administrative structure of the nagari, particularly at the main trading stations, subject to new stresses. On the expulsion of the Acehnese panglima from the west coast, for instance, the local raja who replaced them were often Dutch nominees without the necessary local sanction. Conflict between the authority of the raja, whose position was enhanced by external influences, and the adat and genealogical leanings of the penghulu at supra-village level was one of the permanent sources of conflict in the rantau. This factor explains the almost continuous state of civil war along the coast preceding the imposition of firmer Dutch control upon the outbreak of the Padri War.

In the extremities of the western rantau, in Inderapura and its original dependency of Anak Sungai, the rajaship reached the full cycle of evolution partly because of their distance from the core region and partly because of economic reasons. Through the wealth accrued from pepper, which up till the mid-seventeenth century came mainly from Inderapura, the raja acquired sufficient wealth and influence to emerge as a powerful authority with Muhammad Syah assuming the title of "Sultan." With Inderapura´s rise as a separate kingdom, the penghulu kota became menteri with the important function of acting as the ruler´s councillors and advisors. The menteri both of XX kota (Inderapura) and XIV kota (Mukomuko), however, were constantly wary of the authoritarian leanings of the ruler and fought hard to preserve Minangkabau institutional traditions. The situation led to civil war and the eventual break-away of the southern territory of Anak Sungai as a separate Sultanate under British patronage (Kathirithamby-Wells 1976:71-76). Affairs did not bode well for the first Sultan of Anak Sungai, Gulemat (1691-1716), a British protege. It was not until Merah Bangun, an Inderapura prince, was appointed with appropriate sanction from the Menteri Dua Puluh Kota and the Datuk Lima Kota that the line was legitimized (Kathirithamby-Wells 1976:83).

It is interesting that in the UUMM no mention is made of the title of Sultan, and the ruler of Anak Sungai is referred to simply as the "Rajah," a mere shadow of Tuanku. Yet, despite the Minangkabau origins of insitutional traditions in Anak Sungai, there was a clear ambivalence in the system where "feudal" characteristics had evolved. Unlike the ruler at Pagarruyung who made no substantial claims of revenues and services from his subjects, the chiefs at Anak Sungai—comprising the Menteri Empat Belas Kota of Mukomuko, the Datuk Lima Kota of Bantal, and the Peroatin nan kurang Satu Enam Puluh (fifty-nine peroatin or village heads)—followed an order of precedence in rendering services to the Sultan. The Menteri Empat Belas Kota held the highest rank and, accordingly, took charge of court affairs, including protocol: "[T]o carry and to place (as the dishes at an entertainment), to arrange and put in order, to estimate and serve out accordingly, to furnish attendants, and people to do the work, to support [the ruler´s] dignity; these are the duties of the Ampatblas." The Datuk Lima Kota came next in order. They were obliged to keep the ruler supplied with building materials, such as rattan and attap, and were in charge of security. The Peroatin nan kurang Satu Enam Puluh came last in order of rank. Besides looking after the day-to-day affairs of the dusun, they were the chief intermediaries between the dusun and the court and were obliged to report to the menteri any defiance to the ruler´s authority. They were also, strictly speaking, responsible for the collection and presentation at court of an annual tribute from each dusun, of a bambu of rice, a fowl, a (Spanish) dollar, sirch and betel-nut. The UUMM, however, makes special mention of the fact that the presentation of food and money was not "a token of respect and honor, but is paid as a tribute" by special arrangement and by custom (UUMM

1822:10-12). The reason for this could be because the fifty-nine _peroatin_ who administered the area to the south of Bantal, strictly speaking, belonged outside the sphere of Minangkabau influence to the tribal south. The tribute was, in any case, not collected with any regularity and became, effectively, a token of submission to the ruler (Kathirithamby-Wells 1977:18, 32-33).

The other variation in the implementation of the Minangkabau administrative institutions at Anak Sungai pertained to the conflict between the two _adat_ systems of Ketemenggungan and Perpatih Nan Sebatang. The _UUMM_, which states that there were three "usages" or customs established in Minangkabau, attributes the third to the customary traditions of the raja who, as final authority, exercised the _adat_ Ketemenggungan (_UUMM_ 1822:6-7), associated with Tanah Datar and considered to have a more superior position in the _darat_ (Dobbin 1974:336). In describing the laws prevalent in the Inderapura and Anak Sungai regions, however, the _UUMM_ speaks of the conflict between the two law systems as remaining unresolved. "[O]pinions were divided on this subject, quarrels were unsettled, disputes undecided and the custom of Perpati Sebatang was partially established according to the pleasure of individuals ..." (_UUMM_ 1822:10). This presumably alludes to the unstable conditions prevalent in the region as a result of the difficulties the Sultan faced in establishing his total authority because of constant opposition from the menteri, the guardians of the more egalitarian traditions. These tensions were present even during the lifetime of Singa Maharaja, who recited the _Undang Undang MukoMuko_, and were precipitated by strong Company support for Sultan Khalifatullah Inayat Syah (17891816). With the help of the British Resident, E. R. Elphinstone, the rebellious chiefs were brought to court and the gravity of _derhaka_ recorded for posterity in no less than three _syair_ found in MS Cod. Or. 6051. One of them, _Syair Datuk Danau Seorang_ pertains specifically to the disloyalty of Maharaja Diraja (Kathirithamby-Wells and Yusoff Hashim 1980:9-10).

It is evident from the _UUMM_ that Minangkabau _adat_ and institutions served as a basic model for government in the Anak Sungai Sultanate. The first part of the _UUMM_ describes the classic forms of Minangkabau administrative structure in the _rantau_ as recorded, without change, by posterity. The second part of the _UUMM_ which pertains specifically to Mukomuko betrays some changes and adaptations. The latter would have been composed only with the genesis of the Anak Sungai Sultanate, not earlier than the late seventeenth century and a generation or two before the time of Singa Maharaja. It is only in the "Origin and descent of the Rajahs of Indrapura and Moco Moco" which follows the <u>UUMM</u> that Singa Maharaja takes license to update the genealogy to the rulers, carrying it to the reign of Sultan Hidayatullah (1816-32).

There are, indeed, factors other than personal power and economic motives which go to explain the political conflicts of the coastal <u>nagari</u> during the pre-colonial and early colonial eras. Minangkabau institutional forms were a potent force and conditioned political affairs to a large degree until the effective substitution, during the nineteenth century, of native authority by colonial authority. Historical processes in the Sultanates of Inderapura and Anak Sungai illustrate the validity of Minangkabau institutional models as exceeding the functions of pure myth to operate within the realms of real government in the <u>rantau</u>. More than this, through the shadow which the Tuanku at Pagarruyung cast on the peripheral areas of the Alam Minangkabau may be traced, to some extent at least, the actual substance and durability of his illustrious credentials.

Appendix

TRANSLATION OF THE UNDANG UNDANG OF MOCO MOCO [1822]

[Source: *Malayan Miscellanies*, II, No. XIII (Benkulen,
1822):1-13). Except Malay terminology which has been
italicized, the text remains as in the original]

Introduction

This Undang Undang was committed to writing from the
recitation of Singa Maharaja of Munjota, the oldest of the
mantries of Moco Moco, and almost the only person now living
who is able to recite the whole. He stated it to have been
carefully taught him by his father as handed down from his
ancestors, and he was particularly solicitous that in writing
it down no word should be altered even where the sense
appeared obscure and to require emendation, for such he said
were the words in which it was composed by his fore-fathers,
and it did not become their children to add to or take away
from them. It is composed in a kind of measured prose broken
into stanzas, and it is recited in the manner of verse, by
which means it was no doubt better impressed upon the memory.
The brevity and conciseness of the expression, and the
constant allusion to customs and its circumstances supposed to
be familiarly known, but which require explanation to be made
intelligible to foreigners, render it difficult to follow its
letter and spirit in a translation, but it deserves to be
preserved as a curious and original specimen of traditionary
literature. It contains many words belonging to the dialect
of Menangkarbau, and which are unknown to the modern Malay.
As I am not aware that the peculiarities of the Menangkarbau
language have as yet been noticed or exhibited, it may not be
uninteresting to give a short comparative vocabulary in
illustration of the difference between it and common Malay.

The original stories and traditions of the Malays have
almost all been disfigured in later times by the interpolation
of shreds of Mohammedan fable, and in their ambition to trace
the descent of their sovereigns from orthodox personages such
as Adam, Solomon, and Iskander, who figure in the pages of the
Koran, their pagan ancestors have been suffered to pass into
undeserved oblivion. The names of Katumunggungan and Perpati
Sabatang are among the few that have been preserved from a
period antecedent to the introduction of Mohammedanism, and
their institutions have never given way to the code of the
Koran, but remain unaltered to the present time. They are

conceived by the Malays to be two persons, brothers, subordinate to the Maharajah di rajah of Menangkarbau whose capital was then at Priangan padang panjang, but the traditions respecting them are involved in the greatest obscurity. Comparing these names with parallel ones used in Java, there seems some reason to conclude that they are not the names of individuals but of offices, the Tumunggung having anciently been the designation of the officer entrusted with the general management of the country and still conducting the duties of police and municipal regulation in many Malay states, while the Pati or Papati was the minister of the King. In Java, the Tumunggung is the governor of a province; where the government is complete there is generally a Pati Luar and a Pati Dalam; i.e. a minister for foreign affairs, and a minister for the home department, and possibly the term Perpati Sabatang may have reference to the union of both these in one person. This however can only be considered as conjecture.

In one of the Malay traditions of which I have a copy, it is stated that while Priangan padang panjang was yet a wilderness, covered with forest trees and matted with ratans and prickly shrubs, the ancestors of Tatanja Garhana, of Perpetti Sabatang, of Katumunggungan and of Kajarahan, a princess, established their residence in it, clearing the lands and introducing cultivation and civilization. The rest of the story is occupied with the adventures of the princess of Kajarahan and her descendants, who are said to have settled all the Southern districts of Sumatra, such as Passummah, etc., until the arrival of the prince from Roum who, after marrying a daughter descended from Kajarahan, settled in Menangkarbau and founded Pagaruyong the modern capital.

A collection of these traditions, however wild and fabulous, would not be devoid of interest, and would throw some light upon the history of those early periods. A cloud rests upon all that preceded Mohammedanism which it is difficult to penetrate but there is abundant proof that Menangkarbau stood high in power and consideration before that period, and that the customs and usages which still prevail are derived from a very remote antiquity. Some of these are very peculiar, such as the descent of property to the nephew, which obtains to this day, and others which cannot be here enlarged upon.

Translation of the Undang Undang of Moco Moco

The condition of mankind, the descendants of Adam, is to

live on the earth canopied by the heavens in countries under
the sovereign, in towns under __mantries__ or chiefs, and to
follow established usages and customs; their condition is from
God, the custom is from Adam when the sovereignty was
established, the law or usage was also established.

Where was the sovereignty first established?--first in
the country of Roum, secondly in the country of China, thirdly
in Pulo Mas (the golden island) or the land of Menangkarbau;
when the sovereign was established in the land of
Menangkarbau, the law and usage was also established together
with the constitution of the country under its sovereign and
the towns under their __mantries__; moreover, the people were
divided and also the land and forest.

Where is the portion possessed by the Tuanko [tuanku]?--
it extends from Teretta Ayer Etam[8] to Sakilang Ayer Bangy,[9] to
Nibong be lantud mudi,[10] to chupak ber gantong chiri,[11] to
sialang ber lantak bessi,[12] to Durian di taku Rajah,[13] which
is opposite to Tanjong si Malido, to Si Pisau pisau hanjat:[14]
to the west of these boundaries are the ryats or subjects of
the Tuanko of Menangkarbau; to the east are the subjects of
Tuanko Imbang Jaya; the people being thus divided, the law and
usage was established.

What are the usages that were established?--first those
of Katumunggungan, second those of Perpati Sabatang, and third
those that relate to the Rajah; the usages that relate to the
Rajah or sovereign, and which are observed towards the Tuanku,

---

[8] Ayer Etam is a river between Bantal and Ipu on the West
Coast of Sumatra.
[9] A river situated a little on the north of mount Ophir.
[10] Nibong, a species of palm __Areca tigillaria__ [?], bent in a
direction looking up the river; the name of a town celebrated
for its gold mines, and situated at the conflux of the Masoomi
with the Marangin, the former of which rises in Gunong Mandi
Urei, and the latter descends from the lake of Korinchi.
[11] The Chupa tree with the suspected token.
[12] The honeycomb reached by means of iron pegs driven into the
trees.
[13] The durian tree notched or cut by the king: it is situated
on the Batang hari river, and is the boundary between the
territories of Menangkerbau and Jambi.
[14] __Pisau pisau__ is a carved piece of wood placed on the tops of
houses.

are the salute of a single gun, the use of the umbrella, the receiving of homage in the royal residence or palace; it also belongs to the Tuanku to seek what is just and right, to lean towards the law of the Shuraa, as contained in the Hudees, to lean also towards the Daur or usage of the country, where it is just and right, seeing that the Tuanko is the Key of the law, whose order is not to be resisted, and whose sentence is not to be questioned; when he calls black white [literally a black dendang, a species of bird], it is white, and when he calls white black, it is black; these are the usages relative to the Tuanko.

What are the qualifications displayed by the Tuanko?--he can counteract the effect of spells; distinguish poisons by sight; know the motions of dangerous enemies; overawe the children of men; he is skilled in the science of physiognomy and the knowledge of character, sagacious in comprehending the real object of all that is said, whether open or secret, seeing that the great are envious, and the old are malevolent; these are the qualifications of the Tuanko.

What are the usages applicable to the subjects of the Tuanko?--they are the usages of Katumunggungan, for wounds, pecuniary compensation, for killing, the payment of the bangun; for high crimes, death; for offences, fines; for debts, payment and receipt; for partners, their just shares; for accounts, adjustment;--to notch the tree[15] [ber laku kayu]; to pay fees[16] [ber tahil amas]; to receive sentence when proved; to be acquitted on oath when doubtful; to bestow freely; to purchase fairly; to measure by the chupa and gantang; to cock fight skilfully; to make salt in appropriate places; to fish by fishermen; to have vessels with nakhodas or masters; to pay duties on anchorage [ubar ubar gantang kamudi];[17] to receive fees on weighing; to pay tribute at the foot of the throne of the Tuanku; these are the usages which are observed and enforced in the kingdom of Menangkarbau.

---

[15] This alludes to the custom of recording solemn agreements by cutting a notch in a tree on the spot where the engagements are concluded; hence the name of Durian di taku Rajah, above mentioned, having been cut by the king in commemoration of the settlement of boundaries.
[16] Literally to weigh the gold, the fees of the courts having usually been paid in gold which was weighed in courts.
[17] Literally, "the ubar ubar (medusa) clinging to the rudder," a figurative expression for harbor duties.

Who are the people that pay tribute at the foot of the throne of the Tuanko?--they are the people of Renna[18] nen lima pulo, the Darat nen ampat langgam, or land of the four provinces, Priangan padang panjang, Gugur kota Anou, Kubong uga blas kota, even to Renna Sungei Pagu and the Renna Batang Bekuwe, being the territories of the kingdom of Menangkarbau.

Who are they that pay the tribute of "tukup bubung" (shelter of the roof), at the foot of the throne of the Tuanko?--the Bandahara of Sungy Trub, the Makhudam of Simani, the Tuan Kadii of Padang ginting, and the Indermah of Suruasa; these are the people who pay the tribute of tukup bubung at the foot of the throne of the Tuanko in token of submission and allegiance.

What is the reason of this tribute being paid at the foot of the throne of the Tuanko?--it is compensation for [literally "causing to float"] the ship overlaid with gold, which was lost in the contest with Sikatimuno on the shoals of the burning mountain, on arriving from the country of Roum, the crown of the world, and which was navigated by Nakhoda kaya; a ship which was inlaid with diamonds and rubies, equal in price to the price of a kingdom, and comparable in value to the crown of the son of Solomon.

These usages of the Darat descended along the rivers even to the coast districts of Anak Sungei; that is to say, the usages and customs observed in the neighbourhood of Gunung Berapi, in Sianak, Kota Gedang; Priangan padang panjang, Tikoo, Pariaman, Pau, Padang, Kota tangah, Bayang, Trusan, passed down the main stream of the river, beyond the Bandar nen Sapulo,[19] and through fire and water,[20] arrived at Tello Dayapura, or the country of the Duapulo[21] [the twenty].[22]

---

[18] _Renna_ is a term applied to lands lower than the Darat, or central land of Menangkarbau.
[19] "The ten ports"--the name of the country between Indrapura and Padang.
[20] Literally, "if it rained, it rained, and if it was hot, it was hot."
[21] Indrapura is so called from being under twenty _mantries_ or chiefs; Moco Moco is in like manner called the Tana nen ampatbilas or the country of the fourteen (_mantries_).
[22] The interior of Indrapura is under six _mantries_, the coast is under an equal number, and the intermediate districts are

Being arrived at the country of the Duapulo, there was established the rajah together with the law, usage, and constitution of the country under the sovereign, the towns under mantries: moreover, the people were divided in the country of the Duapulo; having passed the main stream of the river and come to the point of Ujong Tanjong, division arose concerning the usage and custom; those of Katumunggungan said, if compensation is not paid for wounds, and bangun for murder, there is an end of the people; those of Perpati Sabatang said, if for every wound compensation is paid, and for every murder, the bangun, there is an end of the people; those of Katumunggungan said, if they who wound are not to pay compensation, nor they who murder the bangun, better let us return to Menangkarbau and to the country of the Duapulo, where the country is under the Sovereign, the towns under mantries, high crimes are punished with death and offences with fines; those of Perpati Sabatang said, if compensation is to be paid for wounds, and the bangun for murder, that is the custom of the men of Ujong Tanjong,[23] of Tapa Selulong, and of Batu Mendamei, the custom of robbers and plunderers; men whose weapons are great stone hammers, clubs or the roots of the Langgadei [a species of Rhizophora], thorny stems of the Rukam [Flacourtia], maces to strike along and across, with whom what is strong is uppermost and what is weak is lowermost; opinions were divided on this subject, quarrels were unsettled, disputes undecided, and the custom of Perpati Sabatang was partially established according to the pleasure of individuals; pass now to the country of the Ampat-blas [fourteen] where was established the Rajah together with the usage, custom and constitution; the people were also divided.

Who are the subjects of the Tuanko?--they are the people of the Ampat-blas, of the Lima kota, and of the Proatin nen korang satu anam pulo [sixty save one], these are the subjects of the Tuanko in the country of the Ampat-blas, the law and usage was also established.

What are the usages that were established?

[The next three paragraphs are a repetition of what has been

---

under eight.
[23] Tanjong signifies those descending branches which are thrown out by the Rhizophora (?) Indian fig, etc. and take root on touching the ground.

-136-

Who are the people that pay tribute at the foot of the
throne of the Tuanko?--they are the sixty save one Proatins;
with respect to the usages, they are equally followed by all,
but there is an order of precedence among the subjects of the
Tuanko, the Ampatblas being considered the elder, the Lima
Kota the next, and the sixty save one Proatins the youngest of
all.

Thereafter, when matters arise whether good or bad in
the royal residence, what are the duties of the Ampatblas?--
they are, to carry and to place (as the dishes at an
entertainment) to arrange and put in order, to estimate and
serve out accordingly, to furnish attendants and people to do
the work, to support his dignity; these are the duties of the
Ampatblas.

What are the duties of the Lima Kota?--to present a
handful of earth, a roll of ratan, a lath of attap,[24] to keep
guard lying on the ground, and exposed to the dews; these are
the duties of the Lima Kota.

What are the duties of the sixty save one Proatins?--if
enemies come from the sea, or from the hills, if there are
chiefs who are rebellious, or subjects who throw off their
allegience, to proclaim and declare them to the Ampatblas for
the orders of the Tuanko; they are to dig trenches, build
walls, plant ranjaus, to keep guard, lying on the ground and
exposed to the dews, if there are men among them hard of skin
and large of bone, they are to be Dibalangs [guards of honor];
these are the duties of the Proatins; a further service is
also due from them; to reckon the months and years, and at the
end of each year each Proatin is to present of rice one
bamboo, of poultry one fowl, of money one dollar, together
with siri and betel nut.[25]

---

[24] Attaps are made of the leaves of various kinds of palms and
are employed for the roofs of houses. The meaning of this
phrase is that they are to furnish materials of the Raja's
house.
[25] The tribute from the Proatins was established on the
cession of the country in satisfaction for the death of a
Rajah of Indrapura who was killed at Urei.

What is the designation of this presentation of rice,
fowls, money, etc.?--it is not a token of respect and honor,
but is paid as a tribute; it is not an innovation or new
institution, but aggreeable to a custom of ancient standing
derived from the Darat, Rajah succeeding to the Rajah and
Mantri to Mantri, and has come to the country of the Ampatblas
which is called Ujong Pagaruyong, the representative of
Menangkarbau, whose sovereign is the highest and most glorious
King, a descendant of Sultan Iskandar Alum who resided on the
summit of Gunong Seilan, the king of all worlds who is
renowned from where the sun sets to where he rises, who is
known all over the world from the coast to the interior, he it
is who can traverse the whole expanse of ocean, and the space
between heaven and earth, he wears the crown of the son of
Solomon, has the Payong ubur ubur[26] carried over him and
possesses the sword called Semandang giri.

Origin and descent of the Rajahs of Indrapura and Moco Moco

There were three brothers, sons of Chindermata, of whom
the youngest governed at Batang pili or Jambi, the middle one
in Bugis country, and the eldest at Indrapura by the
appellation of Tuanko ber Darah puti [of the white blood]; he
it was who made a compact with the alligator who attended him
from the Bugis country, at the time that he left Pagaruyong
and visited his two brothers before settling at Indrapura.

On the death of Tuanko ber Darah puti, he was succeeded
by Tuanko ber tampat di laman; on his disappearance, there
followed seven Rajahs of another race, after which the
succession reverted to the Menangkarbau family, i.e. to Tuanko
di Punggo, next to Tuanko pulang deri Jawa, then to his son
Tuanko ngungu [the toothless] who was succeeded by Sultan
Iskandar of the race of the seven Rajahs above mentioned, and
he again by sultan Sidi the son of Tuanko ngungu, who was
succeeded by the Tuanko Padusi [a female] the mother of the
present Tuanko.

The origin of the Rajahs of Moco Moco is as follows; at
one time there was much trouble and vexation on many accounts
among the fourteen Mantris, and much oppression exercised
towards them, till at length they complained to Menangkarbau.
From thence they were directed to receive the son of the

---

[26] The umbrella so named from having a resemblance to the
Medusa.

Tuanko of Pariaman by name Sultan Sidi Sherif who established himself at Dusun Pase on the Quallo of Munjota; his son Tuanko Rajah Etam succeeded, after whom came the son of Tuanko di Punggo who was killed at Urei, his residence was at Sungei Sagga in the interior of Munjota. Then followed Sultan Gulomat from Indrapura, who fixed his residence at dusun Kalapa Munjota; next Tuanko sungut [whiskered] also from Indrapura, who resided at Pase, next Tuanko Khatib besar, also from Indrapura, who resided at Bantal, after whom came Tuanko Gedang, a son of Tuanko di Punggo, who fixed the capital at Moco Moco. He was succeeded by his son Marasiling, whose son Sultan Tukdir allah succeeded, and to him his son Sultan Hidayat allah.

ISLAM, HISTORY, AND SOCIAL CHANGE IN
MINANGKABAU

Taufik Abdullah
LEKNAS - LIPI

A Minangkabau might brush aside the often repeated question posed by "foreign" observers. How could a matrilineal
society such as Minangkabau become one of the most thoroughly
Islamized ethnic groups in the Malay world?   The Minangkabau
might know that one of the central themes of the intellectual
history of Minangkabau is the search for the formulation of
relationship between adat and Islam; nevertheless the legalist
connotations of this question force him to make an inappropriate contrast between the foundation of his matrilineal social
system and the patrilineal bias of Islamic law but also he
would feel that the ideological formulation that has been
reached is made without cultural significance.   If this question does not incite his ethnic pride on "the genius of Minangkabau" to synthesize contradictions harmoniously (for example, Nasroen 1957), he might feel that the question forces
him to clearly locate himself in the legal plurality of Minangkabau. If he is quite knowledgeable he would not only be
reminded of the successive religious movements, which unfail-
ingly posed serious questions to the religious validity of the
matrilineal system, but also of the many family conflicts that
occur as the direct consequence of the legal pluralism. But
let me just cite a famous example.
    At the end of the 19th century Sjekh Achmad Chatib, a
Minangkabau ulama (learned Muslim leader), who was imam (religious functionary) of the Syafiite school at the Grand Mosque,
in Mecca, launched his orthodox movement.   Through his numerous writings, many of which were interpretations of authoritative religious texts, he wanted to purify religious life and
to reform Minangkabau society in accordance with Islamic precepts. A true legalist at heart, he felt nothing but contempt
for what he thought to be a half-hearted conversion. He fur-
iously attacked the prevalent tareket (mystic orders) and the
matrilineal inheritance system.   Tareket religious practices
were, to him, heretical.   Even the tareket of Naqshabandiah,
whose doctrinal tenet was widely considered to be one of the
closest to the mainstream of the orthodox doctrine, was not
spared from his doctrinal assaults.   The Naqshabandiah tenet

-141-

that the teacher is the intermediary between the students, the devotees, and God, was, according to him, a bida'ah, a religiously unlawful innovation (Gobéé & Adrianse 1965 [1845-56]; Achmad Chatib 1965).

In one of his books Achmad Chatib stated that the whole foundation of Minangkabau society was blasphemous. The matrilineal inheritance system was tantamount to the robbery of the orphans--they were disposed of their rightful property. Naturally this legalistic orthodox doctrine posed serious problems to the government which was still in the process of making Minangkabau into an integrated part of the pax-neerlandica. After all, religious controversy would presumably force one to have a closer look at one's own religious treasury and any attempt to question the validity of existing social foundations would most probably lead one to re-search for its inherent greatness. Whatever the possibility, the consequence of this religious controversy was certainly not conducive for the gradual penetration of Dutch economic and political power. Therefore, the local government sought the possibility of "codifying" Minangkabau adat-law--a plan that was criticized by Snouck Hurgronje (Adatrechtbundel 1911, 22). The greatness of adat, he said, lies in its ability to adjust itself to changing situations. The "codification" of adat would only make it a static law. As such, as a mid-19th century colonial policy maker also argued (Kielstra 1892:272-303), adat would not be able to cope with the continuing thrust of Islam in the social fabric. And, of course, Islam was a "volcano," as one put it, to be contained.

But it was not the concern of the government that really mattered. Syekh Bayang, a leader of the Naqshabandiah, aptly countered Syekh Achmad Chatib's opposition to Minangkabau inheritance law (Schrieke 1919-1921). If it was true, he asked, that the Minangkabaus, due to their adat system, had illegally acquired their properties, then, the Syekh in his turn had also been living in sin. For had he not received alms and contributions from the Minangkabau pilgrims? These gifts came from the "cursed" properties.

In 1904 Syekh Achmad Chatib's step was radically followed by Haji Yahya from Solok. In defiance to penghulu's authority he exhorted people to abandon their adat inheritance system. Social turmoil created by this exhortation led the government to exile Haji Yahya. And it was the last outburst of a religiously inspired opposition to adat inheritance law.

The simple question sarcastically asked by Syekh Bayang, I think, clearly demonstrates the inadequacy of a legalistic approach in dealing with the place of Islam in Minangkabau. Syekh Bayang, of course, could have added more devastating questions. The debate could as well have ended up by Achmad

Chatib's self-denial. And that is exactly what finally happened. He never set foot in his homeland again. Syekh Bayang's sharp rebuttal might have been triggered by Achmad Chatib's attack on his _tarekat_ school, the Naqshabandiah; his defense of _adat_, nevertheless, emphasized the intellectual propensity to look at Islam as a system of meaning rather than a set of regulations.

The Naqshabandiah, more than other _tarekat_ schools, emphasized the religiously correct behavior as a way to attain the highest gnostic order, but, not unlike the others, it also offered its definition of the world, the Minangkabau world, from religious perspective. As such the validity of _adat_ as a system of conduct was strengthened, but at the same time relativized. _Adat_ was valid only as long as it was not conceived to have directly confronted religion. But the elusive nature of the religiously valid behavior continued, since it was also based on the applicability of the dual concept of _mungkin_ (possible) and _patut_ (proper) (Abdullah 1970).

The significance of Achmad Chatib's legalistic assault was later, in the early 20th century, somewhat replicated by the emergence of the modernist orthodox movement.

Unlike Achmad Chatib who went to the _rantau_--a holy one, to be sure--not only physically but mentally as well, the modernist reformers, known as the _Kaum Muda_--who, not unlike the Padri reformers of the early 19th century, only went to the _rantau_ as preparations for their self prescribed roles in Minangkabau--did not question _adat_ inheritance law in its totality. They, not unlike the _ulama_ of the _Kaum Tua_, the traditionalist _ulama_, who in the 1930s explicitly expressed their legal _fatwa_ on this matter, formulated the solution in accordance with the actual practices in some areas, such as these reported by Verkerk Pistorius as early as the 1860s (Verkerk Pistorius 1871:131-132). Instead of rejecting the validity of the foundation of the Minangkabau social system-- how could a matrilineal system survive if its basis of continuity was discarded?--the modernist reformers, who not only aimed at creating a religiously right guided society, but also made Islam the basis of entering the "progressive world" as well (Abdullah 1971), supported the notion of differentiating inherited properties into two categories, the _pusaka tinggi_ and _pusaka rendah_. If the former should remain as it was--that is matrilineally inherited--the second, which was personally earned by the deceased, should be transferred in accordance with the Islamic inheritance law. Naturally it is not as simple as it may sound. The matrilineally inherited property should also be religiously interpreted; otherwise, its validity would remain in doubt. It should be considered, as one of the Kaum Muda suggested, as waqaf, a communal property for the sake of the well-being of the members of the community. But, of course, as various studies have shown (von Benda-Beckmann 1979a) and many efforts to reconfirm this formulation have demonstrated (Naim 1968), the reality is far more complex.

This is, indeed, a repetitious discussion, so that one might be tempted to comment, "who does not know about that"? I would be the first to raise my hands to acknowledge defeat. An important fact, however, should be emphasized. The ideological foundations of the series of religious reform movements remained the same, so that the further Islamization of the society should not necessarily result in the negation of the Minangkabau world. After the crisis of the initial period was over, the trend to regain normalcy began. The main purpose of this rather well-known expose is, first of all, to register my vote of "no confidence" in a strictly cultural approach to understanding changes that have been taking place in Minangkabau conceptions of both types of inherited properties. For it seems to me that Islam is more the formulator than the cause of the process. At the same time, I think, it is unrealistic to look at the continuity—or should I say the survival?—of the matrilineal social system and its fundamental prerequisites simply from a one-sided economic point of view.

My problem is, therefore, quite simple. If I say that I am interested in inquiring into the role of Islam in the process of change in Minangkabau, I could again be accused of asking an already outdated scholarly question. But let me first of all give another illustration. In a social survey conducted in selected rural and urban areas of Minangkabau, it was found out among other things that the majority of the respondents felt that "the most respected persons" in their surroundings were the ulama, the penghulu, and the government officials. The latter, it should be noted, was "really" the poor third, particularly if one compares the percentage they received with that of the ulama. The religiously educated persons were also thought to be the ideal sons-in-law. But the same survey also found out that not only most of the respondents preferred to send their children to the university they also would like to have university graduates as their sons-in-law (Kato 1977). My tentative conclusion to these little findings is that while people might still continue to be committed to the old notion of what the ideal should be, they could simultaneously entertain "new wishes" or "new dreams."

If this case, which is admittedly incomplete in itself, can be applied to religious affairs, one could assume that in spite of the deeper impact of economic and technological

-144-

changes in the social relationship, the desire to maintain the commitment to religious ideas does not necessarily diminish. Or to put it differently, although the process toward a clearer structural manifestation of secularization seems to be on the increase, a tendency to block the possible trend toward the secularization of consciousness is even stronger (Berger 1967:111-113). This last statement, naturally cannot be defended by the above example; it could, however, be easily verified by careful observation of social and ideological trends in Minangkabau. It is, it should also be noted, by no means a unique Minangkabau phenomenon.

Perhaps it is true that "myth is a cosmic map of the interesting territories of reality and fantasy" (O'Flaherty 1980:94). Some myths might be very personal experiences in the sense that their sphere of reality is much determined by familiarity with the culturally defined notion of "common sense," but other myths might be felt to be rationally sensible and be empirically plausible. The first type of myths usually express themselves through imaginary and metaphysical media--thus one could learn that the first king, through magical means, descended from heaven. The mode of discourse of the second type of myth, on the other hand, gives the notion of worldly factuality. This latter type of myth in other words, has what I can call historical plausibility.

A myth in the latter sense may be an unverified historical event. Without losing its mnemonic function, this type of myth does sometimes invite historical curiosity, which, understandably enough, causes it very often to be subjected to the conventional questions of "what, where, when, who, and how?"

Eliade suggested that a culturally significant historical event in due time could have undergone a process of transformations (Eliade 1959)--history became myth--but a group of history lecturers of the Teachers' Training Institute a Padang (in 1970) was determined to recover, so to speak, "history as it really was." Starting from various myths (that is from unverified histories) they conducted their "historical" investigation. Unable to undertake conventional historical research, for lack of authentic historical sources in the ordinary sense and, untrained, perhaps, in anthropological methods of studying myth, they simply used a "survey research" method. This is naturally an inappropriate method with which to begin, but the findings, nonetheless, are interesting.

Most of the respondents of this so-called historical research were the penghulu, who also happened to be the local leaders of the newly established LKAAM (Lembaga Kerapatan Adat

-145-

<u>Alam Minangkabau</u>—Council of Adat of the Minangkabau World). Since the questions were taken from the various versions of <u>tambo</u>, traditional historiography, the familiarity of the respondents with the subject-matter could be expected. But the team found out to its chagrin that the respondents could not agree on the "what, where, when, and who" of alleged historical events. Such and such per cent of the respondents thought that an event took place in the 11th century; others thought otherwise. Such and such per cent were convinced that the first king of Minangkabau was Mr. So and So, while others thought he must be a different person. And so on.

Although interesting as intellectual entertainment, there is nothing extraordinary in this finding. It only points out that although the <u>penghulu</u> are by definition traditional guardians of Minangkabau's myth of concern and share similar historical consciousness, their knowledge of the past--that is, as it was conceived to be the "past"--was, at best, scanty. There is no doubt that the expertise of the <u>penghulu</u> on the various aspects of Minangkabau society and tradition varied considerably, but the fragmented knowledge of the unverified history is also due to the fact that there are several versions of the <u>tambo</u>. Local differences and interpolations are very common to traditions which were originally orally transmitted. It should be emphasized, however, that the written versions began to be produced and reproduced after Islam, with its networks of <u>surau</u>, had made its headway into the Minangkabau heartland. Therefore, almost all available texts had been in different degrees Islamized. Local varieties in many ways indicate that the Islamization process of the tradition were very much local affairs. Local varieties were determined by doctrinal orientations and, perhaps, also by social statuses of the new group of the definers of reality, the <u>ulama</u>.

One of the most important unverified histories is the so-called Bukit Marapalam Agreement. More than <u>tambo</u>, the historicity of this "event" seems plausible. Its historicity might simply be "remembered," not "discovered," let alone "invented," as an historian might have commented (Lewis 1976). It is said that "sometime in the past," a covenant was sealed between the representatives of the Minangkabau royalty and several <u>penghulu</u> on the one side and <u>ulama</u> the other. They agreed that Minangkabau should be governed by Islamic and <u>adat</u> norms and regulations. But how? We have two answers. Some <u>penghulu</u> would say that the original agreement was that "<u>adat</u> is based on <u>syarak</u> (religion), <u>syarak</u> is based on <u>adat</u>." But all <u>ulama</u> and some other <u>penghulu</u> would emphasize an aphorism more oriented to Islam, that is "<u>adat</u> is based on <u>syarak</u>, <u>syarak</u> is based on <u>kitabullah</u>". This aphorism, which might indicate a latter stage in Islamization, is usually supported by another one, that "religion designs, adat applies."

One might doubt whether the origins of these aphorisms, whatever the emphases were, could be historically traced. But let them be as what they are. If the event did take place, when was that? To this question we could be sure that we would have an experience similar to that of the group of history lecturers mentioned earlier. One local historian might say that it occurred in the 19th century, during the Padri War, but others would argue for much earlier dates. Again no history could be verified.

But, who were the penghulu and from which nagari did they come? Did the royal representatives have the right to seal such an agreement and make it applicable to the whole alam Minangkabau? No such questions, however, were ever asked publicly. But, then, how about the "invitation" of some royal representatives and several penghulu from Saruaso (Luhak Tanah Datar) to the Dutch Padang in 1821 to support them on behalf of the Minangkabau people in their struggle against the Kaum Putih, the Padri reformers? If this is the question, we could be sure that ulama, penghulu, and cerdik pandai "intellectuals" alike would convincingly argue that the "invitation" was illegitimate. How many adat legal reasonings had been put forward to reject the legitimacy of such an "invitation"? And indeed, even general de Stuers, the Dutch military commander, himself concurred with such a view.

Appropriateness and propriety (alur dan patut) according to adat have always been determinant factors in judging any event of social significance. Economic rationales (Oki 1977) might also be put forward to explain the breakout of the scattered anti-tax rebellions and mass-demonstrations of 1908; it is clear, however, that the actors simply reacted on the basis of their cultural interpretation of their situation. Their sense of appropriateness and propriety had been offended. Similar themes would be repeated again and again in the rhetoric of political opposition to colonial power well until the beginning of the National Revolution of 1945. One could, perhaps, react to one's immediate objective environment, but the reaction it seems, always has to be both formulated and rationalized from one's cultural paradigm. At least that was the case in Minangkabau.

But again, how about the Bukit Marapalam Agreement? The absence of the above quoted questions indicates not only the cultural acceptance of the formula (questions were not asked because the formula was fundamentally right) but also the nature of the Islamization process and the encounter of Islam with existing social values and arrangements. Islam did not begin the conversion of Minangkabau by addressing itself to structural problems. At the early stage of the process, Islam was basically "anti-structure" if _adat_ could be taken to represent "structure" (Turner 1972). But let me illustrate this point in comparative perspective.

History (that is as far as it could be "reconstructed" from available evidence) and traditional historiography (that is a history subjectively conceived and a world-view mythically enacted) might not give similar pictures of the past, and I hasten to add that they usually don't. But in many "essential" episodes or phenomena (of course these terms can be applied after the hierarchy of significance has been established) they do quite often share basic similarities, albeit with different modes of description. One such "essential" episode was the early stage of the Islamic encounter with the existing structure. This episode can be called the formative period of the Islamic tradition.

From the comparative perspective, both historically and "culturally" (that is from the perspective of traditional historiography) it can be seen first that Islam in Minangkabau, unlike that in Aceh, did not establish a supra-village political organization. Islam did not begin by introducing new political organization. If there ever was a Sultanate or a Kingdom of Minangkabau, it did not derive its origin from the coming of Islam, as was the case in Aceh, as illustrated in the _Hikayat Raja-raja Pasai_ or the _tarsilah_ in the Sulu world. Second, the early stage of the development of Islamic traditions was not laid down by an almost abrupt conversion of the _kraton_, the center of power. Unlike Makassar (Mattulada 1975; Noorduyn 1956) and Patani (Teeuw & Wyatt 1970) and probably also Malacca (Wake 1964), Minangkabau never had the coastal political center which also served as the entrepot of Muslim traders. The gradual process of Islamization, third, did not reach its decisive climax with the conquest of the _kraton_ by force, as was the case in Java (de Graaf & Pigeaud 1974).

Unlike Aceh, Minangkabau tradition did not perceive the beginning of its world, to be sure, with the coming of Islam. The central power of Makassar (Goa-Tallo double kingdoms) was culturally and politically compelled to convey Islam by persuasion and threat of force as "the real truth" to the neighboring realms; more importantly, it provided structural arrangements for the newly accepted religion. Minangkabau, however, did not have to undergo such experiences in the formative period of its Islamic tradition. Minangkabau, furthermore, unlike the successive sultanates in Java--from the coastal and maritime Demak to the inland and agrarian Mataram--did not have to engage itself in the perpetuation of the unbroken chain of political legitimacy. Nor did it

conspicuously entertain similar fascination with the notion of
continuity, for the sake of the validity of existing power,
that even forced the _literati_ of Mataram to review incessantly
the definition of the world in the face of unavoidable
changing situations (Ricklefs 1976).

Neither from the various versions of traditional historiography (_tambo_) nor from historical evidence could the
political predominance of the royalty in the heartland of
Minangkabau (_darek_ or the "region of three _luhaks_") be ascer-
tained. Both potential sources, however, do indicate that the
royalty had considerable political influence on the coast (the
rantau areas). Whatever the real character of the royalty, it
can be assumed that the institution itself seems to symbolize
the cultural integration of Minangkabau. Although the nature
of the politically fragmented yet culturally united world in
the unrecorded past of Minangkabau still has to be determined,
tambo and oral traditions clearly show that the early Islamization process followed, perhaps simultaneously, two paths.
The first was through the continuing flow of wandering _ulamas_
(for example, van Ronkel 1919), many of whom might as well be
traders and, later, returnees from _rantau_. Since the 17th
century the network of _surau_ or religious schools also began
to make their impacts on Minangkabau religious lives. Through
these types of processes, without the sanction of political
power as was the case with Makassar or with some parts of
Java, where one could find petty principalities ruled by
ulama (de Graaf & Pigeaud 1974), Islam reached the _nagaris_.
The acceptance and the degree of commitment, that is emotional
attachment of its adherents, were very much determined by the
specific circumstances of the _nagari_ themselves.

Second, and more important for our purpose, is the redefinition of the Minangkabau world. The cosmogony of Minangkabau was "reformulated" and the origin of its world was
Islamized. The notion of Minangkabau-ness would finally find
its unity in the metaphysical concept of "Nur Muhammad" (the
light of Muhammad), from which this real, observable world
emanated. Within this framework the cultural concept of the
Kings of Three Seats (_Rajo Tigo Selo_) could be seen. While
the _Rajo Alam_ (The King of the World) represented the idea of
the unity of the Minangkabau, the other two kings, the king of
Adat (_Rajo Adat_) and the King of Religion (_Rajo Ibadat_) were
the representatives of the ideological foundations on which
the _Alam Minangkabau_ based itself (de Josselin de Jong 1960).

The fascination with the definition of the world rather
than the structure of the society, both in terms of its arrangement and its religious validity, was to remain one of the
most dominating themes of the history of Islam in Minangkabau.
This intellectual propensity, as most of the _tambo_ clearly

suggest, not only maintained and strengthened the notion of a culturally unified and politically "federated" (that is the existence of some links between nagari, either hierarchical or otherwise, is suggested) alam Minangkabau but also emphasized the ever-expanding notion of the world (Abdullah 1972). It is understandable, therefore, that the single most obvious similar theme in the numerous myths of origin of the nagari is the movement of people—the early settlers were the travellers who came from their original homeland, that is Pariangan Padang Panjang (Adat Monography). But again, how about the Bukit Marapalam Agreement?

If the above observation has any validity, then I would venture to suggest that the answer to the historical problems of this historically plausible event should be sought in the already indicated Minangkabau attitude toward history. History is not simply a reconstructed event of the past but a meaningful experience of the past. An event can only be historically significant if it also culturally meaningful. Hence why should the Bukit Marapalam Agreement be subjected to those questions which derived their origin from notion of the appropriateness of the world? The basic question itself is already the answer—the agreement is both norm and destiny.

Although historical certainty is a virtue, historical fairness is essential to the continuity of the world. In other words, it is not the accuracy of the description of the past event that really matters (who could be sure about the past, anyway?), but the notion that something of significance for the present and the future had taken place in the past. As long as the historical knowledge can be socially and culturally sanctioned, why should one bother about the non-essential matters, such as the questions of "who and when exactly?"

In comparative perspective, I would suggest that the Minangkabau experience can be taken as an example of a conversion process which started by Islamizing the world. It did not condemn the existing order, but gave it new significance. Once this process began, Islam sought to find social institutions to be legitimated. The ontological status of such social institutions, in other words, was supported by placing them within a sacred frame of reference (Berger 1967:42). In the process the heterogenetic character of Islam was transformed into an orthogenetic one. The main thrust of the conversion was not how society should be rearranged or restructured but rather how society should be conceived. Islam provided new systems of meaning, on the basis of which reality should be understood, rather than regulations of conduct. Historically, the nature of the process of conversion in the early stage of Islamization can be seen in the predominance of the tarekat schools, rather than the legalistic orthodox ulama. (The tendency of some scholars to make a clear difference between "conversion" and "Islamization," I think, has the "Orientalistic" inclination that Edward Said writes about.)

Instead of the establishment of a new political entity, Islam created a spiritual community which bound its members with "the rope of God." It was a community in which religious values and norms were to form the basis of the legitimate paradigm. The continuity and the versatility of this spiritual community, however, were determined by the commitment of its adherents and the capacity of guardians to strengthen the force of religion in personal life and to broaden its scope in social relations (Geertz 1968). Several mechanisms would be needed for such a purpose (Mol 1977). The potentiality for all these requirements to actualize themselves, nevertheless, was also very much dependent on the internal structure of the spiritual community—i.e. the different degrees of the religiously prescribed social responsibilities—and the social economic environment.

The test to this community came when economic change began to take place, while Minangkabau remained politically fragmented (Dobbin 1977). Could the guardians of religion, the ulama and the religious schools, continue to be politically inactive while formal political structure was not able to function adequately? This inability, furthermore, had not only disturbed whatever social harmony there was, but also posed a direct challenge to the role of conduct nurtured by the spiritual community.

The relative vacuum of power in the supra-village sphere at a time when the Minangkabau interior was beginning to undergo economic change finally forced some ulama and their religious schools to involve themselves in political affairs. The increased frequency of trading activities, between the interior and the coast, demanded safer communications between the nagari, which, however, could not be met by the fragmented political system of Minangkabau. At the end of the 18th century, as a memoir of Syekh Jalaluddin (de Hollander 1847) clearly suggests, in some parts of Agam, ulama and their religious schools and students, directly put themselves as the vanguards of justice in the supra-village sphere.

It is a matter of interpretation—whether the ulama reacted to this situation because of their concern with the continuing relevancies of the values safeguarded by the spiritual community or whether it was simply due to the dynamics of change created by economic opportunities. But once the concern for the functioning of religious values was set in motion, other inherent dynamics of religion began to manifest themselves. A reform movement, which demanded the total reflection of doctrinal teaching in personal as well as social lives, had begun.

Economic changes and the relative vacuum of power in the supra-village sphere made the need for the consolidation of the notion of the spiritual community greater. Ironically, however, this need caused the anti-structural propensity of the community to be put into question—the ulama felt the urge to consider power as a possible alternative. This was the situation of the early 19th century Padri movement. Naturally, in order to understand this movement other historical circumstances should not be ignored. The universal character of Islam made this religion very vulnerable to the influences from the center of the Islamic world. The intensification of the Padri movement which eventually drove Minangkabau to years of civil and religious strife, took its radical and sometimes extreme posture particularly after the return of the three Wahabi-influenced ulamas. The involvement of the Dutch (1821), however, not only distorted the indigenous character of the conflict, but also disrupted whatever social and cultural consequences of the conflict.

An advantage of studying history is that we are dealing with a "finished chapter"—we know the outcome of the event. On the basis of this assumption the farewell advice of Tuanku Imam Bondjol, the Padri leader in the valley of Alahan Panjang, to his son can, perhaps, be taken as an indication of the mood of the time at the end of the Padri War. "The best friend," he was reported to have said in the memoir of his son, is "the learned [ulama?], who knows what to believe and what not to believe. Furthermore, acknowledge the authority of the penghulu, follow his regulations; those who are not obeyed are not worthy penghulu, they are only the bearers of titles. Be as strongly loyal as possible to adat and if your [religious] knowledge is not adequate, study the twenty qualities of Allah" (van Ronkel 1915:1116). The integrity of the society and the spiritual community could be achieved and maintained if the penghulu, that is the holders of political power, were trustworthy, and if the ulama remained in their function to remind people of "what was wrong and what was right." But more importantly, if something was wrong, one should "study the twenty qualities of Allah." In other words, one should always return to tauhid, the oneness of God.

The unrecorded past—in the modern sense of the words—of the interior of the Minangkabau was over. Many records make it clear that ulama, or whoever were considered to be such (Haji, etc), were excluded from adat and administrative power, although their influences cut across the nagari boundaries. Never since then has any event of social significance taken place without references to religion or religious leaders. The Padri War in many ways was a turning point in the history of Minangkabau. It not only ended up with the conquest of the Minangkabau region by the Dutch, but also the abolition of the Minangkabau monarchy. The breakdown of this sacred integrative institution, however, did not by any means disintegrate the cultural concept of the unity of <u>alam Minangkabau</u>. The new meaning of <u>alam</u> <u>Minangkabau</u> as being the world that was supported by the two sacred pillars, namely Islam and <u>adat</u>, had by that time been entrenched in the Minangkabau consciousness.

If anything, the involvement of the Dutch in the religious and civil conflict only strengthened that notion. After all, by the beginning of the 1830's, when the influence of the Wahabi movement in the Arab Peninsula was eroding, the process to recover the period of normalcy, when the precept of "using the ladder to go upstairs, using stairs to go down," began to take shape. The memoirs of Tuanku Imam Bondjol is but one example of this trend.

But as an historical event the Padri episode illustrates the crisis of the purely anti-structural character of the spiritual community and the participation of its guardians in supra-village politics. It shows the first important attempt to consolidate the community in the face of economic and political changes. By historical hindsight, I think, this episode also prepared Minangkabau and its religion to face further and more serious challenges to the functioning of non-structural notions of the spiritual community.

I was tempted to give illustrations of how Islam, the professed religion of the Minangkabau, legitimated or motivated changes of social significance. But let me conclude this presentation with an observation, a cursory one perhaps.

Regardless of any moral connotations that can be attached to colonialism, it disrupted whatever homogeneity there was in a "traditional" society. One of the consequences of colonialism was the increased plurality of the society, which among other things created the need for a clear identification of self. Self-identification becomes even more important once the unbridgeable differences between ruler and ruled become definitely affirmed.

In this situation, some concerned individuals might establish voluntary associations or join existing ones. In many instances these voluntary associations also filled the roles of solidarity groups. Students of history or political science who are very often forced to rely on records might even be tempted to see history from the "ups and downs" of

these organizations. Important actors in political affairs
were usually identified by looking at the kind of organization
they belonged to. In this case one could easily agree with an
observation that out of nine signatories of the historic
Jakarta Charter (1945), for example, there were four Islamic
leaders.   The rest should be categorized as being "secular
leaders," for the simple reason that they neither based their
struggle on Islam nor they joined Islamic political parties.
It should be emphasized, however, that except one who was a
Christian, all of them were Moslems.

But could we also use this rather formalistic approach
in dealing with the situation in Minangkabau?

Let me give an illustration. As luck would have it, I
was invited by some former top revolutionary leaders in West
Sumatra to give my supposedly "expert opinion" on how to write
"the history of the revolution" in the region.   When I made a
comment that there were relatively few Islamic leaders at the
top leadership of the revolution, they looked at me in ap-
prehension. "I am a graduate of the Thawalib schools, "said
the former Commander of the T.N.I. Regional division: "Do I
belong to the category you just mentioned?"   Naturally, I was
reminded of the information in the history book that the real
founder, though not the pioneer, of the so-called Communist
Party in West Sumatra was an ulama, a teacher of a modernist
religious school.   And how many instances can be given to
emphasize how odd was the observation I just mentioned?

One could simply identify oneself by anything and join a
suitable solidarity group, but the internal capacity of the
identification of self is based on a commonly shared definition of self.   Identification is the label with which you
want people to recognize you, but the definition of self is
related to the basic traits of your identity.   In other words
the label that is self identification is more a political and
ideological category than a religious or cultural one. Or to
put it differently, if religion can be conceived to have two
mutually inclusive aspects (Geertz 1968) then one could say
that self-identification is more a reflection of its structural rather than its cultural aspect. Self identification in
its official forms in participation in voluntary associations
or solidarity groups is a way to place oneself in a certain
place in the social and political constellation.   As such the
commitment to an identification is determined by the degree of
confidence one has about the extent of which the cultural
definition of self has already been secured.

The emergence of a nation state, Indonesia, on the ruins
of the Netherlands Indies, which had for the first time in
history brought together the numerous ethnic groups under one
administrative and political entity, has certainly intensified

the tendency toward a more pluralistic society. But the boundary of the notion of "our" society has also been considerably expanded and become more ambiguous. The border between a political and cultural society has yet to be analytically considered. But as it stands now, cultural interpretations of politics are still to be reckoned with in understanding modern Indonesia.

In this situation we can perceive that while the process toward the "perfection" of the political national integration is rapidly gaining momentum and the emergence of a "national culture"--culture as a symbol communication--has become more apparent, the desire to maintain primordial identity is not diminished. But to make a long story short, whatever economic changes that have taken place so far, there has always been an inclination among Minangkabau to safeguard their matrilineal social system. It is a sacred system; it has been religiously legitimated.

Looking from this perspective I would argue that Minangkabau traditional propensity to ideologize, so to speak, the tradition of _merantau_, such as is reflected in the various _adat_ teachings, and to romanticize the adventure of going to the _rantau_, beautifully depicted by many _kaba_ and sung by traditional as well "modern" Minangkabau songs, can to some extent be related to the function of _rantau_ to the system. The _rantau_ provides whatever outlets needed to release the pressure caused by the system in the period of economic changes. Islam as the legitimating value and _rantau_ as an outlet as well a structural solution, to my mind, which is most probably not entirely unbiased, would be the most determinant factors in the continuity of this matrilineal system.

ISLAMIZATION IN KERINCI

C. W. Watson
University of Kent

Kerinci lies on the southern borders of Minangkabau territory, and although Kerinci cannot be described as falling within the ambit of Minangkabau, there is historical evidence of Minangkabau migration into the area. In preparing this paper on the Islamization of Kerinci, I was very much aware of the Minangkabau material which, at several points, seemed to describe exactly what had occurred in Kerinci. Yet in other respects there were differences, and these differences suggested to me that one might do well to re-examine the Minangkabau evidence.

The intention of this paper became, then, two-fold: first, to provide a description of the process of Islamization in Kerinci leading to a consideration of what factors were important in this process; second, to offer some suggestions about the potential explanatory value of such factors in relation to the Minangkabau material. There is, consequently, throughout the paper a constant dialectic between the reconstruction of events in Kerinci and those in Minangkabau. The best way to present that dialectic for the benefit of those familiar with Minangkabau history seemed to me to present some observations on weaknesses or lacunae in recent writing about Minangkabau and thus to show how the Kerinci events can be used to explore hypotheses in relation to Minangkabau.

This inevitably means that the paper is unbalanced in appearance; the first part dealing with Minangkabau seems not to have any direct connection with what follows, but I hope that the observant reader will realize that not only is my description of events in Kerinci framed very much in the perspective of what has been written about Minangkabau, but that it also tries by implication to extend that perspective and point a way to new directions for research.

The starting point for anyone trying to come to grips with an understanding of what happened in the Minangkabau Highlands at the turn of the eighteenth century is clearly Christine Dobbin's series of articles (1974, 1975, 1977). The reason why her 1977 article in particular occasioned so much interest when it appeared was that, for the first time, here was an attempt to link the history of the Padri Wars with the economic development of the region. Prior to this article the events of the period had been described all too simplistically in terms of the personalities involved in what were considered religious conflicts between factions representing adat and revivalist Islamic movements. This type of account had never been very satisfactory, and Dobbin's article showed exactly how, as many people had suspected, the events of the period had to be set in some socio-economic context if they were to be properly understood.

In general, I strongly endorse this approach, and if I make any critical remarks below, it is certainly not with the intention of denying the importance of the article and its overall soundness. I do, however, have one or two reservations about some of the specific interpretations of the material, and I want to state these at the outset, both in order to suggest that Dobbin's analysis requires further refinement and also to make clear the reasons for introducing certain lines of enquiry in my own description of Kerinci.

Re-reading Dobbin's 1977 article more critically after the first excited response to it, one, or perhaps I should say I, was struck by the lack of a theological or religious dimension to the analysis. In part, one can understand this as a reaction against the earlier interpretations which tended to emphasize just this aspect of the events (see, for example, Mansoer et al. 1970:119f.), but Dobbin's implicitly polemical response to the previous accounts has been too extreme. Her description of the economic motivations behind the rise of Islamic reformism without any apparent acknowledgment of the momentum of its own which a religious movement can generate, leaves one with the impression that the materialistic explanation is just a bit too facile. One looks in vain through her descriptions of the traditional political organization and the socio-economic development of the region for some account of the practice of religion in the society. Inevitably, one supposes, the sources here must be rather poor, but some attempt at a description beyond the usual mention of religious hostility to gambling and drinking should be made.

Another unsatisfactory part of Dobbin's account (as given in the 1975 article) is the reconstruction of traditional authority in the eighteenth century. Without going into this in detail I have the impression that the European sources which she quotes describing aspects of the political organization of the villages failed to perceive the real nature of village government. Wanting to see everything in hierarchical terms, the European observers selected the figure of the penghulu (the descent group elder) as the central official around whom to construct a model of political organization. I am dubious, however, whether this interpretation accurately reflects the true situation. Furthermore, the descriptions of the functions of junior descent group elders (penghulu kecil), coupled with the universal accounts of the near anarchy which often seems to have existed in the villages, suggest that political organization was not all that clearly defined. The powers of the penghulu appear to have been limited very much to their own groups, and although there may well have been a nominal supra-descent group village council, it is clear that the most important institutions within the village worked according to the sanctions of kinship.

Dobbin's argument is that there are two linked reasons for the rise of reformism: first, traditional hostility to aristocratic features of the political organization which became more pronounced as the gold trade declined and with it the power of the royal family; second, the rise in prosperity of hill villages as a consequence of the cultivation of cash crops which led to increased inter-village rivalry in the new climate of economic opportunity. The reformers sprang from the class of nouveaux riches entrepreneurs determined to safeguard their interests through the zealous promulgation of syari'a law.

This account, it seems to me, does not give sufficient weight to other considerations. I do not know the historical Minangkabau evidence at first hand so I cannot take up in detail these points, but there are certain questions which immediately arise. Was there no internal conflict within the villages?[1] Given the descent group structure within the villages and the superficiality of titles of authority, one can imagine that some rivalry must have existed. One knows from other Malay societies of the existence of what might be termed "big men" in Polynesia, orang kaya in Malay, men whose status and authority within the village derived not from ascribed position but from personally achieved wealth. If this competition between a hereditary elite from the principal descent group segment and, on the other side, a set of economically powerful individuals was, as I strongly suspect, a structural feature of the social organization of the villages, then to what extent did either group make use of religion as a source of legitimation for its own position?

Furthermore, the distinction between upland hill villages and lowland villages in the rice-growing valley, sugges-

---

[1] In fairness to Dobbin, it should be noted that in her 1974 article (p. 323) she does, in fact, mention such conflict. In her 1977 article, however, she does not, in my opinion, attach sufficient importance to it.

tive though it is in terms of ecological aspects of the conflicts which arose, does not explain some curious features of inter-village warfare. The traditional battles between villages according to the literature have a ritualistic air about them and, in some cases, the conflicts appear to have been quite stylized. Secondly, villages which engaged in these battles were usually contiguous. My own research in Kerinci suggests that fighting broke out often as a consequence of boundary disputes. Thus, it is not two villages deriving their livelihoods from different agricultural or economic pursuits which come into conflict, but those which in fact share the same ecological features. The conflict is, then, about access to rice fields. Differences in religious beliefs simply add another dimension, not to conflicts arising out of changed economic circumstances, but to traditional disputes over boundaries.

The last observation brings me to another point. Perhaps one should look as much at demographic pressure on land as on upland-lowland distinctions in order to account for the emergence of religious leaders. In contemporary times we have seen that an area such as Koto Gadang can give birth to an extraordinary number of Indonesia's intellectual elite. The reason for this appears to be that riceland there is limited, and people have had to search for a livelihood outside the village. In the twentieth century the obvious avenue to both professional status and economic security is education. In the late eighteenth and early nineteenth centuries, religious education—as well as petty trading, of course—must have provided equivalent opportunities. One can imagine circumstances in which young men from villages with limited riceland went to areas to learn a living either by trade or by pursuing a religious vocation. One accepts, of course, that centers of trade were also centers of religious instruction. According to this hypothesis, then, one would expect to find religious teachers coming in the first instance, that is before the idea of association with Islamic revivalism had gained much currency as a source of power and prestige, from villages where riceland was limited. This I am proposing as an alternative to Dobbin's view that it was traders from upland villages who first espoused revivalism.

One reason for questioning Dobbin's account in this respect is the weakness of the argument relating to why traders were drawn to revivalism. My own suggestion is that when it was indeed traders who supported the cause of Islamic reform, this was because they saw it as a source of political legitimization which would enhance their social standing. Dobbin, on the other hand, maintains that it was the appeal of Islamic law, _fiqh_, with its provisions for fair trading, which attracted the new entrepreneurs. Her evidence for this is the Hikayat Jalaluddin which she cites frequently. I feel unhappy about one source being used in this way to make a general case for a complex situation. Following the same line of argument Dobbin goes on to state that another impulse behind the adoption of Islamic law was the search for strong sanctions against the depredations of bandits.

This argument seems plausible enough but there are one or two a priori reasons for questioning it. It implies that there were no proper commercial codes in existence at the time, and this in turn suggests that trading must have been at a rather rudimentary level since no such codes of conduct had evolved. But we know very well that there existed trade in the area long before this, and it is hard to imagine that over the centuries no acceptable practices for trading both internally and with outsiders had evolved. Traditional codes of law, after all, include cheating (lancung kicuh) and sharp practice among the principal crimes in the society. Similarly, theft (maling-curi), civil disturbance (dago-dagi), and banditry (rebut-rampas) are also prominent among the eight major crimes (delapan pucuk larangan). It is hard, therefore, to accept that the championing of Islamic law was a novel attempt to facilitate commercial endeavor and enhance general security.

My observations on Dobbin's interpretation of events, and I should stress that they are intended as observations rather than as proper criticisms, indicate the lines of my own thinking about the Islamization of Central Sumatra. In my account of what appears to have happened in Kerinci, I tentatively suggest ways of looking at the rise of reformism which I see as being complementary to those put forward in Dobbin's analysis. In particular, the issues which I touch upon to a greater or lesser degree as the evidence permits are: the nature of the village polity; the cleavages within village society and their implications for the spread of Islam; and, finally, the way in which syari'a was appropriated and accomodated within the ritual practices of the society.

The Earliest Evidence of Islam in Kerinci

The earliest evidence we have of the existence of Islam in Kerinci are letters in Malay written in Arabic script from Jambi princes to village elders in Kerinci dated around AH 1100 (1688 A.D.) It seems that it was about this time, if not shortly before, that the Sultan of Jambi was extending his influence from the environs of Jambi into the hinterland (Tideman 1938:78), perhaps as a consequence of European pressure being exerted on him from the east, and Kerinci lay on the perimeter of the area which he was attempting to claim as part of the territory of the Sultanate. By means of emissaries sent from outposts of the Sultanate such as Muaro Masumai (the present day Bangko) the ploy was to win the Kerinci elders over to accepting Jambi overlordship by issuing royal characters (piagam) by which their position as village chiefs was recognized and the boundaries of their territory formally defined. At the same time the Sultan was also trying to introduce Islam or, where it had already been introduced, to bring some orthodoxy into the observance of Islamic precepts. The tone of the extant letters suggests that Islam must have been first introduced into some areas in Kerinci at the latest by the middle of the seventeenth century, although whether it was brought by itinerant teachers or by Kerinci people themselves returning after a long sojourn in areas already under Islamic influence is not clear.

A good example of a document combining political purpose with religious exhortation is a letter from Pangeran Sukarta dated AH 1192 (1778 A.D.) addressed to the several Depati[2] of Sungai Penuh. The first part of the letter is a piagam setting out the boundaries of the territory under the control of the Depati and stating that the Depati have a mandate to institute royal justice (mendirikan hukum raja). The last part of the letter deals with specific religious matters and is worth quoting in full.[3]

> ....Furthermore, the princely word of Pangeran Sukarta ringing out in all Kerinci is: let the syari'a law be established in Kerinci. And the Pangeran especially commends to the attention of the four Depati, that it, Depati Setiudo, Depati Payung Negeri, Depati Purwa Negaro, and Depati Sungai Penuh, that which is brought by Kiyai Depati Simpan Negeri and Depati Suto Negaro together with Mangku Depati and Fakih Muhammad, namely that the Pangeran forbids that which is forbidden by syari'a and what is bad according to syari'a are in particular four things: first, if there is death let there not be a procession with drums, gongs, clarionets, and guns; second, let not men and women come together in

---

2 Depati is the Javanese title bestowed on descent group elders by Jambi princes.
3 I am grateful to Dr. P. Voorhoeve for correcting some mistakes in an earlier translation of this letter. He is, of course, in no way responsible for any errors which may remain.

one place and sing and dance; second [sic] do not pay
homage to spirits and devils and stones and trees and
suchlike; third, do not marry a woman without her wali
agreeing; fourth, do not eat or drink that which is
forbidden; and do not do anything else such as this
which is not permitted by syari'a.

In no circumstances let there be done what is forbidden.
This is the royal command of the Pangeran which he
orders to be issued to all the Depati and Malin in
Kerinci.

And whosoever does not want to abide by the syari'a let
him be punished by all the Malin coming to agreement
[The text here seems to be corrupt and I make of it what
sense I can. C.W.W.] with the Depati and Mangku together
with the Menteri so that the judgement of syari'a law is
upheld. This is the royal command of Pangeran Sukarta.

In no circumstances let there be any transgression.

Greetings to end the letter. ╱

He who wrote this piagam is Tuan Haji Imam Abdul Rauf as
commanded by His Royal Highness Pangeran Sukarta Negara.
(Tambo p. 3)

This letter gives us a good impression of the state of
things at the time. There was apparently regular communication between the Jambi princes and the Depati in Kerinci, and
Islamic teachers appear to have played an important intermediary role. One notes the presence in Kerinci of Fakih
Muhammad. There is no evidence exactly who the latter was,
but it seems likely that he was sent to Kerinci from Jambi for
the purpose of giving religious instruction.

Another letter, dated AH 1208 (1793) from three Jambi
pangeran to a Depati in Rawang (Tambo, pp. 34f.) makes clear
the intention to replace customary law by syari'a and states
that religious instructors are being sent to this end. This
dispatch of teachers gives us an interesting insight into how
Islam was spread to remote areas as a consequence of missionary zeal.

Evidence From European Sources

From European sources (SFR and a treaty with the Dutch
in 1666) we also know that from the mid-seventeenth century,

-163-

people from Kerinci were coming down to the West Coast for trading purposes and thus were coming into contact with the Sultanates of Indrapura and Moko-Moko. We do not know, however, whether these trading trips, besides obviously exposing Kerinci people to the practice of Islam led directly to conversions.

A detailed report written in 1818 by an Englishman, Thomas Barnes, who had visited Kerinci, permits us to make a few deductions about the state of Islam in the area at the time. In the first place, he mentions that Kerinci people regularly leave Kerinci for long periods with the intention of earning money on the West Coast which suggests that at that date at least there were probably Kerinci communities on the coast where people were coming into prolonged contact with their Muslim neighbors. He also mentions the existence of several Padri in Kerinci and names one or two of them including a certain Raja Ibrahim. Although there is some uncertainty whether the term here refers to Islamic reformers of the type who were then involved in religious conflict in West Sumatra or simply to teachers, this does establish that at this time there were people in Kerinci spreading religious ideas. Something else which Barnes mentions is the difficulty he had of obtaining permission to pass by mosques, again an indication that by this time Islam had become established. (See Barnes 1818.)

Fifty years later a report by an American traveller (Bickmore 1868:471) leads one to conclude that Islamic reformism had reached the area since mention is made of the zeal with which Islamic teachers returning from the pilgrimage pursued their cause in the villages round the shores of Lake Kerinci—in fact, Bickmore even suggests that the Padri reformers originated from Kerinci. Although this evidence is second-hand, since it is based on accounts which Bickmore heard, there is no reason to doubt it. Crawfurd too had heard that in Kerinci there were bands of religious zealots and mentioned this in his Dictionary (1856).

Additional evidence of the existence of Islamic reformers in Kerinci is to be found in McNair's account of Perak (1878) in which he mentions that the Kerinci immigrants who settled there—who seem to have come from Rawang in north Kerinci—were extremely religious and dressed in white, considering themselves better Muslims than their neighbors (p. 132). Snouck Hurgronje, incidentally, also mentions in The Achehnese (1906 I:297) that although Achehnese women were supposed to marry only Achehnese men, an exception was made for marriages to ulama from Kerinci who were considered to be exceptionally pious.

It is clear, then, that by the mid-nineteenth century at

the latest there were villages in Kerinci which had not only become Muslim but which had also come under the influence of the reform movement. How deeply Islam affected the day-to-day lives of the villagers, it is, however, difficult to say. The evidence of books of religious instruction preserved as pusaka in some villages gives the impression that theological ideas were very much confounded with magic and superstition in the popular imagination (see Tambo pp. 60ff.).

The overall view which one gets from these documents and from the incidental mentions of religion quoted above is that Islam had become widespread throughout the region, but that for most villagers, as for Muslims elsewhere in Sumatra and in the Malayan Peninsula (see the accounts of Wilkinson 1906 and Snouck Hurgronje 1913), being a Muslim meant primarily a profession of belonging to a community of Muslims and following certain ritual observances rather than holding a coherent set of doctrinal ideas.

Interpreting the Evidence

The First Stage of the Reception of Islam

Several writers have made the point that it is the sense of belonging to a religious community which is at the same time an elite, which seems to have prompted people to convert to Islam. If we are to accept this as a plausible hypothesis of what occurred in Kerinci, namely that villagers were converted to Islam out of a desire to be ranked with the village elite, we need to know first whether the structure of village society was such that talk of elites and stratification is appropriate.

In the first place, as we have seen, Islam was associated with the Sultans of Jambi, and it was the latter who were claiming through the issuing of piagam the power of being able to confirm the authority of the various Depati of the Kerinci villages. What the extent of the traditional authority of the Depati—or their equivalent—was before direct contact with Jambi, is uncertain, but it seems reasonable to conjecture that it was very circumscribed. The Depati seem to have been little more than the heads of small local descent groups, the position of the elder passing according to matrilineal principles—at least in north Kerinci—from mother's brother to sister's son.

As appointed heads of descent groups they were respected throughout the community, but their authority and the sanctions they were able to impose on individuals were limited to the confines of their own descent groups. There was no one who had overall authority within the village.

At some point early contact with Jambi seems to have given senior status to some of these descent group heads by conferring on them the titles of Depati. In this way they slowly began to acquire greater power within the village as a whole, at least as far as appearances were concerned. The next step was to establish a more elaborate structure of government by creating further official posts such as <u>Mangku</u> and <u>Mantri</u> and setting out a code of practice for judicial procedure. This is what the Jambi princes did in the letters and documents addressed to the Depati who, together in council, now enjoyed formal political power with the ability to enforce their decisions, exact fines, etc. This strengthened political position they owed to the Sultan of Jambi who, through the mystification of characters and the bestowal of titles had, as it were, simply created a hierarchy of village government by fiat.

When the idea of Islam was introduced, perhaps by a zealously religious Sultan, either concurrently with the original village reorganization or at some later date, then the adoption of this new set of beliefs as part of the winning of legitimation was, one presumes, eagerly accepted by the Depati. Conversion to Islam meant no dramatic change in their lives and made no great demands of them. On the contrary, it helped their political position within the village because it provided them with a source of supra-village authority to which they could appeal to confirm their exercise of judicial control.

In this respect, the attempts of the Sultans to make the <u>syari'a</u> law universally applicable are interesting because this is an area where one might expect to find that the Depati and their officers would welcome innovations which gave them more absolute power as interpreters of the new law, but where, on the other hand, there would be resistance from the villagers used to the flexibility of traditional procedures. The contrast between the two types of law should not, however, be exaggerated since, as has been pointed out in the African context, there is often considerable similarity of approach between Islamic law and many codes of customary law: both give great emphasis to torts and greatly restrict what comes under the category of criminal cases. Where changes were introduced into the traditional system was in those instances where Islamic law declared an issue criminal which, under customary law, would either have been treated differently or ignored altogether: matters of adultery or the drinking of alcohol. Another point of difference was that under Islamic law there was a possibility of the death penalty, something which seems to have been unknown in customary law. (Some traditional legendary accounts even suggest that customary law was specifically devised to supersede the practice of revenge killing which had earlier prevailed. Thus the whole elaborate system of traditional fines can, in fact, be seen as arising from a reaction to a death penalty.)

In attempting to establish the syari´a in the villages, not only did the Depati have the authority of the absent Sultan to which they could appeal, they also had support in the persons of those religious teachers who had been sent to instruct them. The latter as both religious figures and representatives of the temporal power of the Sultan commanded considerable respect. In addition to their being perhaps clients of the Depati who, it is to be imagined, were responsible for their upkeep (presumably through levies, specifically zakat payments), they also stood to gain directly from the new legal procedures involving payments relating to marriage and divorce. One sees, then, the emergence of an alliance between the traditional Depati and the new religious figures giving each other mutual support and pressing home their political advantage by promulgating an ideology which ratified their position: Islam. In these circumstances it was not questions of theology or belief which mattered initially but the creation of solidarity within a Muslim brotherhood through communal participation in organized ritual.

The Second Stage

The reasons why the Depati figures chose to adopt Islam and acknowledge Jambi overlordship in order to consolidate their authority are, then, easy to perceive. The position becomes even clearer when we consider the precariousness of their traditional position within the village polity and how important it was for them to have recognition from an outside power. This polity has been called ultra-democratic in that families of three or four generations´ depth were more or less autonomous units within village society with their own internal codes of conduct regulated by family elders. When it came to inter-family and inter-village disputes, it seems that procedures for arbitration often broke down and there was feuding and rivalry of the kind which, for example, characterizes the culture of mountain societies in the Philippines. Thus a man could not always rely on his position as a Depati or upon any appeal to law to win a hearing for his judicial decisions. The society was going through a transitional stage, it seems, moving from a rather crude, arbitrary form of law-making where revenge was the guiding principle to a more considered attitude to law as a body of principles regulating social order and administered by hereditary officials.

In most cases, villages comprised the families of four or five descent groups which had come to settle there at different times. The Depati title would be linked usually to the senior branch of the descent group of the original settlers. The hereditary principle of the descent of titles and the concomitant right to the leadership of the descent group was not a simple transfer from mother's brother to sister's son. It appears that a number of factors were taken into account: which branch of the family by virtue of the principle of rotation (giliran) was entitled to be the next title-holder; which of the men within that branch were the most suitable candidates for election to the post. Thus there was some degree of flexibility in deciding who the next Depati would be, and the principle of rotation, in particular, meant that it was impossible to establish anything like a ruling family. In some villages where there was clear-cut segmentation at certain stages of genealogical expansion; instead of rotating a title, it was decided to share the title among the various segmentary divisions, adding a suffix to the principal title to indicate that this agreement to share had taken place. Thus one has, for example, the families of Depati Setiobawo Tuo—the tuo title indicating the senior branch—and Depati Setiobawo Putih, both earlier combined in the one group of Depati Setiobawo. Furthermore, the descent groups which had settled in the village more recently were sometimes unwilling to merge themselves under the umbrella of the original descent group and sought independent political existence. In some cases, for circumstantial reasons which are no longer clearly known, they appear to have been granted a separate Depati title; in others, although they were given a separate charter, the title was one which they shared with the other descent groups with, again, only the suffix differing. Thus in the village of Pondok Tinggi, for example, the Depati of all the four descent groups which reside in the village bear the primary title of Depati Payung. The fact of sharing a title in this way effectively put all the descent groups and all segments within them on a political par.

One can see then, that with arrangements such as this, in particular with the emphasis on the political and legal independence of descent groups and even of families within the groups, there was considerable mobility with regard to access to power and prestige, and ultimately the Depati title did not per se carry enough weight to ensure any autocratic government within the village.

The balance of government and political power, however, tipped temporarily in favor of the Depati and their immediate matrilineal families as a consequence of the recognition of

Jambi suzerainty. One may speculate that there arose at this time an attempt to create a village elite comprising the elders of the senior branches of the principle descent groups in alliance with religious teachers. The next stage in the Islamization of the area, the emergence of the revivalist or so-called putih movement can be interpreted as a challenge to this established authority in an attempt to decentralize village government once more. Thus, paradoxically it may appear, the reformers were representative of the older, traditional structures of social organization. This requires some explanation.

One reason why, in pre-Islamic times, the Depati never became a powerful autocratic body was that they never controlled the economic resources of the community and, despite some income derived from fines and community service, they were not always the wealthiest men in the village. From the earliest mention of Kerinci in the records, it seems that the principle source of wealth was trade, with Kerinci men going back and forth to the West Coast and Jambi taking a variety of forest products and also gold. Kerinci gold was in fact well-known throughout Sumatra, and although it seems that it did not originally come from Kerinci, but from neighboring areas, it was men from Kerinci who acquired it and traded it. There was from early times a great prestige to be gotten from wealth and the possession of material goods, and this led Kerinci people to become temporary migrants working away from Kerinci for long periods or going on trading expeditions in order to acquire the wealth which would bring them status when they returned to their villages. Before the coming of Islam, this wealth could only be translated into material possessions: luxury goods (e.g. cloth and guns), gold and silver items, and, it seems, rice fields taken in pawn. There also appears to have existed an institution of debt-slaves, but this never seems to have been extensive.

There were, then, so-called rich men (orang kaya) in the community who could be considered a wealthy elite. They were not, however, an established institutional body like the Depati, and their fortunes were soon fragmented by inheritance. They were in no sense a corporate group, and their rise and fall depended on the success or failure of their trading ventures in the rantau. Some of these men may well have been Depati themselves, but others presumably represented, whenever they resided in the villages, an alternative authority to the Depati, with small bands of clients and relatives, a useful check against any arbitrary exercise of political power by the Depati.

Simply as orang kaya, however, they had none of the legitimating titles of insignia which would give them power by right. The Depati, on the other hand, had their _piagam_ from Jambi, and the authority of Islam to validate their claims to leadership. But it must have been noticeable, too, that as Islamic values became common throughout the society those religious instructors who had come to reside in the villages, although having no traditional claims to prestige or status, had acquired the latter simply through their association with Islam and having been on the pilgrimage. The _orang kaya_, then, quickly perceived that through the simple expedient of going on the pilgrimage they were in a position to challenge Depati authority by appealing to Islam and the kudos of the _haji_ title.

This, in fact, seems to have been what happened from the early years of the nineteenth century. Favorable geographical and economic conditions in Kerinci allowed many people the opportunity to become wealthy through trade and, in addition, it seems that the desire to be an _orang kaya_ and, at a later date, the goal of the pilgrimage, provided the incentive to be thrifty and save as much as possible. There are several accounts of this strong desire of Kerinci people to accumulate wealth. By all accounts then, there was a steady stream of people going on the pilgrimage, some of them settling first in Malaya to earn the money for the journey.

For some of these returning _haji_ the spirit of the reform, which they had encountered in the Islamic world of the time, must have come as grist to their mills in their desire to establish themselves back in village society. Not only could they claim the right to a hearing through their being _haji_, they could even claim through their special knowledge of the true meaning of Islam to have greater right to the leadership of the community than the ignorant Depati whose shallowness they could condemn. Doubtless there were others too who were genuinely inspired by religious motives and a desire to spread the true faith.

One can surmise how easily this challenge to established authority conducted in terms of a religious conflict of views must have erupted beyond the confines of the villages and led to strife and fighting within the region. The obscure oral accounts one hears today of inter-village warfare in the nineteenth century do not mention the dimensions of the disputes, but one can plausibly imagine that as religious ferver grew in the region, differences in belief became independent causes of dispute. The one account of strife that I did hear, during the course of fieldwork, between _hitam_ and _putih_ factions mentioned warfare between the northern part of Kerinci representing the reformers (_putih_) and the southern region who were considered _hitam_.

The evidence does not allow one to draw any definitive

conclusions here, but it is worth noting that the southern region is that which came more directly under Jambi influence than the slightly more remote northern villages and was perhaps more centralized. It is noticeable too that the northern village of Rawang from where the early religious leaders appear to have sprung, was the most densely populated at the time and there appears to have been emigration from there since the nineteenth century. This is a case of what I argued earlier one might expect: demographic pressure on limited riceland leading people both to pursue trade more actively and to become religious teachers.

To return to the question of open conflict both within the villages and between villages, however, one should not, as far as Kerinci is concerned, exaggerate the amount of violence and unrest. The peculiar structure of village government meant that the conflicts rarely became acute. Not only was there the possibility of mobility between interest groups, with the Depati also having the possibility of becoming _haji_ and the _orang kaya_ being elected to official positions, but the size of the village communities was so small (200-400) that the ethics of kinship amity must have often prevented any serious dissension from breaking out. And in those cases where it did erupt, there is evidence that the recourse was simply for one of the disputing parties to move out of the village and establish himself and his family elsewhere.

In sum then, what one sees is a period of social unrest in the region which is ostensibly about differences of belief and religious practice but is really about the structure of village government. Once the challenge to the autocracy of the Depati has been successful and the passions of religious enthusiasm, which in the interim have acquired an autonomy of their own, have subsided, the village society settles down to its former state organized around the principles of minimal descent group government.

Evidence from the Late Nineteenth Century

From about 1875, as a consequence of increasing Dutch interest in Kerinci, we find a number of systematic reports on the region compiled by colonial officials from the accounts they elicited from Kerinci traders who came down to the coast at Moko-Moko and Indrapura. Religion is one of the items which is regularly mentioned in these reports. In the first of these, which was especially written for the benefit of the famous Midden-Sumatra expedition, which originally intended to explore Kerinci, there is a description of the state of things in 1872. Referring to religious practice the report states:

-171-

Islam is beginning gradually to spread throughout the land and of course the influence of the so-called hajis does not lag far behind. Tanah Rawang, in particular, is Muslim, and it is also beginning to spread in Sulak.

Delicts such as adultery and theft are also punished according to the Koran....

[Education] is limited to the so-called menghaji (Koranic recital) and only a few priests [sic] understand and read Malay and that, poorly. Provided a Kerinci man can recite but a short Arabic prayer he is considered a teacher—haji—in his land. (TNAG Bij.I. i60f.)

A few years later another report was produced, written by the Controleur of Indrapura, W. C. Hoogkamer, in 1876. This contained more detail than the earlier report and the following remarks were made about religion.

The religious officials (geestlijkheid) seem to take great advantage of the ordinary man, since they are able to raise the amount of zakat and fitrah to a great degree and adapt everything to raise their status above others.

They also take a portion of the marriage fees.

Most Kerinci people are earnest but rather blind (domme) followers of Islam.

Kamun, Tanjung Pau, and Ujung Pasir (near Tanah Kampung) are an exception in this respect.

Their people follow the religion of the ancestral heathen gods or Dewa-Dewa. The Kerinci call this religion Asé Pelaro which seems for the most part to be like the religion of the Pasemah and the Kubu.

The bringing of offerings to dead ancestors and dewa-dewa together with the performance of fantastic dances are the main prescriptions of the outward observance of the religion.

It is also in those villages that one finds written, or rather incised, on bamboo, spells and formulas—although the Kerinci man in general is very superstitious, and an unbounded faith is placed on the words of magicians and wizards (<u>wigchelaars en bezweerders</u>). (VBG 1880:65)

What is particularly interesting about the information given here are the remarks to the effect that there are still some villages which are not Muslim and that, in general, the people are very superstitious.

The next report on conditions in Kerinci appeared in 1898 and was written by the then Controleur of Indrapura, E. A. Klerks. In this account, which is by far the most detailed in its description of the region, various aspects of religious practice and the influence of Islamic ideas on the day-to-day lives of the villagers are mentioned; and, taken together, they provide an illuminating insight into the changes which must have occurred in the twenty year interval since the writing of the previous reports.

The information given in the report about religion and the position of religious officials in the villages can be summarized as follows. Islamic influence in the area has become more pronounced and has led, for example, to the decline of cock-fighting as a pastime (p.82). Despite this growing influence, however, there is no evidence of fanaticism. Singing and dancing still occur. Returned <u>haji</u> do not appear to be very militant (p.81) and in judicial matters there are no religious figures who sit on councils or arbitrate in matters of law. In matters of marriage and divorce, however, religious authorities play an important role, as one might have expected, since they officiated at the ceremonies for a fee. There is an institution whereby a woman can be formally separated from her husband at her own bidding, and this separation is symbolized by the <u>imam</u> splitting a piece of wood. A proper divorce, however, can only take place if the husband pronounces the <u>talak</u> (the Islamic formula for divorce) and if he is initially unwilling to do this he can usually be persuaded by the wife's relatives to pronounce the <u>talak</u> for an agreed sum. This is known as <u>menjual talak</u> (p.75). There are mosques in every village in Kerinci and each mosque is administered by a number of mosque officials: <u>imam</u>, <u>khatib</u>, <u>bilal</u>. In addition, each descent group also has its own set of religious officials, and these take it in turn to officiate at Friday prayers and special feast days. One mark of religious officials seems to be that they shave their hair (p.53). Circumcision and incision are practiced. Theft and adultery are not punished according to the Islamic code. There still exist one or two <u>kramat</u> (sacred) places where offerings are made to spirits, but there are fewer of these than formerly. As far as education is concerned, this is "limited exclusively to learning how to read from the Koran and to a knowledge of the rituals of Islam." People from some villages go to Padang to get a religious education but in Sungai Penuh and Rawang there are religious teachers, returned _haji_, who give instruction.

Not much comment need be added to this. Since one is never sure to which areas within Kerinci the specific mentions of religion refer, either in this report or in the previous ones, there are problems when it comes to comparing the references. Insofar as it is possible to make any comparisons, the direction of change seems to be towards more tolerance in some matters and a gradual acceptance of Islamic prohibition in others. The consumption of alcoholic drinks is reported to have ceased and, like the decline in cock-fighting, this is directly attributable to Islamic preaching. One notices, however, that both these activities are rather peripheral to the culture of the people--although it should be admitted that cock-fighting was said to be very popular--and there are no positive injunctions in _adat_ enjoining people to drink or gamble. In those matters where there are specific prescriptions laid down in customary law, we see that _adat_ has not been superseded by _syari'a_, whereas earlier reports had tended to suggest that this was happening. Klerks also mentions that the death penalty is unknown. What seems to have happened, then, is that although there may have been some attempts to replace customary law, these have not ultimately succeeded. And since the procedure for litigation existing prior to the introduction of Islam seems to have been, at least in the ideal, sufficiently sophisticated and well-organized, there appears to have been a reluctance to accept the innovations of _syari'a_ and the interventions of religious personnel to replace what was already satisfactory.

In some areas, involving not so much prohibitions as the regulation of rites, there has been compromise. The ceremonies of marriage and divorce are a combination of Islamic and traditional ritual. The institution of _jual talak_ is particularly interesting since it represents, from the orthodox Islamic point of view, a curious compromise whereby the strength of the woman's position in marriage according to the traditional evaluation is safeguarded while at the same time the Islamic formula is respected. Only in one domestic matter does there appear to be no attempt to introduce the provisions of _syari'a_ and that is in relation to inheritance. Traditional arrangements for the division of property were never questioned, it appears, perhaps because they were finally adapted to the socio-economic pattern of organization of the community. (This was, one imagines, readily perceived by the religious instructors of the villages who were either native to the region or from neighboring areas where the system was similar. Their perceptions, therefore, were different from the foreign ulama who preached in Aceh and who could see little of value in the traditional system and were anxious to establish a system of direct inheritance by a man's sons.) Matters of inheritance and the devolution of property then, which are central to the socio-economic life of the community, are more likely--all other things being equal--to determine legal practice than to subject to arbitrary changes of law proposed from without. When principles relating to property do change, it seems to be as a direct result of changes in the economic infrastructure as has become apparent in recent times.

Clearly, to judge from Klerk's report, where Islam has had the most impact on the society has been in the incorporation of its ritual into daily life. This is immediately noticeable in the references to the mosques which have sprung up in the villages and in the description of the organization of religious officials, both within the village as a whole and within the individual descent groups. Each is given a specific function, and thus the religious life of the community is carefully orchestrated; and, through the ritual of Friday prayer and the collection of contributions for the spiritual welfare of the community, the institutions of religion acquire great significance in the routine of the village.

It is not, one notes, the theological content of the religion which appeals to the people. As far as one can judge from the brief remarks about religious education consisting merely of learning to recite a few Arabic prayers, questions of belief and dogma are very secondary. It is the appropriation of the ritual formulae which matters. One can speculate on various reasons why this should be so. To my mind, the readiness with which this element is accommodated can be attributed to the way in which it appears to be consonant and continuous with much pre-Islamic ritual: spells (jampi-jampi), incantations (mantra), and innovations (seruan), which are so much a part of Malay culture (cf. Skeat's Malay Magic). The ritual, therefore, provides an effortless way of moving from the conceptual world of the old beliefs to the new universal religion.

Similar reasons can be found to explain why the ideal of the pilgrimage should have become so popular. I have suggested above that there might have been political reasons which gave people the incentive to return to the community as haji, but another way of looking at this novel desire is to see it in terms of two pre-Islamic traditions: first, that of the ascetic who retires from the community and meditates alone to gain spiritual wisdom and magico-mystical power, still a strong motif in Sumatran culture but often neglected by scholars because of the stress on this form of religious behavior as defining Javanese religion; and second, the tradition of seeking wealth and knowledge in the _rantau_ away from the homeland. Both these traditions appear to coalesce in the experience of the _haji_. In the first place, the pilgrims return with new religious status, not because they have acquired greater knowledge of their religion, but because the act of the pilgrimage itself has conferred on them new spiritual power. This change in their religious status is outwardly symbolized by the donning of new garments, in particular the white turban. At the same time this religious authority can be exploited for political and economic advantages since the opinion of a _haji_ carries weight in the community. And in the second place, it should be remembered that the actual journey to Mecca is often combined with trading ventures so that the returned pilgrim not only brings back a religious title, but also considerable material goods. If we see it in this light, as a natural extension of values long held in the community, it is hardly surprising that going on the pilgrimage was one of the elements of Islam which was taken up with the greatest enthusiasm in this isolated mountain region.

A final point to be made is that despite the early stress on orthodoxy represented by the Jambi letters, it seems that Islamic principles did not oust the performance of pre-Islamic rituals. This is not immediately obvious from Klerk's account although there is there the mention of _kramat_ places. A better idea does, however, emerge from a short comment by Kooreman, Controleur at Moko-Moko. In part of a report published in 1893, he writes of Kerinci _adat_ practices. His informant was a certain H. Abdoerahman from Rawang, said to be a person of great influence and probably a Depati. The description he gives of the rites which are performed in relation to the _pusaka_ (heirloom) objects kept in the village is worth quoting in full.

> In the loft of the houses belonging to the Depati of the Mendapo, by the main post usually decorated with paintwork and carving are to be found miniature houses curtained with colored cottons. In those miniature houses which are reached by means of a ladder are kept objects which originate from the _orang tua-tua_, or ancestors in the Malay sense, of the Depati.

> These objects called _pusaka_ consist of old manuscripts written in _Encong_ writing on bark or bamboo, pieces of clothing, weapons, gongs and stones, and are considered to belong to the women (_vrouwen_) of the Depati called co-Depati [?] who function as priestesses. They come

and burn incense regularly and bring yellow rice and
they scatter baked rice on the pusaka at which ceremony
they are accompanied by two other women known as dayang-
dayang. Usually old songs are sung as an accompaniment.

The pusaka are greatly respected by the people. They
bring offerings there and it is usual to make solemn
oaths and promises there. Nothing may be done with the
pusaka unless the women mentioned above are present.
Some of the objects, including the Encong writings, may
not be seen or touched by anyone other than these women-
-and then only in weighty circumstances such as a war,
epidemics or other misfortunes, on the occasion of
receiving a Raja, the appointment of a new Depati etc.
when they may be brought down.

On these occasions a buffalo must be slaughtered and
then in the presence of the female Depati and to the accompaniment of shouting and singing, the burning of incense, the scattering of rice, the shooting of guns, the
beating of gongs and drums, the pusaka are taken out of
their special miniature houses and paraded round the
village, during which time the dayang-dayang dance. With
the same ceremony they are returned to their place in
the loft. The pusaka also possess sawah known as sawah
rapat which are cultivated by the people, and the harvest of which is intended for the Depati who is obliged
to see to the board and lodging of notable visitors to
the village. (Kooreman 1893:184f.)

Haji Abdoerahman clearly saw that there was something
anomalous about these ceremonies being performed by a Muslim
people since Kooreman takes the trouble to comment on the
above that: "According to Haji Abdoerahman, all these customs
are still strictly observed even though all the people have
been converted to Islam."
    The impression we are left with, then, is that the
religious life of the community at the end of the nineteenth
century, even in those villages which were considered to be
especially pious such as Rawang, consisted largely of the performance of rituals which were valued both as a focus of communal organization and as a means of persuading nonmaterial
forces through appeal and conciliatory offerings to intervene
in the day-to-day routines of life in the village. Theological concepts remained rudimentary and there was nothing which
might be called a coherent and systematic world view to which
the society subscribed. Morality and ethics were very much an
extension of attitudes and values relating to the organization

of kinship and expressed through various adages and proverbial principles; and the law appears to have been an ad hoc matter administered by councils of elders who were more or less respected.

Conclusion

Drawing together the various divergent strands in this account of the Islamization of Kerinci, I would argue that the historical progress of Islam in the area can be perceived as taking place according to three stages. First, Islam is introduced from Jambi at the same time as an attempt is being made to create a rudimentary political centralized authority with descent group heads (Depati) being confirmed as village chiefs subordinate to the Jambi royal family. At this stage, Islam, as the religion of Jambi along with the bestowal of titles and official insignia, is part of the ideological superstructure which works to legitimate the new village hierarchy. Subsequently, as Islamic ideas which had initially made little difference to the ritual practices within the village begin to take hold, those men (orang kaya) in the society who are economically powerful but who do not have easy access to officially recognized political titles, see that Islamic ideas and the social prestige of individual haji can be turned back upon title holders and established authority. Their espousal of revivalist ideas can then be seen as the exploitation of religious sentiments to justify their challenge to the village establishment which had once used the same religious ideology but differently interpreted to conform its own status.

Internal strife within villages soon gives to religious issues a momentum of their own, and the question of religious orthodoxy becomes perhaps a dimension added to the character or traditional inter-village disputes which one perceives as having existed from pre-Islamic times. Finally, in the third stage of the reception of Islam, after a period of sometimes quite violent social conflict in which the issue of religious orthodoxy is sometimes a central feature, sometimes a peripheral one, a modus vivendi is reached when the political situation within the villages has returned to a state in which again it is the autonomy of the descent group which is the controlling principle of organization, and centralized authority is only of nominal importance.

According to this interpretation, Islam, in whatever guise, mystic Sufi or orthodox Wahabi, is often used in central Sumatra in appeals to legitimate political power, and the particular ritual practices which are ultimately adopted by the whole community are those which enhance the ordered social life of the village irrespective of theological correctness.

Acknowledgements. Earlier drafts of this paper were presented in seminars in the Universities of Hull and Canterbury, and I am grateful to various people in those two places who made helpful comments on some of the ideas. I am also grateful to Lynn Thomas for comments on the version presented to the Amsterdam symposium.

The research on which this paper is based was funded by the Evans Fund, The SSRC of the United Kingdom, and the Ministry of Education of the Netherlands.

POLITICAL HISTORY AND SOCIAL CHANGE IN MINANGKABAU:
INFORMATION FROM LITERARY WORKS

Umar Junus
University of Malaya

A literary work may provide us with important information about the society from which it comes. Works of literature are means by which their authors internalize and interpret their social-cultural circumstances. The descriptive
capacity of literature enables it to convey a sense of social
circumstances which an ordinary sociological researcher might
otherwise find difficult to assess. However, there are corresponding dangers that impede interpretation. For example,
literary works do not describe social realities as coherent
wholes; they do not directly give a picture of a social structure. Literary descriptions are not only fragmented, but refracted as well.

The promise and the danger of interpreting society from
literature follow from the nature of literary work. A work of
fiction is regarded here as a further development of narrative story-telling; a narrative story relates events (Walter
Benjamin 1976).[1] So the correspondence to reality of fiction
must be seen in the first place as constrained by the particular events dealt with in the work. In any relation of specific events, there will be deviation from societal norms,
yielding a certain disequilibrium, to use Tzvetan Todorov's
term (1977:111).

Relating events, furthermore, necessarily involves interpreting them, and an interpretation is quite subjective,
depending in part upon the author's sense of his or her social-cultural background. It cannot be tied merely to what one
actually sees, but rather also embodies what the author wants
to see. As a result, there may be different interpretations

---

[1] A kaba pretends to tell a true story of an actual event as
mentioned in its title page. Some novels on Minangkabau
society also have such pretention because they share the story
of some kabas as well as a reference to a happening, located
in a particular space and time, an historical event. A novel
can be regarded as a reaction towards an historical event.

of the same set of circumstances, refracted through the author's understanding stemming from his or her background.

An important source of this background is the culture's complex of myths. One's interpretation of reality is bound to these myths, as a result of primary and secondary socialization (see, for example, Berger & Luckmann 1971). In socialization, some myths are transmitted, others created; some are inferred, others explicit.

Myth is a medium through which we understand and internalize our culture (according to Roland Barthe's interpretation [1973]). By this interpretation, our life is seen to be regulated by a complex of myths, some of which are contradictory to one another. We are afraid of deviating from behavior described in a particular myth because of its prediction of failure, which might include condemnation or unhappiness. One who has trespassed such boundaries might experience the sanction of guilt feelings. A Minangkabau of a certain period of time, for example, might be afraid of doing something against his mother's wishes lest he meet the fate of Malin Kandung in the famous myth.

One who knows no other world outside his own society believes a myth to be the truth. He does not dare test its validity. Ignoring the fact that a myth is a generalization derived from a particular incident which is not exactly the same as the events he experiences, he believes the myth's sanctions to be applicable in his circumstances. The myth of Malin Kandung is believed to apply to a person who acts against maternal wishes, irrespective of his or her intentions.

A myth is told and conceptualized. A simple story might become a myth if it is told repeatedly and if it molds a certain concept in its audience.[2] A literary work may also become mythical. It may be a "myth of concern" if it holds the status quo, confirming existing conditions and resisting change; or a "myth of freedom" if it propagates changes of existing conditions, espousing the replacement of old conditions with new ones.

A literary work may be regarded here as a myth related to the social cultural conditions prelavent in the world of its writer, who faces events within this world. There are,

---

[2] A newspaper reports (New Strait Times, Jan 20, 1981) on how a myth of "supersex" was created by reading materials and how these have affected sexual life in America.

then, three possibilities as to how his conceptualization might proceed. He might see an event as resulting from failure of existing norms, or as the second alternative, as the result of existing norms which need a change. Finally, he might do his best just to see it as it is, without suggesting a diagnosis or solution.

A literary work is a world of ideas. It expresses an ideology and a world view, and may therefore be used as a means of indoctrination. This use of literary works is very important to Minangkabau people since the social system leaves much to personal interpretation, as is the case also with Javanese society (cf. Hildred Geertz 1961:4). Minangkabau family structure also creates problems of interpersonal relationships, which add to the field available for literary evaluation.

A man is on the one hand a subordinate to his mother, but is on the other hand superior to her as her _mamak_ (mother's brother) responsible for her welfare. She is dependent on him, as he provides her with security. He then holds two contrasting positions which he must consider every time he makes a decision.

It becomes more complicated if we also consider his relationship to his wife and children. He is caught between two different obligations: towards his mother and his matrilineal kin on the one hand, and towards his wife and children on the other. A failure to fulfill these two obligations satisfactorily will put him in a difficult position. To prevent this, one must interpret the implications of the whole system. A literary work is very useful in this interpretation.

A literary work is also important to understanding a non-stable or changing society. Minangkabau has endured continuous social-cultural change for quite a long time, especially in the 20th century. As a result, there have been confrontations and mutual reinforcements among several ideologies.

According to some views of Islamic kinship theory, for example, there is a possible confrontation between the Minangkabau social system and the tenets of Islamic Law. A father and his children belong to one family unit but they are of two different descent units in the Minangkabau system. Nevertheless, the two systems complement each other. The lack of a supernaturally derived power prevents a _mamak_ from exercising his control over his _kemenakan_ (sister's children). He must borrow the hand of a father who has been given such power by Islam. For example, in _Pertemuan_ (Abbas Pamoencak nS,1927),

-183-

Masri's father lends his power to Masri's mamak in order to force a marriage between Masri and the mamak's daughter. We find several such confrontations in Minangkabau literature between ideologies of Islam and Minangkabau, such as the novels of Hamka. Another such confrontation occurs between the traditional and the modern world and is expressed in most novels on Minangkabau. The difference between a woman's view and that of a man regarding the Minangkabau system forms another dichotomy resulting from a changing society. (These phenomena reflect a political history and social change. The same phenomena can also be seen in literary works which I shall examine in this paper.)

Minangkabau society is described in two literary genres. The first is Kaba, a traditional Minangkabau narrative story in Minangkabau language; and secondly, the novel written in Indonesian Malay.[3]

Kaba is a dying tradition since it is no longer developing, although these stories were printed in the 20's and reprinted in the 60's when the novel on Minangkabau people began to emerge. There are both old kaba and new ones regarding recent events in the late 19th century or early 20th century. There are at least four kabas which relate the same story as corresponding novels. They are Kaba Sutan Lembak Tuah dengan Siti Rabiatun and Sengasara Membawa Nikmat (Tulis Sutan Sati 1928), Kaba Siti Nurlela, and Pertemuan, Kaba Si Sabariah and Karena Mentua (N. St. Iskander 1932), and Amai Cilako and Salah Pilih (1928) respectively. In addition to that, Hulubalang Raja is simply a rearrangement of Kaba Sutan Manangkerang, published in 1885 by J.L. van den Toorn.

There are both classical and new kaba, which we will henceforth refer to as ck and nk respectively. A ck is a kaba which relates a story derived from a long oral tradition. Its structure differs from that of an nk, so that even a kaba relating a story of the not too distant past can be classified as a ck as long as it has such a structure.

A ck has the following characteristics:

1. There is a sequence of Equilibrium (=E), then Disequilibrium (=D), followed by Equilibrium.
2. The presence of a "stranger," usually a tyrant, causes the D.
3. He could be a complete stranger, or
4. a father.

---

[3] A list of kabas and novels, not complete, is provided in the Appendix to this paper.

5. The son of a mother who was "evicted" returns to work "revenge" upon the "stranger" and to bring back the E, that is the (re)establishment of mamakship.
6. In case of (3), there is a reunion of a family consisting of the mother, father, brother, sister, and mother's brother while in the case of (4) it will exclude a father.
7. It tells of a power struggle between two opposing sides.

A new or nonclassical kaba relates the story of an immediate past, at the end of the 19th century or at the first quarter of the 20th century. It has the following characteristics:

1. There is a sequence of (E-D) D-E.
2. The D is caused by, respectively:
   a. the absence of a mamak (mother's brother; mother's mother's brother);
   b. the absence of a responsible mamak as the culprit simply sold the family property for his own pleasures and exercised his right by forgetting his duty or his obligation towards his maternal kin;
   c. a son who is more interested in enjoying life by spending lavishly upon the dwindling property, and in so doing, forgetting his obligations toward his matrilineal kin;
3. The son later transforms himself into a rich merchant by accumulating wealth and property in addition to his regaining the lost family property. It is somewhat a reestablishment of mamakship.
4. There is a problem of interpretation of rights and duty. There might be a tendency to emphasize one's right by forgetting one's duty but in the final analysis, a duty is more important than a right. A right may only be exercized after complete fulfillment of duty, thus demonstrating the greater importance of duty.
5. The story is concluded with the reunion of a mother, brother, sister, and father. The existence of a sister always leads to a family reunion. (cf. Junus 1980).

There are three types of novels: the early (eN), the later (lN), and the new novel (nN) respectively, each with its own characteristics.
An eN has the following characteristics:

1. The sequence of E-D (-E).
2. The presence of a stranger causes a D. He might be (a) a complete stranger, a tyrant, or (b) a father, or (c) a (non-relative) lover or marriage partner.
3. There is an attempt at a reunion of a family, usually a matrilineal family.

Exemplifying the importance of a stranger's role as an antagonist, two novels by Selasih, a woman writer, tell a story about a character who is victimized by a stranger until he or she is given protection by his/her matrilineal family (cf. Junus 1977).

1N on the other hand has a different set of features, such as:

1. A sequence of El-D (E2) with El=E2
2. The responsibility for the D is attributed to the traditional system as understood by the older people, which accentuates one's duty towards the family to the point where it seems one has no right at all.
3. A separation of kinship ties by establishing a union with a non-relative. The importance of right has won the battle.

There are two types of 1N. Most 1Ns are written by western educated novelists who usually work for the Dutch government. The protagonist in these novels is an educated Minangkabau who works for the Dutch. However, there are some novels written by non-western educated novelists not working for the Dutch, such as Hamka. The protagonist in these is usually a non-western educated man who does not work for the Dutch (cf. Junus 1977).

An nN[4] has the following characteristics:

1. A sequence of (E-) D-E.

---

[4] I take the liberty to include as well a short story since the number of novels in Minangkabau society was limited during this period. The novel had, as a matter of fact, gone meran- tau since they dealt with a human or Indonesian problem. The location of Kemarau, (1967) is Minangkabau; it however deals more with a human problem rather than a problem of a Minangkabau vis-à-vis his society. Its relevance to our problem now is the willingness to return home, an attachment to kampung.

2. An attachment to a modern value, such as the importance of love and a corresponding disregard for the
   traditional system, which could cause a D. There is
   a tendency toward intentional neglect of obligations
   to matrilineal kin. The protagonist is more interested in his right, including his right to material
   support from his mamak in pursuing his education.
3. The conclusion is a reunion of family by his accepting the traditional system.

A comparison between ck and nk can be seen in Figure 1
(next page). It can be seen that both kaba propagate traditional values: the importance of mamakship, and of duty and
family unity. Kaba are different from novels, as a comparison
between a novel and a kaba relating the same incident might
show. Kaba Siti Nurlela tells us about an establishment of
mamakship as a brother takes care of his sister and mother.
It ends with a family reunion. These two elements are absent
from Pertemuan. Although Sengasara Membawa Nikmat concludes
with Midun returning home as a demang, and reuniting with the
family, he also takes a foreign wife, a "stranger." It
differs from Kaba Sutan Lembak Tuah in that Lembak Tuah does
not take a foreign wife. He marries his fiancee who was
chosen by his family in a traditional way.

However, there are some changes from a ck to an nk. An
nk no longer continues suspicion of a stranger as such a
person is no longer presupposed to be bad. On the contrary,
he might be very helpful. The change shows a greater degree
of openness in the society to foreign elements. It is a non-
responsible mamak who creates a D, since he is more interested
in exercising his right by simply forgetting his duty. In
contrast, his kemenakan does the following:

   i. regains the lost family property and adds to it;
   ii. acts as a responsible mamak by emphasizing his duty
       rather than his right.

The nk is then an indoctrination of how as a mamak, one
should act. Such literature attempted to address a problem
which existed during the late 19th and early 20th centuries.
   A mamak simply forgot his duty or obligation. He was
only interested in exercising his "right" as he was a bad man.
He was enjoying himself due to an unhealthy influence from his
environment or from the way he was brought up. Or he misin-
terpreted the "law" as was the case with Dr. Andiko in Kaba
Sultan Lanjungan.

	cK	nK
	a stranger is bad	a non-responsible mamak is bad
Variables	a power struggle	an interpretation of mamak´s right & duty
	acquiring super-natural power	accumulating wealth

	a search for a responsible, duty-oriented mamak
Constants	a family reunion
	against the abuse of power

Figure 1: Comparison of cK and nK

Kaba are indoctrinations of their audience, which consisted of noneducated Minangkabau, usually parewas--the
adolescent group which was caught between two worlds, the
traditional and the modern. They faced a temptation to emphasize the enjoyment of life by exercising their rights and
their obligations to improve their own future.

This literature is also an interpretation of Minangkabau
"ideology" since the society is now open to a different world.
It is the second element in an nk, the neglect of obligation
to matrilineal kin, which replaces the power struggle in a ck.
The disappearance of a power struggle is related to the disappearance of an evil stranger who would like to crush the
opposing family.

The element of supernatural power also disappears as the
struggle in an nk no longer has anything to do with that. It
is now competition in accumulating wealth and property that is
important; one will be regarded as a respectable mamak if he
can provide well for his matrilineal kin. This is in line
with the theme of the obligation of a mamak toward his matrilineal kin, since it is understood in these kabas that one is
obliged to provide them with material welfare by both preserving and adding to the inherited property. Poverty is considered a disgrace among the village folk; and the poor famil-

ies are pariahs. There is always competition within the family between two brothers or two sisters, although the latter
is not mentioned in nk <u>kabas</u>.

An eN is not really different from a ck, except that a
non-supernatural power takes the place of a supernatural one.
E can be viewed as continuations from ck (cf. Junus 1974:714).
The replacement of a supernatural power with a non-supernatural one is due to the adaptation of the ck to the conditions of
20th century life, with a rational outlook replacing a non-ra-
tional one. No further explanation regarding a ck and an eN
is necessary.

It is more interesting to compare an nk and an 1N, or an
eN with an 1N, as can be seen in figures 2 (below) and 3 (next
page).

	:	nK	:	1N
Variables	:	a search for a tradi- itional <u>mamak</u> who is duty-bound	:	a condemnation of a traditional <u>mamak</u> as one who is more inter- ested in rights than in duty
Constant	:	against the abuse of power		

Figure 2:   Comparison of nK and 1N

A comparison between nk and 1N shows us that nK is a
myth of concern, defending the traditional system, while an 1N
is a myth of freedom, discrediting the traditional system. An
1N shows an effort to establish a new tie with a "stranger" by
at least weakening the tie with the traditional relatives. It
may go beyond this, by breaking the family tie as can be seen
in <u>Memutuskan Pertalian</u> (Tulis St. Sati 1932) and <u>Salah Pilih</u>
(Iskandar 1928), unless the family is ready to compromise by
accepting and legitimizing the new tie. For example, the
village-folk in <u>Sakah Pilih</u> are ready to compromise by
accepting the marriage between Asri and Asnah, both of whom
belong to the same exogamous matrilineal unit. This shows acceptance of a non-traditional world. The protagonist is no
longer a part of his traditional background, but a part of a

	:	eN	:	1N
Variables	:	presence of a bad stranger	:	presence of a bad <u>mamak</u> who forces someone to fulfill his duty toward his matrilineal kin
	:	family unity	:	family disunity
Constants	:	against the abuse of power presence of an educated man for the "modern" man, money is no longer an important factor for happiness (it may be hated); emphasis is on right rather than duty		

Figure 3: Comparison of eN with 1N

new world, a modern one perhaps. He now dares to depart from his traditional family, no longer depending on them, but entering another world, a better one.[5]

There is a factor responsible for this. The protagonist in an nk is a merchant or a farmer who changes himself into a

---

[5] It is interesting to note the difference of membership within a nuclear family in a <u>kaba</u> and in a novel. There is a preference in <u>kaba</u> for a mother to have a son and a daughter and a development of a brother-sister relationship. It guarantees happiness as can be seen in my note no. 13 (in Junus 1980a). In novels, on the contrary, there is a preference for a family with only one child, a son or a daughter, only which in a <u>kaba</u> tends to have an unhappy ending: 14 out of 27 novels have an unhappy ending, while 4 have an indecisive ending. Only 9 have happy endings. Most novels end with the failure to reconcile with the traditional family life.

petty trader. He is a part of the traditional establishment, who is accumulating wealth for the sake of his family, something of which they can be proud. He believes that the element of luck is responsible for his success, although he must do his best to pursue it. If the luck is not with him, his effort may be useless, in which case he must return to the fold of his traditional family for help.

The protagonist in an lN differs in that he is somewhat educated and has a secure job with the government. He is quite sure that he need not return to the family for help since his future in a non-traditional world seems certain. Accordingly, an lN is dealing with a more modern, educated man, originating from a Minangkabau family. He sees only the duties involved in Minangkabau society but not the rights it reserves for its members.

There are now two different world views, that of educated Minangkabau and that of non-educated ones. Due to the availability of an alternative world which he considers to be a better one, an educated Minangkabau simply forgets the traditional world. The introduction of "westernization" has changed the structure of the Minangkabau society, and produced people who are willing to emerge from the traditional world of duty and enter the modern one in which they think they can exercise their rights.[6]

The eN started a new tradition of the educated protagonist. The educated man, however, is not really independent from the traditional world. In the novel, he might be either victimized by traditional power, or be compelled to return to his family after failing in the modern world. Samsulbahri in Siti Nurbaya (Marah Rusli 1922), falling victim to a traditional power, is an example of the former case, while Nasrlin in Kalau Tak Untung (Selasih 1933) exemplifies the latter.

There are two explanations of the above situation in an eN. The novel either follows the tradition established by a cK, or it deals with an early stage of the introduction of western elements to the Minangkabau society. The protagonist is either not fully able to free himself from the traditional ties which are still very strong, or he is not sure of his position in the new world. He is caught between his emotional attachment to his traditional background and his rational tie with the modernized society, as were the Indonesian poets

---

[6] Rusmala in Rusmala Dewi (Hardjosemarto & Madjo Indo 1932) simply refused to pay her obligation towards her mamak who had paid his obligation towards her in her difficult situation because she hated the system.

before the war (Junus 1980).

An nN shows a different picture of this conflict. The D is caused by the protagonist's embracing the modern elements in society which makes him reject a priori the traditional system. He demonstrates this by emphasizing rights rather than duty. His commitment to a modern value forces him to reject his mother's brother's daughter as his future bride, since marrying her is in accordance with the traditional system which he wishes to avoid. He forgets his obligation toward his mamak whose behavior toward his kemenakan contrasts with the neglect of the latter.[7] Finally, the E is re-established by the protagonist's reunion with the family. He is now willing to marry his mother's brother's daughter. He remembers his obligation toward his mamak, which alone makes an nN different from an lN.[8]

A contrastive analysis between an lN and nN shows that:

a. lN's were written during the peak of the period of emphasis on modernization, which was understood to be superior to the traditional world. Everything modern was associated with happiness and freedom in exercising one's rights. Tradition, however, was associated with the humiliation of obligations without any rights.

b. nN's were written after some revolution of the modern and traditional worlds. Writers, having lost some of their previous prejudices, saw the modern world as an alternative to the traditional one, but not necessarily superior to it. A character might conclude that forgetting tradition was not necessary in order to live in the modern world. For example, he might enjoy the benefits of modern life and still marry his mother's brother's daughter. Additional-

---

[7] There are two different attitudes a young educated Minangkabau might have. He might condemn his mamak who fails to fulfill his obligations towards him. On the other hand, he might refuse to acknowledge his obligations towards his mamak who has done everything for his future. He refuses, for example, to marry his mother's brother's daughter as he is now a "modern man," free to choose his own wife.

[8] Rusmala, for example, did not appreciate what her mamak did for her, due to her prejudice that it was part of a "rotten" system.

ly, the traditional lifestyle is no longer seen as backward, but has been modernized itself. The girl had changed from (rambut) seperti ekor kambing "(the hair is arranged) like a horse's tail" (cf. A.A. Navis 1977).[9] nN's were written during the time when there were two different movements. The drive toward modernization was prevalent among villagers living within the traditional society, and was no longer considered a problem. On the other hand, there was a movement among those who had been living outside the traditional world to return to it, bringing with them a more modern atmosphere.[10]

By integrating the time factor into the difference between an lN and an nN it can be seen that:

T1 (associated with lN): a drive toward modernization,

---

[9] The first expression has a bad connotation associated with backwardness, while the second has a modern one.

[10] There are two different cultural movements in Minangkabau at present. One is the cultural movement of the elite group while the other is non-elite. The elite group would like to reassert its identity by discovering something from the tradition and by bringing the traditional elements into a modern world. The non-elite group, on the other hand, would like to modernize itself by incorporating imported elements into its cultural life. I would like to mention two cultural phenomena: a. There are some new buildings in Padang and other towns in Minangkabau with Minangkabau architecture, the very architecture that is disappearing from village life. The new houses in villages are taking after imported architecture. b. The modern dramas by Wisran Hadi are trying to use the elements of randai without losing their identity of being modern dramas. A randai, on the other hand, has elements of modern drama incorporated into its performance (cf. Junus 1981). As a comparison, I would like to mention a tendency, ordinary in Indonesia. A village girl abandons her traditional shampoo as she is now under the influence of a TV advertisement which introduces her to a "modern" (it means better) shampoo. On the contrary, a "modernized" city woman prefers a traditional shampoo (it may be prepared in a modern way) to a modern one. She seems to believe in the traditional wisdom. These two movements are represented in the development of kaba and novel, two genres of different origins.

with the modern world regarded as superior to the
traditional one;

T2 (associated with nN): an anti-climax for T1. There
was a better understanding regarding the modern and
the traditional worlds. Modernization no longer
presented a conflict as village folk did their best
to modernize themselves as a matter of course. At
the same time, there was the drive to "redefine the
traditional value."

The difference between an lN and an nN thereby shows the
cultural movements of two different times. An lN is related
to the pre-war conditions, and an nN to the situation after
1960. It shows two cultural outlooks which are related to
social changes and the political history of the Minangkabau
people.

A literary work expresses the "ideology" of its writer.
Writing from the point of view of a woman, Selasih feels
secure within the traditional world. Her novels express
suspicion of strangers, who are regarded as a threat, ready to
humiliate the protagonist. It is only a traditional family
tie that gives her protection. Yusnani in <u>Pengaruh Keadaan</u>
(Selasih 1937) leads a miserable life among strangers (her
father, her step-mother, and her half-sister) until she is
saved by her brother who acts as her <u>mamak</u>. Thus, Selasih
voices a typical woman's view regarding her traditional world.
Due to differing socio-cultural backgrounds, Hamka and
N. St. Iskandar express different ideologies although they are
somewhat related (cf. Junus 1977). Hamka was to some degree
affiliated with a national movement against Dutch colonialism.
Therefore, in Hamka's novels a western educated man who works
for the Dutch government is not portrayed in a positive light.
Rather, Hamka portrays benevolent, self-made, self-employed
characters independent of the Dutch government. This also
relates to the manner in which Hamka interprets his social-
cultural background. He himself is self-made as well as self-
employed.
Iskandar, on the other hand, had a western education and
works for the Dutch government.
A character in Hamka's novels is not very different from
one in a <u>kaba</u> in that he starts his own business as a
peddler.[11] This relates to the fact that Hamka follows the

---

[11] We have to take a note here that Hamka was also a <u>kaba</u>
"writer": see <u>Kaba Siti Sabariah</u>.

tradition of improving oneself, as advocated in a <u>kaba</u>.

This illustrates the point that we must regard every opinion expressed in a literary work as originating from its writer. Thus, a novelist expresses a different viewpoint from that of a <u>kaba</u> story-teller due to the differences in their socio-cultural backgrounds.

A <u>kaba</u> story-teller has the following socio-cultural backgrounds:

a. He is part of the traditional world in that:
   1. He follows the tradition by composing a <u>kaba</u>;
   2. He is apt to be much involved in village life;
   3. He is attached ideologically to the traditional world which is responsible for his composing a <u>kaba</u>.
b. One need not be educated in the modern way in order to compose a <u>kaba</u>, and so he is apt to be regarded as uneducated.

A novelist, on the other hand, represents a different world. He has the following socio-cultural background:

a. He is no longer a part of the traditional world. He writes a novel, a non-traditional genre. It is in Indonesian Malay rather than in Minangkabau language. He lives in a different world as he is no longer a part of the village life where the traditional system is in operation.
b. He has endured a different socio-cultural process as he has educated himself in the western way. He has a different knowledge system from that of a traditional Minangkabau.

The differences between an 1N and an nk relate to the socio-cultural differences between the authors of the respective genres. However, everything should be taken as "ideology" rather than reality.

An 1N might tell us that the traditional system is no longer operational since it fails to regulate the marriage system. It might be true as far as that novel is concerned, but it is not necessarily a reality in the society. The traditional system is always there, practiced by those in the villages.[12] The situation in a novel is from the point of

---

[12] It also endures change although it may not be so impressive and rather slow. It is less strict now. Before there might

view of an educated Minangkabau rather than that of the Minangkabau society as a whole. A kaba is, on the other hand, related to the world of non-educated Minangkabau, those who are still a part of the traditional village life. Due to those differences, it is very interesting to note the development of each genre.

There is a development from a ck to an nk which is related to the world of non-educated or less educated Minangkabau people. A stranger is no longer the factor responsible for a D as an nk. The E is re-established if the protagonist is successful in becoming a very rich merchant. Additionally, the village is no longer an enclosed society. There is no restriction regarding the marriage partner although the obligation to subscribe to the welfare of matrilineal kin still exists.[13] This development shows how the traditional society has changed its outlook. It is a political as well as a social change.

There is also a development from the eN to the lN and the nN, which is related to the world of educated Minangkabau. There are three steps in its development:

1st step as in an eN: there is a suspicion of strangers although there is also the attempt to incorporate a particular stranger in domestic family life (cf. Junus 1976).

2nd step as in an lN: there is no suspicion of the stranger; rather, he is accepted as an equal. In fact, the traditional system is blamed for every unhappiness.

3rd step as in an nN: there is an attempt at reconciliation with the traditional system. Attachment to a modern value is viewed as resulting from prejudice against the traditional system, propagated by the lN. This attitude is responsible for the disintegration of the family unity and is regarded as immoral. The characters conclude that they have an obligation toward the traditional system as part of

---

have been total rejection of changes, now they are willing to have compromise. They no longer condemn a person who does not follow the traditonal system. A stranger is now acceptable. He is no longer a bad person.

[13] One seems to simply agree to the choice of a spouse made by one's family. Or the family simply accepts one's choice of a spouse. The family cannot express their disagreement as they depend on him.

those they have towards Minangkabau.

A comparison between the development of _kaba_ and novel shows two different cultural movements. One is a movement among the non-educated or non-elite Minangkabau toward modernization and freedom from what are seen as duties without corresponding freedoms. The other is among the elite, educated Minangkabau, who would like to return to the traditional system, or at least re-evaluate it in a more positive light.

In order to see a complete picture of this literature, we must consider the problem of its intended audience.

A _kaba_ is in Minangkabau language, and is told orally by a story-teller or in a _randai_ performance. This fact limits its audience to those who understand the language. Also, this form does not appeal to every Minangkabau. The audience is more or less limited to:

a.   Those who are not educated or whose education is limited. This is a logical consequence of the _kaba_ being part of the village life in which those who have left the village to become educated are no longer involved.
b.   Those who have leisure time; people who do not have to attend to family business in the evening, since they are not engaged in domestic life.
c.   A group of young people who may be called _parewa_. They have the following characteristics:
1.   They have yet to decide whether they will become farmers or merchants.
2.   Therefore, they simply enjoy life without any consideration regarding the future. They request money from their mothers without any consideration of how this money is to be raised. This may result in selling the family inheritance until nothing is left for their livelihood.
3.   They spend their time chatting, playing, and gambling, rather than engaging in domestic life.

This explains why a _kaba_ relates a story of how a _parewa_ becomes a successful businessman. It expresses to the youth the Minangkabau "ideology," that duties are more important than rights, as well as the necessity of fulfilling obligations toward mothers, sisters, and _kemenakans_, providing them with material welfare. The _kaba_ attempts to teach the _parewa_ their right to the family property and to do their duty.

A novel is, on the other hand, intended for a different

audience.   Since it is written in Indonesian Malay, the
audience is not limited to Minangkabau people. As a matter of
fact, only a fraction of the Minangkabau people would be able
to read this language; that is, the educated.   This education
means the reader is aware of the existence of another world
which he might prefer to his own tradition. The novel orients
such a reader to a different world, and therefore is a "rite
of modernization," to borrow the term used by James L. Peacock
(1968). As such, it may be said that the novel discredits the
traditional Minangkabau systems or the practice within a Minangkabau family life.[14]

     To its non-Minangkabau audience, the novel is an apology
for the strangeness of the Minangkabau people in dealing with
foreigners. It explains that this attitude relates to their
social-cultural origin against which they are now rebelling.
It is a manifesto for the emergence of a new breed of Minangkabau, the educated ones.   There is a need for such an
apology, as they are now ready to integrate with people of
different origins.[15] The novel shows, then, an openness and

---

[14] In Kalau Tak Untung, one's dependence on his/her traditional family on the one hand and his/her rebellion towards the
practices within the society on the other develops into a dilemma. Due to his discontent regarding his family's decision
barring him from marrying a degraded (materially) Rasmani and
forcing him to marry his mother's brother's daughter, Masrul
chose to marry a "stranger." His marriage was a failure. He
also failed to return to Rasmani, who died waiting for Masrul's proposal. Masrul was not sure whether he should propose
to Rasmani or not for several reasons:
a. she had been rejected by his family before due to her
    poverty;
b. it was no longer a pure love since he already had a wife
    married by "love";
c. he was not sure whether Rasmani was willing to be his "se-
    cond" wife.
The situations were really a dilemma for Masrul.
[15] The Minangkabau people, or the novelists of Minangkabau
origin, were the first to realize it. They had already
realized it in the 20's. Other people were rather late to
realize it; they did so in the 70's. There was a protest a-
gainst the ethnocentricity of Batak people (Marianne Katoppo
1979) and the Toraja people (Ris Prasetyo 1979) expressed by
outsiders. The protest against the Batak preference for marrying within the traditional circle was also mentioned by
Ashadi Siregar (1975). Putuwijaya also expressed his protest

willingness to be part of modern cosmopolitan society.[16]

To summarize, the difference between the intended audience of a <u>kaba</u> and that of a novel again shows the existence of two different worlds, the traditional and the modern. A <u>kaba</u> indoctrinates the reader as to how one should act in order to preserve the traditional lifestyle. However, it also shows that the system is not rigid, but rather is capable of adapting to change. Therefore, the <u>kaba</u> is not completely excluded from the wave of modernization.

A novel, on the other hand, teaches how one should behave in a modernized society. Novels have gone to the extent of condemning the traditional values since as part of an undesirable lifestyle, this is a rebellion against the traditional system, especially as it regards choosing a marriage partner. Such novels express the desire for freedom (cf. Junus 1974). However, more recently there has been a revival of traditional values. The new novels express the view that the traditional world should be seen as rational, without the prejudice which was expressed in the previous ones.

This study shows us a history of politics and social change in Minangkabau society such as that with which a literary source might provide us, which may be compared with information from other sources.

---

against the Balinese tradition (1972) but it had nothing to do with the dealing with an outsider. However, he did realize that it prevented him from fully integrating himself into a non-traditional life (Putuwijaya 1973).
[16] It can be seen in the development from an eN to lN and nN since they show three steps of development.

APPENDIX

A tentative list of kabas and novels, not exhaustive:

A. CLASSICAL KABAS

Kaba si Ali Amat (van Ophuijsen), Leiden: Trap, 1895.

Anggun nan Tugga Magek Jabang dengan Puti Gondoriah Ambas
   Mahkota & A. Damhoeri), Bukit Tinggi: Pustaka Indonesia,
   1966 (2nd ed).

Bujang Paman (St. Pangaduan & Dj.M.St. Perpatih), Bukit
   Tinggi: Banjanus, 1963 (7th ed).

Cinduo Mato dan Bundo Kandueng (Sj. St. R. Endah), Bukit
   Tinggi: Pustuka Indonesia, 1961(?) (3rd ed.).

Si Gadih Ranti dengan si Bunjang Saman (Sj. St. Radjo Endah),
   Bukit Tinggi: Pustaka Indonesia, 1961 (5th ed.).

Puti Gondoriah (Sj. St. Radjo Endah), Bukit Tinggi: Pustaka
   Indonesia, (5th ed.).

Intan Pengirieng dan Buyueng Pakue (A.M.A. Mudo & Dj.M.St.
   Perpatih), Bukit Tinggi: Tsamaratulichwan, 1962 (5th ed.).

Kambang Luari (St. Pangaduan, St. Mantari, Ahmad Chatib & Dj.
   M. St. Perpatih), Bukit Tinggi: Tsamaratulichwan, 1961 (6th
   ed.).

Sutan Lembak Tuah dengan Siti Rabiatun (Sj. St. R. Endah),
   Bukit Tinggi: Pustaka Indonesia, 1961 (2nd ed.).

Malin Deman dengan Puti Bungsu (Dj.M.St. Perpatih), Bukit
   Tinggi: Bajanus, 1965.

Mamak si Hetong (van Ophuijsen), Leiden: Trap, 1892.

Magek Manandin (St. Pangaduan & Dj. M. St. Perpatih), Bukit
   Tinggi, Tsamaratulichwan, 1961 (11th ed.).

Sutan Manangkerang (van den Toorn), BKI, 103 deel, 1885.

Manju Ari (van den Toorn), VBG XLV, afl. 1, 1891.

Murai Batu (van Hasselt) dalam De Talen en Letterkunde van

Midden Sumatra, Leiden: Brill, 1881.

Puti Nilam Cayo dengan Dang Tuangku Gombang Alam (Sj. Radjo Endah), Bukit Tinggi: Pustaka Indonesia, 1961 (2nd ed.).

Si Rambun Jalue (Hamerster), Jakarta: Balai Pustaka, 1920.

Rambun Pamenan (Sutan Mankudun & Iljas Sutan Pangaduan), Bukit Tinggi: Tsamaratulichwan, 1961.

Sabai nan Aluih (M. Rasjid Manggis Dt. Radjo Panghoeloe), Bukit Tinggi: Arga, 1964.

Puti Sari Bunian dengan Tuangku Sutan Duano (Sj. Bt. R. Endah), Bukit Tinggi: Tsamaratulichwan, 1961 (8th ed.).

Mara Sudin dengan Siti Salamah (Sj. St. R. Endah), Bukit Tinggi: Pustaka Panorama, 1955.

Siti Syamsiah (Sj. St. Radjo Endah), Bukit Tinggi: Indah , 1961 (4th ed.).

Manuscripts at the Library of the University of Leiden:

Bujang Muhamad Kadin (MS. OR. 5975)

Gombang Patuanan (MS. OR. 6084/5972; 6077B)

Liwang Duwani (MS. OR. 5973)

Sutan Palembang (OR. 12.162, Mal. 6788, Oph. 40)

Sarek Mulie (MS. OR. 6074A)

si Tabuang (MS. OR. 6084)

Talipuek Layue (MS. OR. 6078B)

B. NON CLASSICAL KABAS

Amai Cilako (Sj. St. R. Endah), Bukit Tinggi: Indah, 1961 (3rd ed.).

Siti Baheram (Sj. St. R. Endah & Irsda Muljana), Bukit Tinggi: Arga, 1964.

Bujang Parisau (Sj. St. R. Endah), Bukit Tinggi: Indah, 1962.

<u>Sutan Jainun</u> (Sj. St. R. Endah), Bukit Tinggi: Indah, 1961.

<u>Siti Kalasun</u> (Sj. St. R. Endah), Bukit Tinggi: Pustaka
  Indonesia, 1962 (2nd ed.).

<u>Sutan Lanjungan</u> (Bahar Dt. Nagari Bass), Payakumbuh: Eleonara,
  1964 (2 vols.).

<u>Siti Mariam</u> (A St. Diandjung & A. D. Adjung), Bukit Tinggi:
  Indah (2 vols.).

<u>Si Marantang</u> (Sj. St. R. Endah, A. St. Diandjung & A. St.
  Batuah nan Tinggi), Bukit Tinggi: Indah, 1966.

<u>Siti Nuriyah dengan Sutan Amiruddin</u> (Sj. St. R. Endah), Bukit
  Tinggi: Pustaka Indonesia, 1961 (2nd ed.). [Can be
  regarded as a classical <u>kaba</u> as well.]

<u>Siti Nurlela</u> (Sj. St. R. Endah), Bukit Tinggi: Indah, 1961
  (3rd ed.).

<u>Rancak Di Labuh</u> (Dt. Paduko Alam [di Indonesiakan oleh A. R.
  Yogi]), Bukit Tinggi: Fa. H.S.M. Sulaiman, 1955.

<u>Reno Gadih</u> (Sj. St. R. Endah), Bukit Tinggi: Indah, 1961.

<u>Si Sabariah</u> (Dt. Indomo), Bukit Tinggi: Tsamaratulichwan, 1957
  (4th ed.).

<u>Talipuek Layue</u> (Sj. St. R. Endah), Bukit Tinggi: Indah, 1962.

<u>Siti Teladan</u> (Sj. St. R. Endah), Bukit Tinggi: Pustaka
  Indonesia, 1962 (2nd ed.).

C. Early Novels

Iskandar, Nur St. (1932) <u>Hulubalang Raja</u>, Jakarta: Balai
  Pustaka.

Muis, Abdul (1928) <u>Salah Asuhan</u>, Jakarta: Balai Pustaka.

Rusli, Marah (1922) <u>Siti Nurbaya</u>, Jakarta: Balai Pustaka.

Selasih (1933) <u>Kalau Tak Untung</u>, Jakarta: Balai Pustaka.

Selasih (1937) <u>Pengaruh Keadaan</u>, Jakarta: Balai Pustaka.

Tulis St. Sati (1928) <u>Sengasara Membawa Nikmat</u>, Jakarta: Balai

Pustaka.

D. Later Novels

Abbas Pamuncak n.s. (1927) _Pertemuan_, Jakarta: Balai Pustaka (2 novels).

Enri M. (1940) _Karena Anak Kadung_, Jakarta: Balai Pustaka.

Harjosumarto, S. & Aman Dt. Majo Indo (1932) _Rusmala Dewi_, Jakarta: Balai Pustaka.

Iskandar, N. St. (1928) _Salah Pilih_, Jakarta: Balai Pustaka.

Iskandar, N. St. (1932) _Karena Mentua_, Jakarta: Balai Pustaka.

Tulis St. Sati (1932) _Memutuskan Pertalian_, Jakarta: Balai Pustaka.

E. New Novels

Datuk Batuah Nurdin Yacub (1967) _Panggilan Tanah Kelahiran_, Jakarta: Balai Pustaka.

Iljas, ny. Johanisoen (1964) _Anggia Murni_, Jakarta: Balai Pustaka.

Navis, A.A. (1967) _Kemarau_, Bukit Tinggi: Nusantara.

Navis, A.A. (1970) _Saraswati, si gadis dalam sunyi_, Jakarta: Pradnyaparamita.

Navis, A.A. (1977) "Kawin," _Album Cerpen Femina_ 3.

<u>**PART III: POLITICS AND ECONOMICS IN HISTORICAL PERSPECTIVE**</u>

ECONOMIC CONSTRAINTS, SOCIAL CHANGE,
AND THE COMMUNIST UPRISING IN WEST SUMATRA (1926-1927):
A CRITICAL REVIEW OF B. J. O. SCHRIEKE'S WEST COAST REPORT

Akira Oki
Nagoya Shoka Daigku

Introduction

In the introduction to his book written in 1974, entitled Peasants, Politics, and Revolution, J. S. Migdal puts
the question: "Why have politics and revolution often been
analyzed outside the context of the specific pressures peasants face in their relations with other classes?" As one of
the reasons for this, he explains:

First has been the eagerness of Western social scientists to dismiss Marx. This has led them to relegate
the role of economic constraints and class pressures to
a secondary place in favor of an approach emphasizing
the importance of culture, values, and norms. (Migdal
1974:22)

This attitude is particularly conspicuous in America,
where, as noted by D. K. Emmerson, Marxism is virtually "illegitimate," and where the political and cultural approaches are
predominant in the study of the Southeast Asian history
(1980:62-64). Second, Migdal points out that in the application of anthropological methods all too little effort has been
made to analyze single peasant villages in terms of the economic pressures generated by larger international and national
forces (1974:23). Marxist or not, we cannot deny the general
truth of Migdal's observations.

Migdal's argument also applies to previous studies of
the communist uprising in West Sumatra in 1926-1927. The
situation there is rather ironic because economic pressures
and constraints have not been studied seriously in spite of
the fact that the uprising was strongly inspired by Marxist
ideas including "impoverishment." There are real reasons why
most studies of the uprising have so far focused not on
economic, but heavily on political aspects such as details of
the events, activities of political organizations and ideologies (see, for example, Blumberger 1931:Ch.7; McVey 1965;

Mintz 1959:171-239). Second, it erupted under the leadership of the Partai Komunis Indonesia (Indonesian Communist Party) as early as 1926-27. Third, it was the first anti-Dutch revolt in the colonial era which encompassed several regions. Finally, the uprising occurred in the midst of an export boom which may have diverted scholars from the analysis of economic constraints. In short, the uprising appears to be an epoch-making political event in Indonesian history in the eyes of scholars. However, political aspects were not the whole story of the uprising. As with any other historical event, it involved interactions of social, cultural, and economic aspects.

When we try to find immediate causes of the uprising from a short-term viewpoint, ideologies and activities of eminent leaders and political organizations became important objects of analysis, which have been amply studied. However, it is difficult to believe that such an epoch-making uprising happened only as a result of ideologies.[1] The primary purpose of this paper is directed not toward how communist ideas permeated among the population, or how the leaders organized the revolt, but toward why the ideologies and the leaders could be accepted by the population in terms of their socio-economic backgrounds, paying due attention to economic constraints, particularly poverty. Although the number of those who actually participated in the uprising was small in comparison with the total population, we can expect that the uprising reflected wide-spread dissatisfaction among the population. This socio-economic approach may enable us to evaluate the meaning of the uprising in the context of a long-term social change of the Minangkabau society in general. I do not claim that this paper is the first to apply the socio-economic approach. On the contrary, B. J. O. Schrieke has already done admirable work in the West Coast Report (Schrieke et al. 1928, Part I, Sociological Section; see Schrieke 1955), which is in fact the only study in this field. Before going into details of the Report, a brief description is given below.

An attempt to disseminate Marxist ideas in West Sumatra was made by the PKI in 1920, the same year as the party was formed. A male graduate of a school in Singapore was sent to West Sumatra to function as a link between Batavia (Jakarta) and West Sumatra (IPO 1925a; Mailrapport 1926a). The influence of the party was strengthened by instigating protest

---

[1] I agree with Ogburn, who criticized the traditional view which attributed much importance to the great individual in all political and social forces. See the section on "The Great Man versus Social Forces," in Ogburn 1964.

meetings against the Dutch plan of introducing a land tax system into this region at the end of 1922 and early 1923 (Mailrapport 1924). From this time onwards, the party succeeded in rapidly establishing branches and other connected organizations such as Sarekat Hitam (Black Association) and Sarekat Rakyat (People's Association) (Mailrapport 1926b, 1927c). By the beginning of 1925, Suliki, one of the communist centers in West Sumatra, was proudly called a "small soviet" by communists and sympathizers (IPO 1926a). It was a time when, reportedly, even children in the countryside were singing the "International" (Mailrapport 1926b).

Reaction to the rapid development of the communist movement came from the Dutch colonial government and conservative adat (customary law) chiefs, most importantly, penghulus (chiefs of matrilineages). Police arrested communists or supposed communists extensively in proportion to the development of the movement (IPO 1925b). Some 430 persons had been detained in West Sumatra by September 1925. A Minangkabau newspaper accused the government of arresting people on the basis of information given by those who knew nothing of communism (IPO 1926d). In the face of the spread of communist influence, conservative penghulus felt that their authority was threatened. The most common reaction of these penghulus was to denounce the Marxist idea as contradicting both adat and Islam. Many penghulus organized meetings to divert the villagers from the communists, with some success (IPO 1926e). By the end of 1925, the rumor of a communist revolt had spread throughout West Sumatra. In the following year, the communists and their sympathizers began to assault village heads and native and Dutch officials, particularly in Padang Panjang, Pariaman, Alahan Panjang, Silungkang, Sawah Lunto, and Sijungjung (Mailrapport 1927a). Scattered uprisings broke out in Batavia and the residence of Banten in West Java in December 1926, although Tan Malaka was opposed to these uprisings. In West Sumatra, revolts were attempted only on the eve of New Year's Day, most vehemently in the Sawah Lunto region, including Silungkang (for description of the uprising, see again Blumberger:Ch.7; McVey 1965; Mintz 1959:171-239).

A. Schrieke's Methodology: Socio-Economic Analysis

Shortly after its suppression, a committee was formed to investigate the uprising by order of the Governor General. Schrieke was an important member of the committee in charge of West Sumatra. This committee completed its four-part report in 1928: Part I, the Political Section and Sociological Section; Part II, Economic Conditions of the People and the Tax

Burden; Part III, Administration; and Part IV, Summary. Schrieke was directly involved in writing Parts I, III, and IV, but not Part II.[2] Of these, Part II is different in nature from the other parts insofar as it is a collection of data on taxes and income of the population rather than an analysis or evaluation of the uprising. What is referred to as "Schrieke's West Coast Report" in this paper denotes Part I, the Sociological Section, unless otherwise indicated. It is of note that Schrieke was not involved in writing Part II (which was written by Fievez de Malines van Ginkel), the economic section, which may be relevant to his weakness in the analysis of economic circumstances.

Schrieke seems to regard the fundamental background of the uprising to be the fact that the penetration of a monetarized economy, especially at the turn of the 20th century, had been eroding the old nagari (village) system which, in turn, had produced wide-spread social instability. I agree with the basic lines of this viewpoint. According to his analysis, before this erosion began, Minangkabau was formed out of many villages called nagaris which can be considered as "small territorial republics" (territoriale republiekjes), i.e. village communities with a high degree of autonomy. The village administration in the old nagari was carried out by the village adat council, a collective body of the adat chiefs, notably the penghulus. In the social sphere, the village community was crystallized around the strong cohesion of matrilineal families. The village economy was seen as a "closed production economy" (de gesloten productenhuishouding) based on the communal ownership of hereditary landed property by the matrilineally extended family, or simply family land, most importantly irrigated rice fields or sawahs (Schrieke 1955:95–96). In short, Schrieke defined the traditional Minangkabau society as having consisted of the nagaris, which were autonomous and sustained by a self-sufficient economy, based on rice cultivation in the sawahs of family land. Thus, Schrieke regarded the change of the old village system as a change in Minangkabau society in general.

---

[2] The original titles for the Parts are: Deel I, Politiek Gedeelte, Algemeene Richtlijnen voor de Toekomst [see English translations in Benda and McVey 1960, the Political Section; Schrieke 1955:83–166, the Sociological Section]; Deel II, De Economische Toestand en de Belastingdruk met betreeking to de Inlandsche Bevolking van Sumtara's Westkust, written by Fievez de Malines van Ginkel; Deel III, Bestuur en Aanverwante Aangelegenheden; and Part IV, Samenvatting.

Since all the aspects of the village community are inter-dependent, a change in any aspect would, in theory, cause a change of the village structure and thus of the Minangkabau society as a whole. However, Schrieke's analysis proceeds in the following order: (1) the penetration of a monetary economy beginning with the introduction of money taxes (income tax and slaughter tax) in 1908; (2) the expansion of export crop cultivation stimulated by the increased demand for tropical products from Europe; (3) the change in the land system; (4) the development of individualism; and (5) the relaxation of the old village order, as exemplified by the weakening of the authority of the penghulus. We should not miss the point that Schrieke described Minangkabau social change in this specific order. For the changes from (1) to (3) are arranged neither by a time sequence per se nor at random, but rather by the logic of Schrieke's theory. In other words, in the chain of causal relationships of social change, Schrieke reckoned the change in economy to be the initial cause which further generated social, political, and cultural changes. In this sense the introduction of monetary taxation in 1908 is viewed as a significant turning point, not only in terms of economic change, but also for social change in general. This does not mean that in Schrieke's view the West Sumatran economy was entirely a "closed production economy" before 1908, though Schrieke did not elaborate this point. Even during the Cultivation System of coffee (1847-1908) the monetary economy was slowly penetrating into the West Sumatran economy and to that extent social change was also taking place. We will come back to this point later in more detail. Nevertheless, it would be reasonable to view the year 1908 as a turning point of social change in West Sumatra.

After effects of the five points mentioned above had been examined, Schrieke argued that the nagari, the basic unit of Minangkabau, in the 1920's was in a transitional stage of change from a closed society to an open society where the new and the old coexisted but without achieving harmony. This transitional stage was creating a variety of grievances among the population: for some, changes were too fast, and for others they were too slow. For instance, penghulus were dissatisfied with their ever-diminishing authority; educated young people were frustrated because they were not being given satisfactory positions within the framework of the adat system in the village, as they thought they were superior to the penghulus intellectually; Islamic leaders were dissatisfied with the oppression of the colonial government; the "middle-class" people were irritated because they were not being given social status corresponding to their economic strength; and the masses (orang banyak) were dissatisfied with taxes (Schrieke 1955:126, 130-134, 160-161). The PKI could draw support from the population by ascribing the source of all these grievances to Dutch colonial rule and by presenting the symbolic magical word, <u>kemerdekaan</u> (freedom).[3]

Schrieke may be correct in relating the fundamental causes of the uprising to the unstable situation of a society in transition. Since so many historical writings on political events have lacked such a perspective as Schrieke's, it is important to stress its value as a much needed putting of local and political events into the broader context of socio-economic change.[4] Viewed carefully, however, there are points in Schrieke's argument which call for reassessment. First, the importance of differing economic circumstances in various parts of West Sumatra is ignored when, in fact, these were closely related to the uprising. Second, widening inequities in the distribution of wealth between the rich and the poor are overlooked. Third, the resentment of the population against taxation is viewed as a psychological phenomenon rather than as a serious expression of the actual weight of the tax burden, particularly on the poor. Fourth, the change in the land ownership system is overestimated either through the use of incorrect data or by making wrong inferences, and consequently the extent of social change is somewhat exaggerated. Considering the fact that the land system was one of the most important pillers of the social system, the fourth point constitutes a serious weakness in Schrieke's argument. I consider the correction of these points very important because Schrieke's account had the effect of bringing some confusion into later Minangkabau studies (see the concluding section of this paper). In the following paragraphs we will first scrutinize the above four points, and then discuss the relationship between socio-economic change and the uprising.

1. The Development of Differing Economic Circumstances

The West Sumatran economy had become dynamically involved in international trade since the end of the 18th century, stimulated by the opening of Panang in 1786 and of Singapore in 1819, and by the appearance at the end of the 19th century of American ships mainly in search of coffee, the cultivation

---

[3] Schrieke 1955:161; in the original, the spelling is "kemerdikaan" rather than "kemerdekaan."
[4] Quite contrary to Winus' assertion, the socio-economic approach has been adopted little in Southeast Asian studies. For his argument, see Winus 1980.

of which was then rapidly expanding in hilly regions of the highlands.[5] However, the development of a commercial economy was seriously hampered by disturbances due to the Islamic reformist movement, the padri war (1803-1837) and Dutch military intervention in the war. After bringing the war to a conclusion, the Dutch introduced the Cultivation System in 1847 which continued until 1908.

Under the Cultivation System, peasants had to set up coffee gardens and deliver their produce to the Dutch at low fixed prices. Together with the ban on the export of rice and the closing of the trade route to the east (both of which commenced in the mid-19th century), the Cultivation System considerably impeded the development of free economic activity (Schrieke 1955:96-97). However, although Schrieke overlooks it, the market economy was in fact making some progress even before 1908. For instance, the trade with the east coast of Sumatra was continuing via riverways in spite of Dutch intervention.[6] The Cultivation System certainly suppressed free economic activity on the one hand, but it also played the role of sowing the seed of economic evolution on the other. It had the effect of spreading coffee cultivation whereby the peasants became accustomed to the cultivation of export crops in general towards the end of the 19th century. Furthermore, the peasants came to earn cash income no matter how low the prices at which they had to deliver their produce of coffee.

There is another unmistakably significant effect of the Cultivation System. Since the System was more intensively applied to hilly villages more suitable for coffee cultivation than to plains villages where rice cultivation was still the major economic activity, differing economic circumstances appeared within West Sumatra.[7] This difference was widened after the abolition of the System in 1908 as peasants became free to cultivate any crop they wanted.

With the introduction of monetary taxes in March 1908 (initially a two per cent income tax on adult men and slaughter taxes) in addition to the existing corvée labor, people were driven to earn cash income. Forced by the payment of taxes and stimulated by the increased demand for tropical products in the international market, the production of export

---

[5] The economic circumstances at that time are admirably described by Christine Dobbin 1977.
[6] See Lulofs 1904. The West Sumatran coffee was exported mainly via the Kampar River under the name of "Kampar Coffee."
[7] The most detailed account of these circumstances can be found in Graves 1971.

crops (coffee, gambier or _gambir_, coconuts, rubber) kept expanding towards the year of the uprising, with a peak of
expansion in 1925. Although it is not our purpose here to
explain why and how the expansion of the export crop production was made possible, three points deserve special attention. First, there were land reserves in West Sumatra, particularly in outlying regions of the highlands, enough to
expand export crops without sacrificing food production.
Second, the rapid spread of village and local credit institutions in the 1910's facilitated the provision of necessary
capital. Third, the expansion of export crop cultivation in
West Sumatra was chiefly achieved by small holdings of Minangkabau peasants instead of European estates. There even emerged enterprises set up entirely by Minangkabaus for export
crops, obtaining credit from governmental credit institutions,
employing laborers and issuing shares. The West Sumatran
economy was changing in the direction of capitalism (Oki
1977:Ch.2).

The evolution of the West Sumatran economy occurred
unevenly in various parts of the region and among various
strata of the society. As shown on Map 1 (page 215), the
centers of export crop cultivation were located in outlying
regions both of the highlands and lowlands, surrounding the
rice producing core uplands or _darat_. Schrieke vividly
described the successful development of export crop cultivation for each case, but he failed to visualize the loca-
tional and ecological settings of the centers.

Like the regional differences in the crops cultivated,
there was also a varying degree of monetarization in West
Sumatra. Although comprehensive data are not available, the
sample figures in Table 1 (page 216) may give a rough idea of
this by the time of the uprising. The proportion of cash
income to total income varied from the highest 99.86% of
Padang to the lowest 66.4% of Alahan Panjang, an area of high
altitude and one of the most economically backward. It is of
interest that the proportion of Grobogan district in Central
Java, poor but close to the big commercial center of Semarang,
was only 56% at the time (Schrieke et al. 1928 Deel II:19,
note 1), thus much lower than that of Alahan Panjang. This
suggests that a monetary economy penetrated more deeply in
West Sumatra even in economically backward areas.

Map 1: The Major Export-Crop Growing Regions in West Sumatra

Siak River

Bangkinang
(rubber)

Talu
(coffee,rubber)

Upper Kampar
(gambier)

Lubuk Sikaping
(coffee,rubber)

Kampar River

Eastern Fringe
Regions (rubber)

Pariaman (coconuts)

Kuantan-Indragiri
River

Batang Hari
River

Muara Labuh
(coffee,rubber)

Painan-
Balaisalasa
(coffee,rubber)

Indrapura-Tapan
(coffee,rubber,
coconuts)

Korinci
(coffee)

Export Crop Cultivation Centers

Rice Cultivating Core Uplands (darat)

Barisan Mountain Range

Table 1
The Proportion of Cash Income to Total Income (percent): 1926

Towns and Surroundings			Rural Areas	
1a. Padang*	(town)	99.86	4. Maninjau*	80.37
1b. "	(surroundings)	75.74	5. Lubuk Sikaping*	85.87
2a. Pariaman*	(town)	99.80	6. Suliki*	71.05
2b. "	(surroundings)	92.64	7. Alahan Panjang*	66.64
3. Old Agam*		85.52	8. Muara Labuh*	76.62
			9. Korninci*	75.74

Source: Schrieke et al. 1928 Deel II: blz.19.
*Sub-division (Onderafdeling)

2. The Underestimation of Widening Inequities

Most scholars have tended to underestimate the relationship between poverty and the communist revolt. Schrieke
remarked that the ordinary members of the movement were recruited from the poorest strata of the peasant population in
the over-populated areas (such as Pariaman, Old Agam) and the
poorest, economically most backward districts (Sawah Lunto
Sub-Division, the land east of Lake Singkarak) (Schrieke
1955:133). However, in the final Part of the West Coast
Report, he, as one of its writers, remarked that the economic
circumstances of West Sumatra were favorable and that poverty
did not constitute an important factor (Schrieke et al. 1928
Deel IV:92). H. J. Benda and R. McVey, the co-translators of
the West Coast Report (Part I, Political Section) deny the
relationship more explicitly:

> The revolts were certainly not bred in misery among
> poverty-stricken or exploited peasants and laborers
> living under the yoke of Western capitalism. Tenancy,
> population pressure and the proletarianization of coolie
> labor—generally the most common causes of agrarian un-
> rest in Asia—were absent in both areas (Banten and West
> Sumatra) that nurtured the insurrections. (Benda and
> McVey 1960:xx)

It is not surprising that the problem of poverty has
been ignored, because the uprising occurred in the midst of an
export boom in West Sumatra which was a relatively wealthy

part of Indonesia at that time. This seeming paradox can be solved only when we consider widening inequities among the population in the wake of the spread of monetary economy.

<u>Table 2</u>
Economic Stratification: Annual Income Per Adult Male in 1926 (f.=Guilder)

=Year=	Below f.300	f.300– f.600	f.600– f.1,000	f.1,000– f.2,400	Above f.2,400
1908	98.45%	1.05%	0.50%	none	none
	342,542	3,647	1,746	none	none
1917	97.45%	2.21%	0.26%	0.07%	0.01%
	303,372	6,891	807	219	36
1926	72.65%	22.12%	3.64%	1.41%	0.18%
	264,094	80,409	13,294	5,119	661

Source: Schrieke et al. 1928 Deel II:38
Note: The upper figure indicates the percentage, and the lower figure shows the actual number of taxpayers for each year.

Table 2 (above) clearly shows increasing inequities in the distribution of income in West Sumatra between 1908 and 1926. When the monetary taxation was introduced in 1908, the majority (98.45%) belonged to the low income group (less than f.300).[8] While the proportion of the low income group had diminished to about 75% by 1926, the income groups between f.300 and f.1,000—"middle class" according to the West Sumatran standard—had increased from 1.55% in 1908 to 25.76% by 1926.   Furthermore, of the rich groups earning more than f.1,000 none existed in 1908, but by 1926 the percentage 1.59%.   Here we cannot miss the irrevocable trend towards economic stratification in the relatively homogeneous Minangkabau society. During this period, when there were people who were improving their economic position on the one hand, a large proportion of people remained low income earners. The

---

[8] The annual income of f.300 by an adult man, with an average of four dependents, was just sufficient for a livelihood. However, many of the income group below f.300 seemed to have incomes around f.120, which was sufficient only for food.

latter may have felt their living more difficult than before due to tax payments, the infiltration of imported commodities into daily life, and their relatively worse off position.

In addition to the economic stratification discussed above, regional inequities of income also advanced between 1908 and 1926. Table 3 (page 219) shows regional differences in per-capita income, dividing West Sumatra into six categories. Category I included only the Muara Labuh sub-division (onderafdeling), and Category II, only the Korinci subdivision. These two categories represented the most prosperous areas with an extensive export crop cultivation as well as substantial land for rice cultivation. Among Category III were the big commercial centers of the highlands, their surroundings, and the prosperous areas engaged in export crop growing and transit trade, both in the highlands and the lowlands. The areas in Category IV were medium in terms of per-capita income, comprising local commercial centers (except Padang, the capital of West Sumatra) and outlying regions of export growing in the highlands. Categories V and VI, comprising about 37% of the total population (Schrieke et al. 1928 Deel II:12, 166, 178), can be characterized as the poor areas left behind by the benefits of monetary economy, because the ecological and geographical settings were not favorable either for rice or export-crop cultivation, and because the opportunities for non-agricultural activities (commerce, wage labor, and other industries) were limited.[9] It must be stressed here that poor regions often became the centers for communist activities (see again Table 3, page 219).

3. The Underestimation of the Tax Burden

In Part IV of the West Coast Report, Schrieke, together with other co-authors, made three conclusions on the taxation issue: (1) the tax burden in West Sumatra was quite light; (2) the family relationships of Minangkabau society served to promote a relatively equal sharing of the burden; (3) taxation was not an especially sensitive issue in the uprising (Schrieke et al. 1928 Deel IV:92). Considering the strong cohesion of the extended family system in West Sumatra, the

---

[9] Detailed names of places included in the respective categories are given in Schrieke et al. 1928 Deel II:152-169.

Table 3
Regional Differences in the Average Per-Capita Annual Income

Categories	Ave. Annual Per-Capita Income	Sources of Income (percent)		
		Food	Export & Cash Crops	Others
I	f.167.33	23.78	29.35	48.67
II	f.116.01	54.84	36.48	8.68
III*	f.114.47			
a.		17.40	30.60	51.90
b		26.46	5.19	68.98
IV*	f. 82.00			
c.		25.03	5.99	68.35
d.		13.24	19.18	67.58
V*	f. 55.50			
e.		53.24	7.35	39.41
f.		43.63	16.42	39.95
VI*	f. 39.55			
g.		70.95	2.65	26.40
h.		84.25	11.45	4.30

Source: Schrieke et al. 1928 Deel II:17, 151-169

*As the aggregate figures of percentages of the constituent income sources are not available, figures are given for certain places in respective categories quoted in Westkust Rapport (pp.151-169): a.(southern part of Lubuk Sikaping sub-district--onderdistrict--); b.(The Old Agam sub-division-onderafdeling--except the nagari (VII Lurah); c.(relatively wealthy 9 villages in the Maninjau sub-division);d.(the Rao sub-district); e.(relatively wealthy 9 flat villages in the Suliki subdivision); f.(wealthy 7 villages in the Alahan Panjang subdivision); g.(the Alahan Panjang sub-division excluding the villages in f.); h(the poorest in the Suliki sub-division).

second point might be, in theory, possible, though no evidence to support it is presented in any part of the Report. In any case, points (1) and (3) are unacceptable. We will examine these two points below in the process of examining the ways in which communist influence penetrated into West Sumatra, and the tax burden itself.

After the violent anti-tax rebellion in 1908 (Oki 1977:68-82), there were no serious revolts relating to taxation until 1914 when a revolt was planned by Islamic leaders, three of whom had been detained in connection with the 1908 rebellion and released by 1912. Although the attempted revolt was abortive, it is of note that the rebel leaders were able to recruit followers by agitating about the rise of taxes (Mailrapport 1914). As predicted by the leaders, the income tax doubled from 2 to 4 percent in 1915 (Staatsblad 1914 no.132, 1915 no.190,191). The population was stirred up by the rise in the taxation rate because it occurred when the economy was suddenly struck by the recession caused by World War I.

In addition, the Nagari Ordinance, enacted in 1915, converted such customary dues collected by the _nagari_ (e.g. _serayo_ or occasional labor service, and _urang iyurang_ or occasional money contributions) into _de facto_ regular government taxes, which also evoked wide-spread dissatisfaction among the population (Oki 1977:82-91). Moreover, we must remember that the communists succeeded in drawing the support of the population by criticizing the Dutch plan of introducing the land tax system into West Sumatra in 1922 and 1923 as mentioned above.

Taxation evoked social unrest in many other ways. The Dutch severly punished those who did not pay taxes. Those convicted had to collect gravel for road construction and be watched doing so by fellow villagers. Both those being punished and those watching felt the treatment humiliating. As a result, resentment against taxation and the Dutch tended to become stronger among poor people and in poor regions, which had a greater proportion of arrears than other areas (Mailrapport 1927d). The taxpayers felt it unjust also that the village head and all native officials were exempt from tax and corvee, although most of them were often wealthier than the average taxpayers.[10] The arrogant attitude of the district

---

[10] Around 1926, 39% of village heads had incomes above f.600, while only 5% of non-_penghulus_ earned more than f.600 per year (Schrieke et al. 1928 Deel II:47, 117).

head at the time of tax collection further aggravated the hostility of the villagers. The hostility was stronger when a district head knew nothing about the _adat_ of the district of which he was in charge, and when the inhabitants regarded him as having no sympathy with them. Indeed, the position of the district head came to be taken more and more by the educated rather than by one of the chiefs of the home district.[11] When arresting those in arrears, Dutch and native officials often regarded the offenders as "red." As noted by a Minangkabau official and Indonesian newspapers, those arrested and punished gradually became sympathetic to communists (Mailrapport 1926a; IPO 1926b, 1926c). The foregoing may be enough to show how closely the taxation issue was related to the expansion of communist influence, particularly among poor people.

Now we need to look into the actual burden of taxation, taking here only the direct money tax (i.e. income tax) as an example; however, we should not forget that the population was also burdened with other taxes including a direct tax in labor (i.e., corvée) or its commutation money, slaughter tax, and other indirect taxes. Table 4 (below, this page) shows that the absolute value of income tax had steadily increased since 1908, though with some fluctuations.

Table 4
Average Assessment of Income Tax Per Adult Male
(Value in Guilders)

Year	1908	1909	1910	1911	1912	1913	1914	1915	1916	1917	1918
Value	1.73	2.11	2.65	2.60	3.06	3.24	3.40	2.25	5.60	5.17	5.30

Year	1919	1920	1921	1922	1923	1924	1925	1926
Value	4.95	4.31	4.36	4.72	4.52	4.71	5.44	6.15

Source: Schrieke et al. Deel II:38

Furthermore, we should not overlook the fact that the assessment was not adjusted to economic conditions. Between 1915 and 1916, during the wartime recession, the average assessment rose suddenly by 100 percent. The assessment values for 1916 and 1918, both recession years, were larger than those for the short-lived postwar boom of 1918-20, or

---

[11] In 1926, of 26 district heads, only 7 were _penghulus_; of 52 sub-district heads, 8 were _penghulus_ (Schrieke et al. 1928 Deel III:19-20, 72-74).

even 1924, when the economy began to recover. Under these circumstances the strong antagonism of the population towards taxation should be interpreted as a serious expression of the actual weight of the tax burden. The communist propaganda of freedom from taxation was certainly convincing to the lower strata of the society such as wage laborers in towns and plantations, peasants of poor regions, and petty traders.

4. The Exaggeration and Overestimation of Social Change

As was stated at the beginning of this paper, "social change" is used here to denote the structural change of the village. Although a variety of matters are included in this category, we will limit our discussion (a) to the land system, as the most important physical foundation, and (b) to the authority of the penghulus, as the socio-political basis of the customary order of the village.

a. Change in the land system

A brief description of the land system in the Minang-kabau village may be helpful for understanding the following discussion. The land in a village was divided into three types: the family land, the individual land, and the village communal land. The family land was inherited from the ances-tors of the matrilineally extended family, the most important land being the sawahs. Although it was communally controlled by the lineage as a whole, it was not cultivated communally by the members, but by sub-lineages, each of which was allotted a certain portion. Although the sub-lineages could use the por-tion freely, they were required obtain permission from the lineage as a whole, particularly the penghulu, before pawning it. Since the family land was inherited through the maternal line, from mother to daughter, it functioned as symbol of social unity and as the basis of the inheritance system, as well as being the most important source of livelihood. The sale of the family land was most strictly limited, if not im-possible, and even the pawning of it was allowed only on the occasions stipulated by adat. The individual land here refers to the land acquired personally either through purchase or by a person's own effort. An individual could use and dispose of the land freely while he was alive but when he died it was inherited customarily by his sister's children or kemanakans instead of his own children. Once inherited, it became part of the family land. The village land consisted of unculti-vated land reserves over which the village exercised the ultimate right of disposal (hak ulayat), and the land for village facilities.[12] This type of land was closely related to the village autonomy. Schrieke focused on changes in the system of the family and individual land.

i. family land

According to Schrieke, the regulations on the pledging of family land were not rigidly observed even before the introduction of monetary taxation. For instance, inquiries made in 1906 and 1907 in Batipuh-X Kota and Sawah Lunto revealed that the strict classical rules governing pledges were already regarded as belonging to the customs of previous times, and the valid motive for pledging of family land was recognized as being "an urgent lack of the necessities of life," at variance with the adat. After 1908, this tendency was further accelerated by taxation, and the desire to purchase luxuries, take a trip by motor car at the end of the fasting month, and so forth. The development of export crop cultivation and commercial activities also promoted the relaxation of old regulations on pledging. When the prices of export crops sharply dropped (e.g. copra prices in 1920; Kamer 1931:6-7), cultivators and merchants in Pariaman sometimes were forced to pledge their family land due to economic difficulties, of course violating adat (Schrieke 1955:107-110).

Schrieke's argument that the regulations on the pledging of family were relaxed seems to be persuasive and based on sound ground.   However, pledging is after all a temporary transfer of usufructuary rights and therefore the relaxation of adat in this category alone is insufficient to claim a substantial change in the system of family land. Being well aware of this, Schrieke further referred to the dilution of adat on the permanent disposal of family land. He maintained that all family land in the nagari Air Dingin (in Alahan Panjang) was converted into individual land because of pawning and because the traditional adat regulations were neglected, even though the regulations were still perceived as a legal norm (Schrieke 1955:110). If this had really happened, Schrieke's assertion would have become very persuasive. In 1934, however, a Dutch official made an investigation in this nagari and found that the effects contradicted Schrieke's account. According to the investigation, there had been a big fire in this nagari in 1910. To build new adat houses, about half of the family land of rice fields had been pawned, but it had mostly been redeemed by the time of the 1934 investiga-

---

[12] For a discussion of the land system in West Sumatra, see Oki 1977: Chapter IV.

tion. It is not clear why Schrieke misunderstood the situation. Perhaps he took temporarily pawned family land to be individual land, as a person who obtained land from others through pawning tended to regard the land as his individual land. In reality, however, the land could be termed individual land only until the original owner redeemed it. In this nagari the sale of family land was admitted only on one occasion, a case in which all family members had died (AB 1934). Hence the conversion of all family land of this nagari into individual land was never a possibility: Schrieke was incorrect on this point.

ii. individual land

In relation to individual land, an important change could be seen in the tendency for a greater proportion of individual land to be given to one's own children during one's own lifetime—a procedure which was called hibah under Islamic law—with less objection from the kemanakan. A person obtained individual land through purchase and personal effort, most importantly for export-crop gardens which were normally away from the residence of the maternal family, and were maintained by the individual's own family. According to Schrieke, the penetration of a monetary economy in Minangkabau and independent economic activities concomitant to the economy promoted individualism, a nuclear family, and an increasing freedom of individual land from the intervention of the maternal family (Schrieke 1955:114-117). As far as individual land is concerned, this seems to have been an irrevocable trend.

The Minangkabau social system was, without doubt, changing in its material basis, the land tenure system. The rigid regulations on the family land, crucial to the cohesion of matrilineal family ties, were relaxed to the extent to which it became possible to pawn at variance with the adat, and to that extent the strong family tie was weakened. However, contrary to Schrieke's account, the change did not proceed to the extent of selling of family land. Had family land really been sold, not only the matrilineal family ties but also the social relationships of the village community as a whole might have disintegrated. However, such has not happened so far. Next we will examine social change through the decline of the authority of penghulus.

b. Social change: the weakening of social ties

In the village communal life the penghulus played a multiple role: as custodians of family property, the authorities of _adat_, judges of legal matters, protectors of family members in times of economic difficulties, and the leaders of all matters concerning the welfare and security of the village. In broad social terms, they constituted a political force within Minangkabau society as a whole, an "_adat_ aristocracy." In Schrieke´s view, the decline of the authority of the _penghulus_ meant the disintegration of the Minangkabau society and Minangkabau world. Schrieke found two major sources causative of the decline, one being Dutch colonial administration, and the other being modernization.

The Dutch administration had undermined the _adat_-based authority of the _penghulus_ since the late 19th century with the imposition of a number of native officials over their heads, for more effective administrative purposes, especially for the execution of the Cultivation System. Under these native officials, _penghulus_ often functioned as subordinates. Although _penghulus_ were not government officials, they were obliged to put pressure upon their fellow villagers to deliver coffee under the Cultivation System and pay money taxes after 1908. This situation inevitably made the position of the _penghulus_ very unpopular. While the _penghulus_ were burdened with taxation matters by the government, they were often bypassed by native officials: For instance, when the village head or a native official wanted to meet villagers, the former directly met the latter, thereby bypassing _penghulus_ (Schrieke 1955:139). This added to their loss of face and prestige in the eyes of the villagers.

The Nagari Ordinance of 1915 further damaged the authority of the _penghulus_. There are two significant points to be discussed here in connection with the Ordinance. First, the Dutch newly instituted the village council (_nagariraad_) to function as an administrative body which consisted only of the so-called "core-_penghulus_," supposed to be the _penghulus_ belonging to the families of the original founders of the village. The new council brought a dual authority into the village, thus lessening the relative importance of the _adat_ council, and the importance of the _penghulus_ in general, as well. It should also be noted that the division of the _penghulus_ into two groups, the "core" and the "non-core," introduced antagonism among them and contributed to the disunity of the village community. Second, the Ordinance deprived the _penghulus_ of their privilege to enjoy the customary dues (_uang adat_). This meant a serious injury to _penghulu_ authority in a purely _adat_ sphere, as well as the loss of an important source of income.[13]

Schrieke further discussed the erosion of the authority of the penghulus in the process of modernization in Minangkabau. Educated young people and the younger generations (kaum muda) became increasingly critical of the older generations (kaum kuno) and of the old adat system, personified by the penghulus. To be a penghulu was no longer attractive because he was only burdened with government obligations while he was not privileged as a government official. In short, the advantages accrued from the prestige of the position were not considered equal to the disadvantages attached to the function. The remarkable decline in respect for the penghulus is described by Schrieke:

> And so it may happen that of various candidates—a clever one, a rich one, a daring one, and a stupid one—the stupid one is selected for penghulu-ship. For the rich one is too busy with his own affairs, the clever one does not really care for the job as he wants to leave the village or settle down as a religious teacher, and the stupid one will cause the least trouble to anybody. (Schrieke 1955:139)

Schrieke has convincingly demonstrated the degree of social change in West Sumatra before the communist uprising. It is also of note that the above quotation illustrates the lack of importance of penghulu-ship among those who were not engaged in rice cultivation. This is congruent with his basic argument that the commercial (or monetary) economy promoted the erosion of the adat order. In trying to make his argument persuasive, he presented evidence for social change from such regions as Alahan Panjang, Silungkang, the nagari Kota Lawas (in the Maninjau district), Pangkalan Kota Baru (north-east outlying regions of the highlands), XX Kota Kampar (eastern fringe area of the highlands), Batipuh and X Kota (the Padang Panjang district), Sawah Lunto, and Indrapura (further south of the coast area) (Schrieke 1955:107–110, 114–142). Most of these regions were deficient in sawah, and therefore the population was often engaged in economic activities other than rice cultivation including wage labor, textile industry, cash crop cultivation, and commerce. By underestimating the regional differences, however, Schrieke assumed that social change had taken place generally in West Sumatra. Although he briefly refers to regional differences, by his definition this

---

[13] Schrieke 1955; for the Nagari Ordinance, see Stap 1917; for adat dues, see Oki 1977:19–23.

only signifies the local variations of adat, for instance, regulations to select penghulus rather than the degree of social change (Schrieke 1955:139).

Apart from the social differences, Schrieke's analysis of individualization was somewhat exaggerated. For instance, the growing tendency towards the one-family system does not necessarily indicate a remarkable change of communal adat order as a whole unless the matrilineal family relationship between the segmented family branches, the descent system, and the regulations on the disposal of family land were substantially undermined. Of these, the last aspect is vitally significant. However, the crucial evidence which Schrieke presented--the case of nagari Air Dingin--has been proved incorrect, as mentioned before.

Some additional remarks are necessary in connection with the decline of the authority of the penghulus. In trying to fulfill their duties assigned by the government (tax collection for instance), penghulus sometimes resorted to such measures as refusing to give permission for pilgrimage to Mecca or to hold a marriage ceremony, to those who had not paid their taxes. This conduct might lead us to think that the authority of the penghulus was strengthened, rather than weakened, by the government.[14] However, we must be careful about such arguments. It should not be forgotten here that the traditional authority of the penghulus was based on their control over the lineage property (pusaka), most importantly sawahs, and voluntary support of the villagers, and was legitimated by the adat. The involvement of the penghulus in the colonial administration may have added some administrative power, which was outside the framework of adat, but it also reduced their traditional authority at the same time. For such conduct of the penghulus as mentioned above must surely have reduced the respect of the villagers for the penghulus, and thus their voluntary support. It was often the case in colonial policy to make use of traditional chiefs as an administrative tool in this way.[15] When judging the relative strength or weakness of the authority of the penghulus, we must take account of the balance between the increase of administrative power attached by the government and the decrease of customary authority. In this sense, I agree with

---

[14] Kahn (1976) argues that the authority of the penghulus was strengthened by the Dutch administration (cf. von Benda-Beckmann and von Benda-Beckmann, this volume).
[15] A good example of this can be seen in Kathirithamby-Wells 1977:30-31.

Schrieke to the extent that he concluded there was a general decline of the authority of the penghulus, though I consider that there were regional differences in the degree of the decline depending chiefly on the major economic activities of the region concerned, whether rice growing or others.

B. Economic Constraints, Social Change, and the Communist Uprising

In the foregoing paragraphs we have examined social instability and grievances in terms of socio-economic change in Minangkabau society in a transitional stage of change, critically following Schrieke's argument. We have also discussed the varying degrees of socio-economic change in various parts of West Sumatra and the existence of poor people who were left behind by the benefits brought from the development of a capitalist economy. Our final question is whether there existed any connection between economic constraints, social change, and the uprising. It goes without saying that the causes of the communist revolt were complicated. However, some important aspects in relation to the above question can be seen from a close investigation of communist centers where the communist movement was particularly active, namely the Padang, Pariaman, Silungkang, Sawah Lunto, Sijinjung, Alahan Panjang, Old Agam, and Suliki regions, and the town of Padang Panjang (see Map 2, page 229).

From the economic point of view, these communist centers can be divided into two groups. The first included Sijunjung, Sawah Lunto, Silungkang, Singkarak, Alahan Panjang, Suliki, and Maninjau. These regions were unsuitable both for rice cultivation and export crop cultivation due to bad ecological and geographical conditions. For example, Sijunjung, Sawah Lunto, Maninjau, and Singkarak were hilly regions with a scarcity of arable land, particularly flat land for sawah, while Alahan Panjang was too cool to grow rice due to its altitude, even though some plains villages in this region did have flat land. Male inhabitants of these regions tended to leave home as traders and wage laborers (Schrieke et al. 1928 Deel II: 164-169). In the Silungkang area, the textile industry had some significance and many inhabitants were engaged in the home industry and cloth trade. Comparable to Silungkang was the Suliki region which was another center of the textile industry[16] in West Sumatra in the 20th century. Both in Silung-

---

[16] See Oki 1979.

Map 2: Location of Centers for the Communist Movement in
       West Sumatra

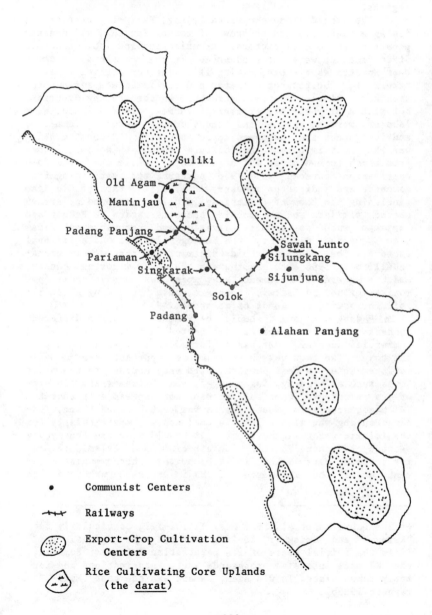

- • Communist Centers
- ╍╍╍ Railways
- ⬭ Export-Crop Cultivation Centers
- ⬭ Rice Cultivating Core Uplands (the _darat_)

kang and Suliki, merchants were becoming an important social and economic force. Finally, all of these belonged to poor regions.

The second group comprised Padang, Pariaman, part of the Old Agam district, and the town of Padang Panjang, all densely populated commercial centers. Urbanization and socio-economic stratification were most advanced in the Padang district in West Sumatra as a whole, making it easier for Marxist ideas to take root. The town of Pariaman and its immediate surrounding area had a similar economic structure to the Padang district, but with a slightly higher average income. In Pariaman, wage laborers were engaged in indigenous coconut gardens, commerce, and indigenous and European copra industry. Coconut growing was the most important agriculture around this town, income from which formed about 45% of the total, while that from food cultivation covered only 9.8 percent, the rest coming from commerce and indigenous industry in 1926.[17] Part of Old Agam (including the town of Bukittinggi and its surrounding areas) shared similar socio-economic characteristics to Padang and Pariaman such as commercialization and economic stratification. Of the Old Agam, the Kamang district had additional factors. The people of this district had the memory of tax rebellion in 1908 when Kamang was the most important center, and the modernist movement (kaum muda) was active under communist-influenced Islamic teachers, both providing a fertile soil for sowing the seeds of communism.[18]

Padang Panjang should be mentioned in a different context from the regions delineated above. As it was a commercial center, merchants formed an influential group in the town. The town was, however, more important as a communications center in West Sumatra, with easy access to the major towns such as Padang, Bukittinggi, and Batusangkar. In view of its strategic location, it was not unreasonable that the PKI headquarters in West Sumatra was established there. Padang Panjang was also a intellectual center, particularly for the Islamic reformist movement. It should be noted that young members of Sumatra Thawalib (an association of Islamic reformist schools, established in 1918) joined the communist movement under the influence of Haji Datuk Batuah (Abdullah

---

[17] See Schrieke et al. 1928 Deel II:151-171, particularly for "Kring V" and "Kring VI" dealing with the poor regions.
[18] At the initial state of its penetration into West Sumatra, the PKI made intensive propaganda where insurrections had formerly taken place. In Old Agam, Kamang was the case (Mailrapport 1926b).

1971:37-45). What, then, were the social and political implications of the economic characteristics of these communist
centers?

The foregoing examination of the communist-influenced
regions has made it clear that the majority of the inhabitants
of the first group and lower strata of the second group were
poor even during the export boom, and that merchants constituted an important social and economic force. The communist
slogan of "freedom from taxation" and the Marxist theory of
"impoverishment" must have been convincing particularly to the
poor inhabitants. Understandably, the PKI deliberately made
intensive propaganda campaigns in the poor regions such as
Padang, Pariaman and Old Agam, especially to the poorest
people of overpopulated areas of West Sumatra (Tropen Museum
m.s.:28). There seems to have been some relationship between
the relative importance of merchants and the expansion of the
communist movement in the commercial centers. Petty traders
were bitterly hit by the recession in 1920-22 and became sympathetic to communist allegations against the Dutch and European capitalists. The economic recovery after 1924 increased
not only the economic, but also the social and political
strength of the merchants. However, they could neither obtain
status corresponding to their economic strength in the adat
hierarchy nor participate in local administration since they
were rejected by both the Dutch and the penghulus. As in the
case of Silungkang, the communist slogan of "Equality for all"
(sama rata sama rasa) was accepted by these dissatisfied merchants (Benda and McVey 1960:102).

In the social sphere, the major communist-influenced
regions shared two common features. First, these regions were
located outside the rice-growing plains villages in the
nucleus (darat) of the highlands (except the Old Agam district). Was this simply coincidence? It is significant to
note here that, although most penghulus tried to rebuff the
communists by criticizing their ideas as contradicting the
adat, it was in the darat that the communist movement was relatively most sluggish. This suggests that the influence of
the penghulus was stronger in the darat than in outlying regions (rantau); Penghulus in the darat used adat as a counter-
ideology to communism. Second, the communist centers were
located along or not far from the railways, thus they had very
easy access to major roads. This location suggests that the
movement advanced where communication was easy and the society
was relatively open to outside influence. Moreover, the railway business had produced a modern-type proletariat which had
organized what was then the only trade union in West Sumatra.
Members of the trade union formed one of the core groups which
joined the communist movement (Mailrapport 1927b).

The distinctions between the regions rich in _sawah_ and poor in _sawah_, and the _darat_ and _rantau_--here understood as socio-economic categories--should, however, not be drawn too sharply in relation to the development of the communist movement. The conflict between _penghulu_ on the one hand, and merchants and the less privileged on the other should also be understood in a relative sense. In fact, the communist movement spread to regions other than those discussed above, such as in the _nagari_ Padang Luar near Padang Panjang, under the influence of one of the most important communist leaders, Haji Datuk Batuah who was born in the _nagari_ (Oki 1979). _Penghulus_ were not always against communism and commercialism. There were some who were merchants and some who participated in the communist movement. For its own part, the PKI tinged its propaganda with Islamic and even _adat_ elements. For instance, the communists criticized the Dutch for depriving the population of their customary territorial rights, or _hak ula-yat nagari_, for the Ombilin mines in Sawah Lunto (Schrieke 1955:164). The communist slogan of _kemerdekaan_ appealed not only to the inhabitants of the communist centers but also to those in other regions. In short, grievances against the Dutch and instability existed everywhere and among every social and economic group. Nevertheless, the regional specifications are helpful for analytical purposes for they focus the problems clearly. In spite of some exceptions, we can say that the communist influence penetrated particularly into poor agrarian regions outside the core uplands and also commercial centers which contained a lot of poor people. To conclude, social change and economic constraints were certainly relevant to the communist uprising in 1926-27 in West Sumatra.

Conclusion

I believe Schrieke's account of the communist uprising in West Sumatra (Part I, Sociological Section) to be a milestone among historical studies of Indonesia insofar as it viewed a political event in the light of social change in Minangkabau, relating all aspects of society--political, cultural, social, and economic. Schrieke was correct in relating the fundamental causes of the uprising to the unstable situation of the Minangkabau society in a state of change. He interpreted the social change as the result of the modernization process chiefly generated by the penetration of capitalistic economy and a spirit of capitalism, as happened in Europe. Whether or not we use the term "modernization," capitalistic economy would certainly change the social system based on a pre-capitalistic economy. Quite differently from

Europe, however, capitalistic economy and foreign elements—including Marxist ideas—were to a considerable extent brought to and even forced upon the population by a foreign government within the framework of colonial rule in the case of West Sumatra. What Schrieke saw in the modernization process in the area were mainly changes desirable for a capitalistic market economy, including individualism, the weakening of the traditional social system, the emergence of a "middle class," and so forth. By viewing it this way, his attention was diverted from the problem of poverty and widening inequities among the population. Whether consciously or unconsciously, it was more convenient for him not to take the framework of colonial rule into serious consideration. Under colonial rule the population was burdened with taxes and corvee labor while profits from products of West Sumatra ultimately fell into the hands of the Dutch and a number of other Europeans because they handled most of the foreign trade of colonial Indonesia.

Schrieke's account of the communist uprising had the effect of bringing some confusion into later Minangkabau studies. J. S. Kahn correctly pointed out:

> The student of modern Minangkabau society is, however, faced with a curious paradox. While Schrieke, writing of the period after the turn of the century, discussed the breakdown of matriliny, and while predictions of its demise are frequent, matrilineal organization seems to retain an important place in modern Minangkabau. (Kahn 1976:64-65)

The "curious paradox," as discussed by Kahn himself, can be resolved when viewed from a different perspective: Schrieke dealt with the Minangkabau of the first two and a half decades of the century when the economy was experiencing a most drastic change in the direction of a capitalistic economy, stimulated by the export boom. After the end of the 1920's, however, the economy successively faced a series of outside pressures, all of which had the effect of drawing the economy back towards a subsistence level: The Great depression of the 1930's, the Japanese occupation, economic disturbances in connection with the struggle for independence, and civil wars after Indonesian independence. In short, Minangkabau has not experienced a fundamental change in economy, especially in the mode of production, until now.[19] Consequently, it is quite

---

[19] The production of export crops has been slowly reviving recently. However, the production level is still far below that

understandable that the matrilineal social system still "survives."

In the analysis of a society or historical event, socio-economic interpretation is not always the only (or most important) approach. However, I stress the importance of socio-economic interpretation in the study of Minangkabau in view of the fact that this society has been studied overwhelmingly in its cultural and political aspects. Furthermore, no social system or culture or political event can exist in the absolute vacuum of socio-economic conditions. Considering the above, I believe that the socio-economic approach may throw new light upon Minangkabau study.

---

of the 1920s. For example, the export of coffee, one of the most rapidly expanding crops, in 1977 amounted to 8,898 tons in contrast to the 18,900 tons in 1928. This decline becomes much sharper when we take into account the difference in population between these two years: 1.9 million in 1929, and 3.2 million in 1977 (Propinsi Sumatera Barat 1977:523, Table Q.I.4; Kamer 1931:32).

TRANSFORMATION AND CHANGE IN MINANGKABAU

Franz von Benda-Beckmann
LBH Wageningen
and
Keebet von Benda-Beckmann
Erasmus University, Rotterdam

Introduction

Forty years ago, Korn (1941) complained about the strange course the study of Minangkabau _adat_ had taken and the sad state of affairs which these studies had produced: fundamental misunderstandings of Minangkabau society and its law, and misconceived and patently unjust applications of _adat_ laws in the colonial courts. This concerned not only the (mis)understanding of the present state of _adat_ law, as Korn pointed out, but also affected the understanding and interpretation of social and legal change in Minangkabau. More recently, Kahn (1976, 1980a, 1980b) has again argued, from a slightly different point of view, that the interpretations of social change in Minangkabau are misconceived, as they proceed from a false historical baseline: that is the idea of the "traditional matrilineal system" of Minangkabau, which in his view was basically the product of early Dutch colonial domination. He warned of the dangers inherent in the uncritical use of earlier Dutch writings on Minangkabau _adat_ law and contended that its reconsideration must start with its deconstruction as it is portrayed in the discourse of earlier Indonesianists (1980b:82).

With this paper we wish to contribute our share to this deconstruction of _adat_ and _adat_ law of Minangkabau. Like Korn and Kahn we are convinced that many of the earlier interpretations of Minangkabau _adat_ and Minangkabau social organization are misconceived, and that these misconceptions lie at the root of equally misconceived analyses of change in Minangkabau. Like Korn and Kahn, we shall in particular focus upon changes in the complex of rules and institutions relating to property holding, inheritance, and succession to positions of socio-political authority known as _adat pusako_, the _adat_ of matrilineal heritage. In our analysis we shall consider two sources of potential distortion. One of them has already been emphasized by Kahn: disregard of the effects of the colonial government's administrative and economic policies. Kahn argues that the _adat_ and social organization described in 19th century writings and reproduced since then was not the system as it existed prior to Dutch colonial rule, or the turmoil of the Padri War which Minangkabau had experienced during the previous 20 years. The image of the traditional matrilineal system was to a large extent, if not completely, the product of traceable Dutch interventions in political and economic life. Whether or not one shares Kahn's conclusions as to the effects of Dutch measures, his general point is an important one which must lead to a critical reexamination of Dutch writings. We should like to discuss another element of potential distortion to be considered in the deconstruction. Minangkabau _adat_ has been described and interpreted largely in terms of western—usually Dutch—legal thinking. We shall try to show how interpretations of Minangkabau social forms, both by lawyers and social scientists, have been western in character and how these have influenced conceptions of social and legal change in Minangkabau.

In our attempt to add to the understanding of socio-legal and economic developments in 19th and 20th century Minangkabau we shall proceed in the following manner. We shall first indicate our historical baseline by outlining the rules and institutions of the _adat pusako_ as we think it existed in the early 19th century, at the close of the Padri war but before the actual systematic colonization of the Padang Highlands by the Dutch. The main parts of our paper will then focus on the impact which Dutch administrative and economic policy had on the _adat pusako_ and the socio-economic activities related to it, as well as on the nature of legal and social change occurring during the first half of the 20th century. The discussion of both questions, particularly the first, leads us into a complex dialogue with Kahn's ideas about the actual state of 19th century Minangkabau. Briefly, the divergence between Kahn's and our interpretations is the following: we do not think that the "traditional matrilineal Minangkabau society," with corporate kin groups in which there was equal access to lineage property based on common ownership, ever existed. We rather think that it only existed in some stereotyped summary reproductions of Minangkabau _adat_ and society, and that we must work with a much more differentiated picture of Minangkabau law and social organization. Kahn, on the other hand, thinks that such a traditional system did exist, but that the system written about was not it but was instead basically the product of 19th century economic and administrative policy of the Dutch. He therefore takes other interpretations of change to task for not proceeding from a correct historical baseline. Our impression is that Kahn himself fell victim to the transformed descriptions of Minangkabau <u>adat</u> which he takes as descriptions of actual conditions. Furthermore, the factors which in Kahn's view essentially produced the traditional system, in our view rather contributed to a disintegration of the actual system as we conceive it.

It is understandable, then, that our different interpretations result in different analyses as to the character of changes flowing from the new economic and administrative policy in the early 20th century. To be sure, Kahn's interpretation of Minangkabau socio-economic changes differs from the previous interpretations of Schrieke and Maretin. For example, whereas Schrieke and Maretin see rural capitalism emerge as the locally dominant mode of production, Kahn sees petty commodity production emerge instead. The three basically agree, nevertheless, in portraying 19th century changes as dramatic and far-reaching, as fundamental departures. We on the other hand begin with a different interpretation than they of Minangkabau social forms prior to the 19th century; we see the 19th century changes as somewhat less dramatic than they, and we see some continuities where they see departures. We recognize that our views also carry elements of speculation, which are attendant upon any historical reconstruction. Nevertheless, we think that a careful reading of available sources brings us closer than Kahn to an accurate account; fortunately 19th century Minangkabau is relatively well documented, especially the second half of the century, so we can form a rather detailed picture of central elements of its social and economic organization.[1]

It will be one of our major criticisms of the writings of Kahn, Schrieke, and Maretin that some of their more important interpretations of Minangkabau history perpetuate biases inherent in the earlier writings on the subject. Especially important are the biases inherent in western legal thinking, by which we mean much more than jurisprudence alone. One must be wary of ethnocentrisms in legal thought whether they take the form of diffuse and vague or highly precise and professionalized notions of what law, rights, and kindred concepts mean and how they relate to social practices and organizations. Early writers, including anthropologists and colonial judges, were often unaware of the conceptual mistakes

---

[1] Even though most of the 19th century sources were written in the last third of the century, we can assume that a great part of the descriptions reflect Minangkabau prior to much influence by the colonial administration.

engendered by the mistranslations based in their ethnocentrisms, a point recently repeated in legal anthropology
but which was previously well recognized by some among the
Dutch _adat_ law scholars.[2]   Whereas an uncritical use of
specific or professional western legal concepts can easily
lead to "jamming into categories" (Nader 1965) or unwarranted
"backward translation" (Bohannan 1969) and thereby to distor-
tions of purported descriptions of social life, an unspecific
general use of terms can be equally misleading by virtue of
vague or diffuse descriptions, leaving a reader to guess an
author's intentions (cf. Hooker 1975:23).

Although there is a wide range of what western legal
thinking means for the individual scholars concerned, they
usually agree upon several basic, mainly structural, characteristics of western law. These are that western law is the
product of a society which is politically organized in the
form of a state and characterized by a high degree of social
differentiation and functional specialization or division of
labor. It is to a high degree externally and internally differentiated. External differentiation makes law as a whole a
relatively autonomous category of cognitive and normative conceptions distinct from other categories, such as ethics, morals, and good manners. It also demarcates a sphere of legal
behavior which is differentiated from other spheres such as
the social, economic, and political. Western law is internally differentiated in the sense that there are a number of
distinctions among spheres or fields of law such as public and
private, criminal and civil, substantive and procedural, property and inheritance law, that of things, of obligations, of
persons, and so forth. Furthermore, western law has a specific notion of subjective rights, legally defined as pro-

---

[2] Compare Nader 1965; Gluckman 1969; Bohannan 1969; Vansina
1965. For the older Dutch literature see Van Vollenhoven
1909. It should be noted, however, that the use of western
concepts can also contribute to a refinement of the analysis
of non-western concepts and institutions. A good example is
Willinck 1909, who scrupulously compared some Minangkabau
notions of _harato pusako_ with the Dutch notion of common
ownership and _hibah_ with Dutch and Roman notions of donations.
He was severely criticized for his comparisons. However, his
critics did not recognize the differentiated descriptions and
understandings of Minangkabau institutions, wrapped up as they
were in long exposees on Roman and German law and in strongly
expressed dislike for the Minangkabau culture. For similar
analyses of Barotse material, see Gluckman 1972, 1973.

tected interests which give the entitled person a claim, ultimately to be effectuated in court.

These structural characteristics of western law and the preoccupation with subjective rights, especially the various types of ownership, should be kept in mind when considering writings on Minangkabau _adat_ and _adat_ law. In Minangkabau _adat_, as in most Indonesian _adat_ systems, there is no conception of "_adat_ law." _Adat_ is internally differentiated,[3] but the folk system of classification has no category for "law," nor do any of the folk categories correspond to an analytic conception of law in general. However, there are many rules, concepts, and principles which would fit in almost any analytical concept of law designed for comparative analysis. Besides, some of the _adat_ classifications are almost completely legal in character.[4] The term _adat law_ (_adatrecht_, _hukum adat_) is a Dutch invention.[5] In Van Vollenhoven's writings it was designed to refer to the law in _adat_. Van Vollenhoven was well aware of the fact that _adat_ law was not only "_oosters_" ("oriental") in content, but that it also differed considerably from western law in its formal and structural properties. He chose to use the term _adatrecht_ precisely to express that _adat_ law could only in part be differentiated within _adat_ (1918:9). But in spite of this insight and his, certainly for his time, unparalleled understanding of the nature and working of law in the Indonesian _adat_ systems, the law in _adat_ was gradually transformed into a separate category, _adat_ law. It came to be interpreted and applied in a context of western legal thinking. As we shall show, interpretations of _adat_ biased by western legal thinking also pervaded the specific literature on Minangkabau _adat_, thereby creating a partly transformed _adat_ or _adat_ law different from that produced and reproduced in villages. Some sources show a remarkable precision in describing indigenous terms and institutions.[6] The use of some key terms with a

---

[3] See Dt. Sidi Bandaro 1965; R.M. Dt. Rajo penghulu 1971:100-ff; Nasroen 1957; F. von Benda-Beckmann 1979a:115ff. As Kahn has emphasized again recently, this law in _adat_ by no means exhausts the empirical and analytically distinguishable referents of the concept _adat_. One must therefore take care to make such distinctions as that between the law in _adat_ and _adat_ in the sense of behavior patterns (1980b:81).

[4] For example, the two _cupak_, the four _kato_, the four laws (_cupak nan duo_, _kato nan ampek_, _undang nan ampek_); see Dt. Sidi Bandaro 1965.

[5] See Van Vollenhoven 1918:1ff. and 1928.

technical legal meaning in western law may have blinded later writers to the actual ethnography.[7]

But apart from that there were the transformations resulting from the political struggles for the recognition of indigenous law and rights by the dominant colonial legal system.[8] The term _adatrecht_ itself became important in this struggle. But central to the discussions concerning the introduction of agrarian legislation in the 1870s were the terms "_beschikkingsrecht_" (the communal right of avail of Indonesian communities) and "_inlands bezitrecht_" (native right of possession). Throughout the colonial era these terms were the focus around which the question of recognition was centered.[9]

In order to have _adat_ rights to land recognized, it was essential to stress their similarities with Dutch rights to land. Thus, these neologisms, although designed to avoid direct translation of _adat_ phenomena into Dutch terms, more often than not were in their structural characteristics as western as the Dutch legal terms—as we shall see in the analysis of the literature on Minangkabau. The effects were multiplied when these terms not only were used as political tools, but also as a standard terminology to describe the various _adat_ laws in Indonesia. The transformation of _adat_ into _adat_ law finally took on a new dimension when it was used and reinterpreted in the colonial courts.[10] The courts were themselves a western legal institution working a western law of procedure. In this context _adat_ rules and principles were divested of their procedural elements. The _adat_ processes of decision-making and realization of rights in interaction processes simply _could not_ be reproduced in the western-style courts. Furthermore, detailed and unbiased descriptions of

---

6 See for example Verkerk Pistorius 1871; Stibbe 1869; Résumé 1872. Earlier literature does not give very detailed information.
7 See e.g. van der Toorn 1881. For similar reasons, Willinck (1909) was misunderstood.
8 The emphasis on the legal aspect of _adat_ was also directed against the widely held opinion that the indigenous law of the Indonesians was, in principle, Islamic law. For references to and a critical discussion of this view, see Van Vollenhoven 1918:19ff, 1928:110ff.
9 Cf. Van Vollenhoven 1919; Logemann and Ter Haar 1927; Korn and Van Dijk 1946; Nolst Trenité 1920; 's Jacobs 1945; cf. Burns 1978.
10 For a recent analysis of Ter Haar's influence, see Strijbosch 1980. See also Woodman 1969:129ff., 1981.

the law in _adat_ were in the court context transformed into "_adat_ law."[11]

It is therefore important to distinguish between the law in _adat_ as conceived and operated in the village sphere, and _adat_ law as conceived in the courts and the literature. A description and analysis of legal change in Minangkabau must pay attention to both. As has been pointed out by Kahn, it would be misleading to assume that these two levels of _adat_ were and are isomorphic but it would also be a mistake to assume that they are unrelated to each other (1980b:82). The courts' _adat_ law has been shaped by the law in _adat_ and has in turn influenced it and its development.[12] And both have been influenced, often differentially, by non-legal factors.

Western legal thinking is not confined to certain assumptions about the nature of legal rules and their application in adjudicative processes. It also extends to the relation between law and behavior, and in a diachronic perspective, to the relation between law/legal change and social and economic change. Some comments must therefore be added on the relation between law and behavior, both in its synchronic and diachronic dimension. A clear understanding of this relation is fundamental for our later discussion of change, and for our argument against other interpretations.

Statements of the relationship between law and behavior are often dominated by clichés. Characteristic of these clichés and the assumptions on which they rest is a preoccupation with prescriptive rules. In this thinking, behavior is related to law simply in terms of conformity or deviance. Another cliché is that if social behavior patterns change, law will in principle also change. If law does not change, it is conceived of as lagging behind social or economic development.[13] This limited view disregards the fact that law does not only have prescriptive and validatory uses, but also always has room made in it for relatively autonomous conduct. Within this range of autonomy, new patterns of social and economic behavior can emerge without necessarily changing the law or creating a lag.[14]

---

[11] This problem is extensively discussed in K. von Benda-Beckmann 1981, 1982. See also Woodman 1969:129ff., 1981.
[12] For an early analysis see Ter Haar 1929.
[13] Compare Abel's (1973) discussion of the "gap" problem.
[14] The classic study of the relation between legal and economic change is Renner's study of the institutions of private law and their social function (1929). In his analysis of the change from petty commodity production to capitalism in West-

These simplistic models, which are not confined to legal
thinking but are as frequently encountered in general anthropological theories,[15] prepare the ground for a new set of
transformations. They encourage unwarranted inferences as to
actual behavior patterns based on legal rules, or the reverse,
inferences regarding legal rules based on observations of behavior. In our attempts to reconstruct the state of law and
social and economic organization in Minangkabau, we must
therefore take particular care that the domain of adat law and
ideology and that of actual social and economic activities
remain separate, and to avoid reductionist inferences both
from the state of adat/adat law to economic life, and in the
reverse direction. This is all the more important and difficult, since the term "adat" itself can refer to social phenomena in both domains (cf. Kahn 1980b:82).

Minangkabau Property Law in the Early 19th Century

Introduction

Minangkabau property and inheritance law in the 19th
century--leaving open for now the question of just what were
the conditions in the villages temporarily governed by the
Padri--was essentially defined as adat. It was part of the
adat pusako complex of rules and principles which was dominated by the social, political, and economic relations within
the nagari.
Before trying to reconstruct the content and structure
of this legal complex, let us first, in order to avoid misunderstandings, comment on the problem of the dominant system
of law. We do not wish to argue that the adat of the 19th
century was something like a pure adat of a timeless golden
age. For many years prior to the Padri war and the subsequent
Dutch colonial domination, adat as a legal system existed in a
dual relationship with a concurrent system, Islamic law. This
relationship was dual in two senses, first in that elements of

---

ern Europe, he demonstrated that important socio-economic
change can occur in a field where conduct is not legally prescribed ("change of function") without this change being yet
reflected in or leading to a change of legal rules ("change of
norms").
[15] They have also largely dominated the assumptions of struc-
tural-functionalism and are characteristic of many Marxist interpretations; see Cerroni 1972; Poulantzas 1972.

Islamic law and legal language have been incorporated into adat, a process which probably began well before the Padri war and which continues until the present time. Secondly, even when Islamic elements were not translated into adat, or accepted beside it in everyday village life, Islamic law as a separate system was also accepted and reproduced in Minangkabau.

The relationship between adat and Islamic law has, so far as we know, varied considerably in the history of Minangkabau, before the Padri war as well as under Dutch colonial rule and after independence. This relationship has varied with the relative power of the proponents of the system and with the economic and political bases for this power (cf. Taufik Abdullah 1971, 1972). Following Dobbin (1977:27f.), we can assume that during the latter decades of the 18th century a definite attempt to give more force to Islamic law in property and economic legal affairs culminated in the Padri War. But there is no evidence from which we may infer that Islamic law as a whole ever succeeded in superseding adat as a system of property and inheritance law. We may assume, on the other hand, that probably well before the Padri war, adat as a system was influenced by Islamic law and that this particularly may have been the case in those nagari which for a longer period came under actual Padri government. However, as far as we know, the elements of Islamic law were in general translated into adat, incorporated into adat, or accepted beside adat as village law.

For example, the establishment of Islam as the dominant religion resulted in the creation of religious offices. But these offices, malim or chatib adat, subsequently became suku offices, to be inherited matrilineally. Large parts of Islamic marriage law and burial customs were accepted into village law, not replacing adat but added to adat rules and customs. Many legal concepts of Islamic law, like hak (right), milik (property, ownership), hibah (gift), warith (heir) were used in adat. Moreover, comparison of the adat expressed in Islamic terms, and the meaning these terms have in Islamic law itself reveals that the original adat conceptions were not suppressed by Islamic legal institutions: Warith in Islamic law are the Koranic heirs and a person's agnates—in Minangkabau warith denotes matrilineal kin and matrilineal heirs. Hibah in Islamic law is a contract which must become effective during the donor's lifetime, and the donor is not restricted as to the amount of his or her gift. In Minangkabau adat hibah is revocable and becomes effective only at the donor's death; the donor is severely restricted with respect to the amount of the gift. Hak and milik were similarly adapted into the context of adat (cf. F. von Benda-

Beckmann 1979a:162, 322).

Before, and also to a large extent after the Padri war, the power bases of Islamic legal influence lay outside the system of _nagari_ government; the economic relations on which Islamic legal influence could build were mainly inter-_nagari_ or inter-regional trade relations. From this position, it was difficult to attempt to redefine the legal system of property relations, particularly a legal system which was so interwoven with intra-_nagari_ social and political relations. It is likely that when the Padri moved to occupy political power _within_ the _nagari_, more force was given to Islamic law than previously, but there is little evidence from which to speculate. Apparently not even the Padri tried to abolish the _pusako_ system as a system of property law.[16] The restoration of _adat_ law and order following the military defeat of the Padri was certainly not a complete return to the situation which existed before the outbreak of the civil war. We know that in some cases the Padri domination left its clear marks on the political organization of the _nagari_.[17] But we can gather from early post-war descriptions such as that of Francis (1839) that the restoration of the "_soekoe bestuur_" (_suku_ government) and the _adat pusako_ system and _adat_ization of Islamic/Padri influences seem to have been successful. The military defeat of the Padri and the presence of Dutch troops and administrative officials were essential conditions for this restoration, and we shall discuss the impact of the Dutch administration on the _adat pusako_ system in a later section of this paper. But in the third decade of the 19th century, the legal system pertaining to _nagari_ government and property was essentially _adat_, with the first influences of the new rulers and additional influences from Islam. Before we consider what the effects were of the developing economic and political

---

[16] See HAMKA 1968:33. About later Islamic efforts to replace the _adat_ property and inheritance law, see Prins 1953, 1954; HAMKA 1968; Anas 1968; F. von Benda-Beckmann 1979a:323ff. For further material concerning the pre-Padri era, see Kielstra 1887a; Dobbin 1975, 1977.

[17] In Bukit Hijau, a system of territorial divisions linked to the mosques (_sidang_) has survived as a combined form of government with Islamic and _adat_ functionaries. Whether it was used as a purely theocratic form of government during the period Bukit Hijau was occupied by the Padri unfortunately is not known; see K. and F. von Benda-Beckmann 1978a:80; F. von Benda-Beckmann 1979a:80. See for similar survivals AB 39:212ff.

conditions in the coming years, and during the <u>Cultuurstelsel</u>
in particular, let us first try to outline the basic
principles of the <u>adat pusako</u> complex.

1. The System of <u>Adat Pusako</u>

Each villager is, on the basis of matrifiliation, incorporated into a number of groups which are generally structured
by or modeled on the principle of matrilineal descent. There
are groups of different sizes, the smaller groups usually
being segments of the more inclusive ones. True matrilineal
descent groups of any size and genealogical depth are called
<u>jurai</u>. In the most frequent use of the term, however, <u>jurai</u>
denotes the sub-branches within the groups which are headed by
a <u>penghulu</u> (<u>penghulu andiko</u>) who is an acknowledged member of
the <u>adat</u> council. These groups we shall call "lineages" (see
for an overview of the different terms, de Josselin de Jong
1951:49ff.). As lineage membership was relevant for <u>nagari</u>
citizenship, residence, access to agrarian productive resources, economic cooperation, and ceremonies, it seems
justified to view them as the basic socio-political units.
Their members are characterized in <u>adat</u> as "being of" or
"having in common" among others, one <u>penghulu</u>, (<u>sapenghulu</u>),
one <u>penghulu</u> title (<u>sasako</u>), one heritage (<u>sapusako</u>), one
property (<u>saharato</u>), one graveyard (<u>sapandam sapakuburan</u>), and
one forest (<u>sahutan karch</u>).

A lineage could be a true matrilineal descent group, but
could also be internally stratified. Internal lineage
stratification came into existence when persons of different
social and political rank—strangers and descendants of former
slaves—were incorporated as lineage members. Since strangers
and the descendants of former slaves could only acquire
citizenship in a <u>nagari</u> through lineage membership, many
lineages have been stratified sometime in their history. In
the course of time, however, such ex-stranger or ex-slave
<u>jurai</u> were usually given independent lineage status with their
own <u>penghulu</u>, as a result of which the membership of the
original lineage was again reduced to matrilineally linked
blood relatives, and the former internal stratification was
raised to the level of inter-lineage stratification (see also
F. von Benda-Beckmann 1979a:61ff.).

Supra-lineage organization and institutions of <u>nagari</u>
government vary considerably throughout Minangkabau. It is
common to the socio-political organization of all <u>nagari</u> that
each lineage and lineage member is affiliated to and part of
one of the named groups called <u>suku</u> or <u>suku pusako</u> on the
basis of real or putative common matrilineal descent, in most

parts of Minangkabau (but Kampueng in 50 Koto, see De Rooij 1890). Suku are supposed to have originally been Minangkabau-wide matriclans. These groups were exogamous and constituted units within which inter-lineage inheritances of property (harato pusako) occurred and which handled disputes about property and matters of succession. These suku structures were also used for the politico-administrative organization of the nagari. Lineages and groups of closely related lineages were, however, in many nagari also grouped together in politico-administrative units which cross-cut suku lines and combined component groups of different suku pusako. Such units were called hindu (adat) or also suku (adat).[18] The actual political organization of most nagari consisted of varying combinations of these two group-forming principles. Emphasis on the hindu/suku adat principle seems to have been characteristic for the traditional Koto-Piliang system of government in which all suku (clan) segments were united in four suku (administrative) units. In these nagari, repre-sentatives of the "4 suku" also formed the highest governmen-tal institution. In the Bodi-Caniago tradition, the highest governmental institution, the Karapatan Adat Nagari, was

---

[18] This multiple meaning of suku led to controversies among the Dutch scholars and administrators of Minangkabau, the parties variously asserting that suku were clans or adminis-trative unions of clan segments. For the view that suku were originally clans, see Stibbe and Kroesen in Résumé 1872; for the contrary view, that suku were administrative associations of clans at the very beginning of Minangkabau nagari organiza-tion, see De Rooij 1890 and Leyds 1926.

In our opinion, both kinds of groups must have existed in the early stages of Minangkabau political organization. For the recognition of the two different kinds of groups in early Bukit Hijau, see the account of the nagari foundation in F. von Benda-Beckmann 1979a:72ff. The same distinction is reported in the account of the foundation of Nagari Tanjung Sungayang, which is considered one of the oldest nagari in Minangkabau. Dt. Sanggoeno Dirajo describes how the leaders of the genealogical groups "make" suku adat (1920:82ff.).

The distinction between suku(pusako) and suku adat/hindu adat apparently obtains in all Minangkabau nagari, though the groups are often labelled with the same term (suku) or still other terms. For an overview, see Kemal 1964. For a more systematic description of the political organization of nagari Bukit Hijau, see F. von Benda-Beckmann 1979a:61ff., and K. and F. von Benda-Beckmann 1978.

formed by all lineage heads (penghulu andiko). But in the 19th century, the political organization of most nagari seems to have included elements of the two classical systems.[19]

These variations in political organization accounted for similar variations in the socio-political control over the nagari-territory. Roughly speaking, the territory of the nagari was divided into two categories of land: (1) the land which was inherited property (harato pusako) of a lineage, mainly land under cultivation and used for house-sites, and (2) ulayat land, land not permanently exploited agriculturally, particularly uncleared forest. The control over these lands was vested in the penghulu as representatives of the nagari, their suku, or their lineages, depending upon the political organization of the respective nagari.[20]

The lineage was a unit in its external relations--which concerned common representation in nagari governmental and administrative affairs by its penghulu andiko, common liability for compensation in serious criminal matters, common rules of exogamy, and common representation in transactions about the pusako property of its members with members of other lineages. In its external relations all inherited property held by the lineage members was attributed to the lineage or to its penghulu(ship), the symbol of group unity and leadership.

It would be wrong to infer from this external unity that all members--or even blood relatives--would be equally entitled to all pusako property. Internally the lineage and in particular its members' property relations usually were differentiated.[21] In a true matrilineal descent group this was a result of the mechanisms of internal distribution and allocation of pusako property and of inheritance. Only those lineage members for whom the property was actually harato pusako turun temurun, i.e. the direct matrilineal descendants of the person(s) who originally acquired a particular property, had a right to be considered in the distribution. This could be all lineage members. But usually there were several complexes of such property held by smaller jurai within one

---

[19] Cf. Westenek 1918a; De Waal 1889; Kemal 1964.
[20] For accounts of ulayat land and the relationships to it in Minangkabau, see Résumé 1872:11ff; Kroesen 1874:15; Willinck 1909:637ff.; Westenek 1918a:15. The community's right over ulayat was termed beschikkingsrecht ("communal right of avail") by the Dutch adat law scholars; see Van Vollenhoven 1918:263, 1919; Logemann and Ter Haar 1927.
[21] For a more comprehensive description of the adat system of property and inheritance, see F. von Benda-Beckmann 1979a.

lineage. Such complexes came into existence when a member inherited self-acquired property (harato pancaharian) which then became pusako for him or her and for his or her descendants. Or it could originate from a temporary gift (hibah) of pusako property from a member's bako, the father's matrilineage to his child, its anak pisang (see below). Whereas such property was externally included in the lineage's pusako, and represented by the penghulu, internally only the descendants of the ex-pancaharian property or the recipients of a gift—as long as it did not return—were entitled to its economic exploitation.

However, the main portion of the lineage property usually was harato pusako turun temurun for all lineage members. The relation of the group members to their pusako was an unspecified "having" or "holding in common," which was expressed through possessive pronomina or references to the group. This "having in common" was the legal basis for acquiring concrete rights to use and exploit pusako property; it was not identical with these concrete rights. Concrete rights could only be acquired as a result of a decision-making process, ideally organized by the group head and resulting in a consensual decision of all adult group members (sakato).

The most important concrete rights were the ganggam bauntuek, the pambaoan, and the dapatan. They were all temporary in character, for definitive division of pusako property within the lineage was not allowed. When it did occur, it meant a division of the group holding common harato pusako as well, i.e. a cleavage of the lineage into two lineages, each of which was then saharato sapusako.

The ganggam bauntuek was ideally distributed to jurai of equal genealogical depth. It remained in the jurai unless a redistribution occurred. The ganggam bauntuek gave its recipients, in principle both men and women, the exclusive right to use the property. The actual use was determined by the jurai. It was generally women who exploited ganggam bauntuek property, but men could be given pambaoan property out of the ganggam bauntuek stock. The actual distribution of ganggam bauntuek depended upon the concrete needs of a woman or jurai—for example, the number of children, female children in particular, the economic situation of the women and of their husbands, additional opportunities to exploit other land by way of pambaoan or a gift (hibah). Changes in the circumstances making a distribution uneven would necessitate a redistribution. This constituted the temporary nature of the ganggam bauntuek. Redistribution also required a consensual decision by all adult lineage members. In practice such attempts often seem to have led to quarrels and ultimately to cleavages, after which the former ganggam bauntuek holding units became

lineages, each holding their own harato pusako turun temurun.
The allocation of pambaoan and dapatan had a more temporary
character.

Pambaoan could be given to a married man for exclusive
use in his nuclear family.   After his death, pambaoan in
principle reverted to the group which had given it (pambaoan
kumbali). If the relations between the man´s lineage and his
children—between bako and their anak pisang—were good, the
bako could decide to leave the property with the children for
a longer time, or the transfer could be formalized as a privileged loan or temporary gift. Decisions about pambaoan were
made unanimously by the lineage.   Whether pambaoan should be
given, in what amounts and for how long, depended on the
concrete circumstances of the situation—the economic situation of the man´s wife, the relation between her group and
that of her husband, and the possibility of eventual further
marriages to strengthen the inter-group relationship.

Dapatan was pusako property usually given to women at
the time of marriage or shortly after.   Prior to marriage,
women had no separate household there within the rumah gadang,
but worked and consumed together with their mothers. After
divorce or the woman´s death, the dapatan remained with the
group which had allocated it.

In a stratified lineage, there was an additional differentiation, for lower ranking lineage members were entitled
only to a gift (pambarian) but not to a share in the processes
of distribution (pambahagian). The lineage´s core members,
the blood relatives, would decide how much of the lineage´s
property would be given to the lower ranking members. This
property remained subject to the ultimate control of the core
members and the penghulu, and the recipients were not allowed
to pawn it.   If the blood relatives of the lineage were extinct, their pusako property could be transmitted to the lower
ranking lineage members. This was, however, no automatic process but rather required the consent of the extinct core
group´s matrilineally related relatives in other lineages.
The lower ranking lineage members were in principle excluded
from succeeding to the lineage´s sako, the penghulu title.
Within their group, however, the property they had been given
was treated as "their" pusako and this property complex was
subject to the same rules about distribution, allocation, and
inheritance as pusako in general.

Alienations of pusako property were severely restricted.
Pusako was heritage, acquired by the ancestors, to be used by
the present generation and to be passed on to future generations of group members.   "Aienyo bulieh diminum – buahnyo bulieh dimakan – batangnyo tatap tingga," i.e. "Its water may be
drunk, its fruit be eaten, but its stem remains forever." In

principle, only temporary alienations were allowed and these had either to be based upon existing special social relationships or to create such ties. One category has already been mentioned: transfers of pusako property to the group's anak pisang. Various types of such transfers were known under various terms (cf. F. von Benda-Beckmann 1979a:176ff.). Some resembled a pawning or privileged loan, others were closer in nature to a temporary gift. The property was sometimes given for as long as the children live, salamo hiduik anak. In this case the land reverted to the bako after the death of the (last) anak pisang. Alternatively, allocation was to the anak pisang's jurai in continuity. In this case the property would revert to the bako only if the children's jurai became extinct.

The other important category of temporary alienations were pagang gadai transactions, usually translated as "grondverpanding" by the Dutch or "pawning," "pledging" in English (see Guyt 1936; cf. F. von Benda-Beckmann 1979a:169ff.). Through these transactions, the pawner (panggadai) transferred the right to use the land in exchange for a sum of money or gold to the pawnee (pamagang). In classical adat, pawnings were allowed only in four cases: when a lineage required money for the marriage feast of a female member, for the installation of a penghulu, for a burial, and for the reparation of the rumah gadang. Pagang gadai transactions ideally had to be based upon social relations of matrilineal kinship, but it seems that in practice other grounds were also accepted.[22] The prospective pawner, the head of the group lineage needing money, had to try first to pawn the pusako to members of related lineages in his suku. Only if none of them was willing to give money and take the land could it be pawned to unrelated groups. Pawning of pusako required the consent of all members of the group who held the pusako in question as common pusako turun temurun. The transaction involved also a ceremony, in which the penghulu and the holders of the neighboring plots of land participated, and by their participation indicated that the transaction was in accordance with adat—a process called "preventive law care" by the Dutch scholars of adat law.[23] The location of the ceremony was relevant to the additional consequences of the pawning. The ceremony had to be held in the house of the pawnee. But male pawnees had two

---

[22] Cf. Résumé 1872:19; F. von Benda-Beckmann 1979a:170; see also Joustra 1923:118; Guyt 1936:59.
[23] See Logemann 1924; Holleman 1920; Van Vollenhoven 1931; Ter Harr 1934, 1937.

houses, the "house of the children" and "the house of the
kamanakan," i.e. the house of their wife's (lineage) and that
of their own lineage. The choice of location indicated who
would benefit from the transaction and would receive the
pawned property if the pawnee should die before the moment
that it was redeemed.

Redemption (tabuih) terminated the pawning relationship.
The right to redeem could not be abrogated in adat and was not
subject to limitation.[24]

The pawned property kept its pusako status for the
pawner's lineage. For the pawnee, the right to use the land
was determined by the status of the money invested. If the
money/gold was pusako or bungo pusako, the use-right for the
pawnee also was considered pusako. If the money was pancaharian—self-acquired property—the right to use the land
had the same status.

The pagang gadai relationship could also be ended by the
"transfer of the pawning," mangisah gadai, to a new pawnee.
In this case, the pawner might think that the relationship
should be terminated, as otherwise the new pawnee might claim
that the the land is his pusako property. If the pawner did
not have the means to redeem the property, he could decide to
transfer the gadai to a third person, a transaction often also
used to "deepen the pawning," i.e. to increase the pawning
sum. The initiative to terminate the relationship could also
come from the pawnee. If he wanted his money back, he could
offer the land for redemption to the pawner. If this offer
were not accepted, the pawnee himself could, with the pawner's
consent, initiate the transfer to a new pawnee. However, if
the pawner had refused an offer to redeem his property, he
could not then withhold his consent (F. von Benda-Beckmann
1979a:174).

2. Personally-Acquired Property

Property which was not inherited but acquired by a person's own efforts, such as newly cultivated land, trade earnings, and the products of one's own creative labor, was called
harato pancaharian. The property complex acquired by a married couple during their marriage was termed harato suarang
(individual property). In the system of adat pusako, self-
acquired goods were considered to be "pusako in chrysalis
state" (Willinck 1909:58f.). The adat status of these pro-

---

[24] See Wilken 1926:417; F. von Benda-Beckmann 1979a:172ff.

perty objects was temporary. Once the individual property holder had died, the property was inherited by the members of his _jurai_.[25]

In exchange transactions, Minangkabau individuals could dispose freely of their _pancaharian_ property. Disposition in the form of gifts, in practice gifts from a father to his children, which presented a threat of withdrawal of future _pusako_ from his _jurai_, were subject to _adat_ restrictions. Such gifts, generally termed _hibah_, were allowed and valid only _satahu saizin ahli warih_, with the "knowledge and consent" of the lineage members who were the future heirs to this property, and with the "cooperation" of the _penghulu_. _Satahu saizin_ might be better translated as "acknowledgement;" it did not refer so much to the result of a process of perception as to a social process of giving and receiving knowledge.[26]

3. Concepts, Rules, and Decisions

The dominant rules and values of the _pusako_ system were clearly expressed in the _adat_ conceptual system of property categories and relationships. Property objects and relations were dominated by the idea of the continuity of lineages and their heritage, _pusako_. Heritage (_pusako_), rather than material property objects (_harato_), stood at the apex of the universe of valuable goods, material and immaterial. Property objects were defined by their use value in relation to that continuity, and were distinguished by the means (actual labor) by which they had originally been acquired and by reference to the relative distance in time from the moment of their acquisition. _Pusako_ property was distinguished into the following categories:

> (a) _harato pusako tambilang ruyuang_--the _pusako_ property dug up from the trunk of the palm tree; the land originally cultivated by the ancestors, i.e., the real _pusako turun temurun_ of the lineage.

> (b) _harato pusako tambilang ameh_--the _pusako_ property acquired by gold or money; former _pancaharian_ goods, bought or pawned property.

---

[25] For more detailed descriptions, see Willinck 1909:776ff; Sarolea 1920; F. von Benda-Beckmann 1979a:151, 155f.
[26] See Logemann 1924:123; F. von Benda-Beckmann 1979a:193; K. von Benda-Beckmann 1982.

(c) <u>harato pusako tambilang basi</u>--land dug up with the iron hoe; recently cultivated land.

(d) <u>harato pusako tambilang budi</u> (<u>tambilang kai´tan</u>, <u>harato hibah</u>)--<u>pusako</u> or property acquired on the basis of good social relationships; land given to strangers and descendants of former slaves who were incorporated into the lineage, or land acquired by temporary gifts.

Using these categories of <u>pusako</u>, the legally relevant differential property relations within the <u>saharato sapusako</u> group may appropriately be expressed.

In the conceptual world of Minangkabau <u>adat</u>, temporary social units and relationships (marriage, patrifiliation, individual lives), and the property relations based upon them (<u>pambaoan</u>, <u>suarang</u>, <u>pancaharian</u>; temporary gifts to <u>anak pisang</u>) were overshadowed and absorbed in the diachronic notion of <u>pusako</u> continuity. All property was <u>pusako</u> in the diachronic dimension. This diachronic conceptualization of property was so dominant that <u>harato pancaharian</u> was, and to a certain extent still is (for empirical data, see F. von Benda-Beckmann 1979a:194ff.), identified and referred to as one category of <u>pusako</u> property (<u>tambilang basi/ameh</u>). In the diachronic dimension <u>pancaharian</u> is <u>pusako</u> because it will be <u>pusako</u>.

The <u>adat</u> rules and principles about property relations, distribution, allocation, pawnings, gifts, and so forth share some important traits. To varying degrees, they permit such actions or transactions to take place, state conditions concerning their validity, and prescribe the process in which they are to be carried out. But there are scarcely any strict rules stating <u>whether</u> these transactions should take place and to what concrete result they should lead. Both depend on a social process of decision-making in which the concrete circumstances of the situation must be considered--it is "<u>tergantung situasi dan kondisi</u>," as Minangkabau say nowadays. The relevance of certain types of circumstances is indicated by principles most of which have already been mentioned: the concrete needs of individuals or groups, the location of a pawning transaction, and the actual social relationships between individuals or groups. Which circumstances are the most relevant in a specific case, whether they lead to a constructive decision, and to what decision they lead must be determined in a concrete interaction process leading to a consensus (<u>sakato</u>) of the decision-makers. This action/interaction element is implicitly or explicitly integrated in the rules,[27] which rules cannot be conceived as standing apart from this action/interaction element. Under different circumstances--and these are different in nearly every case--the same rule thus can lead to different results.

What holds true for rules also holds true for the conceptions of "rights." Rights in Minangkabau _adat_ were not objective, as are rights in western law, which one either has or does not have and which can be actualized independently of "circumstances." The actualization of rights also depends upon decisions: the action/interaction element is also integrated into them. It is therefore understandable that the relations between persons and property objects are not conceptualized in terms of abstract rights in _adat_.

The Impact of the Colonial Administration

The presence of the Dutch troops and the gradual defeat of the Padri forces set the scene for the restoration of _adat_ law and order in the Minangkabau _nagari_. Although the buildup of the Dutch colonial administration introduced new elements into the socio-political organization of the _nagari_ and created unprecedented forms of super-_nagari_ governmental structures, the _nagari_ retained or returned to a socio-political organization essentially based upon the principles of the _adat pusako_. In some _nagari_, traces of Padri governmental institutions were retained, but these also were "_adat_-ized" in the course of time. Whereas the Dutch had consciously supported the "_adat_ party" against the Padri, and in their subsequent policy aimed at keeping the influence of Islamic functionaries to a minimum, they had little sympathy for the actual nature and content of the _adat_ system with its _suku_ government and matrilineal succession and inheritance rules. In their eyes, the _nagari_ were ungovernable with such a political structure, and they immediately tried to change the system by creating new political offices on the village and supra-village levels, in order to devise a new form of local government and create a workable link between their own administration and the local population. That no more far-reaching attempts to change the Minangkabau socio-political organization were made was due mainly to a lack of economic, personal, and political resources. It certainly did not stem from a positive evaluation of the _adat pusako_ system. As early as 1837, Francis commented:

---

27 See also K. von Benda-Beckmann 1980, 1981.

Many times we have tried to convince the Malays how difficult it was to deal with the _suku_ administration and how imperative it was to replace it with a hierarchical multi-level form of government. But their stubbornness and ambition did not make this possible, and thus the _suku_ administration has remained intact despite several organizations.

Neither the tyrannical government of the Padri nor the system introduced by us has been able to extinguish their general preference for the _suku_ government. (1839:128)

It therefore seems to be justified to assume that although the Dutch presence was a necessary condition for the restoration of the _adat_ system, this restoration during the 1820s and 1830s actually occurred against or despite the Dutch preference for a more "rational" hierarchical and unicentric local government organization.[28]

During the following decades, however, the Dutch administrative and economic policy brought forth important

---

[28] See also Verkerk Pistorius 1868:353ff. In his lament over the _adat suku_ government, the _adat pusako_ system, and the disappointing functioning of the Dutch created functionaries, Verkerk Pistorius even doubted that the Dutch had made the right choice when siding with the _adat_ party against the Padri:

But also the Padri did not have sufficient time to take far-reaching and persisting measures. If we had cooperated with them, if we had used their influence in place of protecting the insignificant influence of the opponents and thereby these old and obsolete institutions [i.e. of the _adat pusako_, vBB]—how much better would the prospects now be for the the well-being and the future of the native. We had no reason to be afraid of the Islamic functionaries' power; we could have subjected it to our ideas and later, if necessary, could have subjugated it completely. (1868:345)

It should be noted though that Verkerk Pistorius, like other Dutch officials who thought of the _adat pusako_ system as an obstacle to good government and development, pleaded for bringing the present governmental system more into line with _adat_ principles. Cf. Graves 1981:29ff. For more material about the Dutch policy in the first half of the 19th century, see Kielstra 1887b, 1888, 1889.

changes in the socio-political and economic structures and activities. The systematic establishment of a pseudo-traditional administrative system based upon the offices of <u>Tuangku Laras</u>, <u>penghulu kepala</u>, and <u>penghulu suku</u> (<u>rodi</u>), the introduction of the system of forced cultivation and delivery of coffee (1847), the introduction of a new judicial system officially doing away with <u>nagari</u> justice (1875), and the declaration of unused land to state domain (1874) significantly changed the political and economic context in which the Minangkabau property and inheritance law operated. According to Kahn, "...the culture system, based upon state control of land and forced cultivation of crops, served to reinforce the process of feudalization and stagnation in the indigenous commercial economy and to solidify certain aspects of local social organization." The result, in his eyes, was a static system of corporate lineage organization, based upon common ownership of and access to land and to what he calls the development of traditional Minangkabau society (1980a:163f.; 1976:87f.).

In our view, this hypothesized impact on lineage structure and land holding and distribution is not plausible. While the gradual encroachment of the Dutch colonial administration undoubtedly led to significant changes in the politico-administrative and economic context in which the system of land holding and distribution operated, it is difficult to see how it could have produced the "traditional matrilineal Minangkabau society" envisaged by Kahn.

The new administration failed. It never created the effective link to the villages for which the Dutch had hoped (cf. Francis 1839; Verkerk Pistorius 1868; Kroesen 1874; de Rooij 1890). Although the offices introduced by the Dutch were quickly "domesticated" (Graves 1981) by the Minangkabau, they could never actually replace the system of authority based upon <u>adat</u>. The result was a dualistic form of <u>nagari</u> government, which still is characteristic for contemporary Minangkabau (see Sjofjan Thalib 1974; K. von Benda-Beckmann 1981). The government consists of new or quasi-<u>adat</u> offices established by the Dutch on the one hand and genuine <u>adat</u> offices on the other. The <u>adat penghulu</u> in principle retained much of their authority and power. But in fact their functions were in part transformed and reduced and their actual power undermined, since some aspects of political decision-making processes were assumed by supra-<u>nagari</u> institutions. Other aspects, such as command over some economic activities of lineage members, were transferred to the <u>penghulu kepala</u> and the <u>penghulu suku rodi</u>.[29] The latter did not, however,

successfully usurp supervision of _pusako_ and the proper _adat_
activities (see Kroesen 1874; Verkerk Pistorius 1868; de Rooij
1890). None of the new or remodeled political units--the ar-
tificially created _laras_-district, the administrative _nagari_
under the _penghulu kepala_, and the "culture system _suku_" under
the _penghulu suku rodi_--ever became a unit characterized by
common ownership of land or a group within which there was
equal access to land. Nineteenth century administrators
generally noticed that the new functionaries did not exercise
land control rights, except for the cases in which they had
been in office as _penghulu adat_ before their appointment
(Kroesen 1874:8; see also Verkerk Pistorius 1868; de Rooij
1890). In those cases in which they used their position of
power to engage in land politics, it certainly was not to
promote equal access to land. From the very beginning of
Dutch colonial rule the Dutch officials reported the manner in
which the new local officials manipulated their external
sources of power in order to enrich themselves or their
lineage.[30]

To support his hypothesis of an actual creation, or, at
least, intensification, of communal property relations, Kahn
draws inferences from the situation in Java. De Kat Angelino
(1931:436) had suggested with regard to the effects of the
culture system on Java "that the redistribution of land, often
thought to be a product of an earlier, communal system of land
tenure, was in fact a consequence of the Culture System itself, which made access to subsistence land more important
than ever" (Kahn 1980a:167, citing Kat Angelino 1931). Noting
that in "[i]n Java, the combination of sugar-growing and the

---

[29] Kahn does not share the assumption that the imposed system
of government had a deleterious effect upon the position of
the _penghulu_ (1976:85). The facts and reasons given by him,
however, do not demonstrate anything to the contrary. If pre-
colonial forms of village organization, including much of Minangkabau property and inheritance law, and specifically including the _penghulu_'s function in land distribution, were
retained (1976:86), if the _penghulu_ could retain a degree of
judicial power, and if they were not made entirely powerless
by the new system of administration (1976:87), all this certainly does not suggest that the _panghulu_ were more powerful
than or as powerful as they had been in pre-colonial times.
[30] See Francis 1839:128; Verkerk Pistorius 1868; during the
years 1870-1874 alone, for example, 17 _Tuangku Laras_ and 54
penghulu kepala were deposed by the Dutch (Mailrapport no.
575, 22.6.1875).

cultivation of rice was intended to preserve a separate subsistence sphere," and that "[v]illage lands, in effect owned
by the colonial government, were divided up regardless of the
local structure of land ownership," Kahn maintains that
"coffee cultivation in Sumatra was organized" not "in estate
fashion, but rather by individual coffee-planters." Nevertheless, the Sumatran situation was very similar to that of Java,
as "over-all ownership of land throughout the East Indies lay
with the government..." (1980a:166).

It seems to us that this hypothesis, and the facts it
presupposes, are untenable. To begin with, there was never
overall state ownership of village land in West Sumatra.
Until 1874, when the so-called Sumatra Domain Declaration was
issued, state ownership of land existed in no way whatsoever.
The Domain Declaration, when introduced formally, certainly
did not cover all village land. Article 1 stated:

> All waste land [woeste gronden] in the Sumatran dis-
> tricts under direct Government rule are part of the
> State's domain, unless members of the indigenous pop-
> ulation exercise rights over it which are derived from
> the right of reclamation [ontginningsrecht]. Except for
> the cultivation rights of the population, the right of
> disposal is exclusively vested in the government.[31]

It was generally assumed that the ulayat lands in the
nagari had become state domain through this declaration.
However, this assumption of ownership seems to a large extent
to have existed on paper only. The declaration had been kept
"secret"; it was not brought to the notice of the adat leaders
(Korn en Van Dijk 1946:26; AB 11:80). In 1904, the assistant-
resident of the XIII and IX Kota's summarized the state of affairs as follows:

> The Director of Justice [in Batavia] relies on the
> domain declaration and seems to think that it has made
> the right of avail [beschikkingsrecht] of the native
> heads over the ulayat lands obsolete, or in any case
> subject to the Government's rights of disposal.
> According to him, the old adat, being inconsistent with

---

[31] Regeling der wijze van uitgifte van onbebouwde gronden in
de gouvernementslanden van Sumatra, Staatsblad 1874:94f. On
the different legal interpretations of these provisions, see
Van Vollenhoven 1919:53ff. See also Logemann and Ter Haar
1927:106.

the regulations, must not be adhered to anymore. I do
not wish to give a judgment on this difficult position,
but would like to state that the Local Government has
never given notice of the domain declaration to the
native heads, precisely because the declaration was inconsistent with <u>adat</u>. In practice, the heads have not
felt much or anything of the declaration, and the
Colonial Government itself has not implemented the declaration in the strict sense, probably for the same
reasons which led the Local Government of the <u>Resi-
dentie</u> to keep the declaration secret from the native
heads.[32]

Whereas land used for coffee cultivation to some extent
may have been <u>ulayat</u> land, rice land which was the <u>pusako</u> of
the lineages certainly did not fall under any form of state
ownership. While the combination of state control of land and
the culture system economy on Java may have had the effect of
creating new forms of communal ownership, it never did so in
West Sumatra.

It is equally misleading to conclude that if "the
colonial government also sought to encourage communal access
to rice land" (Kahn 1980a:166) and/or if "local officials were
therefore encouraged to administer carefully the allocation of
land on the basis of adat" (1980a:167), the colonial administration actually did take appropriate measures to ensure
this or that local officials actually did so. From what we
know, the contrary is more likely: that Minangkabau officials
rather promoted unequal access to land by using the Dutch
connection in <u>nagari</u> property politics. Besides, the Dutch
colonial administrators and courts in the 19th century did not
usually interfere in internal lineage property affairs. The
Dutch courts systematically refused to hear lineage internal
disputes about <u>pusako</u> property (Guyt 1936:145f.). And if the
Dutch interfered at all, they tended to uphold the, also in
Kahn's view, pre-colonial status-based differentiation in
lineage internal property relations (AB 11:74ff.).

Equally mistaken is Kahn's idea that by registering and
then limiting the number of <u>penghulu</u>, "the Dutch further
regulated the forms of local kinship organization in order to
fulfill the needs of the colonial government" (1980a:168).
Again, this would have been the Dutch intention. But like

---

[32] AB 11:80. For a good illustration of the practice, see the
case history described in AB 11:74ff., partly reproduced in F.
von Benda-Beckmann 1979a:259ff. See also Oki 1977:109ff.

most administrative measures of the Dutch, it resulted rather
in the opposite of the intended goal. The Dutch prohibition
on creating new penghuluships, rather than creating or intensifying corporate groups with communal ownership, seriously
affected the adat mechanisms of group splitting and group
formation (see F. von Benda-Beckmann 1979a:65ff., 365f.;
Graves 1981:41). Instead of splitting the penghulu headed
lineage which held "one sako and one harato pusako" in accordance with the adat principle that "what has become too large
must be shortened, what has become unclear must be clari-
fied,"[33] the "one-property-holding" groups became much too
large for the adat mechanisms of allocation and distribution
of land to be carried out successfully. Within the Dutch-
recognized penghulu lineage, subdivisions developed with a
great deal of autonomy in property matters. Whereas in Dutch
adat these groups could not become penghulu headed lineages,
such groups generally claimed and often established a new
title according to village adat. Thus a new ambiguity
concerning the status of groups and their property complexes
was introduced which became a dominant theme in village
politics. The more such groups developed and the more they in
time split themselves, the more difficult it became to settle
the succession to the penghuluships and to maintain lineage
control over the separate pusako complexes and the idea that
all members of a penghulu lineage were really "of one
property."

Instead of creating or intensifying the development of
corporate lineages with common ownership and equal access to
land, the Dutch measures led to an increasing dissociation of
penghulu headed groups and groups which were actually saharato
sapusako (a single group with respect to its inherited property). This development was also fed by the impact which the
culture system economy had on Minangkabau property relationships, in particular by the increasing monetization of
property relationships to land.

This monetization must not be equated with (increasing)
trade or other economic activities based upon exchange rather
than (re-)distribution of goods, nor with the monetization of
the Minangkabau economy as a whole. There is evidence that
trade played an important role in the overall Minangkabau
economy well before colonial rule, and that the years 1780-
1830 were characterized by a new trade boom in many areas of

---

33 "Pajang dikarek-buntak dikapiang." For a discussion of the
mechanisms of group splitting, see Kooreman 1902:917; Willinck
1909:353; F. von Benda-Beckmann 1979a:66ff.

Minangkabau (Dobbin 1977). At the end of the 18th century considerable quantities of coinage were introduced into the Minangkabau economy for the first time, offering an alternative to the traditional methods of barter and of exchange calculation, based on a system of gold weights (Dobbin 1977:24). But trade, and the money flow which accompanied it, was mainly an inter-<u>nagari</u> or inter-regional affair. The money earned in trade was usually invested in new exchange relations or in the acquisition of consumer goods. Under colonial rule, the monetization of the economy continued, but important changes occurred which changed the direction of the money flow and its impact on property relations. Inter-<u>nagari</u> commercial activities decreased. With this the possibilities of earning money in consumer goods or new inter-<u>nagari</u> trade also decreased as did the opportunities of investing money in consumer goods or new inter-<u>nagari</u> exchange relations. Through concentration on coffee cultivation, new money was introduced, money that in general was also held individually (see Kahn 1976:82). Since the import of new commodities, and trade in general, was restricted by the Dutch, the money flow was more or less forced into the <u>nagari</u>, where it affected the <u>nagari</u> economy and social life internally. Also affected was the system of <u>adat</u> property law which was based upon these relations.

The basic way in which money could affect internal <u>nagari</u> property relations was the system of pawning, transfers of pawnings, and redemptions. There is clear evidence that pawnings were frequent during the period of the Culture System. In 1874, Kroesen reported:

> Innumerable are the disputes about land ownership, which are the consequence of temporary alienation by means of pawning. Both parties, often the heirs in the second or third generation of the original pawner/pawnee try to prove the original right of their ancestors. The witnesses are usually dead, and what the heirs declare to have heard by tradition is usually insufficient to clarify the issue. (1874:19)

The 19th century observers were surprised by the extent to which pawnings occurred, and they could not conceive of the economic rationality behind the pawnings—a point faintly echoed by Kahn´s question of why villagers should have had any interest in rice land transactions over and above their subsistence needs (1980b:87). One should not overlook the fact that pawnings were generally initiated by the pawners who were in need of money for consumption purposes, among which were the four classical <u>adat</u> reasons: the costs of a burial, the wedding of a female lineage member, the construction of an adat house, and the installation of a penghulu. It is quite plausible that the stagnating economy and reduction of the overall money flow actually contributed to an increase in pawnings as families living off rice production and trade were increasingly cut off from the sources of earning money or gold.

The mechanisms for monetarization were pawning, redemption, and pawning transfers. The transfers of pawnings, in particular, made it possible to transfer exploitation rights on pusako property without adherence to the restrictions which adat imposed on pawnings. In the degree to which pancaharian money was invested in these transactions they led to the "pancaharianization" of pusako. This did not concern pancaharian rights to other lineages' pusako property only, but also to the holding of pancaharian-exploitation rights in one's own group's harato pusako. For if the whole group did not want or was unable to redeem the pusako, then individual group members could not be prevented from doing so in order to acquire the right, though temporarily, to use and exploit the pusako property exclusively. In adat, such transfers were not termed "redemption" but rather "transfer of the gadai" (mangisah gadai). This terminology indicated that the pusako-relationship of the whole group (for whom the property in question was turun temurun) and their right to redeem and redistribute the property were not affected by the pancaharianization of one's own pusako.

Thus the basis was laid for a new type of differentiation of pusako property relations, based upon money investment. The importance of the processes of distribution within the whole group was reduced, and actual exploitation rights were brought to smaller social units. In both respects, the authority which the penghulu could exercise over their lineage's pusako property was undermined.

In sum, we can state that (a) in early 19th century Minangkabau, there did not exist a system of static, penghulu focused lineages, the property of which was held in common ownership giving each lineage member equal access to land, and that (b) the Dutch administrative and economic policy did not create such a system or intensify its development; but on the contrary, Dutch policy created the conditions for the gradual dissolution of political and socio-economic groups and for the emergence of a new type of internal lineage differentiation in access to land.

20th Century Developments

In the early decades of the 20th century, economic and

legal developments changed the impact of the monetization and pancaharianization of relations to pusako property significantly. The system of forced cultivation was abandoned and replaced by money taxation. Minangkabau was opened up to the influx of foreign commodities and the administrative and commercial sectors expanded. New needs for money and new means of earning money were thereby created. As far as we can tell from the available sources, the new economic conditions led to an increasing monetization of the relationships to pusako property, which considerably affected the operation of the adat mechanisms of land distribution and allocation. For "pusako held with money" was not subject to ganggam bauntuek (re)distribution in the group for which the property originally was, and in principle remained, common pusako property. The adat mechanisms, however, were not replaced. They continued to operate, but in the smaller lineage segments, expanding through time, which held the use-rights to the pusako land on the basis of invested money.

The impact of the monetization of relationships to pusako land became even greater when the adat and adat law restrictions on dispositions over pancaharian property were relaxed. In the second and third decade of the 20th century, the adat principle requiring the consent or acknowledgement of the penghulu and all adult lineage members for a gift of pancaharian was dropped and the freedom of disposition was generally accepted both in village adat and the courts' adat law.[34] Pancaharianized use-rights to pusako now could freely be transferred to a man's own children. In theory at least, most pusako property could be held individually and be transferred within the conjugal family, though in theory and practice such transfers were only temporary and their effect could be undone if the members of the group holding pusako rights exercised them. A new dimension was added to this development when in the 1960s village adat and court adat law definitively accepted intestate inheritance rights of children in their father's pancaharian property, even though this new rule still operates only within the nuclear family. Outside this circle the matrilineal system of inheritance rules is still intact. Also, once pancaharian property has been inherited by children, it becomes pusako in their lineage segment and is forthwith inherited matrilineally (cf. Kato 1977:268).

Ironically enough, corporate lineages with common

---

[34] See F. von Benda-Beckmann 1979a:328 with case references; in particular see the decisions in the case of the inheritance of dr. Muchtar, TR 131:82ff.

ownership and equal access to land were being created precisely during that time in which, in the eyes of contemporary and later observers, the matrilineal system was breaking down. When the tax system was introduced in 1908, the units made responsible for the payment of taxes were the groups which were considered by the Dutch to own pusako property in common. For these groups, the Dutch created a standard term, kaum. The kaum was represented by its head, whom the Dutch styled mamak kepala waris, "the mamak who is the head of the heirs, i.e. lineage members." The kaum with its common harato pusako and its mamak kepala waris also became the standard legal body which dominated, and still dominates,[35] court proceedings over pusako property. This terminology has been a constant source of confusion.[36] The word kaum refers to groups of different size (penghulu lineages, sublineages) in different nagari, yet all kaum are treated according to the same rules in the court system (cf. K. von Benda-Beckmann 1982:29).

Thus for the first time, lower level units of adat socio-political organization which in adat held pusako in common in the sense that they constituted one property-complex in their external relations, were directly linked to external administrative and judicial institutions of the colonial system. From that time onwards, Dutch administrative attention switched from the penghulu suku (rodi) to "the mamaks"-- mamak the manager, mamak the creditor, mamak the manipulator of pusako property. Schrieke's report and several court judgments from the first decades of the 20th century give a vivid impression of the manipulation of pusako property by mamak kepala waris (Schrieke 1955; Guyt 1936:145-155; Oki 1977:128).

The role of the mamak in the property affairs of their lineage members was strengthened by a new wave of adat interpretation which reflects the Dutch desire to have individual persons responsible for the pusako complex also in non-tax matters. This was the "recognition" that in the four classical adat situations a mamak kepala waris could pawn the pusako property of his kaum without the consent or acknowledgment of even the closest kaum members. The formulation of this new adat rule seems to have been more or less a one man show. It was asserted by Guyt in his dissertation Grondver-

---

[35] In about 50% of all civil disputes at least one party acted as mamak kepala waris. See K. von Benda-Beckmann 1981:125. In pusako disputes this percentage was much higher.
[36] See K. von Benda-Beckmann 1981:143-4.

panding in Minangkabau (1936:70-74), based upon some ambiguous statements in the literature and some recent court judgments (Landraad Pariaman 1926; Landraad Fort de Kock 1933; Landraad Payakumbuh 1933). However, the chairman of the courts handing down the explicit statements of the new rule in the last two cases had been Guyt himself—a fact not mentioned in his dissertation.[37] This interpretation has not been upheld in post-Independence Minangkabau.

The Transformation of Adat

The creation of the "kaum as owner of its pusako" in the early 20th century was a marking point in a development in which adat property relationships had been transformed by western legal thinking. This development and the mechanisms of transformation must be well understood, because the transformed adat notions gradually became an independent adat law system of increasing relevance in practical property affairs, but also because they heavily influenced later interpretations of social change in Minangkabau.

The influence of Dutch legal thinking in the description and interpretation of Minangkabau adat is most evident in the attempt to conceive of property categories and relationships in western notions of rights, and, in particular, of ownership (eigendom). A good impression of the degree to which this was done can be won by reading through the 19th century sources collected in the Pandecten van het Adatrecht.[38] This review shows that even where the adat system is largely described in its own and not in technical legal terms,[39] the descriptions are ultimately summarized in terms of eigendom. Basically, harato pancaharian was considered to be individual ownership, pusako property common or family ownership.

Once this thinking became manifest, it had consequences at several levels of interpretation. In Dutch law, ownership is an institution of the private as distinct from the public

---

[37] See Guyt 1936:72; TR 126:75, 140:218, 140:226; compare also Ter Haar's postscript in 140:225.

[38] Vol. I (1914) on the beschikkingsrecht ("communal right of avail") and Vol. III (1916) on the inlandsch bezitsrecht ("native right of ownership [possession] of land"), in which excerpts from the writings of 20 and 23 authors have been collected.

[39] See for instance Verkerk Pistorius 1871; Résumé 1872; Kroesen 1874; Wilken 1883.

law sphere. Dutch law, of course, recognizes also public legal relations to property, land in particular, of sovereignty over territory, public control and administration of land vested in the state and its administrative agencies. The state, or less inclusive public corporations, can also be owners in the sense of private law—but this is something very different from its exercise of public legal rights.

In this conceptual frame, the much less differentiated public and private aspects of _adat_ property relations could not be adequately expressed. The communities' relations to _ulayat_ land posed a particular problem, since the state had assumed sovereignty, and in 1870-1874, also private ownership of land not held in ownership by Indonesians. The discussions occurring in the 1870's, and after the introduction of the Domain Declarations, show the dilemma with which the colonial lawyers were confronted: either the relations to _ulayat_ were sovereign rights, and had then been replaced by the state's rights, or else they were private ownership rights, in which case they would be exempt from the Domain Declaration. The relations to _ulayat_ land fitted neither category well, and so there ensued long and politically and economically motivated controversies about what consequences should be held to follow.[40] The West Sumatran practice is largely known: the colonial government considered _ulayat_ land to fall under the state's domain, though the population was allowed to exercise rights of cultivation (_ontginningsrecht_); the local government was strongly opposed to this interpretation and was extremely hesitant to interfere with _ulayat_ land.

In the dichotomous framework of public-private law, the relationships to _ulayat_ land thus were assimilated into Dutch public rights. _Pusako_ relations were reduced to the dimension of private law. Lineages which in their external property relations formed a unit in _adat_, i.e. mainly in public and political matters, were thus conceived of as property holding units in terms of private law also. All the _pusako_ properties held by the lineage's members formed one property complex. Translated into western notions of rights, it was only logical that the _familie_ (lineage, _kaum_) was considered to be a legal

---

[40] For different interpretations by officials in Minangkabau, see Verkerk Pistorius 1871 and Willinck 1909; see also Oki 1977:109f. For the discussion on the national colonial level, often with reference to the Minangkabau case, see Van Vollenhoven 1919; Logemann and Ter Haar 1927; Korn and Van Dijk 1946; 's Jacob 1945; Nolst Trenité 1912, 1920. Cf. Burns 1978.

body holding property in common ownership. It was a "rechts-gemeenschap" with common property and common administration.

Although there existed fairly detailed and differentiated accounts of the internal system of property relations, these were also transformed by the same logic: the right of ownership in Dutch law is the most absolute right which includes the right to use and to exploit the property objects being owned. Lesser rights must be derived from ownership. The concrete adat rights flowing from ganggam bauntuek distribution and pambaoan/dapatan allocation were translated into such rights, e.g. gebruiksrecht (right of use), but this presupposed the existence of a legal body, the familie, which was different from the sum of its members. Within the unit of common ownership of pusako, there could not be a smaller unit having equal rights to a part of the common property complex. Consequently, only the familie, the lineage, was considered to be a rechtsgemeenschap, and not the lineage segment, the jurai (see Van Vollenhoven 1918:250).[41]

The introduction of the neologism "inlandsch bezitrecht" did not lessen or otherwise change the effects of this transformation. It was a well-meant effort to conceive of "oriental" rights in oriental terms and to explicate the difference between the adat concepts and the western term eigendom. But this "orientalization" of eigendom concerned the external aspects of the rights of property holding units, be they individuals or groups; i.e. differences in the rights to dispose of property by way of sale, gift, etc. (see Van Vollenhoven 1918:264). It did not affect the idea that the group was holding one property in common on the basis of a common right.

Thus the important and legally relevant distinctions within the pusako property complex in adat could not be adequately expressed. The distribution and allocation of ganggam bauntuek, pambaoan, and dapatan were pushed into the background. By the same logic the inheritance of ganggam bauntuek and pancaharian property was also transformed.

This was done in two ways: Through inheritance the pancaharian right was transferred. The receiver had to be a legal person, capable of holding rights. We have seen that only the family, the lineage, was such a unit, not a lineage

---

[41] Different, and much more differentiated, was the description and interpretation given by Willinck (1909), who very systematically related the adat notions to the Dutch eigendom notions and who particularly also analyzed the differences in the internal rights and mechanisms of distribution.

segment. Thus, the individual ownership (<u>harato pancaharian</u>) had to become common ownership (<u>harato pusako</u>) of the whole lineage. <u>Ganggam bauntuek</u>, on the other hand, could not be inherited at all, because it was not held by a legal person, but by a segment only.[42] This led some authors to deny the possibility of inheritance-like transfers at all and to construe the changes in property relations on the model of accrual and decrease derived from western (Germanic) notions of common ownership.

> The Malayan law does not have the right of inheritance, nor does it know heirs. Each time a family member dies, the remaining members' shares increase, and each time a new member is born into the family, the other members' shares in the <u>pusako</u> decrease. <u>Harta pentjarian</u> becomes part of the <u>pusako</u> as soon as the person who had acquired it dies. But also here we cannot speak of "inheritance." The <u>pentjarian</u> is <u>ipso jure</u> joined with the <u>pusako</u> as a consequence of the death, but does not fall as inheritance to the persons entitled in the <u>pusako</u>.[43]

In these interpretations, the existence of the internal lineage differentiations of the <u>pusako</u> complex described earlier could not be maintained.

It must be noted that the interpretations given above are the result of a systematic interpretation of <u>adat</u> in terms of Dutch jurisprudence. They were not fully developed until the early 20th century, which saw the emergence of the <u>adat</u> jurisprudence, in particular in and as a consequence of the work of Van Vollenhoven. Most 19th century descriptions and

---

[42] This view was basically shared by Van Vollenhoven who recognized inheritance only between families (lineages), <u>suku</u>, and <u>nagari</u>, i.e. between <u>rechtsgemeenschappen</u> (1918:250, 261). He also held that <u>pancaharian</u> fell to the <u>familie</u> as a whole; only in the first generation was there a "precedence-in-use" (<u>onderhoudsvoorrang</u>) for the closest matrilineal relatives. In the notes added to the second volume of his <u>Adatrecht van Nederlandsch-Indie</u> (1931:883f.), however, he freely admitted his incorrect interpretation after reading the account of Sarolea (1920) which confirmed Willinck's description. This seems to have gone unnoticed, however, and his influential statement was forthwith reproduced in the literature. Cf. F. von Benda-Beckmann 1979a:190.

[43] AB 6:179; see also Smits and Bosse as quoted in Willinck 1909:769ff.

interpretations did not go so far. Though freely operating in terms of such notions as individual and common ownership, their emphasis remained in detailed ethnographic description rather than pressing the data into a logical system built upon the notions of ownership. Also, in the early 20th century Willinck had given a very detailed description and interpretation of the adat legal system, in which he had freely used Dutch and Roman legal notions. However, he used them as a comparative framework for a better understanding of adat instead of transforming adat notions into them.

Under the influence of the adat jurisprudence, however, these earlier descriptions were further transformed, and Willinck's work was not held in high esteem by the Leiden adat law scholars.[44] A systematic "correction" and adaptation of earlier "wrong" or "unsystematic" descriptions took place when the sources were collected and published in the Pandecten van het Adatrecht. To give one example: In 1871, Verkerk Pistorius had written about pancaharian inheritance:

> All goods left by a deceased, whether he was married or not, fall to the relatives* [sic] to whom he, according to Malayan thinking, is most closely related. The inheritance of the Malay...falls to his brothers and sisters* [sic] and later to the sisters' children but not to his wife and his own children. (1871:45)

In the Pandecten, the words marked with the asterisk were corrected with the annotation: "better: familie (legal person)."[45]

The relations to pusako were further adjusted to Dutch conceptions of property rights by moving away from the diachronic towards the more familiar synchronic dimension as the basis for distinctions. Thus the elaborate distinctions by source of acquisition of pusako property were trivialized. They were reduced to a simple distinction between "high" and "low" pusako property, between harato pusako tinggi and harato pusako rendah, the former being the pusako which since old times had been in the family, and the latter being property

---

[44] Willinck's writing was heavily biased against Islam, matriliny, and "the Minangkabau." Besides he had severely criticized Wilken who was regarded as one of the founding fathers of the Leiden adat law school. See the polemics between Willinck (1911) and Van Ossenbruggen (1911).

[45] Vol. III, 1916:365; for more examples, see annotations on pp. 224, 362-368.

recently made into _pusako_. The basic distinction in the _adat_
law literature became the one between _harato pusako_ and _harato
pancaharian_ (cf. F. von Benda-Beckmann 1979a:351ff.).

This interpretation of _adat_ rules and property relations
increasingly divested _adat_ rules and rights of their element
of orientation to action. The notion of equal shares in the
pusako complex, of decrease and accrual in accordance with the
number of living lineage members, or of equal rights in
pusako of "the entitled person," i.e. _all_ lineage members, did
not leave room for the intellectual and social processes in
which the concrete needs and social relationships of the
persons concerned could become relevant.

Since we lack sufficiently detailed sources, it is
difficult to assess the actual significance of these interpretations and their use by the colonial courts for the
property and inheritance affairs of Minangkabau villagers.
But the changes certainly increased during the first half of
the 20th century. Judging from the available sources[46] and
drawing cautious inferences from our own research in 1974-75,
we discern the following developments:

In the late 1920s the colonial courts started to accept
kaum disputes about _pusako_ property as a matter of principle
(Guyt 1936:146). Although most disputes continued to be dealt
with by the _nagari adat_ councils before they reached the
courts (Guyt 1934), we can assume that the actual number of
court cases increased, and with this the opportunity for the
courts to impose their interpretations in intra-_kaum_ as well
as other _pusako_ disputes. Judging from contemporary
experience, we can, however, assume that even then the
percentage of disputes internal to _kaum_ remained relatively
small and that such cases mainly concerned inter-segment
disputes in which the actual distribution of the _pusako_ was
not submitted to or decided by the court.[47] The court
insisted upon the "_adat_ rule" that in all disputes about
pusako property, the _kaum_ (the owner) must appear in court
represented by its _mamak kepala waris_. Thereby, access to
adat court law was limited in cases where individual _kaum_
members, mostly women, had grievances but could not bring them

---

[46] See e.g. Ter Haar 1929; Guyt 1934, 1936; Korn 1941; the
case law published in TR no. 140.
[47] During 1968-74, only 11% of all _pusako_ disputes in the
courts of Bukit Tinggi, Batu Sangkar, and Payakumbuh concerned
internal lineage disputes (F. von Benda-Beckmann 1979a:307; K.
von Benda-Beckmann 1982; for similar statistical information
from the 1960s, see Tanner 1969, 1971).

to court due to an unwilling mamak (see K. von Benda-Beckmann 1981:144). The courts' adat law application based upon the interpretations outlined in this section, disregarding the internal differentiation of property relationships and paying no attention to circumstances which in adat would have been relevant, resulted in decisions which were quite different from those made in local adat procedures. Treating adat principles as strict rules instead of as principles subject to differential actualization, depending upon different kinds of circumstances, led to the misunderstanding and unjust application of adat law about which Korn complained so bitterly in 1941 (1941:302, 315). Besides, the village institutions of dispute settlement increasingly imitated the decision-making style of the courts (Ter Haar 1929; K. von Benda-Beckmann 1981) through which the Dutch influences were gradually introduced into village life.

The Interpretation of Change

Several social scientists have regarded the end of the system of forced cultivation and the introduction of the tax system as a dramatic turning point in the social and economic history of Minangkabau.[48] In their view, this change was marked by the dissolution of the matrilineal socio-legal system and the rise of the nuclear family (Schrieke et al. 1928; Maretin 1961) or even the development from matriliny to patriliny (Maretin 1961), involving the hypothesized development of inheritance rights in the father's line (Van Vollenhoven 1918:271; Joustra 1923; Schrieke et al. 1928; Maretin 1961; Scholz 1977). Kahn posits a development characterized by increasing individualization of property rights leading to the breakdown of common ownership and equal access to land and to an increasing differentiation of land holdings as a consequence of individualization and dramatically increasing land mobility (Kahn 1980a). Schrieke and Maretin point to the emergence of a new dominant mode of production, rural capitalism (Schrieke et al. 1928; Maretin 1961), and Kahn posits petty commodity production (Kahn 1975, 1980a). However, other recent research has shown that despite considerable change in social and economic behavior, and some significant changes in adat law, one can speak neither of a breakdown of the adat ideological-legal system nor of its loss of practical sig-

---

[48] Mainly Schrieke 1928, 1955; Maretin 1961; Kahn 1975, 1976, 1980a; cf. Scholz 1977.

nificance.[49] Instead there emerges a picture of a much more gradual process of individualization and monetarization of property relationships, and of shifts within rather than away from the matrilineal system.

The weakness of the first kind of interpretation is in exaggerations both of a "traditional matrilineal system" and in inferences of changes in the first three decades of the 20th century: 19th century conditions are seen as too "communal," 20th century conditions as too individualized. As we have tried to demonstrate in this paper, this diachronic comparison proceeds from a false historical baseline: it is based upon conditions of 19th century Minangkabau seen through the eyes of western legal thinking, either as a result of the writer's own bias or as a result of a retrojection of the early 20th century adat law image of the common ownership of pusako by the kaum into the past. Such retrojection was probably facilitated by the apparent paradox that this image was only fully developed at a time when social and economic activity pointed towards greater individualization and differentiation in the access to pusako land. Besides, the comparison was largely a "false comparison" (Van Velsen 1969). It related social and economic behavior to the (assumed) adat ideology of the past; even worse, for this past it assumed that social and economic behavior was consonant with the ideological system.

Moreover the interpretations of the consequences of the observed behavior in the early 20th century, mainly the increasing land mobility, were colored by western legal thinking, based especially on the equation of harato pancaharian with individual ownership. For example, one of Schrieke's important arguments for his break-down prognosis was that in 1927 nearly all land in the Solok region had been pawned and converted into self-acquired property (1955:710). His assumption was that this state of affairs would remain. But, as Prins had pointed out already in 1948, research subsequent to 1927 had shown that most property in the area was pusako property (AB 41:392; Oki 1977:126). Prins correctly pointed out that the use-rights could well be regarded as pancaharian property but that this did not affect the pusako status of the land to which use-rights pertained (1954:52; see also F. von Benda-Beckmann 1979a:422). It must also be kept in mind that the pancaharian-like use-rights

---

[49] Tanner 1971; Thomas 1977; Kato 1977; Oki 1977; F. von Benda-Beckmann 1979a; K. von Benda-Beckmann 1981; Prindiville 1980.

themselves became _pusako_ for the holder's _jurai_ after his death. In Schrieke's interpretation there is an implicit equation of _harato pancaharian_ with individual ownership. This led him to believe that the use-rights, or the land to which they pertained, would in the future retain their individualized status. This would be so with individual ownership but was not the case with _pancaharian_ property.[50]

The distortion of past and present by western legal thinking also led to an exaggerated importance attached to the change in the inheritance rules concerning _pancaharian_, which was incorrectly taken to be the other important nail in the coffin of matriliny (see Schrieke 1955:118; Maretin 1961:193). Here again, the diachronic comparison is false in several respects. It proceeds from a state of Minangkabau society characterized by a strict and "pure" matrilineal system in relation to which any non-matrilineal element is dramatized as "deviance" or "development" (cf. F. von Benda-Beckmann 1979a:-373ff.). But in terms of descent and lineality, the change in _pancaharian_ inheritance is certainly not as drastic as it has been made out to be. Many of what appear to be elements of change were in fact integral parts of the traditional social organization. For example, the traditional system recognized bilateral kinship relations (a point made by Djojodigoeno 1968:262ff.; Fischer 1964), ones not very heavily loaded with social functions. The patrifiliative link between children and father, and through the father to his lineage, was always an integral part of the Minangkabau social system.[51] More important, this link could always be used as a basis for property transfers. Property transfers between a father and his children, or between the _bako_ and its reciprocal _anak_

---

[50] For a similar interpretation, see Scholz 1977:136f.
[51] Korn (1941) and Fischer (1964) in particular have stressed the importance of the father-children/_bako-anak pisang_ relationship as part of the social organization and cautioned against the superficial interpretation in terms of pure matriliny. De Josselin de Jong's interpretation (1951) of the Minangkabau social system as being based upon a system of double unilineal descent is exceptional insofar as it does not subscribe to the naive notion of a formerly exclusively matrilineal Minangkabau, and in that it does not treat the "deviations" from matriliny as "changes." But instead of concentrating upon the bilateral kinship elements and the patrifiliative link, it postulates the existence of a patri_line_ for which the evidence adduced remains unconvincing; cf. Thomas 1977.

<u>pisang</u>, were not a new element nor were they forbidden by
<u>adat</u>--they were only restricted by the way in which the
father's lineage exercised its autonomy in decisionmaking
about such transfers.

The misconstruction of change is most evident in
Schrieke's description (1955:118), which served as a point of
departure for later authors, such as Maretin (1961) and Kahn
(1976). In discussing the changes, Schrieke notes that:

> ...the <u>adat</u> laws of inheritance as applied to acquired
> property display a growing recognition of a new set of
> laws governing intestate inheritance in place of the
> original rule by which property passed to the branch of
> the family in question or the most nearly related
> branches as the case may be.(1955:188)

Schrieke, however, adduces no evidence at all for children's
intestate inheritance; references are made only to property
transfers based upon gifts (<u>hibah</u>) and last wills (<u>umanat</u>).
These are implicitly contrasted to a strictly matrilineal inheritance rule, and so gift practices, arrangements of property transfers after mutual consultation, depending upon the
mutual relations of the families, appear to be something new.
That they are not new is evident from Schrieke's own 19th
century sources (1955:118, note 37; 271) which give a similar
impression, but which also do not speak of intestate inheritance.

But even when in the 1960s[52] intestate inheritance
rights of children were recognized, both on the village level
and in the Indonesian state courts, the impact of the overall
change in inheritance rules on the <u>adat pusako</u> system remained
limited. It must be recalled that <u>pancaharian</u> property is not
continuously individual ownership. Even if once transferred
by way of gift or inheritance to the children, it becomes
<u>pusako</u> property in the children's lineage segment,[53] and as
such follows the continuity outlined by matrilineal inheritance after its short patrifiliative interlude. Besides,
the new inheritance rules only function within the nuclear
family; outside this circle, the matrilineal system is still
intact (cf. Oki 1977:138). To speak of a change of the inheritance system, from a matrilineal to a bilateral or even
patrilineal system, is completely unfounded. Apart from the

---

[52] On the development, see F. von Benda-Beckmann 1979a:335ff.
[53] F. von Benda-Beckmann 1979a:343. See for Padang, Evers
1975.

viricentric bias of such interpretation—pancaharian property held by women was always inherited by their children—the changes did not greatly affect the adat as an ideological and legal system.[54]

This conclusion, of course, is not to deny the changes which have occurred in the social and economic behavior of Minangkabau villagers and in the social and economic significance of the adat property categories. But even these changes should not be dramatized. The residential and socio-economic arrangements which dominate contemporary village life, on the one hand, seem to demonstrate the break-up of the matrilineal system, but simultaneously they reinforce the principles upon which it is based. It has become very rare for a whole sublineage to co-reside in adat longhouses. Most villagers nowadays live in small houses, and the conjugal family, together perhaps with the wife's mother or aunt, forms the dominant residential unit.[55] But the houses in which married men live are always on their wives' pusako land, and any money or labor they invest into them invariably passes to their wives' (lineage). Since the system of residence is effectively governed by adat and pusako, men have no chance of establishing neolocal residence. Men do little work on the pusako lands of their lineage, but spend most of their labor on their wives' pusako or on land which they have temporarily acquired through pawnings, transfers of pawnings, or redemptions. All this comes close to the ideal of a modern nuclear family with the husband and father being free from the bonds of his lineage membership.

But most pancaharian money is invested for the benefit of their wives and daughters and invariably becomes pusako in their (sub)lineage. Thus men contribute to the maintenance of the pusako system through their wives and daughters, and the more they do so, the less they are a danger to their sisters, through whom the pusako system is maintained (see also Tanner 1971:34; Kato 1977:265). Pawnings and transfers of pawnings are frequent and have gradually created a market for temporary use rights to land. But as land mobility increases and land increasingly assumes a monetary value, redemptions and redemption-type transfers of pawnings also increase, because they are an important means of getting access to land. And through redemptions and redemption disputes,[56] the notion of pusako

---

[54] See also Tanner 1971:34; Kato 1977:267ff.; F. von Benda-Beckmann 1979a:373ff., 1980.
[55] Cf. Thomas 1977:59ff.; Scholz 1977:145; Kato 1977:201.
[56] Many land disputes brought to court concern the question of

and the rights based upon matrilineal inheritance are constantly restated.

New Transformations of Property Relationships and Categories

Independence and the subsequent replacement of Dutch judges and administrative officials by Indonesians (Minangkabau people for the most part) did not immediately bring any significant changes in the interpretations of Minangkabau adat in court practice and legal literature (see F. and K. von Benda-Beckmann 1981). Most judges were alienated from village life and had been socialized in western legal thinking during their professional training. The growing Indonesian literature on adat law to a large extent simply reproduced the older Dutch classics like Van Vollenhoven and Ter Haar, and little research on local adat law or its development was carried out. The last decades, however, have seen the emergence of new tendencies in the transformation of adat property relations and categories. The most important one in our view is the redefinition of adat property categories in terms of hak milik (ownership, eigendom) and the weakening or abolition of the rule that pancaharian property becomes pusako property after its holder's death.

These tendencies are fed by two channels. One is the introduction of the Basic Agrarian Law of 1960 and its innumerable implementing regulations. Although professed to be based upon adat, the property categories and relationships defined in it are basically of the Dutch law type.[57] Hak milik, the most (although by no means completely) absolute right in the agrarian law, shows most characteristics of the Dutch eigendom. Although detailed knowledge of the law by Minangkabau villagers is extremely rare and the actual implementation of its regulations in Minangkabau, the registration and conversion of adat rights into the rights defined by the code in particular, is minimal so far (F. von Benda-Beckmann 1979a:281), the law provides a new conceptual frame in which to talk and think about property relationships.

Secondly, until the first decades of the 20th century, the transformation of adat property categories and relationships was practically mainly concerned with the external aspects of property relationships. The transformation of the

_____

which party is entitled to redeem the property in dispute.
[57] See Gautama and Harsono 1972:39f.; Gautama and Hornick 1972:97ff.; Tan 1977.

internal relations to pusako property was basically confined
to descriptions and interpretations in the literature. During
the last 50 years, however, internal group relationships and
adat property categories in general have been increasingly
transformed, both in economic and legal practice. It has
already been mentioned that in the beginning of this century
disputes about internal group relationships to pusako were
opened up to direct judicial intervention. Besides this, the
increase of temporary land transfers based on money investments led to an increase in pancaharian rights to exploit
pusako land. Land disputes have more and more involved both
pusako and pancaharian rights. As a result, new interpretations and redefinitions of pancaharian, as a consequence of
the new rules about disposition and future inheritance, also
affected the rights to pusako. This effaced the sharp distinction between pancaharian and pusako property.

At the same time there are attempts from several quar-
ters to reduce the adat property distinctions to one basic
distinction—harato pusako and harato pancaharian—and to
redefine the legal status of self-acquired property. At the
conference on Minangkabau adat and history held in 1969, a
Minangkabau lawyer proposed that in the future only the
concepts of harato pusako and harato pancaharian should be
recognized; he also proposed abolition of the concept of
pusako rendah. The consequences were stated quite explicitly:

> The harato pusako (which generally have been called
> harato pusako tinggi) which already exist, will be left
> in peace. There will be no further possibility for the
> existence of pusako rendah, as this would lead to an
> increase in pusako tinggi.[58]

Attempts at redefinition were also made during the 1952
conference of the Badan Permusyawaratan Alim Ulama, Ninik
Mamak, dan Cerdik Pandai: Here pancaharian property was among
others defined as the property objects which one has received
by Islamic testamentary dispositions and by way of hibah.[59]

Following the emphasis in Dutch law on the synchronic
sphere of property law, interpreters are also inclined to

---

[58] See F. von Benda-Beckmann 1979a:358. See also the judgment
of the Indonesia Supreme Court in which the new inheritance
rule for pancaharian was stated, Yurisprudensi Indonesia 1969
III:17-33.
[59] Cf. Prins 1953; Tanner 1969; F. von Benda-Beckmann
1979:324ff.

focus on the legal status of property during the holder's lifetime: the full rights of disposition typical for the western notion of individual ownership. _Harato pancaharian_ is therefore sometimes called _hak milik_ (_pribadi_), the Indonesian expression for individual ownership. _Hak milik_ also implies its reified character: it does not only define the relationships to property but also the legal status of the property object. Once the equation _harato pancaharian_ = _hak milik_ has been made, it is only a small step to invoke the _hak milik_ characteristics when an item so characterized is inherited. In westernized legal thinking, _hak milik_ keeps its status after inheritance; it does not become _pusako_ any more. Thus the _adat_ rule according to which self-acquired property becomes _pusako_ is in danger of becoming obsolete. As rights to use _pusako_ often have _pancaharian_ character, these transformations tend to affect and change the rights to _pusako_ themselves and give rise to categories such as "private _pusako_ property" or "property which originates from _harato pancaharian_ and which has according to its development become _hak milik_" (see F. von Benda-Beckmann 1979a:348ff.). These notions cannot be accommodated by the internal logic of the _adat pusako_ any more.

It seems premature to speak as yet of developments implying a new system of _adat_ law. We rather have to do with a gradually emerging tendency which coexists with, and is still dominated by older _adat_ interpretations and practices. Sometimes the tendency is articulated in single court decisions, the fate of which is uncertain (see F. von Benda-Beckmann 1979a:352ff.). Such court cases usually involve the status of men's _pancaharian_ objects as a critical problem; the status of women's _pancaharian_ after death is only very rarely a problem for villagers. So the articulation of the new tendency is limited to non-representative types of cases. Besides, the courts and villagers are usually concerned with _ad hoc_ solutions to problems and not with the creation of a new conceptual system.

However, these tendencies must be followed attentively. The _pusako_ization of _pancaharian_ property is of basic importance for the maintenance of the _pusako_ system, for it guarantees that, through time and inheritance, all property will become _pusako_. If _pusako_ is abolished, the basis is provided for a real breakdown of both the _adat_ ideological system and the behavior relating to it.

COMMERCIALIZATION AND CHANGE IN MINANGKABAU:
A RE-EXAMINATION OF THE HISTORICAL WATERSHED

Joel Kahn
University College, London

In his contribution to the published findings of the government Commission appointed to investigate the causes for the spread of communism in West Sumatra in the 1920s (Schrieke et al. 1928), the sociologist B.J.O. Schrieke advanced the thesis that the period between 1908 and 1912 represented an important watershed in the history of the Residency. The growth in support for the P.K.I. (Indonesian Communist Party), he argued, could be largely attributed to the sudden increase in the pace of economic change that followed the end of forced cultivation and commercial restrictions imposed by the colonial government from the mid-19th century. The decline of commercial monopoly as a cornerstone of colonial economic policy resulted in increased commercialization of the rural economy, which in turn generated intense pressures on traditional social relations and institutions—pressures which allowed an unscrupulous Communist leadership to drum up support through a variety of devious means.

Until quite recently, Schrieke's analyses have been accepted by Indonesianists largely without challenge. His explanations for the success of the P.K.I. in West Sumatra have, for example, been more or less reproduced by Ruth McVey in her otherwise extremely scholarly book on the early history of the P.K.I., while Schrieke's writings on economic change have passed almost unaltered into anthropological discourse through Geertz's important study of processes of social and ecological change in Indonesia (see Geertz 1963:116ff).

However, in the last few years an important element in Schrieke's overall argument has come in for considerable criticism. The criticism comes from a group of younger scholars who have carried out field and/or archival research on West Sumatra in the last decade. Prompted in part by the discovery that Schrieke's predictions concerning the ultimate demise of the Minangkabau system of kinship and social organization have proved either incorrect or substantially oversimplified, and in part by a more detailed examination of economic conditions in 19th century Minangkabau, these writers have subjected Schrieke's periodization of economic and con-

sequent social change to critical scrutiny, undermining as a
consequence the notion that the latter years of the first
decade of this century can in fact be taken to be a significant historical watershed. Ken Young, for example, in a
short report on his ongoing historical research, argues that
Minangkabau peasants experienced a commodity boom at least two
decades before the supposed watershed (Young 1980), while Oki
(1977, and this volume), Benda-Beckmann (1979a), and Kato
(1982) all point to significant degrees of monetization in the
19th century as evidence that the watershed thesis should be
rejected.

While sympathetic to the general aims of these critics,
and particularly to their exposure of the naive Traditional-
Modern periodization that underlies Schrieke's analyses, I
want in this paper to suggest that we should not throw out the
baby with the bathwater by entirely ignoring the specific
effects of the late 19th century economic transformations in
Indonesia that can conveniently be dated to the passage of the
Agrarian Land Laws of the 1870s. For while the effects of
these transformations may have been less directly evident in
West Sumatra than in regions more closely linked to the expansion of foreign capitalist enterprise—an expansion made possible by the Agrarian Land Laws' provisions for the leasing of
land held on traditional rights of tenure to private capital—
they were nonetheless extremely significant in a number of
ways. So significant were these changes for West Sumatra that
it might be argued that the whole tenor of village social,
political, and economic life was transformed in West Sumatra.

I propose in this paper to deal with only one aspect of
this transformation, i.e., its effects on the structure of
peasant enterprises in West Sumatra, although I shall illustrate my argument as well with data collected in the culturally-related area of Negeri Sembilan in Malaysia. It should
also be added that this is very much a preliminary discussion,
since this is the theme of a longer term piece of historical
research currently being carried out on Jambi, Riau, South
Sumatra, and the Lampungs, as well as West Sumatra.

It is clear both from the recent contributions to Minangkabau history cited above, as well as from a wide variety
of other sources that commodity production, exchange, and even
monetization were not introduced into West Sumatra only at the
turn of this century. Indeed integration even within global
circuits of commodity exchange predates the period of the
watershed. Although a good deal of further research is necessary on this point, it seems to me to be safe to assume that
the problem with the writings of the critics such as Kato and
Benda-Beckmann is that they themselves do not go far enough
back in time, linking as they do the commercialization of

Minangkabau to the imposition of forced coffee deliveries in 1847. Be that as it may, it seems to me undeniable that if there was an economic change towards the end of the 1910s, that change is clearly not accurately described as a transition from a "natural" or "subsistence" to a "money" or a "commodity" economy. Indeed it is in all likelihood almost always inaccurate to use the terms natural and monetized to describe either economic epochs, or even economic sectors in the way suggested by dual economy theorists. Furthermore it is also clear that in spite of the emergence of wage labor relations within the peasant economy, and the limited employment of Minangkabau in larger colonial enterprises, economic change in Minangkabau in this century cannot be described in terms of a secular trend towards the emergence of classically capitalist forms of enterprise relying on wage labor.

And yet I would argue that a significant change in the organization of a large number of peasant enterprises has indeed taken place from the first decade of this century, a change that is manifest in the increasing extent to which small-scale enterprises in the region have become dependent on the market for their reproduction. Looked at from the point of view of the peasant enterprise itself, the change can be viewed as a process of market penetration or, put another way, the "commoditization" of production. In other words, while there may not have been significant changes in the internal organization of small enterprises, there has been a shift in the way the productive cycle is renewed, from a situation in which access to productive inputs—land, tools, raw materials, etc.—was obtained through kin group membership, membership in local communities, position in status and gender hierarachies and the like to one in which some or all of these inputs are obtained through commodity exchange. Before examining the causes and implications of this transformation, I shall illustrate the change with material from my own research. It will be noted that in the discussion that follows we are interested in changes in the reproduction of commodity production, and not the shift from subsistence to commodity production.

Peasant Commodity Production in the 19th Century

As we have already seen, production for exchange has in all likelihood long been a feature of the Minangkabau rural economy (See Kahn 1980a). In any case, certainly by the early 19th century, Minangkabau were trading and producing commodities throughout the present-day provincial boundaries. Unfortunately the economic history of 19th century West Sumatra is still to be written in spite of the richness of the archival sources, and this is not the place for a detailed examination of the source materials. What follows is therefore only a very rough sketch of secondary materials.[1]

Perhaps coffee was the most important produced commodity in 19th century West Sumatra. Coffee was already being grown for sale in certain regions of the highlands long before direct Dutch intervention in the Padri wars gave them the administrative base to operate a system of forced deliveries. Indeed it has been suggested that the Padri movement itself was based on the strength of commercial classes in the coffee-producing areas (see Dobbin 1977). One of the first acts of the colonial government, after intervention in the Padri Wars gave the Dutch a military foothold in the highlands, was to send a commissioner from Batavia to investigate ways of increasing coffee production, which had been exported from the early 1800s under colonial monopoly.[2] As a result of his recommendation, a law was passed in 1847 bringing in a system of forced deliveries along the lines of the system developed earlier in western Java. Under the new law it was up to local officials, appointed by the government, to see that every able-bodied man with access to land cultivated a certain number of coffee trees. The cooperation of local officials was secured by granting them a percentage of the revenues on coffee grown in their areas of jurisdiction. Small warehouses were built in most market towns, and the grower was expected to deliver the coffee to the government at these points. In 1862 cultivation was made legally compulsory, and in 1879 the percentage offered to local officials was raised. Peasants were paid a price for the coffee which was set by the colonial government at a level sufficiently low to yield profits in the trade rather than in the production process. All indications are that prices paid to producers were extremely low, often too low even to cover the cost of transport.

In spite of the desire of the government to see all Minangkabau producing coffee for forced delivery, it is clear that circumstances allowed villagers in some areas to evade government pressures and to engage in other kinds of cash-earning activities. Until more detailed work is done it will not be possible to gauge the scope of this "black economy," and yet we can assume that people also raised cattle for the

---

[1] See for example Wolters 1970; Haan 1897; Kroeskamp 1931; Sen 1962; as well as Oki, Kato, and Benda-Beckmann.
[2] For some material on coffee production, see Huitema 1935; Ples 1878.

production and sale of hides, planted other cash crops, and
collected a wide range of forest products--including wood for
fuel and timber for house building--to be sold on local markets. It was no doubt the existence of such alternatives as
late as the 1890s that led the Dutch rather belatedly to
attempt to make up for the loss in revenue by instituting a
tax for those who could or would not grow coffee (Huitema
1935:53f).

There are important areas of debate over the 19th
century regional economy. For example an examination of colonial policy in the region suggests a close relation between
the economic aims (securing a monopoly on the coffee trade,
increasing cultivation, and pegging prices substantially below
world market prices) and the broader social aims of the
colonial power. Hence, for example, the preservation of what
was assumed to be the "traditional" structure of isolated
villages--subsistence orientation, universal access to land
through local kinship groupings, absence of production for the
market, etc.--went hand in hand with the attempt to secure a
monopoly in coffee. It is interesting to examine the implications of this specific colonial context for peasant enterprises in the region. While there is some disagreement on
this issue,[3] it seems that the tendency of these policies
would have been to strengthen subsistence production to the
detriment of commodity production with the important exception
of course of coffee cultivation. Schrieke (1955) for example
describes the almost ridiculous lengths to which the government in West Sumatra went to discourage the trade in rice.
The rules of adat, or customary law as it is usually translated, were also transformed in function if not content by the
colonial authorities in some regions. Through a process of
selection and codification familiar to students of colonial
history elsewhere, Dutch judicial authorities turned a fluid
system of customary practices into a rigid legal code. There
is evidence for other parts of Indonesia that this policy
actually strengthened the subsistence community by increasing
the extent to which all villagers had access to land for subsistence cultivation.[4]   Non-market leveling mechanisms prevented the emergence of an internal market.[5]

---

[3] See Benda-Beckmann 1979a and Kahn 1976, 1980b.
[4] See A.D.A. Kat Angelino 1931b.
[5] Here I am referring specifically to Schrieke's finding that
in spite of attempts by Sumatran villagers to grow rice as a
cash crop for the internal market after the lifting of commercial restrictions, and in spite of an initial rise in rice

But whatever the effects of the Culture System on the development of indigenous commodity production, there is no evidence to suggest that household production was reliant to any great extent on the market for the supply of important productive inputs. The two most significant inputs for the whole range of commodities produced were land and labor. There is no suggestion that wage labor was employed to any great extent—instead labor was probably drawn largely from within the household or from kin and neighborhood groupings. More research is needed to examine the possibility that elites were able to mobilize labor through traditional status hierarchies, in the way suggested for the _sikep_ on Java.[6] The control of land was subjected largely to the rules of _adat_, although it would be a mistake to assume that the allocation of land to commodity-producing units was controlled either by the nagari community as a whole, or by certain elite members of the nagari communities. When such "waste" land was used for obtaining some form of cash income, i.e., for the collection of forest produce for sale or the grazing of cattle, then the ultimate "owner" (whether nagari or _orang basa_) was entitled to a payment known as the _bunga kayu_ (cf. Kroesen 1874; Oki 1977 and this volume).

In short, while no doubt there was considerable variation in the nature of peasant enterprises, most factors favored the emergence of household enterprises in which coffee, or some other commodity, was produced for a (restricted) market, and at the same time a proportion of household labor was engaged in cultivation of rice and other crops for immediate consumption. Cash income, which in the case of coffee cultivators must normally have been very low, was evidently not "invested" in the reproduction of the enterprise, but spent instead on family consumption (salt, cloth) or perhaps by indigenous elites for more luxury consumption.

The contrast between coffee cultivation in the nineteenth century and the production of steel tools—axes, hoes,

---

prices, rice prices fell off rapidly not because of the huge volume of marketed surpluses, but because of a relative oversupply. This can be explained by the widescale persistence of "subsistence production," i.e., non-market, internal distribution of rice.

[6] See Knight 1982. Knight, mistakenly in my view, describes the system as capitalism, although it seems that it was at least made possible by the precapitalist hierarchies already in existence at the time of the imposition of the Culture System in Java (cf. Bremen 1982; Onghokam 1975).

parang (machetes), sickles, and knives—in the modern highland nagari (village) of Sungai Puar at first sight appears to be slight; and yet, as we shall see, the differences are significant. Since I have discussed this case in more detail elsewhere (Kahn 1980a), I shall present only a brief overview here.

Sungai Puar is a Minangkabau nagari with a resident population of just over 9000 in 1971. In the village section of Limo Suku is found the "industry" for which the village is best known. Here smiths forge and finish steel tools which they sell mostly in the nearby market town of Bukit Tinggi, the main point of distribution for markets throughout the island of Sumatra. Smithing is the main occupation of male residents, yet a large proportion of Sungai Puar men and women produce or trade in some commodity for sale in local markets.

Smithing is in fact carried out within a number of different `kinds of enterprise, the three most significant of which were, at the time of my research, individual production, production by owner of enterprise with from two to three wage workers, and kin-based production. As the figures in the table show, individual production was the predominant form, while kin-based production was very little favored.

Table 1
Economic Relations in Smithing: Breakdowns by "class" of total working population (residents and migrants)

Productive Role	Number of Smiths	Percent of Smiths
Owner-worker employing 3-4 workers	24	4.7
Owner-worker employing 1-2 workers	111	21.7
Independent Producer	180	35.2
Wage Worker	117	22.9
Worker with close kinsman	46	9.0
Other	34	6.6

Smithing is carried out entirely with the aim of earning a cash income. Like coffee cultivation in the nineteenth century, moreover, smithing is dominated by very small-scale enterprises, with self employment predominating. This suggests that, as in the 19th century, most such enterprises obtained labor without the existence of a labor market, and that, with some exceptions, there were no monetized labor costs for production.

However, there is a major difference between smithing in the early 1970s and the case described above, since while monetized labor costs remain minimal, other monetary costs are incurred by the producer. In other words, both are cases of a commercialized peasantry producing commodities for a market (in one case a world market, in another largely regional). Yet, in the former, the market-oriented peasant enterprises are reproduced largely through non-market mechanisms, while in the latter, an important proportion of productive inputs are supplied through the market mechanisms.

In the case of smithing, an average of about a half of all revenues brought in from the sale of steelware must be used by the owner/worker to purchase raw materials. The main raw material costs are expenditures on coal and scrap steel. Coal is brought into the village by a small number of traders who purchase it at the Ombilin coal mines in Sawah Lunto. Another group of merchants buys scrap steel in surrounding market towns which comes either from scrapped vehicles or from the unfinished section of the Padang-Pakan Baru railway. Other costs include expenditures for certain tools, anvils, paint, and polishing grit used in the process of finishing forged steel ware. The only "capital" costs met outside the market involve the reproduction of certain items of fixed capital, including some of the hammers used in forging, the small huts within which forging takes place, and the land on which the hut stands. The first two are produced by the smiths themselves, while the huts are built on housing plots classified as the ancestral land of the smith's own lineage (or that of the spouse).

I have pointed out that labor costs are not monetized, and yet to some extent this is an oversimplification. Firstly, there are, as Table 1 demonstrates, a number of enterprises which employ wage labor. Here, however, there is no developed wage form. Rather the "return to labor" (revenues minus money costs) is divided equally among the workers in a forging unit, with an extra share "for the forge." This extra share is intended to cover fixed capital expenditure, but because this is relatively small, the remaining proportion of the extra share is retained by the "employer" as a kind of disguised profit. Even when smithing units were amalgamated within larger enterprises controlled by individual entrepreneurs in the late 1950s (Kahn 1975), this mode of calculation was employed. The system comes closer to piece-work payment than wages in that workers are rewarded according to the volume of output rather than the duration of labor. Thus even when labor costs are essentially monetized, payment according to labor time (the main capitalist mode) is absent.

It would, however, be misleading to speak of an absence of labor costs even for self-employed smiths. Most smiths have worked at other occupations during their lifetimes, and the high rate of temporary migration, as well as the interchange among different local cash-earnings activities, leads to some notion of an acceptable return to labor in commodity production and distribution. As we shall see, there is some difference between this situation and one in which labor input can be treated as though it were totally free of monetary cost.

While smithing, unlike coffee production, has been effectively integrated within the circuit of commodity relations, such is not the case for the village economy as a whole. About 60 percent of households in the village have access to some irrigated land on which rice is cultivated largely for household consumption typically with household labor (more female labor than male). While rice farmers have to make some monetary expenditures even if they cultivate the land themselves (primarily for tools), the main productive inputs are supplied outside the market. Land is inherited in the female line, and while some transfers may take place through a system of pawning, there are strict social obstacles to the development of a land market. Labor is, as we have seen, supplied by women with the help of other family members, and even when land is cultivated by tenants, rent is always paid in kind. In Sungai Puar irrigated land is in short supply, and very few households are self-sufficient in rice. On average, households can meet about 20 percent of their annual rice needs through subsistence cultivation, although the subsistence ratio is higher in other parts of West Sumatra. Thus, while the various forms of commodity production in the village—smithing, carpentry, sewing, mat making, petty trading, etc.—are heavily dependent upon the market for the reproduction of enterprises, there are still areas of the peasant economy that remain isolated from the circuit of commodity circulation. This serves to distinguish the economy of Sungai Puar from the case described below.

Rice Cultivation in Negeri Sembilan, 1975-1976

I have chosen to take my third example not from Minangkabau at all but from the culturally-related area of Negeri Sembilan, Malaysia. The reason for this is that the contrast can best be made with my own research data collected there and because I have no data of comparable detail for Minangkabau itself, although there are indications that very similar changes in the nature of rice cultivation are currently taking place in Minangkabau villages (see Deutser 1981).

Like the Sungai Puar villagers, peasants in the culturally-related area in Malaysia known as Negeri Sembilan expend a considerable proportion of their effort in the production of commodities for the market. The principal form of local commodity production is rubber tapping. Coagulated latex sheets are then sold to shopkeepers. As in the case of blacksmithing, the predominant productive role is that of owner-tapper, although a smaller proportion of villagers sharetap on land owned by someone else. Rubber cultivation is, like smithing, closely integrated within commodity circuits. Tools, land, seedlings, and coagulation equipment are all purchased either directly or through various government credit schemes, although some tap trees on ancestral land. The replanting of rubber holdings, for example, has taken place largely through government loans which are then repaid over a period of years.

The main difference is in rice cultivation. Villagers in Rembau and Tampin districts, like those in Sungai Puar, cultivate rice on irrigated land for household subsistence. In Rembau over 90 percent of such land is classified as pusako, although in the region as a whole it may now be possible to speak of the emergence of a land market. Up to about 1960, rice cultivation in the area conformed in many ways to what Jackson has termed the "traditional pattern" in the inland valleys region of West Malaysia, namely, irrigation by means of brushwood dams or waterwheels, hand preparation of the soil with a hoe, the use of dry nurseries, harvesting with the tuai (a small knife), and threshing by stamping (menghirik) (Jackson 1972). Today, however, there have been important technological changes in rice cultivation. Techniques supplied during the "Green Revolution" have spread relatively rapidly, and local rice farmers increasingly employ chemical fertilizers, herbicides, and pesticides or hire a tractor to plough the fields prior to transplanting. In the years since the adoption of new techniques, there has been little change, however, in the relatively egalitarian pattern of land distribution and the relatively low rates of tenancy. The new techniques do not appear to have had any favorable effect on household output, but their use nonetheless marks an important change. For example, while in the past output was a factor of labor supply, the volume of household demand and the size of holdings, now the success of rice cultivation depends largely on the use of the new inputs. And of course what is most significant about these new inputs is that they cost money, which makes access to cash, rather than access to labor and land, the most important feature of a successful household (Kahn 1981).

Hence while the commodity-producing sector of the Negeri Sembilan peasant economy is in many ways similar to that of West Sumatra, the main difference is that in this case even when goods are produced for household consumption and not sale, their production depends on the market supply of productive inputs. In other words even so-called subsistence production has become integrated within reproductive circuits governed by the commodity form.

The cases outlined above demonstrate differing relations between peasant enterprises and the circulation of commodities. In all the cases a proportion of total individual or household output is sold on the market to be consumed locally (steelware) or overseas (coffee, rubber). The differences therefore are not between "traditional" subsistence-oriented peasants and market-oriented producers. Rather, the most striking difference is the degree and nature of market penetration of production. In nineteenth century Sumatra, productive inputs were supplied almost entirely outside the market through community and kin-based mechanisms of appropriation. There is no evidence of a market in means of production, land, or labor. Craftsmen and women in the 1970s, however, not only produce commodities for sale, but productive units are also substantially reproduced through commodity relations, while the cultivation of rice for household consumption was reproduced outside the commodity circuit. Finally in Negeri Sembilan rubber tapping and rice cultivation are closely integrated within a commodity circuit that involves land and, most importantly, the means of production. Moreover in this last case the commodity circuit that penetrates peasant production is at the same time a world commodity circuit involving capitalist firms and multinational enterprises.

Finally, however, it should be noted that in spite of increased market penetration, there is in one of these cases, a highly developed labor market, at least within the peasant economy itself. The main difference in the nature of labor supply is that only with the system of forced deliveries is labor relatively immobile across different branches of production. This suggests that the process of differentiation which leads to capitalist relations of production in peasant agriculture, which has been extensively described for other parts of the world economy, is not an inevitable consequence of market penetration on the periphery. Indeed on closer examination the differentiation thesis appears to rest on the conflation of three quite different processes: the commodit-

-289-

ization of output, of the means of production, and of labor
power. As these cases demonstrate, these three processes are
not necessarily casually interlinked.

The Implications of Input Commoditization: Peasant Economic Calculation

In the first part of this paper I have attempted to
reformulate the terms of the debate over the question of an
early 19th century watershed in Minangkabau economic history.
While agreeing that Schrieke's periodization is inadequate, I
have also pointed out that evidence of monetization in the
pre-watershed peasant economy in West Sumatra is on its own no
proof that there has been a basic continuity in economic
organization from the coming of the Dutch to the Minangkabau
highlands to the present day. On the contrary, I have suggested that there may well have been an important transformation in the peasant economy in spite of a superficial continuity, and that the transformation has been in the way
small-scale rural enterprises are reproduced. I shall now
turn to an examination of the significance of this transformation, before attempting to uncover its causes.

It has recently been suggested that the inadequacies in
the theory of peasant economy can be overcome once we recognize that the use of blanket terms like peasant, small producer, household production, and the like all lead to a misleading conflation of significantly different forms of peasant
production (see Ennew, et al. 1979). In other words if we are
interested in developing theories about the economic behavior
of specific peasantries, we must have a more refined conceptual apparatus that will allow us to make deductively significant distinctions between different peasantries. One such
set of distinctions concerns the ways in which small commodity
production is reproduced, and a number of writers of peasant
economics have made fruitful use of a distinction between
market and non-market reproduction illustrated above (see Kula
1976; Bernstein 1977, 1979; Friedman 1980). This distinction
has made it possible, for example, to go beyond the all-or-
nothing terms of the positivist and historicist debates that
plague the study of the Indonesian economy (see Boeke et al.
1966), the economy of non-Western societies in general (for-
malists versus substantivists), and the peasant economies of
Southeast Asia (cf. Scott 1976; Popkin 1979), by suggesting
that small producers will behave "rationally" (i.e., in the
manner of a capitalist firm) under certain conditions and not
others. In particular the distinction depends on the differences between economic calculation based on non-monetized

(and non-monetizable) inputs and calculation based on the possible comparison of costs and benefits in quantitative terms (i.e., when all inputs and outputs have at least a potential market).

According to this approach, the differences between 19th century coffee producers, modern blacksmiths, and Malaysian rice farmers are highly significant, since in each case economic calculations will be made differently. There is no space to examine these differences in great depth. Let us then look at three areas in which these forms of small production might differ:

(1) Self-exploitation

The first difference concerns the meaning of self-exploitation.[7] This term, usually taken to mean the increased intensification of labor inputs (beyond the limits which a capitalist enterprise would entertain under similar conditions), in fact could be taken to refer to a broader range of phenomena, i.e., the superexploitation of all productive inputs.

It can be seen that, in the case of nineteenth century Sumatra, factors which typically increased levels of self exploitation—rising consumer/worker ratios, declining output prices, competition with technically more efficient forms of production, etc.—could lead not just to increased levels of labor intensity, but to a superexploitation of all other productive inputs supplied outside the market and hence not valorized in production, in particular, land. Indeed there is evidence that the forced deliveries of coffee did produce overexploitation of land and all its consequences, such that when commercial restrictions were lifted, land suitable for cash crop production had to be sought outside the region where coffee had been grown in the 19th century.[8]

As enterprises become more reliant on the commodity market for their reproduction, however, and raw materials and other means of production acquire a monetary cost, the situation is rather different. Firstly, opportunities for such su-

---

[7] Self-exploitation is developed as a concept for the analysis of peasant economies by A. V. Chayanov (see Chayanov 1966).
[8] This is a process in many ways similar to the destruction of feudal estates in Poland described by Kula, for much the same reasons, and presumably also for what has all too frequently been attributed to natural disaster more recently in places like the Sahel.

perexploitation are decreased. Secondly, self-exploitation (or intensification of labor) increasingly becomes the only alternative--hence suggesting that labor intensification may be even greater as we approach the petty commodity end of the spectrum. Thirdly, when input commoditization results in increased labor mobility, peasants may move into less and less productive (because of low levels of fixed capital costs) branches of production. Fourthly, the potential causes of self-exploitation themselves actually increase, since added to the other causes we now have the deleterious effects of rising input prices.

(2) "Supply Response"

A second, although related, difference between the different types of enterprise concerns the problem of supply response. We have pointed out that some writers have suggested that, due to a subsistence ethic, peasant producers respond "perversely" to price fluctuations. Higher output prices are then expected to lead to a decrease in the volume of output, while lowering of output prices produces the opposite effect.[9] The typology proposed here suggests that this negative supply response is not universal in peasant economies, but that it may occur under certain circumstances. Specifically, increased production in the face of falling prices is likely to take place only when labor is relatively immobile. When labor mobility exists, falling prices can be expected to produce a drop in both enterprize and aggregate production as peasants switch to branches of production in which the "return to labor" is more favorable. Indeed it is precisely under such circumstances that we may expect a social average return to labor to develop, as described above. The converse--i.e., rising prices resulting in falling output--can be assumed to take place only if peasant producers are already achieving desired subsistence levels, something which is increasingly rare in contemporary Southeast Asia.

In any case there is certainly evidence from Southeast Asia and elsewhere to show that under certain conditions peasants do indeed strive to expand output, expand monetary incomes beyond levels required for simple reproduction, and invest in monetary inputs that serve to increase productivity. The literature on Malaysia and Indonesia, with its continuous emphasis on obstacles to growth, subsistence ethics, and the like, needs to be counterbalanced by further research into the

---

[9] See for example, Boeke 1946.

conditions that favor such developments.

(3) Profitability

A further difference concerns the way peasant producers compare the "profitability" of different economic activities. In Negeri Sembilan, for example, the evidence suggests that the commoditization of inputs in rice cultivation has led to a gradual decline in aggregate rice outputs precisely because different kinds of comparisons than previously existed are now possible between the (money) cost of rice cultivation and the price of purchased rice on the one hand, and the money costs of other forms of production (such as rubber tapping) or even wage labor (Kahn 1981) on the other.

This leads to a consideration of a phenomenon that has been mentioned in passing several times in this argument, and that concerns the mobility of labor in an economy in which petty commodity production is a significant form of enterprise. A basic assumption in much of the writings on peasants is that peasants are for one reason or another rather severely restricted in the kinds of economic activities they can undertake and even in the places they can undertake them. Hence, work on the moral economy of the peasantry--the tendency for there to be an inverse correlation between price and output, subsistence-orientations, and the like--frequently takes it for granted that peasants are not free: for example, they may not move out of one kind of production, in which there has been a deterioration in output prices, and into another branch where conditions are more favorable. It is precisely this immobility of peasant labor which prevents an analysis of peasant commodity exchange in terms of value.

However, the commoditization of productive inputs is one of the factors which breaks down the obstacles to mobility, although it can only be said to be one of the preconditions for this mobility to develop. Equally important are the constraints set by wider economic forces, including the presence of more technologically advanced enterprises which make peasant competition either impossible or possible only with extremely high rates of labor intensity. The differences between a situation of labor immobility, and one of labor mobility, however limited, are considerable. Firstly, the mobility of small producers is based on, and in turn accentuates, the tendency for decisions to be arrived at through a comparison of different rates of (money) profitability on the one hand, and different rates of return to labor input on the other. Other things being equal, for example, we might expect peasants to move from branches in which the return to labor is below the social average and into those in which it is equal to or higher than the socially average return to labor. Of course as long as labor power is not fully commoditized, other factors will enter into calculation, and strict labor-time accounting may well not develop. Nevertheless, since individual petty commodity producers experience the drudgery of labor inputs directly, something analogous to the wage as an historically-determined and relatively standardized level around which "returns to labor" in different branches of production tend to vary will emerge. To the extent that such a social average has emerged, we might expect the exchange value of peasant-produced commodities to be proportional to the labor time involved in their production, which in turn further constrains petty commodity producers to produce in terms of socially-necessary labor time. This situation is very different from one in which the relative unimportance of monetary costs of production has not caused qualitatively distinct and concrete forms of labor to merge into a single, abstract, homogeneous category of labor.

Mobility of small producers has the other implication, already mentioned, that decisions will increasingly be based on a comparison of money rates of profitability across different branches of production. Again, other things being equal, we might expect small producers to engage in activities which require the minimum of cash expenditures. Moreover, since market penetration of production has already been assumed to have occurred, small producers can be expected to favor a high turnover--hence favoring branches with relatively higher ratios of circulating capital to fixed capital, rather than vice versa.

I have so far considered the shorter term implications of input commoditization for small-scale peasant enterprises. I have suggested that the distinction between peasant production and petty commodity production is significant from the point of view of the nature and determinants of self-exploitation, the response of small producers to price fluctuations, the kinds of comparisons made between different alternatives, and the determination of prices and ratios between fixed and circulating capital in small production. In the final section of the paper I want to turn to an examination of the historical process of input commoditization itself.

Some Hypotheses Concerning the Causes of Market Penetration

The three causes discussed above, while they cannot be taken to represent stages in some necessary evolutionary sequence, do nonetheless suggest that the most significant process of economic transformation is that described as the penetration of peasant production by the circuit of national and international commodity relations. Having pointed to the significant implications of this process, it is necessary to account for it. What follows is in no way intended to constitute such an explanation. Rather, I shall instead attempt to set out a proposal for further research.

An historical explanation of the phenomenon as it has occurred in specific cases is necessary for reasons outlined above. We have criticized the differentiation thesis precisely for treating the commoditization of production as though it were some inevitable evolutionary process on the world capitalist periphery. A proper understanding must therefore avoid confusing the qualitatively different kinds of input markets that underlie the differentiation thesis. Rather it seems better to assume that market penetration is a consequence of particular economic and political struggles both within the peasantry and between peasants and other classes in concrete social formations. As Marx shows so clearly for the development of capitalist production, the commoditization of labor power is not a natural but an historical development, the end result of a process of proletarianization whereby producers are deprived of/separated from the means of production. Only when the direct producer has no alternative is he/she compelled to sell labor power as a commodity.

Similarly it would seem best to assume that peasants are likely to resist the market penetration of production. Firstly, increased monetary costs of production serve to undermine the (money) rate of profitability of commodity production. Secondly, market penetration takes place only when peasants are no longer able to reproduce themselves outside the market. Hence a land market will not develop simply as a result of the introduction of the "market principle" but when, for example, the communal structures of land distribution have been sufficiently undermined to threaten the reproduction of existing agricultural production.

This proposition can be illustrated for Sumatran coffee producers in the nineteenth century. Whether these peasants were concerned to maximize cash revenues or whether they were interested only in simple reproduction, it is likely that they would have little interest in expanding their cash costs. The "profitability" of coffee cultivation was a result, not of high coffee prices, but of negligible money costs. Any increase in these money costs would quickly undermine socially-defined profit levels. Put another way, the colonial government was able to extract a surplus in the coffee trade, based on paying very low prices to producers, when the land, labor, and means of production employed in coffee cultivation were locked away from the market. In this case the necessarily high rates of exploitation of these inputs could be ensured only through the use of direct political pressure. As long as they had a choice, therefore, we can expect that these peasants would have operated with a minimum of cash outlays.

Any increase in the market penetration of peasant production, therefore, could have only been the result of force in the broad sense. Hence the first significant change was marked not by the natural evolution of the market mechanism in Southeast Asia, but by the imposition of a money tax by colonial governments. Indeed it is not particularly surprising that the imposition of the money tax was strenuously resisted by rural cultivators even when, as in West Sumatra, it was designed to replace forced deliveries. Where there was a relatively low level of market penetration, the imposition of the tax, not surprisingly, forced peasants to produce cash crops for the world rather than the internal market. In Sumatra, for example, the initial response to the tax in some villagers quite quickly turned to more profitable world cash crops such as rubber, tea, coconuts, and coffee when they discovered that even small rice surpluses produced a glut in the market.

Production of cash crops for the world market at the same time did create some opportunities for further specialization. In order to meet the tax burden some peasants could produce commodities such as steelware, textiles, and fruit and vegetables for the internal market which developed in part as a result of the changing division of labor in Sumatra.[10]

Thus the imposition of a money tax explains on the one hand the increased orientation of peasant enterprises and, on the other, a qualitative change in the way enterprises are reproduced. The tax becomes a money cost of production, like rent, and serves to redefine the conditions under which peasant calculation is made. The reorientation and the consequent change in the social division of labor may also explain some degree of market penetration of production, since new economic activities may require non-traditional inputs which can only be purchased on the market.

However, while a tax may increase commercialization of production, a head tax is not on its own a sufficient explanation for a long-term process of market penetration, since the compulsion to pay a tax of this kind does not necessarily undermine the ability of peasants to reproduce their productive activities outside the market. A land tax, such as that levied by the British in Malaya, on the other hand, may have

---

10 Kahn 1980a; Oki 1979; Singarimbum 1975.

longer term effects on the viability of subsistence reproduction since it may, if it is proportional to land area, lead to fragmentation of holdings. Nonetheless, set levels of money taxation are, it would seem, at best a partial explanation for the long-term process described above. Rather, taxation would produce enterprises somewhere in between the peasant petty commodity production extremes, without implying any necessary further process of commoditization.

And yet, as we have seen, the market penetration of peasant enterprises in West Sumatra has considerably increased, even in the last twenty years.

Perhaps the most important factor is one almost entirely overlooked in most of the writing on Minangkabau, largely because its significance was either not appreciated or ignored by Schrieke himself, and this is the factor of land alienation. While as we have seen large-scale proletarianization did not take place in Minangkabau in the early decades of this century, large amounts of land were allocated largely to foreign companies on leasehold (erfpacht) through the provisions of the agrarian legislation for West Sumatra. In the supposedly thinly populated district of Muara Labuh, for example, between 1877 and 1922 the government approved the alienation of 33,677 hectares of "uncultivated" land (a total of 34 separate leases) (document in Korn Collection, number 367). Far from leaving the village economy unaffected, it was reported that already by the late 1910s this had caused considerable hardship for "native" cultivators who could not find enough land for cash cropping (Memorie van Overgave, LeFebvre [see Mailrapport 1919]). Secondly, other land controlled by village councils was declared off limits and allocated as mining concessions to foreign firms. In Alahan Panjang, for example, 102,683 hectares of land was given out to European mining concerns. Thirdly, and in addition to land leased or conceded to private firms, by 1923 106,607,000 hectares of the Residency of Sumatra's West Coast was declared forest reserve, a figure representing 35% of the total land area (Dienst van het Boschweezen 1923). Land under forest reserve could neither be brought into cultivation nor used for the collection of wood, timber, or forest products for sale and, up to the late 1920s, village communities within whose boundaries the forests lay were also deprived largely of their traditional bunga kayu payments as well.

Given that what the colonial government classified as "waste" land in fact formed an important part of the 19th century commodity economy—as a source of "free" products for sale, as land for grazing and shifting cultivation—then the large-scale alienation of land that accompanied the capitalist transformation of the East Indies economy would have had precisely the effect suggested above, i.e., forcing peasant commodity producers to turn to other forms of economic activity such as crafts and petty trade in an effort to meet their needs for a cash income.

The combination of money taxation and land alienation is perhaps the most significant explanation for the important transformation of the Minangkabau peasant economy that took place in the first few decades of this century. In conclusion it is worth examining some reasons why this process has and probably will continue:

(1) The first thing to note is that increased market involvement of the peasant productive process is clearly in the interest of multinational firms. It has become apparent in recent years that while profit levels in peripheral peasant agriculture are rather low, small producers are able both to produce much needed commodities at relatively low prices (Lee 1973), while at the same time forming a profitable market for agricultural inputs supplied by multinational corporations. As C. Payer has recently pointed out, there is an inevitable clash of interests between "self-provisioning" peasantries and the interests of capital (1980). Payer focuses in particular on the way policies advocated by the World Bank have served to undermine self-reproducing peasants who are forced to substitute for traditional techniques through the mechanism of indebtedness. As a result, they may, for instance, become dependent on firms supplying agricultural chemicals.

This process is clearly important, and the means by which such techniques have been introduced during the Green Revolution need closer examination in Southeast Asia. And yet such an explanation is at best incomplete, since it fails to explain precisely how peasants with an interest in minimizing cash expenditures are placed in a position of reliance on such inputs.

(2) One explanation offered is that peasants have become increasingly impoverished by world price fluctuations and, as a result, are forced into debt. Failure to repay the debt locks them into a vicious circle of asset-stripping, increased reliance on the market for the purchase of means of production which leads in turn to increased indebtedness. There is no doubt that this has occurred in Southeast Asia,[11] and yet again the explanation is insufficient since it fails to account for the occurrence of such impoverishment in some places and not others, and more significantly from our point of view, why it occurs in some periods and not others.

---

[11] See Myrdal 1968.

(3)   A similar explanation is embodied in the thesis
that it is population expansion and land fragmentation that
make peasants particularly susceptible to the cycle of indebtedness. Again this has clearly taken place, and yet theories
on population growth also leave a number of things unexplain-
ed. Firstly, of course, the Malthusian assumptions behind the
population growth mechanism make it suspect. Specifically, it
fails to explain particular demographic trends in specific
historical periods. Secondly, Geertz has outlined one way in
which population growth leads to intensification of land use,
labor inputs, and non-market mechanisms of resource distribution. To rely on population growth to explain the opposite
tendency thus requires an explanation for relative population
surplus and a specification of the conditions under which that
leads to increased market penetration.
     (4) An account of why market penetration has occurred
increasingly in this century is implied in writings which
stress the increased divergence between price and output fluctuations brought by reliance on producing for world rather
than local markets. Scott (1976), for example, explains the
breakdown of "moral economy" and traditional redistributional
systems in Southeast Asia as being due at least in part to the
shift from internal to external markets. The consequence has
been that price fluctuations in the latter, being extra-
locally determined, do not make up for annual variation in
output to the same extent that they would if prices were
locally-determined.
     Increased world market penetration of production would,
by this theory, be due to Indonesia's and Malaysia's shift, at
the turn of this century, to the cultivation of world cash
crops, and consequent fluctuation in price and output serving
to dispossess at least some small producers of access to the
means of production, producing the cycle of debt and further
penetration as described above. This hypothesis too deserves
further investigation to see whether the rhythm of market
penetration can be related to the different stages of commodity penetration. However, such a general explanation would
have difficulty accounting for the lack of differentiation
between proletarians and employers of wage labor. In other
words it would probably be insufficient to explain the specific pattern of commoditization that has taken place in particular regions.
     (5) Another important factor in decreasing local forms
of reproduction has been the import of cheap manufactured
goods; it would here be particularly interesting to compare
Indonesia, which has traditionally had tighter restrictions on
imports, with Malaysia, which has had freer policies—a difference partly traceable to differences between Dutch and Bri-

tish colonial policies. It is, however, by no means evident that tight import controls have not in fact led to a transformation of petty commodity production rather than to a reinforcing of the individual pattern of production encompassed by that term (Kahn 1975).

(6) Finally, it cannot be assumed that under all circumstances peasant producers are interested only in simple reproduction. Under certain conditions peasants in Southeast Asia behave more like petty capitalists, expanding production in order to increase money revenues and investment. While research is needed in Southeast Asia into the historical conditions under which this occurs, it seems that increasing output will imply greater monetary costs of production in order to overcome given limits in communal reproductive mechanisms (to acquire more land, more labor, new technologies, etc.).

These are some of the factors which might contribute to the significant transformation in the Southeast Asian peasant economy described above. What should perhaps be noted is that the penetration of commodity relations may be due on the one hand to a deterioration in the conditions of peasant enterprises or, on the other hand, to attempts by peasants to improve these conditions. Neither is there a simple answer to the question of whether the causes are internal or external to the peasant economy. External pressures to commoditize must be met by internal conditions which force such commoditization on peasants whose main interests may lie in minimizing cash expenditures.

Conclusion

What does this discussion lead us to conclude about the debates over the watershed thesis advanced by Schrieke and the processes of social and economic change in 20th century West Sumatra? It seems that the oversimplistic conflation of commercialization and modernization will have to be abandoned. Commodity exchange, often accompanied by the circulation of money, can no longer be taken to be an indicator of either modernization or capitalist penetration. A careful reading of recent anthropological and archaeological analyses of non-Western economies makes it increasingly difficult to believe that there has ever been a pure "natural" economy, while close analyses of contemporary capitalism lead one to reject the notion that Western economies are fully commoditized. Debates over the presence or absence of market exchange, particularly when accompanied by assumptions about the unilineal evolution of "the market principle" are therefore not likely to be helpful for the analysis of concrete trajectories of economic change. This becomes even more true for the case of the societies of Indonesia with their long history of markets, commodity circulation, and even international trade extending back long before the earliest Western contact. The debate over the existence of an economic watershed in Minangkabau after 1908, therefore, will only be resolved in the light of a better understanding of different processes of commoditization--their implications for the short-term dynamic of rural enterprises and their causes. I have proposed here that the late 19th century capitalist transformation of the East Indies economy resulted in a macro-process of input commoditization. This general hypothesis may or may not turn out to be true, although given the present development objectives in Indonesia itself it is hard to imagine that alternatives will emerge.

Nonetheless it is important that these alternatives are borne in mind, to remember that small-scale forms of production are not incompatible with production for the market, or with more communal and democratic forms of enterprise reproduction. The existence of a peasantry in the modern world need not imply either forced collectivization of the labor process or the alienation and forced intensification generated by an increased reliance on world price movements for the very survival of peasant enterprise.

Acknowledgments. This is a revised version of a paper which appeared originally in the Bulletin of Concerned Asian Scholars 14(1), 1982, pp. 3-15, entitled "From Peasants to Petty Commodity Production in Southeast Asia."

The research project "Social Change and Peasant Economy in Sumatra: 1870 to 1980" began in 1981/82 and was generously funded by the British Social Science Research Council, the British Academy, the British Institute in Southeast Asia, and the Nuffield Foundation. For their assistance with the historical research I am particularly indebted to H. de Graaf and the rest of the staff of the Algemeen Rijksarchief in the Hague and to the library staff at the Koninklijk Instituut voor Taal-, Land-, en Volkenkunde in Leiden. I have benefited from discussions of some of the ideas in this paper with John Gledhill, Akira Oki, Esteban Magannon, Wan Zawawi Ibrahim, and Maila Stivens.

The research in Rembau and Tampin in Negeri Sembilan, Malaysia was carried out in 1975-76 with a grant from the S.S.R.C., and was co-sponsored by the Ministry of National Unity and Dr. Kahar Bador of the University of Malaya.

THE IMPACT OF THE INDONESIAN INDEPENDENCE STRUGGLE
ON MINANGKABAU SOCIETY

Audrey Kahin
Cornell University

In the Minangkabau region, as in most other parts of Java and Sumatra during the years 1945-50, the competition between the Dutch and the Republic for the allegiance of the Indonesian people had a strong impact on village society. Although the independence struggle affected many aspects of that society, I will deal here with only one: the changes in nagari (village) leadership.

West Sumatra's history during the four-and-a-half year Indonesian war of independence can be divided into two major phases: the years prior to the second and major Dutch Attack of December 1948, and the months from then until the transfer of sovereignty in December 1949. During the first and longest of these periods, Dutch influence was limited to the Padang coastal plain, and a Residency administration loyal to the Republican leadership in Yogyakarta controlled the rest of West Sumatra. After their second "Police Action" of December 1948, however, the Dutch occupied most major towns of the region, and for the remainder of the struggle they attempted to exert authority over much of the surrounding countryside.[1] During both periods, the policies directed towards gaining the allegiance of the Minangkabau people which the Dutch and local Republicans pursued reflected their divergent views of the traditional structure of Minangkabau society and its most influential components. This paper will provide an analysis of the way in which the Republican government mustered what it perceived to be the basic strengths of Minangkabau village society in order to combat reassertion of Dutch power, and the extent to which it succeeded in this task.

For almost a year following the Japanese surrender, the Minangkabau region was in a constant state of tension and at times of near anarchy. Immediately after Indonesia's Declaration of Independence of August 17, 1945, local political,

---

[1] For the course of events in West Sumatra during this period, see BPSIM 1978; KP 1952; Fatimah Enar 1978; Kahin 1979.

administrative, and religious leaders in Padang set up a Republican government which was able to exert authority over most of the Residency of West Sumatra, even after British troops landed there in mid-October 1945. This local Republican government, in conformity with national policy, adopted a restrained attitude towards the incoming British and Indian troops despite the protection they were providing to the returning Dutch. Dutch internees had been brought to Padang from Bangkinang and other internment camps almost immediately after the Japanese surrender, and other Dutch officials returned with the British forces on October 12. Many of these returnees had been part of the colonial administration in West Sumatra, Dr. L. B. van Straten, for example, who became Dutch Resident, having formerly been controleur in Solok and Pariaman (BPSIM 1978(1):229). There was much popular dissatisfaction in West Sumatra with the policy of restraint which permitted the uncontested return of a Dutch presence, and demands grew that the Republican government and army should respond more decisively against the British who were acting as forerunners of the reimposition of the Dutch colonial administration. The mounting internal pressure for armed confrontation with Allied forces conflicted with the priorities of the new Republican government at both the Residency and national level, and it appeared as if the new Indonesian leaders would be unable to contain the dissatisfaction with their policies. Nevertheless, out of the apparent chaos, an effective Republican government did emerge in the Residency, and after the first nine months of disorder it maintained considerable unity and authority throughout the ensuing four years of struggle.

The task of the new government in establishing its administration, particularly at the district level and below, was always complicated by the popular resentment against all who had held official positions, particularly in the village and the district, during the preceding three-and-a-half years of Japanese occupation. In this period, the local officials had been obliged to act as agents for the Japanese in levying money, supplies, and manpower from the people.[2] Most of them had also held administrative positions under the Dutch, and,

---

[2] These Indonesian officials had been helpless to resist the Japanese demands that they raise supplies from the people: "The Japanese wanted so much rice, so much manpower—we had to collect these things for the Japanese. We even had to collect the people to go to Logas." Interview with Eni Karim, 15 April 1976.

because of their training, were the most technically qualified people to create an administration in the area. At the same time, however, they were the most suspect because of their earlier ties to the Dutch and most resented because of their role under the Japanese. Even those of them who loyally served the Republic found it difficult to throw off the stigma attached to being pegawai tiga zaman--officials of the three periods--Dutch, Japanese, and Republican.

Before the end of August 1945, former members of the Japanese-sponsored Hōkōkai[3] formed themselves into a Residency Komite Nasional Indonesia (KNI--Indonesian National Committee) in Padang, under leadership of the prominent educator, Mohammad Sjafei,[4] who was selected to be the first Republican Resident, and its members then went out to supervise establishment of KNIs at the district (kedemangan) and nagari levels. Initially most of the members of these local KNIs had also belonged to the Hōkōkai, but by late September or October 1945, pressure from different groups, such as the pemuda (young people) and the religious leaders, within several of the nagari, had forced some changes. Although a majority of the former administrators and local Hōkōkai members retained their positions throughout the early months of the Revolution, several fled their posts in fear of reprisals, a few were killed,[5] and many, particularly above the village level, were removed from their positions at the instigation of youth leaders and other activists.

The Resident and his colleagues, and to an even greater extent the Sumatran Governor and provincial government, were eager to have an efficient administrative apparatus operating in the Republican-controlled territories. As many of the men in high Republican positions on Sumatra had received advanced Dutch education and had served in the prewar colonial administration, they usually defended the Dutch-trained lower officials against popular disaffection. Members of the Residency

---

[3] On the Hōkōkai on Java and Sumatra, see Kanahele 1967:142-43, 180-82; for West Sumatra, see Kahin 1979:88-89.
[4] Mohammad Sjafei (1897-1969) was educated at the Sekolah Radja in Bukit Tinggi from 1908 to 1914. A member of the Budi Utomo and later of the Indische Partij, he was associated with the PNI Baru in the 1930s. He founded the INS (Indonesische Nederlandsche School) at Kayutanam in 1926. Under the Japanese he headed the Hōkōkai in West Sumatra and the Chūō Sangi In for all Sumatra.
[5] Interviews with Sultani St. Malako, 20 October 1976; Zainuddin St. Kerajaan, 22 August 1976.

government had to spend much time visiting crisis areas in
West Sumatra, in order to calm anti-government activity either
by removing or transferring former office holders and super-
vising creation of bodies made up of men acceptable to the
local people, or else by persuading the villagers to accept
holdovers from the earlier period. Nevertheless, confrontations between the local officials on the one hand, and the
KNIs, pemuda, and the political organizations on the other,
continually militated against the smooth-running administration the provincial and Residency authorities were trying
to ensure.[6]

By early 1946 leaders in Padang and Bukit Tinggi had
begun to recognize that, if they were to retain the minimal
local support needed to govern the region, they could no
longer rely completely on the Dutch-trained officials, but
would have to bring "popular leaders" (pemimpin rakjat) into
positions of administrative responsibility. At the same time,
however, they still felt the need to retain much of the former
administrative apparatus in order both not to alienate the
whole group of Dutch-trained officials and also to maintain a
degree of efficiency in the day-to-day conduct of the government's affairs. In filling administrative positions, they
then observed guidelines whereby the appointment of a "popular" inexperienced leader would be balanced by that of a
trained administrator, with one of the two being deputy to the
other (BPSIM 1978:151). Those Dutch-trained officials who
were retained in positions at the district level and above,
were usually transferred to regions where they had not served
as members of the Dutch or Japanese administrations.[7]

---

[6] An unpublished typescript from Lubuk Sikaping gives the picture of the situation in Talu during the period. The demang
(title for district chief) was removed by pemuda (youths) in
mid-September after he had attempted to hold on to his power
during the early weeks of Independence. Following his ouster,
tension increased as members of the local population refused
to accept a KNI whose membership was the same as that of the
Hōkōkai. A group from Bukit Tinggi (including civilian
officials and military leaders) came to try to calm the situation. They arranged for the demang to leave the area, and
tried to replace him by the deputy demang. At a district
meeting, he too was rejected, after which a KNI chairman, with
no ties to either the Dutch or Japanese, was finally chosen.
See Lubuk Sikaping 1951b:3-4; Murad 1966:68-71 gives a picture
of formation of the KNI there.
[7] A full list of the Wali Luhak and Demang appointed on 23

In the closing months of 1945, the sporadic antigovernment uprisings in different parts of the region did not pose any real threat to the Residency administration, as there was little coordination among them. This situation began to change, however, from November 1945, when the first political parties were established.[8]   At the village level in West Sumatra the political parties which emerged with greatest strength were those formed by the Muslim organizations, in particular the Masjumi--which incorporated followers of both the Permi and Muhammadiah, the two most important Islamic organizations of the later colonial period.[9]   Most top leaders in the Residency government were not politically aligned with the religious parties, and they recognized the potential of these parties to channel any surge of popular discontent in a challenge to the new government. In March-April 1946, the authority of the Residency government was challenged by two major dissident movements (on the Baso Affair and the Volksfront, see Kahin 1979:135-51). These confrontations further alerted the government to its isolation from the prevalent mood in the region, and the danger that, because of this, other political forces might be able to seize leadership of the anticolonial revolutionary struggle. Although the political situation in the Minangkabau region was never as chaotic as in other parts of Sumatra, the Republican government´s position was sufficiently precarious for it to recognize its urgent need to strengthen its ties with the village-level population.

During the last decades of colonial rule the guidelines for membership of the <u>nagari</u> councils (<u>kerapatan nagari</u>) and

---

January 1946, and their former positions can be found in KP 1952:90, 108-109; and BPSIM 1978:151-54.

[8] Some of the major parties in West Sumatra were established on the following dates: PKI, 12 November 1945; PSII, 18 November 1945; Perti, 26 November 1945; MTKAAM, 20 December 1945; MIT 25 December 1945; Partai Sosialis 23 January 1946 (Fatimah Enar 1978:72).

[9] In West Sumatra the Masjumi was formed in February 1946 from the two organizations which had existed under the Japanese, the Majelis Islam Tinggi (MIT) and the Muhammadiah, which had been allowed to function as a social and educational organization throughout Sumatra under the leadership of A. R. Sutan Mansur. The MIT group incorporated many of the former members of the religious nationalist party, Permi. The traditional religious party Perti, although it had been a member of the MIT, did not join in with the Masjumi.

selection of the _nagari_ heads (_kepala nagari_) had largely been
determined by the colonial administration (see Graves 1981:38-
43; Abdullah 1971:23-24). _Nagari_ heads became beholden to the
Dutch as the major source of their power, and villagers then
grew to view these local leaders less as their own representatives and more as agents of the colonial rulers.[10] An official publication after the transfer of sovereignty described
their role under the Dutch as follows:

> These people who formed the feudal remnants, were
> strengthened by the Dutch government so that they could
> become its tool, for it was clear that they were the
> group that was most obedient to the Dutch government.
> So the contents of real democracy disappeared, and what
> remained was "a mockery of democracy" [_demokrasi pura-
> pura_] which actually signified complete power for the
> adat group as long as they stood on the side of the
> colonial government. (KP 1952:327)[11]

Under the Japanese the moral authority of the local officials,
as mentioned earlier, had been even further eroded.

Recognizing by early 1946 how dissatisfied the people
were with the continuity in local leadership, the Residency
government believed that, if the villagers, in particular members of the religious groups and the _pemuda_, participated in
the selection of their _nagari_ officials, this would strengthen
their ties to the Republican government. The Residency authorities, then, instituted basic changes in the way the
village councils and heads were selected. At its meeting of
March 16-18, 1946 the Residency KNI decided that an election
would be held for _nagari_ councils and _nagari_ heads, and it
appointed a seven-man electoral planning committee. Opposing
the proposal, the major _adat_ party, the MTKAAM (Majelis Tinggi
Kerapatan Adat Alam Minangkabau) at its congress of April 15,
1946, called instead for the addition of several party representatives to the existing _nagari_ councils.[12] In rejecting

---

[10] The Republicans pointed in particular to the ordinance of 3
September 1938 (Stbl. No. 490), "Peraturan Negari Otonoom di-
luar Djawa dan Madura," which defined the authority of the
Nagari Councils and their Heads vis-a-vis the Dutch Resident
and his officials (see KP 1952:324-26).
[11] On the alliance between Dutch authorities and _adat_ groups
and the role of the _penghulu_ in implementing Dutch measures
against the nationalist political groups in West Sumatra in
the 1930s, see Oki 1977:185-86.

this request, the Residency government contended that the MTKAAM's proposal did not sufficiently recognize that achievement of people's sovereignty was the aim of every stratum of the population in the struggle for independence.[13] On May 21 Resident Djamil issued a proclamation calling for direct popular election of representative nagari councils (Dewan Perwakilan Nagari—DPN) and for Wali Nagari (village mayors), to replace the KNIs and Kepala Nagari. The election would be based on universal suffrage for all citizens aged eighteen and over.[14]

The elections for the DPN were held on June 25, 1946, and those for the Wali Nagari on July 10 (Fatimah Enar 1978:-51). The procedures for conducting these elections varied in details (KP 1952:338-40). Usually, however, the nagari KNIs appointed five-man supervisory committees to whom the political parties proposed their candidates. The poltical parties could then campaign in behalf of their nominees. (Not only political parties but also functional groups and different kampung within the nagari could nominate candidates.)[15]

The voting, which was sometimes by secret ballot and

---

[12] The statement of the adat leaders read as follows: "a) Badan Perwakilan Rakyat yang ada sekarang (Kerapatan Negari) telah bersifat kedaulatan rakyat sejati. Penghulu-penghulu dan orang empat jenis wakil rakyat menurt adat ditanam atau diangkat oleh rakyat laki-laki, perempuan, tua dan muda; b) untuk memuaskan supaya Badan Perwakilan Rakyat itu sesuai dengan masyarakat sekarang, diputuskan supaya Kerapatan Negari yang lama ditambah dengan wakil-wakil yang ada dalam negari itu" (BPSIM 1978:599).

[13] KP 1952:330. It was further explained that the new nagari councils would not interfere in adat affairs, which would remain the prerogative of the penghulu and their councils.

[14] The full text of the Proclamation (20/46 of 21 May 1946) outlining arrangements for establishing the nagari councils and what their functions would be can be found in KP 1952:331-36.

[15] In Kambang (Pesisir Selatan/Kerinci) for example, each kampung proposed three candidates for election at the nagari level (Dt. Pintu Langit, 25 August 1976). In Batu Sangkar itself, according to the deputy head of the KNI at that time, a total of 40 groups were each allowed to nominate two representatives in an indirect election aimed at minimizing the influence of the PKI. Out of the 11 candidates selected at the second level, no PKI nominee remained (Zainuddin St. Kerajaan, 22 August 1976).

sometimes by the voter´s oral statement to the election committee, took place at a local center, under supervision of the election committee. Typical of descriptions given by participants of the election procedures in different <u>nagari</u> are the following accounts drawn from three of the <u>kabupaten</u> (districts), Solok, Agam, and Tanah Datar. The first is a description of how the elections were carried out in various <u>nagari</u> in the <u>kecamatan</u> (sub-district) of Singkarak:

> All adults voted for the DPN. The names of the candidates were written on a blackboard. The voter could write his choice on a piece of paper or could give the name of the candidate he liked. There was no restriction on the number of candidates that could be nominated by each group. Later the Wali Nagari was chosen; candidates were usually members of the DPN. There was more than one candidate. This election was usually attended by the camat [sub-district officer]. Sometimes the camat suggested that the unsuccessful candidate should be appointed to a certain position to guarantee internal solidarity in the nagari.[16]

The second is a description · of the election in the <u>nagari</u> of Sungai Buluh (Kab. Agam):

> First, a 5-man committee was formed from elements from the Ninik Mamak [elders in customary law], Cerdik Pandai [intellectuals], and Ulama [religious leaders]. Then this committee carried out its duty for election of members of the DPN. This 5-man committee was appointed based on a decision by a general meeting of the members of the Nagari KNI, and then each party proposed its candidates for seats in the DPN--PKI 2 candidates, Masjumi 3, PSI 1, and three others from the Ninik Mamak, Ulama and Cerdik Pandai, and so on, a total of 24. Then the 5-man committee wrote the lists of names on a blackboard, in public. Then later, on a fixed day all adults came to vote. The method of election was that the people came one by one to the committee and named the list they chose, and the committee wrote the name on the blackboard. Then those that got the most votes got the most seats.

---

[16] Former camat of Singkarak (Kabupaten Solok), Rajab Dt. Rajo Penghulu, 9 October 1976.

To choose the Wali Nagari, these were selected from
members of the DPN. The candidates were Agus Malik,
Karani St. Maarif, and Burhan. The voters again were
the public in the same way as the election for the DPN,
but the one who got the most votes was the one who won,
and it happened to be: Agus Malik. The members of the
DHN were also selected from the DPN, but the people who
chose them were only the members of the DPN.[17]

The third is from the nagari of Lima Kaum, Batu Sangkar,
and is the account of the former Wali Nagari:

The general public took part in the election. The first
election was to choose the DPN. Candidates for the DPN
came from all society leaders made up of ulama, penghulu, cerdik pandai and representatives of the pemuda.
Every suku [matriclan], every society group put up
candidates for the DPN, and they were chosen by members
of each suku and they became the candidates for the DPN.
There were five candidates for the later election
for head of the nagari: M. Salim Dt. Machudum, A. Munaf
Gani, Dt. Tunaro, Dt. Majo Basa, and Dt. Majo Indo.
Before these candidates were chosen, an organizational
committee for the election was appointed from the membership of the DPN. After the campaign the committee
fixed the day for each election to be held. The committee prepared a closed room, and in it three committee
members sat to note which candidates the people chose,
while the other two members of the committee organized
the people outside waiting to vote. Once the election
began, everyone who was entitled to vote, that is everyone aged 17 and over, entered one by one into the room
to make their choice by either naming it or whispering
it to the committee, and the committee noted it down.
After the election was completed, that same day the committee announced the winners of the election. It happened that in the election for village head M. Salim was
chosen as the Wali Nagari, and the other four candidates
became members of the DPN, and one of them, A. Munaf
Gani, was appointed as deputy Wali Nagari. After the
election for the Wali Nagari, the other three candidates
were then chosen by the DPN as members of the Dewan
Harian Nagari.[18]

---

[17] Former Secretary of the KNI of Sungai Buluh, Nizar Habib
St. Rajo Endah, 16 October 1976.

Once elected, then, the Dewan Perwakilan Nagari selected
a working body, the Dewan Harian, from among its members, usually consisting in part of unsuccessful candidates for the
post of Wali Nagari. One of the defeated candidates was also
usually appointed Deputy Wali Nagari.[19] The principal aim
here, and in the attempts to ensure that former members of the
kerapatan nagari retained some role in community affairs, was
to help guarantee solidarity within the nagari and avoid
alienating some traditional leaders who might possibly defect
to the Dutch.[20] Recognizing the dangers posed if many traditional leaders became disaffected, Republican policies were
aimed at minimizing this risk. In parts of Solok, for example, nagari councils, drawn from heads of the more important
families in the nagari were encouraged to act as advisors to
the elected DPN on how best to implement the Council's decisions.[21] In all areas it was emphasized that the new Wali
Nagari and Nagari Councils would not interfere in adat affairs.

Not all the newly established nagari councils were the
outcome of elections, and some merely issued from discussions
and bargaining among the leaders of the strongest groups in
the nagari. This seems to have applied particularly in the
rantau (outlying) areas, for example in parts of Kerinci,[22]
and in some regions on the outskirts of Padang.[23] Even in

---

[18] M. Salim Dt. Machudum (former Wali Nagari of Lima Kaum,
Batu Sangkar), 9 October 1976. These accounts are typical of
ones received from several other regions of Agam, Tanah Datar,
50 Kota, and Solok, and also parts of Pasaman. They are also
similar to the account given in Murad (1966:72-78).
[19] This was a feature of nearly all the elections on which I
have information.
[20] There were several incidents noted of adat leaders who lost
their former positions as a result of these elections being
alienated from the Republic, for example in Pasaman. See Lubuk
Sikaping 1951a:1.
[21] Eni Karim, who was deputy to Bupati Saalah St. Mangkuto of
Solok, said that it was arranged in several nagari there to
have a representative council of penghulu, who, however, had
no executive power, "like the House of Lords" from whom the
DPN members would request advice regarding implementation of
their decisions. Interview, 15 April 1976.
[22] A. J. Bebastani (former kapala Luhak of Kerinci/Indera-
pura), 10 October 1976; St. Masyur Dt. Sati, exDemang of
Sungai Darah.

some nagari in the immediate environs of Padang, however, the Dutch Resident discovered that direct elections had in fact taken place, as he reported after Dutch forces overran the coastal lowlands during their first "Police Action" of July 1947:

> Administration of the nagari has undergone great reorganization over the past years. . . Each nagari is governed by a Dewan Perwakilan Nagari (formerly Kerapatan Nagari) headed by a Wali-Nagari (earlier Pengoeloe Kepala or Kepala nagari). The Dewan Perwakilan Nagari were chosen by the people from candidates put forward by the political parties. The interests of the nagari are therefore no longer promoted by the adat heads but by the PKI, PSII, Partai Sosialis, etc. (Mailrapport 1947a)

He went on to say that in Lubuk Begalung he discovered that only one out of a total of 44 local council members was a penghulu, and noted:

> It is difficult to credit that the old authority of the penghoeloe, that rests not only on personality but also on the magic of defined heredity, should have completely disappeared. (Mailrapport 1947a)

By ending the continuity of leadership of the nagari that had characterized at least the last decades of colonial rule, these elections marked a major shift in power at the lowest level of government. The major beneficiaries in the leadership changes were members of the Masjumi party who now largely replaced the traditional lineage heads at the head of the nagari and in the nagari councils. Mr. Rasjid, who was Republican Resident of West Sumatra at the time, estimates that around 90 percent of the newly elected wali nagari came from the Masjumi, with that party holding a solid majority on most of the nagari councils.[24] For the remainder of the

---

[23] Almunir, 20 July 1976, Abdul Muluk, 15 October 1976, Padang.
[24] Interview with Mr. Sutan Mohammad Rasjid, 18 May 1976. One former camat, on the basis of this experience and his position in the personnel department of the governor's office in 1950 estimates that the ratio between Masjumi and PSI office holders at different levels of the administration was as follows: Wali Nagari 9:1; Camat 7:3; Bupati 3:7. Interview, Bunas Sutan Batuah, 8 October 1976. All informants agreed that it was the

struggle against the Dutch, these nagari representative councils formed the key element of Republican administration at
the local level. They became one of the two pivotal levels of
government in West Sumatra, the other being the Residency.

Nevertheless, the Residency leaders were not satisfied
with the nagari forming the basic unit of government, in large
part because most nagari were too small to be self-supporting.
From early 1947 the Residency administration attempted to
create units that were self-sufficient administratively and
particularly economically by merging clusters of nagari into
autonomous regions (wilajah autonoom).[25] (It was hoped that
the approximately 500 nagari would eventually form 100 autonomous areas which could be self-supporting in both respects.)
Though these efforts continued throughout 1948, the process
never gained much momentum, in large part because it was envisaged that the wilajah autonoom were to be not only economically but also culturally compatible, and the decisions of
the component nagari to join together had to be voluntary. As
a result, the nagari still formed the key units of the Republican administration when the Dutch launched their second
"Police Action" in December 1948. In practice, there were no
organizations that possessed any real power between the nagari and the Residency. Only as individuals did the camat and
bupati (district head) (and sometimes the wedana) exercise
authority, serving principally as supervisory agents--as-

Masjumi that gained overwhelming advantage in the 1946 nagari
elections.
[25] Residency-level dissatisfaction with the operation of the
nagari is evident in the recently published BPSIM, Sedjarah
Perjuangan, which states that, because of the formation of the
DPN the operation of the government became less smooth, in
that so many of those chosen to be members of the DPN and DHN
were men of little experience in administration, and the nagari were too small to be efficient. Although it states that
the clustering of the nagari into wilajah autonoom was gradually being achieved, it acknowledges that only 21 nagari
besar berotonoom (made up of 100 of the nagari) had come into
existence by November 1948 (BPSIM 1978:600-601). (It is possible to speculate that this is a facet of an argument that
took place between the Dutch-trained officials, for example,
Resident Rasjid, and such locally trained leaders as Chatib
Suleiman, whose whole concept of the organization of the defense of the Residency against the Dutch was based on political, economic, and security organizations at the level of
the nagari.)

sessors of the levels of taxation of the component nagari, centers for storing and distributing funds collected by the nagari authorities, and courts of appeal for local, usually civilian-military disputes.

The Dutch anticipated that the changes in the composition of the nagari councils would have alienated not merely the members of the traditionally strongest families, but also a majority of the ordinary villagers. For example, Dutch Resident van Straten gave this assessment to an American military mission visiting Padang in October 1947 (Mailrapport 1947b). The Dutch believed that the Republicans had made a mistake in upsetting adat authority and replacing it by party authority, and forecast that, if Dutch forces were ever militarily strong enough to reimpose Dutch rule, many penghulu, even good nationalists, "would greet our return with joy."

Until December 1948 Dutch efforts to detach groups and individuals from support of the Republic had to be restricted to the Netherlands-controlled area in and around Padang. In 1946 they encouraged foundation of the Persatuan Umum (General Association) in Padang, which, after the first action of July 1947 when Dutch authority was extended to the whole of the coastal plain, was transformed into a Daerah Istimewa Sumatera Barat (DISBA).[26] Leaders of DISBA and the Persatuan Umum had mostly been minor Indonesian officials under colonial rule, and the Dutch Resident admitted that they had little local influence.[27]

Despite their failure to attract recognized local leaders to their side within the areas under their control, the Dutch nevertheless believed that support for the Republic in both the town and the countryside was based on fear rather than any true allegiance.[28] But this assessment evidently

---

[26] This was described as "an association consisting of supporters of a free independent government of Sumatra's West Coast on a democratic basis cooperating with the Netherlands in the spirit of the Linggajati Agreement" (Staf van de Bevelhebber der Landstrijdkrachten n.d.).

[27] The chairman was a retired postal official, Sidi nan Poetih, the secretary was former Asst. Demang Mohd. Joesoef, and the treasurer was another postal official, Abd. Rahim. For the proclamation of the Committee for a Daerah Istimewa Sumatera Barat, see Mailrapport 1947c.

[28] Many Dutch officials continued to contend that no village

-315-

underestimated the degree of popular alienation from the local
adat leaders who had served the colonial administration, and
whose power was often seen to derive from Dutch manipulation
of traditional methods of selection, rather than from the traditional forms themselves.

After the 1946 elections the most important Republican
administrative, taxing (Kahin 1979:232-39, 328-34), and security networks in West Sumatra were built up on the foundation
of the new nagari heads and councils. The security organizations were created in 1947 at the instigation of one of the
outstanding Republican strategists in West Sumatra, Chatib
Suleiman (KP 1952:158; Rifai Abu and A. Suhadi 1976:32-34).
The earliest key element of these was the BPNK (Badan Pengawal
Nagari dan Kota--Body for Guarding the Nagari and Towns) to
which all pemuda between the ages of 17 and 35 who were not
members of the armed forces had to join. Although not given
weapons, members of the BPNK received basic military training
from the regular army (TNI--Tentara Nasional Indonesia) units.
Shortly after formation of the BPNK, officially in January
1948, local security headquarters (MPR--Markas Pertahanan
Rakjat) were established throughout West Sumatra at the three
functioning levels of government, Residency, District, and
Nagari (on the organization of the MPR at each level, see KP
1952:173-79). In the Nagari, the MPRN (Markas Pertahanan
Rakjat Nagari) was headed by the Wali Nagari (whose title
after December 1948 was changed to Wali Nagari Perang, or,
more usually, Wali Perang). The leader of the BPNK was deputy
head of the MPRN and the deputy Wali Nagari was also one of
its leaders. The headquarters was responsible for co-
ordinating all defense efforts in the nagari, and its duties
included overseeing the BPNK (KP 1952:173-79; BPSIM 1978:574-
76). From its inception, but particularly after the second
Dutch attack of December 1948, the BPNK's principal duties
were to guard village security; prepare for a Dutch attack on
the village, coordinate collection and transportation of supplies for the army's front lines, and investigate suspected
internal and external enemies.[29]

---

head was able to exercise authority unless he was also a penghulu: "Among broad sections of the population the disregarding of the adat authorities has never been accepted and orders
of a negari head who is not at the same time a penghulu are
never or rarely obeyed" (Mailrapport 1949b).
[29] Interviews, Daranin Sutan Kayo (Maninjau), 14 August 1976;

When the Dutch assault resulted in the disintegration of the regular army and the flight of all top Residency politicians and officials from the centers of government, the nagari administrations held together, and formed the basis on which the "military government" of West Sumatra was built and from which the guerrilla struggle of 1949 was waged (Kahin 1979:309-34). When the Dutch launched their major attack of December 19, 1948, the Republic's front-line defenses crumbled rapidly; but after a period of panic when many local officials fled their posts, an emergency administrative and security apparatus was soon reestablished in the nagari. The shock and disarray of the early weeks of the attack only briefly crippled the Republican administration, and so long as the Residency "military government" which now had its headquarters in Kototinggi, was able to issue general guidelines, the method of their implementation could be left to the nagari authorities (Instruksi 1949a:12-15 has information on the delineation of the duties of the Wali Nagari).

The BPNK had guard posts at the boundaries of all the villages. These became lookout posts for impending Dutch attacks, customs points for taxing passing traders, and bases from which Republican economic blockades were imposed on the Dutch-occupied towns. This militia acted not merely as the security arm of the local Republican administration, but also provided the major arteries of a communications network that spread throughout the region, with BPNK members acting as couriers for the government and the army (Mailrapport 1949b). In addition to providing an effective barrier to penetration of Dutch influence into the village, the BPNK also acted as a deterrent to former nagari leaders who might wish to switch their allegiance from the Republic back to the Dutch.[30] In performing these tasks the BPNK occasionally abused its position, but the Residency leadership was always alert to the dangers of alienating people in the countryside through arbitrary or brutal behavior by either regular or irregular Republican forces, and in the early days of February 1949 it strengthened the control of the nagari councils over the BPNK. Their rights in the field of security were strictly circum-

---

Sutan Dt. Majo Lelo (Bonjol), 16 August 1976; Nurhakim Taruman (Solok), 17 July 1976; and Instruksi 1949b:19-22.
[30] As a result, this usually only happened when, under the influence of a former village head, the whole nagari wanted to cooperate with the Dutch. A Dutch report notes two instances of this in the region of Payakumbuh in early February 1949 (Mailrapport 1949a).

scribed, and they were placed under more direct supervision of
the Wali Nagari Perang. In all strictly military affairs,
they were under the authority of the local army commander, the
wali perang, and the MPRN (see Instruksi 1949b:18-22).

The defense headquarters and the BPNK played major roles
in creating a situation where the Dutch, having occupied most
of the towns in West Sumatra, came up against a brick wall.
Their communications routes between the occupied towns remained tenuous, and within as well as outside the urban areas,
they continued to encounter organized guerrilla opposition.
Despite the ease of their advance the Netherlands´ forces were
almost totally unable to consolidate their control of the
areas they had occupied, being refused cooperation not only in
the villages but also in the towns. The success of the Republican effort can be seen from the frustration repeatedly expressed by the Dutch Resident in his periodic reports. It
comes through most strongly in that of March 1, 1949, where
after setting out his understanding of the breadth of the
Republic´s administrative, tax, and security apparatus
throughout West Sumatra, he goes on:

> Above all there is everywhere present the town and
> village guards--the Barisan Pengawal Negari dan Kampong
> [sic], so that in no kampung do traitors or spies have a
> chance to organize. It is strongly reminiscent of the
> Netherlands under the German occupation. It is above
> all this BPNK which keeps the supplies of rice from the
> Netherland´s occupied territory, and deals with any
> violations.

> The struggle, stretching from the front to the kampung
> is a true reflection of the ideas Tan Malaka developed
> in his brochure, "Sang Guerilla dan Gerpolek" where he
> sought to emphasize the Murba--the common people. This
> applies not only in distant kampungs, but in those on
> our main roads. . . These examples. . . show the truth
> of a statement that was made in a warung in Padang:
> "The Netherlands army is only strong enough to hold the
> occupied towns; outside of these the TNI, BPNK, and
> guerrillas rule" (Mailrapport 1949b).

Conclusions

The early months of the Revolution witnessed a series of
grudging concessions by Republican leaders in West Sumatra to
the more radical demands of the rural population who rejected
their pragmatic justifications for retaining the existing
administrative framework. After the hardship of the years of

Japanese occupation, the people resented retention of power by officials who had carried out Japanese orders, and with the declaration of independence demanded that there be a real change of personnel and policy direction in West Sumatra. Republican attempts in the face of this to maintain the old order helped precipitate the chaos of the spring of 1946, when the Residency government's authority was challenged by both religious revolts and by the radical socio-economic programs of the Volksfront. The local Republican leadership's position was further undermined by its obedience to national policy in acquiescing to the presence of the British forces in Padang.

Subsequently, when the center of gravity of the Residency government became more radical, with some Volksfront leaders wielding important influence within it, a gradual process began of accommodating to broadly popular demands. Attempts were made to direct the people's potentially anarchic energies away from overturning the established Republican government and instead to channel them into serving the ultimate goal of the independence struggle--namely removal of Dutch power. In order to accomplish this, however, the Republican leadership on Sumatra had to countenance more radical social, economic, and political changes than its Western-trained component had initially been willing to support.

The result was that, within the context of the independence war, there was a real revolution in West Sumatra that brought with it a major alteration, however ephemeral, in the political structure of village society. For at least the duration of the struggle, when Minangkabau society was experiencing one of its greatest periods of stress, power shifted from the adat leaders who had become an essential part of the colonial administrative system to men primarily from the religious parties. More precisely, many of the nagari heads and council members who owed power to their Dutch-defined ascriptive positions in the adat hierarchy had now to yield place, usually to men whose claims to recognition in the village rested on their religious training and role, many of them teachers in either private religious or occasionally government schools. These religious leaders had previously been excluded by the Dutch from exercising any political or administrative authority within their communities.

The change in village leadership was paralleled by a return to a pattern of authority in the region that more closely approximated its traditional, precolonial organization. The nagari was revived as the key unit of government, and the hierarchical system, engineered by the Dutch and maintained by the Japanese, was virtually abolished throughout the period of crisis. The new elected nagari heads and nagari councils became the basis throughout the Residency for build-

ing the local security and tax organizations that provided the
defense and economic sinews of the Republican reaction after
the Dutch penetrated much of the area at the end of 1948. The
social fabric that underlay the revolutionary struggle in West
Sumatra was thus significantly strengthened by a decentralization of authority which accorded more closely with the system
traditionally associated with precolonial Minangkabau. Reassertion of the principle of <u>nagari</u> autonomy, together with the
wider spectrum of representation in its leadership, contributed significantly to the political strength and resiliency
exhibited by the Republic's adherents in their response to the
second Dutch attack.

ABBREVIATIONS

AB	Adatrechtbundels
BKI	Bijdragen tot de Taal-, Land-, en Volkenkunde
BPSIM	Badan Permurnian Sejarah Indonesia-Minangkabau
BURF	Balai Undang Rembau Files
IG	Indische Gids
IPO	Overzicht van de Inlandsche en Maleisch-Chinese Pers
JMBRAS	Journal of the Royal Asiatic Society, Malayan Branch
JPS	Journal of Peasant Studies
JSBRAS	Journal of the Royal Asiatic Society Straits Branch
JSEAH	Journal of Southeast Asian History
KKIA	Koninklijk Koloniaal Instituut te Amsterdam
KP	Kementerian Penerangan.
KT	Koloniaal Tijdschrift.
NSSSF	Negeri Sembilan State Secretariat Files
SFR	Sumatra Factory Records in the India Office Library.
SEMBT	Seminar Internasional mengenai Kesusasteraan, Kesyarakatan, dan Kebudayaan Minangkabau, 4-6 September, Bukit Tinggi, Sumatera Barat, Indonesia.
TR	Indisch Tijdschrift voor het Recht.
TBB	Tijdschrift voor het Binnenlands Bestuur.
TBG	Tijdschrift voor Indische Taal-, Land-, en Volkenkunde, uitgegeven door het Koninklijk Batavias Genootschap van Kunsten en Wetenschappen.
TNAG	Tijdschrift van het Koninklijk Nederlandsch Aardrijkskundig Genootschap.
TNI	Tijdschrift voor Nederlandsch Indië.
UUMM	Undang Undang of Moco Moco
VBG	Verhandelingen van het Bataviaasch Genootschap

Letters in brackets at ends of citations indicate which author(s) in this volume cite given sources.

REFERENCES

A. Wahad Alwee
  1967 Rembau: A Study in Integration and Conflict in Negri
        Sembilan. Centre for Asian Studies, Working Papers in
        Asian Studies, No. 1. Nedlands: University of Western
        Australia. [MP]

AB
  1892 See Kooreman
  1910-55 bezorgd door de Commissie voor het Adatrecht en
        uitgegeven door het Koninklijk Instituut voor Taal-,
        Land-, en Volkenkunde. The Hague: Martinus Nijhoff.
        [BB&BB]
  1911, I. [TA]
  1924 See Logemann 1924
  1934 Omzetting van Poesaka in Pentjarian Grond. 41:392-394.
        [AO]

Abdul Kahar bin Bador
  1963 Kinship and Marriage among the Negeri Sembilan Ma-
        lays. M.A. Thesis, University of London. [MP]

Abdul Samad bin Idris
  1968 Negri Sembilan dan Sejarahnya. Kuala Lumpur: Utusan
        Malaysia Berhad. [MP]

Abdullah, Taufik
  1966 Adat and Islam: An Examination of Conflict in Minang-
        kabau. Indonesia 2:1-24. [LT&BB] [JP] [BB&BB]
  1967 Minangkabau 1900-1927: Preliminary Studies in Social
        Development. M.A. thesis, Cornell University. [MN]
  1970 Some Notes on the Kaba Tjindua Mato: An Example of
        Minangkabau Traditional Literature. Indonesia 9:1-22.
        [JJ] [JP] [NT&LT] [TA] [KW]
  1971 Schools and Politics: The Kaum Muda Movement in West
        Sumatra, 1927-1933. Ithaca, N.Y.: Cornell Modern Indones-
        ia Project. [LT&BB] [TA] [AO] [AK]
  1972 Modernization in the Minangkabau World: West Sumatra
        in the Early Decades of the Twentieth Century. In Culture
        and Politics in Indonesia. C. Holt, ed. pp. 179-245.
        Ithaca, N.Y.: Cornell University Press. [LT&BB] [JP] [MN]
        [TA] [KW]
  1976 The Making of a Schakel Society: The Minangkabau Re-
        gion in the Late 19th Century. Majalah Ilmu-Ilmu Sastra
        Indonesia 6(3):13-29. [NT&LT]

Abel, R.
  1973 Law Books and Books about Law. Stanford Law Review

26:175-228. [BB&BB]

Achmad Chatib, A. Alamah Sjech, bin Abdul Lathif
1965 Fatwa Tentang Tharikat Naqshabandiah. A. Nur Arief,
transl. and ed. Medan: Islamiyah. [TA]

Adat Monographie Dalam Propinsi Sumatra Tengah
c.1950s information on the nagaris, collected by the
Office of the Governor, 1950s. Unpublished. [TA]

Adatrechtbundels. See AB.

al-Ghazali
1979 On the Duties of Brotherhood. Muhtar Holland, transl.
Woodstock, N.Y.: Overlook Press. [MP]

Anas
1968 Masalah Hukum Waris menurut Hukum Adat Minangkabau.
In Menggali Hukum Tanah dan Hukum Waris Minangkabau.
Mochtar Naim, ed. Padang: Center for Minangkabau Studies.
[BB&BB]

Andaya, Leonard
1972-73 Satu Prinsip Baru Penggantian di Pagar Ruyung
diakhir Abad ketujah-belas. Jernal Sejarah (Universiti
Malaya):99-101. [KW]
1971 The Kingdom of Johor, 1641-1728: A Study of Economic
and Political Developments in the Straits of Malacca.
Ph.D. dissertation, Cornell University. [MP]
1975 The Kingdom of Johor, 1641-1728: Economic and Political Developments. Kuala Lumpur. [KW]

Bachtiar, H.W.
1967 Negeri Taram: A Minangkabau Village Community. In
Villages in Indonesia. Koentjaraningrat, ed. pp. 348-85.
Ithaca, N.Y.: Cornell University Press. [JP]

Barnes, J.A.
1962 African Models in the New Guinea Highlands. Man
62(2):5-9. [MP]

Barnes, Thomas
1818 Account of a Journey from Moco-Moco to Pengkalan Jambi through Korinchi in 1818. Malayan Miscellanies. Vol.
2. See also TNAG. [CW]

Barthes, Roland
1973 Mythologies. London: Paladan. [UJ]

Benda, Harry J. and Ruth T. McVey, transl. and eds.
1960 The Communist Uprisings of 1926-1927 in Indonesia:
Key Documents. Ithaca, N.Y.: Cornell Modern Indonesia
Project. [AO]

Benda-Beckmann, F. von
1979a Property in Social Continuity: Continuity and Change
in the Maintenance of Property Relationships Through Time
in Minangkabau, West Sumatra. Verhandelingen van het Koninklijk Instituut voor Taal-, Land- en Volkenkunde 86.
The Hague: Martinus Nijhoff. [JJ] [NT&LT] [JK] [TA]

[BB&BB]
1979b Modernes Recht und Traditionelle Gesellschaften. *Verfassung und Recht in Ubersee* 12:337-351. [BB&BB]
1980 Ayam Gadang toh Batalua? Changing Values in Minang-kabau Property and Inheritance Law and their Relation to Structural Change. Paper presented at the SEMBT. [JP]
Benda-Beckmann, K. von
1981 Forum Shopping and Shopping Forums: Dispute Process-ing in a Minangkabau Village in West Sumatra. *Journal of Legal Pluralism* 19:117-159. [BB&BB]
1982[1980,SEMBT] Traditional Values in a Non-Traditional Context: Adat and State Courts in West Sumatra. *Indonesia Circle* 27:39-50. [JP] [BB&BB]
n.d. Evidence and Legal Reasoning in Minangkabau State Courts. ms. [BB&BB]
Benda-Beckmann, K. and F. von
1978 Residence in a Minangkabau Nagari. *Indonesia Circle* 15:6-17. [JP] [BB&BB]
Benjamin, Walter
1976 The Storyteller and Artisan Cultures. In *Critical Sociology*. Paul Connerton, ed. pp. 277-300. Harmondsworth: Penguin. [UJ]
Berger, Peter L.
1967 *The Social Reality of Religion*. London: Penguin books. [TA]
Berger, Peter L. and Thomas Luckmann
1971 *The Social Construction of Reality*. Harmondsworth: Penguin. [UJ]
Bernstein, H.
1977 Notes on Capital and Peasant. *Review of African Poli-tical Economy*. 10. [JK]
1979 Concepts for the Analysis of Contemporary Peasan-tries. JPS 6(4). [JK]
Berthe, Louis
1970 Parenté, Pouvoir, et Mode de Production. In *Échanges et Communications*. Jean Pouillon and Pierre Maranda, eds. Tomé II. The Hague: Mouton. [JJ]
Bickmore, A.S.
1868 *Travels in the East Indian Archipelago*. London: John Murray. [CW]
Blumberger, J.P.
1931 *De Communistische Beweging in Nederlandsch-Indië*. Haarlem: Willink. [AO]
Boeke, J.H.
1946 *The Evolution of the Netherlands Indies Economy*. N.Y.: International Research Series. [JK]
Boeke, J.H., et al.
1966 *Indonesian Economics*. The Hague: W. van Hoeve. [JK]

Bohannan, P.
1969 Ethnography and Comparison in Legal Anthropology. In
Law in Culture and Society. L. Nader, ed. Chicago:
Aldine. [BB&BB]

BPSIM
1978 Sejarah Perjuangan Kemerdekaan Republik Indonesia di
Minangkabau 1945-50. Jakarta: Badan Permurnian Sejarah
Indonesia-Minangkabau. [AK]

Bremen, J.
1982 The Village on Java and the Early-Colonial State. JPS
9(4). [JK]

Buchler, I.R. and H.A. Selby
1968 Kinship and Social Organization: An Introduction to
Theory and Method. N.Y.: Macmillan Co. [MP]

BURF
1962. [MP]

Burns, P.
1978 Dutch Fantasy or Indonesian Reality: Kabar Serang IV.
pp. 75-109. James Cook University. [BB&BB]

Burridge, K.O.
1959 Siblings in Tangu. Oceania 30(2):128-154. [MP]

Census of Malaysia
1977 Population and Housing Census of Malaysia. Vol I,
Part IV, Basic Population Tables, Negri Sembilan. Kuala
Lumpur. [MP]

Cerroni, U.
1972 Marxismus und Recht--Historisch-Kritische Uber-
legungen. In Marxistische und sozialistische Rechtstheorie. N. Reich, ed. pp. 169-180. Frankfurt am Main:
Fischer Athenaum. [BB&BB]

Chayanov, A.V.
1966 The Theory of Peasant Economy. Homewood, Illinois:
Irwin. [JK]

Collectie Korn
n.d. Documents on Economy of Sawah Lunto, Alahan Panjang,
and Muara Labuh in the Collectie Korn, nos. 352 and 367.
Library of the Koninklijk Instituut voor Taal-, Land-, en
Volkenkunde. [JK]

Collet, O.J.A.
1925 Terres et peuples de Sumatra. Amsterdam. [LT&BB]

Cooper-Cole, F.
1936 Family, Clan, and Phratry in Central Sumatra. In
Essays in Anthropology. R.H. Lowie, ed. pp. 19-27. Berkeley: University of California Press. [LT&BB] [JP]
1945 The Peoples of Malaysia. New York. [LT&BB]

Cordonnier, J.C.
1972 Agriculture et Commerce au Sumatera Barat. Paris:
Mimeographed. [JJ]

Cortesão, A., ed. and transl.
  1944 The Suma Oriental of Tomé Pires...1512-1550. London:
        The Hakluyt Society. [KW]
Crawfurd, John
  1856[1971] A Descriptive Dictionary of the Indian Islands
        and Adjacent Countries. Reprinted Kuala Lumpur: Oxford
        University Press 1971. [See entries under "Rinchi" and
        "Minangkabau."] [CW]
Cunningham, C.E.
  1958 The Postwar Migration of the Toba Bataks to East
        Sumatra. New Haven: Yale University Southeast Asia
        Studies, Cultural Report Series. [MN]
Daghregister, see Kathirithamby-Wells' paper
DeMoubray, G.A.
  1931 Matriarchy in the Malay Peninsula and Neighboring
        Countries. London: Routledge and Sons. [MP]
Deutser, P.
  1981 West Sumatra and South Sulawesi. In Agricultural and
        Rural Development in Indonesia. G.E. Hansen, ed. Boulder,
        Colorado: Westview Press. [JK]
Dienst van het Boschwezen van N.I. 1923. Verslag. [JK]
Djojodigoeno, M.M.
  1968 Bloedverwantschap en Clanverwantschap onder de Min-
        angkabauers. BKI 124:262-272. [BB&BB]
Dobbin, Christine
  1974 Islamic Revivalism in Minangkabau at the Turn of the
        Nineteenth Century. Modern Asian Studies 8(3):319-346.
        [CW]
  1975 The Exercise of Authority in Minangkabau in the late
        Eighteenth Century. In Pre-Colonial State Systems in
        South East Asia. A. Reid and L. Castles, eds. Monographs
        of JMBRAS 6. Kuala Lumpur. [LT&BB] [CW] [BB&BB]
  1977 Economic Change in Minangkabau as a Factor in the
        Rise of the Padri Movement, 1784-1830. Indonesia 23:1-38.
        [LT&BB] [AO] [JK] [CW] [TA] [BB&BB]
Douglas, Mary
  1969 Is Matriliny Doomed in Africa? In Man in Africa. M.
        Douglas and P.M. Kaberry, eds. pp. 121-135. London:
        Tavistock. [JP]
Eerde, J.V. van
  1901 Een huwelijk bij de Minangkabausche Maleiers. TBG
        43:387-511. [LT&BB]
Eliade, Mircea
  1959 Cosmos and History. N.Y.: Harper. [TA]
Embree, John F.
  1950 Thailand--A Loosely Structured Social System. Amer-
        ican Anthropologist 52:181-193. [MP]
Emmerson, Donald K.

1980 Issues in Southeast Asian History: Room for Inter-
pretation--A Review Article. Journal of Asian Studies
40(1):62-64. [AO]

Ennew, J., et al.
1979 "Peasantry" as an Economic Category. JPS 7(2). [JK]

Evans-Pritchard, E.E.
1940 The Nuer: A Descripton of the Modes of Livelihood and
Political Institutions of a Nilotic People. Reprinted
1972, N.Y.: Oxford University Press. [MP]
1951 Kinship and Marriage among the Nuer. Oxford: Oxford
University Press. [MP]

Evers, H.D.
1975 Changing Patterns of Minangkabau Urban Landownership.
BKI 131:86-110. [BB&BB]

Fatimah Enar, d.k.k.
1978 Sumatera Barat, 1945-49. Padang: Pemerintah Daerah
Sumatera Barat. [AK]

Fischer, H. Th.
1964 The Cognates in the Minangkabau Kinship Structure.
Oceania 35:96-110. [BB&BB]

Fox, Robin
1967 Kinship and Marriage: An Anthropological Perspective.
Harmondsworth: Penguin. [JP]

Francis, E.A.
1839 Korte beschrijving van het Nederlandsch grondgebied
ter Westkust van Sumatra. TNI 2:28-45, 90-111, 203-220.
[LT&BB] [BB&BB]

Freeman, J.D.
1955 Iban Agriculture: A Report on the Shifting Cultivation of Hill Rice by the Iban of Sarawak. London. [MN]

Friedman, H.
1980 Household Production and the National Economy. JPS
7(2). [JK]

Gautama, S. and Budi Harsono
1972 Agrarian Law. Bandung: Lembaga Penilitian Hukum dan
Kriminologi Fakultas Hukum, Universitas Padjadjaran Bandung. [BB&BB]

Gautama, S. and R.N. Hornick
1972 An Introduction to Indonesian Law: Unity in Diversity. Bandung: Alumni. [BB&BB]

Geertz, Clifford
1963 Agricultural Involution. Berkeley: University of California Press. [JK]
1968 Islam Observed. Chicago: University of Chicago Press.
[TA]

Geertz, Hildred
1961 The Javanese Family. N.Y.: The Free Press. [UJ]

Gluckman, M.

1969   Concepts in the Comparative Study of Tribal Law. In
        Law in Culture and Society. L. Nader, ed. Chicago:
        Aldine. [BB&BB]
1972   The Ideas in Barotse Jurisprudence, Manchester:
        Manchester University Press. [BB&BB]
1973   The Judicial Process among the Barotse of Northern
        Rhodesia (Zambia), 2nd. Ed. Manchester: Manchester
        University Press. [BB&BB]
Gluckman, M., ed.
1969   Ideas and Procedures in African Customary Law. Lon-
        don: Oxford University Press. [BB&BB]
1972   The Allocation of Responsibility. Manchester: Man-
        chester University Press. [BB&BB]
Gobee, E., and C. Adrianse, eds.
1965   Ambtelijk Adviezen van C. Snouck Hurgronje. Vol. III.
        The Hague: Martinus Nijhoff. [TA]
Gough, K.
1961   The Modern Disintegration of Matrilineal Descent
        Groups. In Matrilineal Kinship. D. Schneider and K.
        Gough, eds. pp. 631-652. Berkeley: University of Cali-
        fornia Press. [JP]
Graaf, H.J. de, and Th. G. Th. Pigeaud
1974   De Eerste Moslimse Vorstendommen op Java. The Hague:
        Martinus Nijhoff. [TA]
Graves, Elizabeth E.
1971   The Ever-Victorious Buffalo: How the Minangkabau of
        Indonesia Solved Their ʹColonial Question.ʹ Ph.D. dis-
        sertation, University of Wisconsin. [AO]
1981   The Minangkabau Response to Dutch Colonial Rule in
        the Nineteenth Century. Monograph Series no. 60, Modern
        Indonesia Project, Southeast Asia Program. Ithaca, N.Y.:
        Cornell Modern Indonesia Project . [BB&BB] [AK]
Gullick, J.M.
1949   Sungei Ujong. JMBRAS 22(2):1-69. [MP]
1951   The Negri Sembilan Economy of the 1890s. JMBRAS
        24(1):38-55. [MP]
1958   Indigenous Political Systems of Western Malaya.
        London: Athlone Press. [MP]
Guyt, H.
1934   Kerapatan-adat. TR 140:127-135. [BB&BB]
1936   Grondverpanding in Minangkabau. Leiden. [LT&BB]
        [BB&BB]
Haan, F. de
1897   Naar Midden Sumatra in 1684. TBG 39:327-366. [KW]
        [JK]
Haar, B. ter
1929   Western Influence on the Law for the Native Popula-
        tion. In The Effect of Western Influence on Native Civil-

izations in the Malay Archipelago. B. Schrieke, ed.
Weltevreden: G. Kolff and Co. [BB&BB]
1934 Welke eisen stelt toepassing van ongeschreven mater-
ieel privaatrecht aan organisatie en procesrecht der Inlandsche rechtbanken? TR 140:35-79. [BB&BB]
1937 Het adatrecht van Nederlandsch-Indie in wetenschap,
practijk en onderwijs. Batavia: Rede. [BB&BB]
HAMKA [Haji Abdul Malik Karim Amrullah; also hamka]
1968 Adat Minangkabau dan Harta Pusakanja. In Menggali
Hukum Tanah dan Hukum Waris Minangkabau. M. Naim, ed.
Padang: Center for Minangkabau Studies. [BB&BB]
Hale, A.
1898 Folklore and the Menangkabau Code in the Negri Sem-
bilan. JSBRAS 31:43-61. [MP]
Hasselt, A.L. van
1882 Volksbeschrijving van Midden-Sumatra. Leiden.
[LT&BB]
Hervey, D.F.A.
1884 Rembau. JSBRAS 13:241-258. [MP]
Hesse, Mary
1980 Revolutions and Reconstructions in the Philosophy of
Science. Bloomington, Indiana: Indiana University Press.
[NT&LT]
Hollander, J.J. de, ed.
1847 Sjech Djilah Eddin: Verhaal van den Aanvang der
Padri-Onlusten op Sumatra. Leiden: E.J. Brill. [TA] [KW]
Holleman, F.D.
1920 Adatrecht van de afdeling Toeloengagoeng. TR 112:375-
402. [BB&BB]
Hollis, Martin and Edward J. Nell
1979 Two Economists. In Philosophy and Economic Theory.
Frank Hahn and Martin Hollis, eds. N.Y.: Oxford University Press. [NT&LT]
Hooker, M.B.
1969 The Relationship Between the Adat and State Constitu-
tions of Negri Sembilan. JMBRAS 42(2):155-172. [MP]
1971 The Early Adat Constitution of Negri Sembilan (1773-
1824). JMBRAS 44(1):104-116. [MP]
1972 Adat Laws in Modern Malaya: Land Tenure, Traditional
Government, and Religion. Kuala Lumpur: Oxford University
Press. [MP]
1975 Legal Pluralism: An Introduction to Colonial and Neo-
Colonial Laws. Oxford: Clarendon Press. [BB&BB]
Huitema, W.F.
1935 De Bevolkingskoffiecultuur op Sumatra. Wageningen: H.
Veen en Zonen. [JK]
Instruksi
1949a Instruksi No. 10/GM/Instr. 31 January 1949, Tugas

Kewadjiban Pamong-Pradja (termasuk Wali2 Negari) di
Sumatera Barat dalam waktu darurat. Himpunan Instruksi.
[AK]

1949b Instruksi No. 13/GM, 2 February 1949, Badan Pengawal
Negeri dan Kota. Himpunan Instruksi Gubernur Militer Da-
erah Sumatera Barat, in Badan Penerangan Staf Gubernur
Militer Daerah Sumatera Tengah, typscript. [AK]

IPO
1925a Warta Hindia, 10 October. No. 45:290. [AO]
1925b Api, 12-17 October. 43:150-153. [AO]
1926a Api, 4-9 January. 3:3-6. [AO]
1926b Sinar Sumatra, 9 March. 25:579-580. [AO]
1926c Oetoesan Melajoe, 18 May. 23:424. [AO]
1926d Sinar Sumatra, 31 May. 25:579-580. [AO]
1926e Radio, 31 May. 25:579. [AO]

Jackson, J.C.
1972 Rice Cultivation in West Malaysia. JMBRAS 45. [JK]
s´ Jacob, E.H.
1945 Landsdomein en Adatrecht. Utrecht: Kemink en Zn.
[BB&BB]

James, W.
1978 Matrifocus on African Women. In Defining Females: The
Nature of Women in Society. S. Ardener, ed. pp. 141-163.
London: Croon Helm. [JP]

Jay, Robert T.
1969 Javanese Villagers. Cambridge, Mass.: MIT Press. [JJ]

Johns, Anthony H., ed. and transl.
1958 Rantjak diLabueh: A Minangkabau Kaba. Ithaca, N.Y.:
Cornell University Southeast Asia Program Data Paper 32.
[JP] [NT&LT]

Josselin de Jong, J.P.B. de
1977[1935] Malay Archipelago as a Field of Ethnological
Study. In Structural Anthropology in the Netherlands.
P.E. de Josselin de Jong, ed. The Hague: Martinus
Nijhoff. Orig. Pub. in Dutch in 1935. [JJ]

Josselin de Jong, P.E. de
1951[1952,1960,1980] Minangkabau and Negri Sembilan:
Socio-Political Structure in Indonesia. Second Edition,
1980. Leiden: IJdo. [1952, The Hague: Martinus Nijhoff]
[1960 printing, Djakarta: Bhratara.] [LT&BB] [JP] [MP]
[TA] [KW] [BB&BB]

1956 The Participants´ View of Their Culture. Reprinted in
Structural Anthropology in the Netherlands, P.E. de Josselin de Jong, ed. pp. 233-252. The Hague: Martinus Nijhoff. [MP]

1960 Islam Versus Adat in Negeri Sembilan (Malaya). BKI
113:158-203. [MP]

1970 Review of Jay 1969. American Anthropologist 72:1128-

1129. [JJ]
1975a Social Organization of Minangkabau. Leiden: Instituut voor Culturele Antropologie en Sociologie der Niet-
   Westerse Volken. [LT&BB]
1975b   The Dynastic Myth of Negri Sembilan (Malaya). BKI
   131:277-308. [LT&BB]
1980a The Concept of the Field of Ethnological Study. In
   The Flow of Life. James J. Fox, ed. Cambridge, Mass.:
   Harvard University Press. [JJ]
1980b Two Essays on Minangkabau Social Organization.
   Leiden: ICA Publication 8. [JJ]
1980c Ruler and Realm. Mededelingen der Koninklijke Neder-
   landse Akademie van Wetenschappen, Afd. Letterkunde NR43-
   1. [JJ]
1980d Deductive Anthropology and Minangkabau. Paper presented at the SEMBT. [JP] [NT&LT]
Joustra, M.
1923 Minangkabau, tweede uitgave. Leiden: M. Nijhoff.
   [LT&BB] [BB&BB]
Junus, Umar
1964 Some Remarks on Minangkabau Social Structure. BKI
   120:293-326. [JJ] [JP]
1971 Kebudajaan Minangkabau. In Manusia dan Kebudjaan di
   Indonesia. Koentjaraningrat, ed. pp. 245-263. Djakarta:
   Djambatan. [JJ] [JP]
1974a Perkembangan novel-novel Indonesia. Kuala Lumpur:
   University of Malaya Press. [UJ]
1974b Review of Culture and Politics in Indonesia, ed. by
   Claire Holt et al., eds. BKI 130:362-72. [UJ]
1976 Dunia Lelaki dan Perempuan: Permasalahan dalam Novel-
   Novel Indonesia. Dewan Bahasa 20:407-423. [JJ]
1977 Masyarakat Minangkabau sebagai dilihat oleh Tiga
   Novelist yang Mempunyai Latar Belakang Socio-Budaya yang
   Berbeza. Dewan Bahasa 21:216-229. [JJ] [UJ]
1979 Realiti dan Mitos dalam "Puti Bungsu." Masa Kini
   1(2). [JJ]
1980a Kaba dan Sistem Sosial Minangkabau: Suatu Problem.
   Paper presented at the SEMBT. [UJ]
1980b Sikap dan Pemikiran dalam Puisi Melayu Moden. Kuala
   Lumpur: Dewan Bahasa Dan Pustaka. [UJ]
1980c Unsur Sosio-Bundaya dalam Sastra Indonesia. Jakarta:
   Sinar Harapan. [JJ]
1981 Catatan Budaya. Dewan Budaya. [UJ]
Kahin, Audrey
1979 Struggle for Independence: West Sumatra in the
   Indonesian National Revolution. Ph.D. dissertation,
   Cornell University. [AK]
Kahn, J.S.

1975 Economic Scale and the Cycle of Petty Commodity Production in West Sumatra. In _Marxist Analyses and Social
Anthropology_. M. Bloch, ed. London: Malaby. [JK] [BB&BB]
1976 'Tradition,' Matriliny, and Change Among the Minangkabau of Indonesia. BKI 132:64-95. [LT&BB] [JP] [AO]
[BB&BB]
1980a _Minangkabau Social Formations: Indonesian Peasants
and the World Economy_. Cambridge Studies in Social Anthropology 30. Cambridge: Cambridge University Press.
[LT&BB] [JP] [JK] [BB&BB]
1980b Review of _Property in Social Continuity_ by Benda-
Beckmann. _Indonesia Circle_ 22:81-88. [JK] [BB&BB]
1981 The Social Context of Technological Change in Four
Malaysian Villages. _Man_ 16(n.s.):542-562. [JK]
Kamer
1931 _Verslag van Kamer van de Koophandel en Nijverheid te
Padang 1930_. (Annual Report of the Department of Commerce
and Industry in the West Sumatran Administration.) Padang: Vorhanding. [AO]
Kanahele, George S.
1967 _The Japanese Occupation of Indonesia: Prelude to
Independence_. Ph.D. dissertation, Cornell University.
[AK]
Kat Angelino, A.D.A. de
1931a _Staatkundig beleid en bestuurszorg in Nederlandsch-
Indie_. 3rd. ed. The Hague: M. Nijhoff. [BB&BB]
1931b _Colonial Policy_. The Hague: M. Nijhoff. [BB&BB] [JK]
Kathirithamby-Wells, J.
1969 Acehnese Control Over West Sumatra Up to the Treaty
of Painan of 1663. JSEAH 10(3):453-79. [KW]
1970 Ahmad Shah Ibn Iskandar and the Late 17th Century
'Holy War' in Indonesia. JMBRAS 43(1):48-63. [KW]
1976 The Inderapura Sultanate: The Foundations of its Rise
and Decline, from the Sixteenth to the Eighteenth Centuries. _Indonesia_ 21:63-84. [KW]
1977 _The British West Sumatran Presidency (1760-85):
Problems of Early Colonial Enterprise_. Kuala Lumpur:
Universiti Malaya. [KW] [AO]
Kathirithamby-Wells, J. and Mohammed Yusoff Hashim
1980 Raden Anom Zainal Abidin: A Nineteenth Century court
Writer of Mukomuko (Benkulen). Paper presented to the 8th
International Association of Historians of Asia, 23 pp.
Kuala Lumpur. [KW]
n.d. _The Syair Mukomuko: An Early Nineteenth Century Sumatran Court Chronicle_. MS in preparation. [KW]
Kato, Tsuyoshi
1977 _Social Change in a Centrifugal Society: The Minang-
kabau of West Sumatra_. Ph.D. dissertation, Cornell

University. [JP] [MN] [TA] [BB&BB]
    1978   Change and Continuity in the Minangkabau Matrilineal
           System. Indonesia 25:1-16. [JP]
    1982   Matriliny and Migration: Evolving Minangkabau Tradi-
           tions in Indonesia. Ithaca: Cornell University Press.
           [JK]
Katoppo, Marianne
    1979   Raumanen. Jakarta: Gaya Favorit Press. [UJ]
Kelly, Raymond
    1977   Etoro Social Structure: A Study in Structural Contra-
           diction. Ann Arbor: University of Michigan Press. [MP]
Kemal, I.
    1964   Sekitar Pemerintahan Nagari Minangkabau dan Perkem-
           bangannja. Padang: Pertjetakan Daerah Sumatera Barat.
           [BB&BB]
Khadijah binte Haji Muhamed
    1978   Migration and the Matrilineal System of Negeri Sem-
           bilan. Ph.D. dissertation, University of Pittsburgh. [MP]
Khoo Kay Kim
    1972   The Western Malay States, 1850-1873: The Effects of
           Commercial Development on Malay Politics. Kuala Lumpur:
           Oxford University Press. [MP]
Kielstra, E.B.
    1887a Onze Kennis van Sumatra's Westkust, Omstreeks de
           helft der achttiende eeuw. BKI 36:499-559. [LT&BB] [KW]
           [BB&BB]
    1887b Sumatra's Westkust van 1819-1825. BKI 36:8-163.
           [LT&BB] [BB&BB]
    1888   Sumatra's Westkust van 1826-1832. BKI 37:216-380.
           [LT&BB] [BB&BB]
    1889   Sumatra's Westkust van 1833-1835. BKI 38:161-249,
           313-379, 467-514. [LT&BB] [BB&BB]
    1892   Sumatra's Westkust sedert 1850. BKI 41:254-330, 622-
           706. [LT&BB] [TA]
Klerks, E.A.
    1898   Geographisch en Ethnographisch Opstel Over de Land-
           schappen Korintji, Serampas en Soengai Tenang. TBG 39:1-
           114. [CW]
Knight, G.R.
    1982   Capitalism and Commodity Production in Java. In Cap-
           italism and Colonial Production. H. Alavi, et al., eds.
           London: Croom Helm. [JK]
Kohler, J.
    1910   Ueber das Recht der Minangkabau auf Sumatra. Zeit-
           schrift fur Vergleichende Rechtswissenschaft 23:250-260.
           [LT&BB]
Kooreman, P.J.
    1892   Aantekeningen van den toenmaligen Assistent-Resident

P.J. Kooreman betreffende de afdeling Painan, in het bij-
zonder betreffende de onderafdeling Indrapoera. AB
11:130-149. [BB&BB]
1893 Aantekeningen betreffende de Korintjische adat. BKI
183ff. [CW]
1902 De rechtspraak in de burgerlijke zaken van de
Maleiërs ter Sumatra's Westkust, voorheen en thans. TNI
3(1):909-930. [BB&BB]
Korn, V.E.
1941 De vrouwelijke mama' in de Minangkabausche familie.
BKI 100:301-338. [LT&BB] [JJ] [NT&LT] [BB&BB]
Korn, V.E. and R. Van Dijk
1946 Adatgrondenrecht en domeininfictie. Twee critieken,
Gorinchem. [BB&BB]
KP
[c.1952] Republik Indonesia Propinsi Sumatera Tengah.
Kementerian Penerangan. [AK]
Kroesen, T.A.L.
1874 Het grondbezit ter Sumatra's Westkust. TNI (4e Serie)
3:1-28. [JK] [BB&BB]
Kroeskamp, H.
1931 De Westkust en Minangkabau, 1665-1668. Utrecht: Fa.
Schotanus en Jens. [KW] [JK]
Kula, W.
1976 An Economic Theory of the Feudal System. London: New
Left Books. [JK]
Lando, Richard P. and Lynn L. Thomas
1983 Hierarchy and Alliance in Two Sumatran Societies. In
Beyond Samosir: Recent Studies of the Batak Peoples of
Sumatra. Rita Smith Kipp and Richard D. Kipp, eds. pp.
53-81. Ohio University Papers in International Studies,
Southeast Asia Series No. 62. Athens, Ohio: Ohio
University Press. [LT&BB]
Landraad Fort de Kock
1933 TR 140(1934):218-226. [BB&BB]
Landraad Pariaman
1926 TR 126(1927):72-79. [BB&BB]
Landraad Payakumbuh
1933 TR 140. [BB&BB]
Lee, G.
1973 Commodity Production and Reproduction Amongst the
Malayan Peasantry. Journal of Contemporary Asia. 3(4).
[JK]
Lévi-Strauss, C.
1969[1949] The Elementary Structures of Kinship. Boston:
Beacon Press. [LT&BB] [JP]
1971 L'Homme Nu. Paris: Plon. [JJ]
Lewis, Bernard

1976 History: Remembered, Discovered, Invented. N.Y.:
Harper. [TA]

Lewis, Diane K.
1962 The Minangkabau Malay of Negeri Sembilan: A Study in
Socio-Cultural Change. Ph.D. dissertation, Cornell
University. [MP]

Leyds, W.J.
1926 Larassen in Minangkabau. Koloniale Studiën 10(1):387-
416. [LT&BB] [KW] [BB&BB]

Linden, J. van der
1855 Het Inlandsch Bestuur in het Gouvernement van Sumatra's Westkust. TBG 4. [KW]

Lister, Martin
1887 The Negri Sembilan: Their Origin and Constitution.
JSBRAS. [MP]
1890 Malay Law in Negri Sembilan. JSBRAS 22:299-319. [MP]
1891 Pantang Larang of Negri Sembilan. JSBRAS 23:142-144.
[MP]

Loeb, E.M.
1934 Patrilineal and Matrilineal Organization in Sumatra.
American Anthropologist 36:26-50. [LT&BB]
1935 Sumatra: Its History and Peoples. Vienna: Institut
fur Voelkerkunde. [LT&BB] [KW]

Logemann, J.H.A.
1924 De Betekenis der Indonesische getuigen. AB 23:114-
133. [BB&BB]

Logemann, J.H.A., and B. ter Haar
1927 Het beschikkingsrecht der Indonesische rechtgemeen-
schappen. Overdruk uit TR 125:347-464. [BB&BB]

Lublinsky, I.
1927 Minang-Kabau: Ein Beitrag zur Entstehung und Weiter-
entwicklung des Matriarchats. Zeitschrift für Ethnologie
59:98-110. [LT&BB]

Lubuk Sikaping
1951a Suka Duka Demokrasi. Unpub. typescript, 10 December
1951. [AK]
1951b Sedjarah Pemerintahan Daerah. Unpub. typescript, 18
December 1951. Kabupaten Pasaman. [AK]

Lulofs, C.
1904 Koffiecultuur en Belasting ter Sumatra's Westkust.
Indisch Gids 26(ii):1642-1643. [AO]

McKinley, Robert H.
1975 A Knife Cutting Water: Child Transfers and Siblingship among Urban Malays. Ph.D. dissertation, University
of Michigan. [MP]

McNair, J.F.A.
1878[1972] Perak and the Malays. Reprinted Kuala Lumpur:
Oxford University Press. [CW]

McVey, Ruth T.
1965 The Rise of Indonesian Communism. Ithaca, N.Y.: Cornell University Press. [AO] [JK]
Mahkamah Agung
1969 Yurisprudensi Indonesia. Jakarta: Mahkamah Agung. [BB&BB]
Mailrapport
1875 no. 575, 22.6.1875. [BB&BB]
1914 Nota betrekkelyke de Samenpaning van Toeankoe Batoeah, Datoek Ampang Basa, Hadji Mohamad Amin en Toeankoe Basa ten doel het Hebbende het in de Wapende Brengen der Ingezetenen ter het in Nederlandsch Indië Gevestigd Gezag. No. 1050. [AO]
1919 Memorie van Overgave: Sumatra's Westkust, J.D.L. LeFebvre No. 2904. [JK]
1924 Letter from Korn to Governor General, Weltevreden, 30 June 1924, No. F183/Geheim, 552/1924; in Verbaal 23 March 1925. [AO]
1926a Dt. Toemmenggoeng, Nota over de Toestand ter Westkust van Sumatra, 16 August 1926. 934/1926. [AO]
1926b Vertaling Rapport van Datoek Batoeah. 1212/1926. [AO]
1927a Letter from Arrends [Resident of West Sumatra] to Governor General, Padang, 31 December 1926. No. 1353,G. 43/1927. [AO]
1927b Process Verbaal Hadji Soeleman. 197/1927. [AO]
1927c Report of Arrends, Padang, 6 April 1926. 602/1927. [AO]
1927d Secret Report of Hamerster, 1 October 1927. 1242/1927. [AO]
1947a Rapport over de periode 24-30 Juli, 1947, signed by L.B. van Straten, Padang, 30 July 1947. No. 52. [AK]
1947b Politiek Verslag, Padang, 23 October 1947. No. 128. [AK]
1947c Politiek Verslag, Padang, 5 November 1947. No. 203. [AK]
1949a Overzicht Situatie, Padang, 7 February 1949. No. 249. [AK]
1949b Overzicht Situatie, Padang, 1 March 1949. No. 263. [AK]
Mansoer, M.D., Amrin Imran, Macdanas Sajwan, Asmaniar Idris, Sidi I. Buchari
1970 Sedjarah Minangkabau. Jakarta: Bhratara. [KW] [CW]
Maretin, J.V.
1961 Disappearance of Matriclan Survivals in Minangkabau Family and Marriage Relations. BKI 117(1):168-195. [JP] [MN] [BB&BB]
Marsden, W.

1811[1966] The History of Sumatra. Third Edition. London.
  Reprinted Kuala Lumpur: Oxford University Press. [KW]
  [CW]

Marshall, Mac
  1981 Introduction: Approaches to Siblingship in Oceania.
    In Siblingship in Oceania: Studies in the Meaning of Kin
    Relations. Mac Marshall, ed. pp. 1-15. Ann Arbor: Univer-
    sity of Michigan Press. [MP]

Mattulada
  1975 Latoa: Satu Lukisan Analitis Terhadap Antropologi-
    Politik Orang Bugis. Dissertation, University of Indo-
    nesia. [TA]

Migdal, Joel S.
  1974 Peasants, Politics, and Revolution: Pressures Toward
    Political and Social Change in the Third World. Prince-
    ton, N.J.: Princeton University Press. [AO]

Mintz, Jeanne S.
  1959 Marxism in Indonesia. In Marxism in Southeast Asia: A
    Study in Four Countries. Frank N. Trager, ed. pp. 171-
    239. Stanford, California: Stanford University Press.
    [AO]

Mol, Hans J.
  1977 Identity and the Sacred: A Sketch for a New Social-
    Scientific Theory of Religion. N.Y.: The Free Press. [TA]

Moyer, David S.
  1980 Paris--Leiden and Other Oppositions. Leiden: ICA
    Publication 16. First Edition, 1976. [JJ]

Murad, D.P., ed.
  1966 Sungaipuar. Jakarta: Jajasan Sungaipuar. [AK]

Murdock, George Peter
  1949 Social Structure. N.Y.: The Macmillan Company.
    [LT&BB]

Myrdal, G.
  1968 Asian Drama. N.Y.: Twentieth Century Fund. [JK]

Nader, L.
  1965 The Anthropological Study of Law. American
    Anthropologist 67(6,Part 2):3-32. [BB&BB]

Nahuijs, H.G.
  1826 Brieven over Bencoolen, Padang, het rijk van Minang-
    kabau... Breda. [KW]

Naim, Mochtar
  1968 Menggali Hukum Adat Minangkabau. Padang: Center for
    Minangkabau Studies. [TA]
  1973 Merantau: Minangkabau Voluntary Migration. Ph.D.
    dissertation, University of Singapore. [mimeographed]
    [JJ] [JP] [MN]
  1979 Merantau: Pola Migrasi Suku Minangkabau. Yogyakarta:
    Gadjah Mada University Press. [Transl. of Naim 1973.]

[MN]
Nasroen, M.
1957 Dasar Falsafah Adat Minangkabau. Djakarta: Bulan
Bintang. [TA] [BB&BB]
Netscher, E.
1880 Padang in het laast der XVIIIe eeuw. VBG 41:1-122.
[KW]
Newbold, T.J.
1839 Political and Statistical Accounts of the British
Settlements in the Straits of Malacca. 2 Vols. London:
John Murray. [MP]
Ng, C.S.H.
1980 The Woven Web: A Brief Look at the Significance of
Adat Dress in a Minangkabau Village. Paper presented at
the SEMBT. [JP]
Nolst Trenité, G.J.
1912 Domeinnota. Batavia. [BB&BB]
1920 Inleiding tot de Agrarisch Wetgeving. [BB&BB]
Noorduyn, J.
1956 De Islamisering van Makassar. BKI 112:247-266. [TA]
NSSSF
1924. [MP]
O'Brien, H.A.
1884 Jelebu. JSBRAS 14:337-343. [MP]
O'Flaherty, Wendy Doniger
1980 Inside and Outside the Mouth of God: the Boundary
Between Myth and Reality. Deadalus 109(2):93-126. [TA]
Ogburn, William F.
1964 On Culture and Social Change: Selected Papers.
Chicago: The University of Chicago Press. [AO]
Oki, Akira
1977 Social Change in the West Sumatran Village: 1908-
1945. Ph.D. dissertation, Australian National University,
Canberra. [TA] [AK] [AO] [JK] [BB&BB]
1979 A Note on the History of the Textile Industry in West
Sumatra. In Between People and Statistics: Essays on Modern Indonesian History. Francien van Rooij et al., eds.
pp. 147-156. The Hague: Martinus Nijhoff. [AO] [JK]
Onghokam
1975 The Residency of Madiun: Priyayi and Peasant During
the Nineteenth Century. Ph.D. dissertation, Yale University. [JK]
Ossenbruggen, F.D.E. van
1911 Mr. G.D. Willinck over wijlen Professor Dr. G.A.
Wilken. Den Haag: Van Dorp and Co. [BB&BB]
Pak, Ok-Kyung
1979 Les Rapport Ethniques dans le Roman Minangkabau
D'Avant-Guerre. Anthropologie et Sociétés 3:141-157. [JJ]

1980 Minangkabau Conceptualization of Male and Female.
Paper presented at the SEMBT. [JP] [NT&LT]

Pandecten
1914-1936 Pendecten van het Adatrecht. Vols. 1-20. KKIA.
Amsterdam: De Bussy. [BB&BB]

Parr, C.W.C. and W.H. Mackray
1910 Rembau, One of the Nine States: Its History, Constitution and Customs. JSBRAS 56. [MP]

Payer, C.
1980 The World Bank and the Small Farmer. Monthly Review
32(2). [JK]

Peacock, James L.
1968 Rites of Modernization. Chicago: University of
Chicago Press. [UJ]

Peletz, Michael G.
1981 Social History and Evolution in the Interrelationship
of Adat and Islam in Rembau, Negeri Sembilan. Institute
of Southeast Asian Studies, Research Notes and Discussions Paper, No. 27. Singapore: Institute for Southeast
Asian Studies. [MP]
1983 A Share of the Harvest: Kinship, Property, and Social
History Among the Malays of Rembau. Ph.D. dissertation:
University of Michigan. [MP]

Ples, D.
1878 De Koffij-Cultuur op Sumatra's Westkust. Batavia:
Ogilvie and Company. [JK]

Poewe, Karla O.
1981 Matrilineal Ideology: Male-Female Dynamics in
Luapula, Zambia. N.Y.: Academic Press. [NT&LT]

Popkin, S.
1979 The Rational Peasant: The Political Economy of Rural
Society in Vietnam. Berkeley: University of California
Press. [JK]

Postel-Coster, Els
1977 The Indonesian Novel as a Source of Anthropological
Data. In Text and Context. Ravindra K. Jain, ed. Phila-
delphia: Institute for the Study of Human Issues. [JJ]

Poulantzas, N.
1972 Aus Anlass der marxistischen Rechtstheorie. In marxistische und sozialistische Rechtstheorie. N. Reich, ed.
pp. 181-199. Frankfurt am Main: Fischer Athenaum. [BB&BB]

Prasetyo, Ris
1979 Hilang Bersama Kabut. Anita 2. [UJ]

Prindiville, J.C.J.
n.d. Food, Form, and Forum: Minangkabau Women as Culinary
Communicators. Forthcoming BKI. [JP]
1980 The Image and Role of Minangkabau Women. Paper presented at the SEMBT. [JP] [NT&LT] [BB&BB]

Prins, J.
    1953   Rondom de oude strijdvraag van Minangkabau.
    Indonesië 7:320-329. [BB&BB]
    1954   Adat en Islamietische Plichtenleer in Indonesie,
    derde druk. The Hague: W. van Hoeve. [BB&BB]
Propinsi Sumatera Barat
    1977   Sumatera Barat Dalam Angka 1977. Padang: Propinsi
    Sumatera Barat. [AO]
Putuwijaya
    1972   Bila Malam Bertambah Malam. Jakarta: Pustaka Jaya.
    [UJ]
    1973   Telegram. Jakarta: Pustaka Jaya. [UJ]
Raad van Justitie Padang
    1930   Hoogerechtschof van Nederlandsch-Indie 9 January
    1930. TR 131:82-105. [BB&BB]
Radcliffe-Brown, A.R.
    1950   Introduction. In African Systems of Kinship and Mar-
    riage. A.R. Radcliffe-Brown and D. Forde, eds. pp. 1-85.
    London: Oxford University Press. [JP]
Radjab, Muhammad
    1950   Semasa Ketjil di Kampung. Djakarta: Balai Pustaka.
    [JJ]
    1969   Sistem Kekerabatan di Minangkabau. Padang: Center for
    Minangkabau Studies. [JJ] [JP]
Raffles, Sophia, ed.
    1935   Memoir of the Life and Public Services of Sir Stam-
    ford Raffles. 2 vols. London. [KW]
Rajo Panghulu, R.M. Dt.
    1971   Minangkabau: Sejarah Ringkas dan Adatnja. Padang: Sri
    Dharma. [BB&BB]
Regeling der Wijze van Uitgifte van Onbebouwde Gronden in the
    Gouvernementslanden van Sumatra. Staatsblad 1874, Nr.
    94f. [BB&BB]
Renner, K.
    1929   Die Rechtsinstitute des Privatrechts und ihre sociale
    Funktion. Tubingen. [BB&BB]
Résumé
    1872   Résumé's van het Onderzoek naar de rechten welke in
    de Gouvernementslanden op Sumatra op de onbebouwde
    gronden worden uitgeoefend. Batavia. [LT&BB] [BB&BB]
Richards, A.I.
    1934   Mother-Right Among the Central Bantu. In Essays Pre-
    sented to C.G. Seligman. E.E. Evans-Pritchard et al.,
    eds. pp. 267-279. London: Kegan Paul, Trench, Trubner and
    Co. [JP]
    1950   Some Types of Family Structure Amongst the Central
    Bantu. In African Systems of Kinship and Marriage. A.R.
    Radcliffe-Brown and D. Forde, eds. pp. 207-251. London:

Oxford University Press. [JP]

Ricklefs, Merle C.
1976 Jogjakarta Under Sultan Mangkubumi 1749-1792. London: Oxford University Press. [TA]

Rifai Abu, Abdullah Suhadi
1976 Chatib Suleman. Projek Biografi Pahlawan Nasional. Jakarta: Departemen P & K. [AK]

Ronkel, Van
1915 Inlandsche Getuigenissen Aangaande den Padri oorlog. TBG 37(11):1099-1119. [TA]
1919 Een Maleisch Getuigenis over den Weg des Islam in Sumatra. BKI 75:363-378. [TA]

Rooij, J.A.F. de
1890 De positie der volkshoofden in een gedeelte der Padangsche Bovenlanden. IG 12:634-681. [LT&BB] [BB&BB]

Rosaldo, Michelle Zimbalist
1974 Women, Culture, and Society: A Theoretical Overview. In Women, Culture, and Society. M. Rosaldo and L. Lamphere, eds. Palo Alto, California: Stanford University Press. [NT&LT]

Sahlins, Marshall D.
1981 Historical Metaphors and Mythical Realities: Structure in the Early History of the Sandwich Islands Kingdom. Ann Arbor: University of Michigan Press. [MP]

Said, Edward W.
1978 Orientalism. N.Y.: Random House. [TA]

Sanggoeno Dirajo, I. Dt.
1920 Mustiko Adat Alam Minangkabau. [BB&BB]

Sarolea, W.H.A.
1920 Minangkabausch Adatrecht: De rechtsbevoegheid van den familietak, zijn goederen en zijn hoofd. TR 112:120-131. [BB&BB]

Schafer, R.
1938 Bestuurmemorie Fort van der Capellen. [KW]

Schneider, David M.
1961 The Distinctive Features of Matrilineal Descent Groups. In Matrilineal Kinship. D. Schneider and K. Gough, eds. pp. 1-29. Berkeley, California: University of California Press. [JP] [NT&LT]
1965 Some Muddles in the Model: Or, How the System Really Works. In The Relevance of Models for Social Anthropology. M. Banton, ed.pp. 25-79. A.S.A. Monograph No. 1. London: Tavistock Publications. [MP]

Schneider, D. and K. Gough, eds.
1961[1974 repr.] Matrilineal Kinship. Berkeley: University of California Press. [LT&BB] [JJ] [MN]

Scholz, U.
1977 Minangkabau: Die Agrarstruktur in West-Sumatra und

<u>Möglichkeiten ihrer Entwicklung</u>. Giessener Geographische
Schriften, Heft 41. Giessen: Selbstverlag des
Geographischen Instituuts der Justus Liebig Universitat.
[BB&BB]

Schrieke, B.J.O.
  1919-21 Bijdrage tot de Bibliografie van de huidige gods-
           dienstige beweging ter Sumatra's Westkust. TBG 59:249-
           325. [TA]
  1955 The Causes and Effects of Communism on the West Coast
        of Sumatra. In <u>Indonesian Sociological Studies: Selected</u>
        <u>Writings of B. Schrieke</u>. Part 1:83-166. The Hague: W. van
        Hoeve. [LT&BB] [AO] [BB&BB] [JK]

Schrieke, B.J.O. et al.
  1928 <u>Rapport van de Commissie van Onderzoek Ingestelt bij</u>
        <u>het Gouvernement Besluit van 13 Februari</u>. ["Westkust
        Rapport."] 4 Parts in 3 Volumes. B.J.O. Schrieke, Fievez
        van Ginkel, Hamerster, Groeneveldt, Van der Plas, Datoek
        Madjolelo, eds. Weltevreden: Landsdrukkerij. [AO] [JK]

Schrieke, B.J.O., ed.
  1929 <u>The Effect of Western Influence on Native Civil-</u>
        <u>ization in the Malay Archipelago</u>. Weltevreden: G. Kolff
        en Co. [LT&BB]

Schrijvers, Joke and Els Postel-Coster
  1977 Minangkabau Women: Change in a Matrilineal Society.
        <u>Archipel: Etudes Interdisciplinaires Sur le Monde Insu-</u>
        <u>lindien</u> 13:79-103. [JP] [NT&LT]

Scott, J.
  1976 <u>The Moral Economy of the Peasant</u>. New Haven: Yale
        University Press. [JK]

Sen, S.P.
  1962 Indian Textiles in South-East Asian Trade in the
        Seventeenth Century. JSEAH 1(2). [JK]

Sidi Bandaro, D.Th. Dt.
  1965 <u>Seluk-Beluk Adat Minangkabau</u>. Jakarta: N.V. Nusantara
        Bukittinggi. [BB&BB]

Singarimbum, M.
  1975 <u>Kinship, Descent and Alliance Among the Karo Batak</u>.
        Berkeley: University of California Press. [JK]

Siregar, Ashadi
  1975 <u>Terminal Cinta Terakhir</u>. Jakarta: Gramedia. [UJ]

s' Jacob, see above, Jacob

Sjofjan Thalib
  1974 <u>Pemerintahan Nagari di Sumatera Barat Dewasa Ini:</u>
        <u>Suatu tinjauan terhadap SK No. 15/GSB/1968</u>. Padang:
        Universitas Andalas, Fakultas Hukum dan Pengetahuan
        Masyarakat. [BB&BB]

Skeat, W.W.
  1900 <u>Malay Magic</u>. London. [CW]

Smith, DeVerne Reed
1983 *Palauan Social Structure*. New Brunswick: Rutgers
University Press. [MP]

Snouck Hurgronje, C.
1906 *The Achehnese*. 2 Vols. A.W.S. O'Sullivan, transl.
Leyden and London: Brill; Luzac. [CW]
1913 *De Islam in Nederlandsch-Indie*. Baarn: Hollandia
Drukkerij. [CW]

Staf van de Bevelhebber der Landstrijdkrachten
n.d. Overzicht Gecontroleerde der Landstrijdkrachten.
Secties Krijgsgeschiedenis. The Hague, File 206-1: 54-55.
[AK]

Stap, H.W.
1917 De Nagari Ordinantie ter Sumatra's Westkust. TBB
53:699-811. [AO]

Statsblaad [see citations in [BB&BB] and [AO]]

Stibbe, S.
1869 Het soekoe-bestuur in de Padangsche Bovenlanden. TNI
(3e serie) 3(deel 1):27-42. [BB&BB]

Strijbosch, A.K.J.M.
1980 *Juristen en de Studie van Volksrecht in Nederlands-
Indië en Angloroon Afrika*. Nijmegen: Publikaties van het
Instituut voor Volksrecht no. VII. [BB&BB]

Swift, Michael G.
1965 *Malay Peasant Society in Jelebu*. London: Athlone
Press. [MP]
1971 Minangkabau and Modernization. In *Anthropology in
Oceania: Essays Presented to Ian Hogbin*. S.R. Hiatt and
C. Jayawardena, eds. pp. 256-267. Sydney: Angus and
Robertson. [JP]

Tambo Kerinci
n.d. A collection of Kerinci Documents transcribed by Dr.
P. Voorhoeve and assistants. In typescript in the Koninklijk Instituut voor Taal-, Land-, en Volkenkunde,
Leiden. Or. 414, 415. [CW]

Tan, K.L.
1977 *De Agrarische Basis Wet 1960: Enige Principes*.
Leiden: Documentatie Bureau voor Overzees Recht. [BB&BB]

Tanner, Nancy
1969 Disputing and Dispute Settlement among the Minangkabau of Indonesia. *Indonesia* 8:21-67. [NT&LT] [BB&BB]
1971 *Minangkabau Disputes*. Ph.D. dissertation, University
of California, Berkeley. [JP] [NT&LT] [BB&BB]
1974 Matrifocality in Indonesia and Africa and Among Black
Americans. In *Women, Culture, and Society*. M. Rosaldo and
L. Lamphere, eds. pp. 129-156. Palo Alto, California:
Stanford University Press. [JP] [NT&LT]
1976 Minangkabau. In *Insular Southeast Asia: Ethnographic*

<u>Studies</u>. Section 7, Sumatra, Vol. I. Frank Le Bar, compiler. pp. 1-82. New Haven: Human Relations Area Files.
[LT&BB] [NT&LT]

1982 The Nuclear Family in Minangkabau Matriliny: Mirror of Disputes. BKI 138(13):129-151. [NT&LT]

Taylor, E.N.
1929 Customary Law of Rembau. JMBRAS 7(1):1-289. [MP]
1948 Aspects of Customary Inheritance in Negri Sembilan. JMBRAS 21(2):41-129. [MP]

Teeuw, A., and D.K. Wyatt
1970 <u>Hikayat Patani: The Story of Patani</u>. The Hague: Martinus Nijhoff. [TA]

Thomas, Lynn L.
1977 Kinship Categories in a Minangkabau Village. Ph.D. dissertation, University of California, Riverside. [NT&LT] [BB&BB] [JP]

Tideman, J.
1938 <u>Djambi</u>. Koninklijk Vereening KKIA. Mededelling No. 42. [CW]

TNAG
1876 Bijbladen I. Documents and reports concerning the Midden-Sumatra expedition, including a translation of the second part of Barnes account promised for <u>Malayan Miscellanies III</u> which was never published. [CW]

Todorov, Tzvetan
1977 <u>The Poetics of Prose</u>. Ithaca, N.Y.: Cornell University Press. [UJ]

Toorn, J.L. van der
1881 Aantekeningen uit het familieleven bij den Maleiër in de Padangsche Bovenlanden. TBG 26:205-233, 514-528. [BB&BB]
1888 <u>Tjindoer Mato: Minangkabausch-Maleische Legende</u>. VBG 45. [JJ]

Tropen Museum
n.d. Militarie Memorie van het Patrouillegebied Padang. ms stored in the Tropen Museum. [AO]

Turner, Victor
1972 <u>The Ritual Process: Structure and Anti-Structure</u>. Chicago: Aldine Publishing Co. [TA]

UUMM
1822 Translation of the Undang Undang of Moco Moco. <u>Malayan Miscellanies</u>. 2(13):1-13. Benkulen. [KW]

Vansina, J.
1965 A Traditional Legal System: The Kuba. In <u>African Law: Adaptation and Development</u>. H. and L. Kuper, eds. Berkeley: University of California Press. [BB&BB]

VBG
1880 Aantekeningen omtrent Midden-Sumatra, Korintji. VBG

58-73. [CW]

Velsen, J. van
   1969 Procedural Informality, Reconciliation and False
         Comparison. In <u>Ideas and Procedures in African Customary</u>
         <u>Law</u>. Max Gluckman, ed. pp. 137-152. London: Oxford
         University Press. [BB&BB]

Verkerk Pistorius, A.W.P.
   1868 Iets over de slaven en afstammelingen van slaven in
         de Padangsche Bovenlanden. TNI (3e serie) 2:423-443.
         [BB&BB]
   1871 <u>Studiën over de Inlandsche Huishouding in de</u>
         <u>Padangsche Bovenlanden</u>. Zaltbommel: Joh. Noman en Zoon.
         [TA] [LT&BB] [BB&BB]

Vollenhoven, C. van
   1909 <u>Miskenningen van het Adatrecht</u>. Leiden: E.J. Brill.
         [BB&BB]
   1918,1931,1933 <u>Het Adatrecht van Nederlandsch-Indie</u>. Vols.
         1(1918), 2(1931), and 3(1933). Leiden: E.J. Brill.
         [BB&BB]
   1919 <u>De Indonesier en zijn Grond</u>. Leiden: E.J. Brill.
         [BB&BB]

Waal, G. de
   1889 Aantekeningen betreffende het Adatbestuur in de
         onderafdeling Soloq. TBG 3:65-83. [BB&BB]

Wake, Christopher H.
   1964 Malacca's Early Kings and the Reception of Islam.
         JSEAH 5(2):104-127. [TA]

Westenek, L.G.
   1918a <u>De Minangkabausche Nagari</u>. Mededelingen van het
          Bureau voor de Bestuurszaken der Buitenbezittingen,
          bewerkt door het Encyclopaedisch bureau, aflevering 17,
          derde uitgave. [LT&BB] [KW] [BB&BB]
   1918b De Inlandsche Bestuurshoofden ter Sumatra's West-
          kust. KT 2:673-693, 828-846. [LT&BB]

Westkust Rapport. See Schrieke et al. 1928.

Wilken, G.A.
   1883 <u>Over de Verwantschap en het Huwelijks- en Erfrecht</u>
         <u>bij de Volken van den Indischen Archipel Beschouwd uit</u>
         <u>het Oogpunt van de Nieuwere Leerstellingen op het Gebied</u>
         <u>der Maatschappelijke Ontwikkelingsgeschiedenis</u>. Leiden:
         Brill. [BB&BB]
   1885 <u>Het animisme bij de Volken van de Indische Archipel</u>.
         Leiden. [LT&BB]
   1926 <u>Opstellen over Adatrecht, uitgegeven door F.D.E. van</u>
         <u>Ossenbruggen</u>. Semarang: Van Dorp en Co. [BB&BB]

Wilkinson, R.J.
   1906 <u>Malay Beliefs</u>. London and Leiden: Luzac; Brill. No. 1
         in the series of Malay Papers. [CW]

1911[1971] Notes on the Negri Sembilan. Reprinted in
Papers on Malay Subjects. R.J. Wilkinson, ed. pp. 277-
321. Kuala Lumpur: Oxford University Press. [MP]
Willinck, G.D.
1909 Het Rechtsleven bij de Minangkabausche Maleiërs.
Leiden: E.J. Brill. [LT&BB] [NT&LT] [KW] [BB&BB]
1911 Non Tali Auxilio! of Wijlen Prof. Dr. G.A. Wilken,
zomede Mr. F.D.E. van Ossen Bruggen en Beider Arbeid op
Vergelijkend Rechtswetenschappelijk Gebied. Zutphen: J.
Nijkamp. [BB&BB]
Winstedt, Richard
1920 Family Relationships in Negri Sembilan. Journal of
the Federated Malay States Museum 9:111-114. [MP]
Winus
1980 Third World Development, Historians of the Expan-
sions, and 'Relevance.' Itinerario 1:77-86. [AO]
Wolters, O.
1970 The Fall of Srivijaya in Malay History. Ithaca, N.Y.:
Cornell University Press. [JK]
Woodman, G.R.
1969 Some Realism about Customary Law—The West African
Experience. Wisconsin Law Review 128(1):128-52. [BB&BB]
1981 Customary Law, Modern Courts, and the Notion of
Institutionalization of Norms in Ghana and Nigeria. Paper
presented at the Bellagio I.U.A.E.S. Symposium on Folk
Law and State Institutions, September 1981. [BB&BB]
Wouden, F.A.E. van
1977[1935] Types of Social Structure in Eastern Indonesia.
Rodney Needham, transl. Koninklijk Instituut voor Taal-,
Land-, en Volkenkunde Translation Series 11. The Hague:
Martinus Nijhoff. [JJ]
Young, K.
1980 The Late Nineteenth Century Commodity Boom in West
Sumatra. Indonesia Circle. [JK]

MONOGRAPHS IN INTERNATIONAL STUDIES

ISBN Prefix 0-89680-

Africa Series

25. Kircherr, Eugene C. ABBYSSINIA TO ZIMBABWE: A
Guide to the Political Units of Africa in the
Period 1947-1978. 1979. 3rd ed. 80pp.
100-4   (82-91908) $ 8.00*

27. Fadiman, Jeffrey A. MOUNTAIN WARRIORS: The
Pre-Colonial Meru of Mt. Kenya. 1976. 82pp.
060-1   (82-91783) $ 4.75*

36. Fadiman, Jeffrey A. THE MOMENT OF CONQUEST:
Meru, Kenya, 1907. 1979. 70pp.
081-4   (82-91874) $ 5.50*

37. Wright, Donald R. ORAL TRADITIONS FROM THE
GAMBIA: Volume I, Mandinka Griots. 1979.
176pp.
083-0   (82-91882) $12.00*

38. Wright, Donald R. ORAL TRADITIONS FROM THE
GAMBIA: Volume II, Family Elders. 1980.
200pp.
084-9   (82-91890) $15.00*

39. Reining, Priscilla. CHALLENGING DESERTIFICA-
TION IN WEST AFRICA: Insights from Landsat into
Carrying Capacity, Cultivation and Settlement
Site Identification in Upper Volta and
Niger. 1979. 180pp., illus.
102-0   (82-91916) $12.00*

41. Lindfors, Bernth. MAZUNGUMZO: Interviews with
East African Writers, Publishers, Editors, and
Scholars. 1981. 179pp.
108-X   (82-91932) $13.00*

42. Spear, Thomas J. TRADITIONS OF ORIGIN AND
THEIR INTERPRETATION: The Mijikenda of Kenya.
1982. xii, 163pp.
109-8   (82-91940) $13.50*

43. Harik, Elsa M. and Donald G. Schilling. THE
POLITICS OF EDUCATION IN COLONIAL ALGERIA AND
KENYA. 1984. 102pp.
117-9   (82-91957) $11.50*

44. Smith, Daniel R. THE INFLUENCE OF THE FABIAN
COLONIAL BUREAU ON THE INDEPENDENCE MOVEMENT IN
TANGANYIKA. 1985. x, 98pp.
125-X   (82-91965) $ 9.00*

45. Keto, C. Tsehloane. AMERICAN-SOUTH AFRICAN
    RELATIONS 1784-1980: Review and Select Biblio-
    graphy. 1985. 159pp.
    128-4   (82-91973) $11.00*

46. Burness, Don, and Mary-Lou Burness, ed.
    WANASEMA: Conversations with African Writers.
    1985. 95pp.
    129-2   (82-91981) $ 9.00*

47. Switzer, Les. MEDIA AND DEPENDENCY IN SOUTH
    AFRICA: A Case Study of the Press and the
    Ciskei "Homeland".
    1985. 80pp.
    130-6   (82-91999)   9.00*

48. Heggoy, Alf Andrew. THE FRENCH CONQUEST OF
    ALGIERS, 1830: An Algerian Oral Tradition.
    1986. 101pp.
    131-4   (82-92005) $ 9.00*

49. Hart, Ursula Kingsmill. TWO LADIES OF COLONIAL
    ALGERIA: The Lives and Times of Aurelie Picard
    and Isabelle Eberhardt. 1987. 156pp.
    143-8   (82-92013) $9.00*

Latin America Series

1. Frei, Eduardo M. THE MANDATE OF HISTORY AND
   CHILE'S FUTURE. Tr. by Miguel d'Escoto.
   Intro. by Thomas Walker. 1977. 79pp.
   066-0   (82-92526) $ 8.00*

4. Martz, Mary Jeanne Reid. THE CENTRAL AMERICAN
   SOCCER WAR: Historical Patterns and Internal
   Dynamics of OAS Settlement Procedures. 1979.
   118pp.
   077-6   (82-92559) $ 8.00*

5. Wiarda, Howard J. CRITICAL ELECTIONS AND
   CRITICAL COUPS: State, Society, and the
   Military in the Processes of Latin American
   Development. 1979. 83pp.
   082-2   (82-92567) $ 7.00*

6. Dietz, Henry A., and Richard Moore. POLITICAL
   PARTICIPATION IN A NON-ELECTORAL SETTING: The
   Urban Poor in Lima, Peru. 1979. viii, 102pp.
   085-7   (82-92575) $ 9.00*

7. Hopgood, James F.   SETTLERS OF BAJAVISTA:
    Social and Economic Adaptation in a Mexican
    Squatter Settlement. 1979. xii, 145pp.
    101-2   (82-92583) $11.00*

8. Clayton, Lawrence A.   CAULKERS AND CARPENTERS
    IN A NEW WORLD: The Shipyards of Colonial
    Guayaquil. 1980. 189pp., illus.
    103-9   (82-92591) $15.00*

9. Tata, Robert J.   STRUCTURAL CHANGES IN PUERTO
    RICO'S ECONOMY: 1947-1976. 1981. xiv, 104pp.
    107-1   (82-92609) $11.75*

10. McCreery, David. DEVELOPMENT AND THE STATE IN
    REFORMA GUATEMALA, 1871-1885. 1983. viii,
    120pp.
    113-6   (82-92617) $ 8.50*

11. O'Shaughnessy, Laura N., and Louis H. Serra.
    CHURCH AND REVOLUTION IN NICARAGUA. 1986.
    118pp.
    126-8   (82-92625) $11.00*

12. Wallace, Brian. OWNERSHIP AND DEVELOPMENT: A
    Comparison of Domestic and Foreign Investment
    in Columbian Manufacturing. 1987. 186pp.
    145-4   (82-92633) $12.00*

Southeast Asia Series

31. Nash, Manning.   PEASANT CITIZENS: Politics,
    Religion, and Modernization in Kelantan,
    Malaysia. 1974. 181pp.
    018-0   (82-90322) $12.00*

38. Bailey, Conner. BROKER, MEDIATOR, PATRON, AND
    KINSMAN: An Historical Analysis of Key Leader-
    ship Roles in a Rural Malaysian District.
    1976. 79pp.
    024-5   (82-90397) $7.00*

40. Van der Veur, Paul W.   FREEMASONRY IN INDONESIA
    FROM RADERMACHER TO SOEKANTO, 1762-1961. 1976.
    37pp.
    026-1   (82-90413) $4.00*

43. Marlay, Ross. POLLUTION AND POLITICS IN THE
    PHILIPPINES. 1977. 121pp.
    029-6   (82-90447) $7.00*

44. Collier, William L., et al. INCOME, EMPLOYMENT AND FOOD SYSTEMS IN JAVANESE COASTAL VILLAGES. 1977. 160pp.
031-8   (82-90454) $10.00*

45. Chew, Sock Foon and MacDougall, John A. FOREVER PLURAL: The Perception and Practice of Inter-Communal Marriage in Singapore. 1977. 61pp.
030-X   (82-90462) $6.00*

47. Wessing, Robert. COSMOLOGY AND SOCIAL BEHAVIOR IN A WEST JAVANESE SETTLEMENT. 1978. 200pp.
072-5   (82-90488) $12.00*

48. Willer, Thomas F., ed. SOUTHEAST ASIAN REFER-ENCES IN THE BRITISH PARLIAMENTARY PAPERS, 1801-1972/73: An Index. 1978. 110pp.
033-4   (82-90496) $ 8.50*

49. Durrenberger, E. Paul. AGRICULTURAL PRODUCTION AND HOUSEHOLD BUDGETS IN A SHAN PEASANT VILLAGE IN NORTHWESTERN THAILAND: A Quantitative Description. 1978. 142pp.
071-7   (82-90504) $9.50*

50. Echauz, Robustiano. SKETCHES OF THE ISLAND OF NEGROS. 1978. 174pp.
070-9   (82-90512) $10.00*

51. Krannich, Ronald L. MAYORS AND MANAGERS IN THAILAND: The Struggle for Political Life in Administrative Settings. 1978. 139pp.
073-3   (82-90520) $ 9.00*

54. Ayal, Eliezar B., ed. THE STUDY OF THAILAND: Analyses of Knowledge, Approaches, and Pros-pects in Anthropology, Art History, Economics, History and Political Science. 1979. 257pp.
079-2   (82-90553) $13.50*

56. Duiker, William J. VIETNAM SINCE THE FALL OF SAIGON. Second edition, revised and enlarged. 1986. 281pp.
133-0   (82-90744) $12.00*

57. Siregar, Susan Rodgers. ADAT, ISLAM, AND CHRISTIANITY IN A BATAK HOMELAND. 1981. 108pp.
110-1   (82-90587) $10.00*

58. Van Esterik, Penny. COGNITION AND DESIGN PRODUCTION IN BAN CHIANG POTTERY. 1981. 90pp.
078-4   (82-90595) $12.00*

59. Foster, Brian L.   COMMERCE AND ETHNIC DIFFER-
ENCES: The Case of the Mons in Thailand.
1982.   x, 93pp.
112-8   (82-90603) $10.00*

60. Frederick, William H., and John H. McGlynn.
REFLECTIONS ON REBELLION: Stories from the
Indonesian Upheavals of 1948 and 1965.   1983.
vi, 168pp.
111-X   (82-90611) $ 9.00*

61. Cady, John F.   CONTACTS WITH BURMA, 1935-1949:
A Personal Account.   1983.   x, 117pp.
114-4   (82-90629) $ 9.00*

62. Kipp, Rita Smith, and Richard D. Kipp, eds.
BEYOND SAMOSIR: Recent Studies of the Batak
Peoples of Sumatra.   1983.   viii, 155pp.
115-2   (82-90637) $ 9.00*

63. Carstens, Sharon, ed.   CULTURAL IDENTITY IN
NORTHERN PENINSULAR MALAYSIA.   1986.   91pp.
116-0   (82-90645) $ 9.00*

64. Dardjowidjojo, Soenjono.   VOCABULARY BUILDING
IN INDONESIAN: An Advanced Reader.   1984.
xviii, 256pp.
118-7   (82-90652) $26.00*

65. Errington, J. Joseph.   LANGUAGE AND SOCIAL
CHANGE IN JAVA: Linguistic Reflexes of Modernization in a Traditional Royal Polity.   1985.
xiv, 198pp.
120-9   (82-90660) $12.00*

66. Binh, Tran Tu.   THE RED EARTH: A Vietnamese
Memoir of Life on a Colonial Rubber Plantation.
Tr. by John Spragens.   Ed. by David Marr.
1985.   xii, 98pp.
119-5   (82-90678) $ 9.00*

67. Pane, Armijn.   SHACKLES.   Tr. by John McGlynn.
Intro. by William H. Frederick.   1985.   xvi,
108pp.
122-5   (82-90686) $ 9.00*

68. Syukri, Ibrahim.   HISTORY OF THE MALAY KINGDOM
OF PATANI.   Tr. by Conner Bailey and John N.
Miksic.   1985.   xx, 98pp.
123-3   (82-90694) $10.50*

69. Keeler, Ward.   JAVANESE: A Cultural Approach.
1984.   xxxvi, 523pp.
121-7   (82-90702) $18.00*

70. Wilson, Constance M., and Lucien M. Hanks. BURMA-THAILAND FRONTIER OVERSIXTEEN DECADES: Three Descriptive Documents. 1985. x, 128pp. 124-1   (82-90710) $10.50*

71. Thomas, Lynn L., and Franz von Benda-Beckmann, eds. CHANGE AND CONTINUITY IN MINANGKABAU: Local, Regional, and Historical Perspectives on West Sumatra. 1986. 363pp. 127-6   (82-90728) $14.00*

72. Reid, Anthony, and Oki Akira, eds. THE JAPANESE EXPERIENCE IN INDONESIA: Selected Memoirs of 1942-1945. 1986. 411pp., 20 illus. 132-2   (82-90736) $18.00*

73. Smirenskaia, Ahanna D. PEASANTS IN ASIA: Social Consciousness and Social Struggle. Tr. by Michael J. Buckley. 1987. 248pp. 134-9   (82-90751) $12.50

74. McArthur, M.S.H. REPORT ON BRUNEI IN 1904. Ed. by A.V.M. Horton. 1987. 304pp. 135-7   (82-90769) $13.50

75. Lockard, Craig Alan. FROM KAMPUNG TO CITY. A Social History of Kuching Malaysia 1820-1970. 1987. 311pp. 136-5   (82-90777) $14.00*

78. Chew, Sock Foon. ETHNICITY AND NATIONALITY IN SINGAPORE. 1987. 229pp. 139-X   (82-90801) $12.50*

79. Walton, Susan Pratt. MODE IN JAVANESE MUSIC. 1987. 279pp. 144-6   (82-90819) $12.00*

80. Nguyen Anh Tuan. SOUTH VIETNAM TRIAL AND EXPERIENCE: A Challenge for Development. 1987. 482pp. 141-1   (82-90827) $15.00*

81. Van der Veur, Paul W., ed. TOWARD A GLORIOUS INDONESIA: Reminiscences and Observations of Dr. Soetomo. 1987. 367pp. 142-X   (82-90835) $13.50*

ORDERING INFORMATION

Orders for titles in the Monographs in International Studies series should be placed through the Ohio University Press/Scott Quadrangle/Athens, Ohio 45701-2979. Individuals must remit pre-payment via check, VISA, MasterCard, CHOICE, or American Express. Individuals ordering from outside of the U.S., please remit in U.S. funds by either International Money Order or check drawn on a U.S. bank. Residents of Ohio please add sales tax. Postage and handling is $2.00 for the first book and $.50 for each additional book. Prices and availability are subject to change without notice.

mother-son kaba[2] 62-ff

"a lot of clucking, but no egg" 64